Varner Families of the South
Volume One

Gerald H. Varner
May 16, 2000

Planned for publication in 1995:

Varner Families of the South
Volume Two

*Varner/Verner Families
of Pendleton District, SC,
and their Descendants*

Varner Families of the South
Volume One

Varner Families
of Oglethorpe County, GA,
and their Descendants

Gerald H. Varner

PUBLISHED BY GERALD H. VARNER
1994

Copyright 1994 by Gerald H. Varner

All rights reserved, including the right of reproduction in whole or in part in any form, without written permission from the publisher.

Published by Gerald H. Varner
    PO Box 91481
    Portland, OR 97291-0481

Library of Congress Catalog Card Number: 94-60607

Manufactured in the United States of America
    ISBN: 0-9642353-0-7 (Volume One)
    ISBN: 0-9642353-1-5 (2 Volume Set)

Dedicated to the memory of my grandfather

Sidney Oliver Varner
(1875-1959)

who lived near many of these Varner families,
in Coosa Co, Alabama, during his childhood years

Contents

Synopsis xvii

Preface 1
    A Message From the Author (1)
    About the Contents of This Book (4)
    About the Topic of Slavery (5)
    Thanks to Those Who Helped (8)
    Sorting the Johns, Georges, Williams, etc. (10)

I--Early Varner Families of NC . . 12
    Westward Movement Turns Southward (13)
    Adam Varner Settles on Uwharrie River (14)
    Adam Varner Left No Will (15)
    John Varner of Rowan Co, NC (16)
    Who Were Adam and John's Parents? (20)
    John Varner, Son of Adam Varner (21)
    Jacob Varner, Son of Adam Varner (23)
    Jacob Varner's Estate (24)
    John Varner, Son of John Varner (26)
    Jacob Varner, Son of John Varner (27)
    Henry Varner: Son of Adam Varner? (28)
    Frederick Varner: Son of Adam Varner? (30)
    Matthew Varner, Son of John Varner (31)
    George Varner, Son of John or Adam Varner (32)
    George Varner Gets Land Grant (33)
    Will of John Varner, Randolph Co, NC (34)
    Will of John Varner, Davidson Co, NC (35)
    Estate Sale of John Varner, Davidson Co, NC (37)
    Will of Jacob Varner, Rowan Co, NC (38)
    George Varner Land Grant in NC (39)

II--George Varner of Oglethorpe Co, GA ... 41
    George Varner Marries Elizabeth Henley (43)
    George Varner, Planter (44)
    George Varner Builds Slave Holdings (46)
    George Varner Writes His Will (49)
    George and Betsy Did Not Attend Local Church (50)
    George and Betsy Varner's Children (52)
    George Varner Land Purchase in Wilkes Co, GA (52)
    George and Betsy Varner Land Sales in GA (53)
    George Varner Serves on Juries (54)
    George Varner's Last Will and Testament (56)
    Appraisal of George Varner's Estate (58)

III--Frederick Varner of Oglethorpe Co, GA ... 62
    Frederick Varner in Georgia (63)
    Frederick Varner Suffers Losses (65)
    Frederick Varner Becomes Church Deacon (68)
    Frederick Varner Leaves No Will (69)
    Children of Frederick and Judah Varner (71)
    Frederick Varner's Service on Juries (73)
    Sheriff Sells Frederick Varner's Land (74)
    Frederick Varner Accused of Misconduct (76)
    Church Minutes Concerning Frederick Varner, Mark Varner, Other Varners and Their Slaves (77)

IV--Matthew Varner of Oglethorpe Co, GA ... 81
    Matthew and Susannah Varner Move to Georgia (82)
    Will Fails To Include Some Children (85)
    Children of Matthew and Susannah Varner (86)

Will of Matthew Varner (88)
Matthew Varner's Will Challenged (89)
Matthew Varner Land Purchases and Sales (91)

V--Children of George Varner .. 92
John Varner, Son of George Varner (92)
William Varner, Son of George Varner (94)
William Varner, Sheriff and Legislator (96)
Children of William Varner (100)
George Varner, Jr., Son of George Varner (102)
Henley Varner, Son of George Varner (104)
Henley Varner, Community Leader (106)
Frederick Varner, Son of George Varner (108)
Susannah Varner, Daughter of George Varner (109)
Elizabeth Varner, Daughter of George Varner (109)
Sarah Varner, Daughter of George Varner (109)
Emily S. Varner, Daughter of George Varner (111)
William Varner Letters (112)
Will of John F. Varner (113)
Appraisal of John F. Varner's Estate (115)

VI--John Varner, Son of George Varner . . . 117
John Varner Becomes a Planter (118)
John and Nancy Varner Move to Alabama (119)
John Varner Elected Clerk of County Court (120)
John Varner Moves to Coosa County, AL (122)
Why Did Varner Families Separate? (123)
Families May Have Parted Friends (124)
John and Nancy Varner Face Problems (126)
John Varner Loses Most of His Wealth (128)
John Varner Purchases 417 Acres of Land (131)
John Varner Purchases 239 Acres of Land (132)

Henley Varner Letter to Brother John Varner (133)
John Varner's Will (135)
John Varner Estate Sale (138)

VII--Children of John Varner and Nancy Powell 142

Amaziah Varner and Martha Pickering (142)
Edward P. Varner and His Descendants (146)
Children of E. P. Varner and Jane Knight (149)
Children of E. P. Varner and Senora Bonnet (151)
William F. Varner and Margaret F. Bonham (152)
Hardaway Varner and Caroline Glenn (157)
Lucy A. Varner and John A. Wilson (159)
Edward P. Varner's Farm Production (159)
Notes From a Pioneer Preacher (160)
Edward P. Varner's Will (161)
William F. Varner Estate Sale (162)

VIII--Azariah Varner, Son of John Varner 164

Azariah Has Health, Financial Problems (165)
Teacher Seeks Payment of Tuition (166)
Merchant Seeks Payment for Goods (168)
Mary Varner's Death Announced (169)
Court Learns Where Children Live (170)
Court Records Identify Slaves (171)
Descendants of Azariah and Mary Varner (173)
Sale of Land Where Azariah Varner Died (181)
1853 Tax Record for Azariah Varner (182)
Law Suits Against Azariah Varner (183)
Trust To Support Azariah Varner's Children (185)

IX--Susan Eliza Varner, Daughter of John Varner   186

John Varner Gives Slaves to Susan (186)
Slave Child Seized and Sold (187)
Witnesses Describe Drinking Problem (189)
Children of Susan and William Varner (192)
Susan Eliza Varner Marries Rufus W. Dacus (200)
John Varner Deeds Slaves to His Daughter (201)
William G. Varner Approves Gift of Slaves (202)
Testimony on Seizure and Sale of Slave Milly (203)
Court Rules in Favor of Susan E. Varner (204)
Testimony of Witness Allen Davis (205)
Testimony of Witness McDaniel Atchison (206)
Testimony of Witness William A. Rice (206)
Testimony of Witness John Varner (207)
John Varner Trust for Susan E. Varner (209)
Tax Record for William G. Varner (211)

X--George H. Varner, Son of John Varner 212

George H. Varner Moves to Mississippi (212)
George H. Varner Copes with Money Problems (214)
George H. Varner Loses Wife and Daughter (217)
George H. Varner Moves to Louisiana (219)
Descendants of George H. Varner (220)

XI--John W. Varner, Son of John Varner 232

John W. Varner Fights in Civil War (234)
Descendants of Cicero Varner (235)
Descendants of Lucien Varner (239)
Descendants of John William Varner (241)

XII--Esselman Varner, Son of John Varner 254

Esselman Joins Confederate Army (255)
Esselman Involved in Court Cases (256)
Children of Esselman and Sarah Varner (258)
Descendants of William A. Varner (259)
Descendants of Manton E. Varner (260)
Descendants of James Hardaway Varner (262)
Descendants of John A. Varner (264)
Descendants of George Henley Varner (264)
1880 Agricultural Census for Esselman Varner (283)
John Varner Charged with Assault and Battery (284)
Esselman Varner's Will (285)
Petition To Probate Esselman Varner's Will (286)

XIII--Frederick Varner, Son of George Varner ... 288

Frederick Varner Moves to Louisiana (288)
Thomas Jefferson Varner and His Children (290)
William Graves Varner and His Family (293)
George W. Varner Found Guilty of Fraud (298)
Frederick Varner's Will (302)
Appraisal of Thomas J. Varner's Estate (304)
Division of Thomas J. Varner's Slaves (305)

XIV--Varner Records in Georgia 307

1800 Federal Census Records (308)
1820 Federal Census Records (309)
1830 Federal Census Records (311)
1840 Federal Census Records (314)
1850 Federal Census Records (316)
Sam Varner Seeks Political Appointment (318)

Early Tax Records, Putnam County (319)
Varner Marriages in Oglethorpe County, GA (323)
Approved Prices for Tavern Keeping in 1799 (324)
Sale of Land in George Varner's Estate (325)
Varner Family Papers (327)

XV--Varner Records in Lowndes Co, AL 329
Census Records for Lowndes County, AL (329)
Notes on Varners in Lowndes Co History (335)
Varner Marriages in Lowndes County (338)
Division of Land by William G. Varner's Heirs (339)

XVI--Varner Records in Coosa County, AL . . . 342
Coosa County, AL, Census Records, 1850-1900 (342)
Cemetery Records, Coosa County, Alabama (354)
Varner Marriages, Coosa County, Alabama (356)
Land Purchases and Sales by Varners (358)

INDEX 361

About the Author 395

Synopsis

Two **Varner** brothers, **Adam and John,** moved from Baltimore, MD, and settled on the Uwharrie and Yadkin rivers in the **North Carolina** wilderness prior to the Revolutionary War. They farmed and raised families there, in **Rowan** (later **Davidson**) and **Randolph** counties.

Three of John and Adam's sons--**George, Frederick,** and **Matthew Varner**--moved their young families to a new wilderness frontier, in **Georgia**, during the 1780's, a few years after the Revolutionary War.

During the early 1800's, **George Varner** became one of the most prosperous planters of **Oglethorpe County, GA.** He used Negro slave labor to build his property holdings, which included nearly 2,000 acres of land and 54 slaves at the time of his death in 1827. George's brothers-- **Frederick and Matthew Varner**--were slave-owning Oglethorpe County planters as well. These three Varners were leading citizens in Oglethorpe County, which was at that time in the heart of the thriving young state of Georgia.

George Varner and his wife **Elizabeth Henley** were parents of nine children. Four of their sons built financial and political empires of their own: **William Varner** in **Putnam Co, GA; Henley Varner** in **Henry Co**, GA; **John Varner** in **Lowndes and Coosa** counties in **Alabama;** and **Frederick Varner** in **Lowndes Co, AL, and Caldwell Par, LA.** William and Henley each served multiple terms in the Georgia Legislature. John was Clerk of the Lowndes County, AL, Court for many years. These four sons of George Varner were also planters; each owned many Negro slaves and large acreages of land.

Two of George Varner's sons--**John and Frederick Varner**--moved their young families to a frontier wilderness on the **Alabama River** in 1819, the year that

Synopsis (continued)

Alabama became a state. John became the first Clerk of the Lowndes County Court when that county was created in 1830. He served in that office for 12 years. John Varner then moved to **Coosa Co, AL,** where he established his fourth plantation in yet another frontier community.

Frederick Varner, son of George Varner and brother of John Varner, owned plantations in **Montgomery** and **Lowndes** counties in Alabama until about 1840 when he moved to a frontier settlement on the **Quachita River** in **Caldwell Parish, LA.**

Major characters, places, and approximate periods of time which this book covers are as follows:

1. Adam and John Varner and their children, Rowan, Randolph, and Davidson counties, NC (1763- 1829).

2. George, Frederick, and Matthew Varner and their children, Oglethorpe Co, GA (1785-1850).

3. Children of George Varner, primarily Putnam and Henry counties, GA (1810 to 1862).

4. John Varner, son of George Varner, Oglethorpe Co, GA (1785-1819), Lowndes Co, AL (1819-1843), and Coosa Co, AL (1843-1869).

5. Children and grandchildren of John Varner, primarily Lowndes and Coosa counties, AL (1819-1920).

6. Descendants of four of John Varner's children, primarily Coosa and Lowndes counties, AL (1840-1994).

6. Frederick Varner, son of George Varner, and his children, Lowndes Co, AL (1819-1840) and Caldwell Par, LA (1840-1865).

Hundreds of additional people who were or are related to these Varners and those who married them are also characters in this book. Places where they were born, married, lived, and died are also mentioned.

Preface

A Message From the Author

Please do not let my address mislead you about my heritage. I am a native of the South, not of the Northwest. I am an Oregonian by adoption only. The Northwest has been kind to me and I am very fond of it, but it was the South that gave me birth and nurtured me during my formative years. When I was 17, I came to the great Northwest as a migrant farm worker. This region, first Washington and then Oregon, was gracious in accepting me as one of its residents. Except for the 19 months I was in military service as World War II was drawing to a close, I have lived in Washington and Oregon ever since.

I was born and grew up in rural Arkansas, in Cleburne County, in the foothills of the Ozarks. That was where my paternal grandfather, Sidney Oliver Varner, settled 100 years ago.

Grandpa Varner grew up in Coosa County, Alabama, next door to many of the Varners whose lives are the subject of this book. But he was not related to any of them by blood. More about that later.

Grandpa was born in Coosa County in 1875. He lived there with his parents and brothers and sisters throughout his childhood years. For reasons that are not clear to present generations, Grandpa Varner left his parents' home in Alabama and moved to Arkansas when he was 18 years old.

Grandpa Varner's father, George Varner, was born in Anderson County, SC. He grew up there and in Franklin County, GA. While a young adult, he moved to Alabama, first to Talladega County but soon thereafter to Coosa County.

If my great grandfather George Varner had not moved to Coosa County, AL, nearly 150 years ago, I would not have written this book, which tells about Varner families who are not related to me! Sounds odd, doesn't it?

Here is how it happened.

My great grandfather George Varner moved to Coosa County, AL, near the time that John Varner and several of his children, who are topics covered in this book, moved from Lowndes County, AL, to Coosa County, AL. My great grandfather George Varner obtained and moved onto a tract of federal land located only two miles from where the John Varner family settled. My great grandfather George Varner continued to live near John Varner, his children, and grandchildren until George died some 40 years later.

The John Varner who lived in Coosa County near where my great grandfather settled had a son named George Varner, who was the same age as my great grandfather George Varner. But, John Varner's son George moved to Franklin County, MS; not to Coosa County, AL! It was my great grandfather George Varner who moved to Coosa County.

By now you can see what happened. While checking old records, including John Varner's will, I was mistakenly led to believe that my great grandfather George Varner was a son of John Varner.

I was right about who my great grandfather George Varner was--my family had passed down some knowledge about him--but I was 100 percent wrong about who his parents and other ancestors were.

How did I learn that I was not related to the family that I was researching?

Janice Palmer, who lives in Pensacola, FL, edits and publishes a Varner Newsletter. In 1992, Ms. Palmer asked me to write a summary of my Varner line for use in her newsletter. In the article, I inserted my great grandfather George Varner on the John Varner family sheet in the place where John Varner's son George Varner belonged.

Preface

A few weeks after my article appeared in the Varner Newsletter, I received a letter from Margaret Varner Barton of Santa Anna, TX. Ms. Barton said that the family I had written about sounded like the one from which her great grandfather GEORGE H. VARNER came! She included copies of family Bible records that her great grandfather George H. Varner had given to one of his children in 1872.

It didn't take much checking to confirm what had suddenly become obvious. My great grandfather George Varner was nothing more than a neighbor to the Varners I had been researching with so much dedication.

After learning the truth, I was momentarily disappointed and somewhat embarrassed. But after reviewing the evidence, I concluded that the error occurred because of unavoidable circumstances and not through careless negligence on my part.

I am so thankful that I learned the truth before I wrote and published this book. Can you imagine how I would feel if the book was printed and distributed with my great grandfather George Varner and his hundreds of descendants included as though we belonged with the John Varner family? I cannot imagine a more distressing experience.

I have expressed my gratitude to Ms. Palmer and Ms. Barton for their respective rolls in bringing this information to my attention. I sincerely appreciate their invaluable contribution.

Do I have regrets about spending so much time and effort researching the Oglethorpe County, GA, Varner families? Not at all. Genealogy is one of my retirement hobbies. It ties in well with my life-long interest in history. I enjoyed going through old records--from musty warehouses to modern air conditioned archives and libraries. Each discovery of Varner information was exciting. I admit that I would not have researched this line of Varners had I not thought it was mine. At least I would not have done it with so much dedication. But I have no regrets that it happened.

Why did I go ahead and write a book about these families? Partly because I had met so many Varners who treated me like kinfolks, and I had promised them and myself that I would write a book. I am hereby keeping that promise. In addition, I enjoy sharing my research discoveries with others, whether kin or not.

About the Contents of This Book

In light of the near disaster explained above, can the information and conclusions contained in this book be trusted? Absolutely. As the hundreds of footnotes attest, I have sorted and organized facts with extreme care.

I have drawn few conclusions from the facts collected, preferring to let the records tell the story. As the reader can see from the footnotes, almost all of the data comes from original records--ones that were written at the time the events happened by people who witnessed the events. I avoided using secondary sources as much as possible; I cited the few that I did use.

Much of the material in this book is extremely interesting. That is true primarily because of the roles the people played in the times, places, and events that are covered. These Varner families--at least those of 100 to 250 years ago--lived during an unusual period of world and American history in a unique part of the world.

They helped create the American nation. They fought in the American Revolutionary War so that the new country could win its independence. They were pioneers on the Western frontier of their day. They were nearby when Indians were driven from lands that white people

PREFACE

wanted to settle. They participated in the practice of slavery. They fought in the nation's bloodiest conflict, the Civil War. They suffered extreme pain, losses, and grief during that war. Even in peacetime, they dealt with personal tragedies--illnesses, death, poverty, alcoholism, and crime.

Generations that followed the Civil War coped with the extreme poverty that engulfed most of the South after the Civil War. They surely experienced the bitterness of reconstruction in years following the war. They saw close-up the racial hatred and segregation that lasted for decades. Today's generations were on or near where much of the action took place during the social revolution of the Civil Rights movement of the past few decades.

About the Topic of Slavery

Deciding how to deal with the topic of slavery in a family history was more difficult than I had thought it would be. Even though the practice of slavery ended several generations ago, I found that putting the names of slave owners in the same narrative with individual slaves quickly became a close and personal experience.

To handle this problem, I decided to report what happened as objectively as possible, based on old records, and, again, let the facts tell the story. Slavery was practiced in America for nearly 250 years (from 1619 to 1865). In comparison, that is nearly twice as long as the 129 years that have passed since slavery was abolished.

We should not and cannot erase the chapter about slavery from our national history or from our family histories. Such early American patriots and leaders as George Washington, Thomas Jefferson, Henry Clay, and Andrew Jackson were among the many prominent national figures who built and/or added to their financial fortunes by using slave labor. The use of slaves was also a prominent part of this Varner family's pre-Civil War history. Thus the practice of slavery needed to be and is included in this book. I have treated it as tactfully and fairly as I know how.

In old records, slaves were identified in a variety of ways. Some records only mentioned the number of slaves on a particular plantation. Other records gave their ages and sex. Wills, estate records, court records, and church membership lists often gave some information in addition to names. Occasionally, mother-child relationships, appraised value, and/or physical descriptions were reported. I included such identifying references that I found about slaves.

What happened to the former Varner slaves after they were freed? Finding an answer to that question was not within the scope of this study. However, I noticed some clues while I was searching source documents.

Black people with the surname Varner[1] appear in many Coosa Co, AL, records for the decades following the Civil War. There are census, marriage, land, and cemetery records, for example. Many blacks named Varner lived in Traveller's Rest Beat, Coosa Co, AL, which is the same census precinct where John Varner and his sons Edward P. Varner and John W. Varner owned slaves.

---

[1]..Former Varner slaves did not necessarily take Varner as their surname. However, Coosa County records, some of which the author recorded, indicate that many of them did.

PREFACE

Many Varners are buried in the Mt. Sinai Cemetery[2], Coosa Co, AL, where many blacks were buried during the decades following the Civil War. This cemetery is near the former Varner plantations. (Presumably, no whites are buried at Mt. Sinai.)

Almost all of the Oglethorpe County, GA, Varner men and their sons and grandsons were slave owners. The sons and grandsons took their slaves with them as they moved to many new locations in the South, including Putnam and Henry counties in Georgia, Lowndes and Coosa counties in Alabama, Caldwell Parish in Louisiana, and Lincoln County in Arkansas.

Many Varners not related to those covered in this book also owned slaves. Some of those who held large numbers of slaves were descendants of another George Varner[3] from Georgia, who resided in Decatur County, GA, and fought from there in the Revolutionary War. This George Varner's sons were slave owners in Baldwin and Pulaski counties in Georgia and Chambers and Macon counties in Alabama. The two sons who moved to Alabama--Alexander Varner to Chambers Co and William Varner to Macon Co--each owned many slaves.

At least three Varners--John, Elizabeth, and Cooper-- owned slaves in Marengo County, AL. The Marengo

---

[2]..Mt. Sinai Cemetery is located on Alabama Highway 27 about one mile north of its junction with U.S. Highway 22 in the Southwest corner of Coosa County.

[3]..This George Varner was an immigrant from Ireland, according to records written by his granddaughters during the 1850's and 1880's. The letters and many other records about this family are at the Alabama State Archives in Montgomery.

County Varners are not believed to have been related to either of the two Varner lines mentioned above.

Neither these other Varner slave owners nor their slaves are covered in this book. I mention them so that other researchers who find black families named Varner will not arbitrarily conclude that they are descended from slaves that were owned by the Oglethorpe Co, GA, Varners or their descendants.

Thanks to Those Who Helped

I gratefully thank those who helped me collect the material included in this book and those who encouraged me while I was working on writing it. Too many helped to mention all of them here, but the following deserve special recognition:

1. My father Oscar Fletcher Varner sparked my interest in family history research by frequently talking about earlier generations of our Varner family.

2. My wife Norma Kathryn "Kay" Peterson Varner helped me with research and traveled with me sometimes while I collected data. She also supported my work as I devoted countless hours, days, weeks, months, and years putting it all together.

3. Freeman and Sula Varner of Weogufka, AL, invited my wife Kay and me into their home and accepted us as kinfolks and friends throughout the years of this work. They have always and continue to treat us to true Southern hospitality, including serving us Southern home cooking and inviting us to sit on the porch with them at evening time and wave at passersby.

4. Ronnie Varner Zak and George Zak of Montgomery, AL, also welcome us into their home. Ronnie helped collect information on 20th Century Varners, too.

5. Virginia Waller Varner and John R. Varner of Hayneville, AL, welcome us warmly also. Driving into historic Lowndes County, going through early records, and visiting the Varners were great experiences every time I went to Hayneville. Virginia also submitted much material on 20th Century Varners who descended from the early day Lowndes County Varners.

6. Linda Varner Goswick of Weogufka, AL, collected and submitted material on many 20th Century Varners who descended from early day Coosa County Varners.

Finally, I wish to thank the institutions where I collected data and the people who work for them. Altogether, I spent the equivalent of two weeks or more at each of the following: the LDS Family History Library, Alabama Department of Archives and History, and Georgia Department of Archives and History. I spent the equivalent of a week or more at each of the following: courthouses in Lowndes County, AL, and Coosa County, AL. I spent several days each at the North Carolina Archives, courthouses in Oglethorpe and Wilkes counties in Georgia, and libraries at the University of Georgia and University of Alabama, the Birmingham Public Library, and the LDS Library in Beaverton, OR. I was at each of the other places listed for shorter periods of time.

I am grateful for the help given by the people and the other resources of the following:

1. LDS (Latter Day Saints) Family History Library, 35 North West Temple St., Salt Lake City, UT 84150.

2. Alabama Department of Archives and History, 624 Washington Avenue, Montgomery, AL 36104.

3. Georgia Department of Archives and History, 330 Capitol Ave. SE, Atlanta, GA 30334.

4. Lowndes County Courthouse, Hayneville, AL.

5. Coosa County Courthouse, Rockford, AL.

6. Oglethorpe County Courthouse, Lexington, GA.

7. North Carolina State Archives, 109 East Jones St., Raleigh, NC 27611.
8. University of Georgia Library, Athens, GA.
9. Wilkes County Courthouse, Washington, GA.
10. Birmingham Public Library, Birmingham, AL.
11. LDS Genealogy Research Library, Beaverton, OR.
12. Rowan County Public Library, Salisbury, NC.
13. University of Alabama Library, Tuscaloosa, AL.
14. Rowan County Courthouse, Salisbury, NC.
15. Davidson County Courthouse, Lexington, NC.
16. Randolph County Courthouse, Asheboro, NC.
17. Caldwell Parish Courthouse, Columbia, LA.
18. Putnam County Courthouse, Eatonton, GA.
19. Wilkes County Public Library, Washington, GA.
20. Montgomery Public Library, Montgomery, AL.
21. Henry County Public Library, McDonough, GA.

Sorting the Johns, Georges, Williams, etc.

A dozen or more men named John Varner are characters in this book. There are also several George Varners and William Varners. And two or more Varners are named each of the following: Frederick, Matthew, James, Jacob, Amaziah, Azariah, Edward, David, and Henley. There are also multiple Elizabeths, Sarahs, Margarets, Marthas, Marys, Harriets, Susannahs, and Nancys.

Sometimes, it is not easy to figure out which Varner with a commonly used first name is which. I have used several techniques, however, to help the reader sort them out.

Early generations frequently used just a first and last name when transacting business that became part of the official records. Later, most used a middle initial and\or a middle name. Whenever one was available, I used a middle name, a middle initial, and\or a maiden name to make it clearer which one I was writing about at a particular time.

To further help the reader separate the various Johns, Georges, and Williams from one another, I have used place names (such as where a person was born or lived) and dates (such as when a person was born, lived, and or died). I have also named parents, spouses, and children. In addition to these features, I have used footnotes to further identify which John, George, or William I am talking about in a particular part of the text.

Other devices that will help the reader recognize people and locate information about them include: (1) chapter titles, (2) sub-headings within chapters, (3) the table of contents, and (4) the index. I worded and organized all of these with the goal of helping identify people for the reader.

Abbreviations

abt--about
aft--after
b.--born
betw--between
cem--cemetery
co--county
d.--died
dau--daughter
LDS--Latter Day Saints
marr--married
par--parish

AL--Alabama
AR--Arkansas
GA--Georgia
LA--Louisiana
MD--Maryland
MS--Mississippi
NC--North Carolina
SC--South Carolina
TN--Tennessee
TX--Texas
VA--Virginia

Chapter I
Early Varner Families of NC

Several Varners[1] settled in the Piedmont region of North Carolina between the end of the French and Indian War (1763) and the beginning of the Revolutionary War (1775). The French and Indian War ended with a decisive victory by England and her American colonies over France and her Indian allies.

People in the English colonies expected this victory to guarantee them freedom to settle the West. They would, they thought, be able to cross the Appalachian Mountains and develop rich new lands, which they hoped to receive either free or at very low prices. The French would no longer pose a threat of taking control of settlers who migrated westward. And without the presence of the French to agitate them, the Indians would be less likely to attack frontier farms and villages.

By 1763, English settlers had been coming to America for more than 150 years, and some areas--including Pennsylvania, Maryland, and Virginia--were becoming crowded, by 18th Century standards. Many people in those areas wanted to gain more living space by moving to new lands in the West. They preferred to seek those goals by crossing the mountains into the Ohio Valley.

But English authorities were concerned about the cost of protecting the settlers on the frontier against Indians and renegade Frenchmen. The French and Indian War had been costly and the English faced the problem of

---

[1]--This book covers only two Varners who settled in North Carolina prior to the Revolutionary War and their descendants. Those two Varners--Adam Varner and John Varner--settled in what was then Rowan County, NC. Other Varners settled in Mecklenburg County and elsewhere in North Carolina.

paying off the huge debts they incurred during the war, which they had fought for seven years (1756-1763) in North America, Europe, and elsewhere in the world.

By defeating the French and their Indian allies, England had gained possession of all the lands extending from the English colonies along the Atlantic seaboard westward to the Mississippi River, except Florida, which was still owned by Spain. The English government anticipated settling the entire region eventually, but not immediately. They wanted to pay the war debts first, before taking on the additional costs of protecting settlers in the West. Consequently, the English government set up the Proclamation Line of 1763, which prohibited settlers from crossing the Appalachian Mountains.

This proclamation did not deter all those who wanted to move west, but it slowed that movement for several years. This was partly because those who would have moved west knew that they could not count on the British Army for protection. But there was a more important reason. There was still unsettled frontier land on the east side of the Appalachians. Much of that was in upstate New York along the Mohawk River and in the Northern and Western regions of New England. But the bulk of it was in the Piedmont Region of North and South Carolina and the portion of Georgia, primarily along the Savannah River, that had been opened to settlers.

Westward Movement Turns Southward

Thus the Westward movement turned Southward, from Pennsylvania and other over-crowded Middle Colonies, and Northward, primarily from New York and Massachusetts. The Southward movement had started earlier with a trickle of migrants. Then it exploded into a torrent of settlers during the 12-year period between the end of the French and Indian War (1763) and the beginning of the American Revolution (1775). This southward migration continued into later decades as well, as descendants of those who moved into the Piedmont Region of the Carolinas and Georgia moved on to settle the rest of Georgia and much of Florida--after 1819 when America obtained possession of it. Before the Southern migration ended, it took a westward turn into Alabama, Mississippi, Louisiana, Arkansas, and Texas.

Adam Varner Settles on Uwharrie River

Adam Varner and **John Varner** and their families were among the thousands of frontier settlers who moved southward from Pennsylvania and Maryland at the close of the French and Indian War.

Adam Varner settled on the Richland Fork of the Uwharrie River in what was then Rowan County, North Carolina in 1763, the year the French and Indian War ended. Adam Varner bought land there on 17 Feb 1763.[1] This farm became a part of Randolph County when it was created in 1779. It is near the Rowan County line in the Northwest corner of Randolph County.

---

[1]--Rowan County, NC, Deed Abstracts. Pages 415-416. Adam Varner bought 289 acres in tract # 10, on the Richland Fork of the Uwharrie River from Henry Eustace McCulloh. 17th Feb 1763. Witnesses were Robert Rainey and Alexander Ford.

The purchase of this land by Adam Varner is also recorded in the minutes of the Rowan County Court of Pleas and Quarter Sessions, Book 5, page 415. "Henry McCulloh sells Tract # 10 West, lying on the Hodges Fork of the Rich Fork of the Uwharrie, containing 289 acres, to Adam Varner. Feb. 17, 1763."

Information about the life of Adam Varner and his family is scant for the first two or three decades they lived in North Carolina. One of the few known documents, the 1779 tax records for Randolph County, reveals that Adam Varner lived in William Millikan's District.[1] He had 290 acres, obviously the same land he acquired in 1763. He had improved 30 acres of it, which suggests that he had cleared it and was farming it. He reported that he owned 5 horses and 15 cattle and that he had four pounds sterling on hand. The total value of his taxable property was 1200 pounds.

Adam Varner Left No Will

Adam Varner died intestate, which means he left no will. No estate records were located. The above mentioned 1779 tax record proves that he was living at that time. In 1783, a deed record notes the transfer of land "adjacent to Widow Varner."[2] Consequently, it is believed that Adam Varner died between 1779 and 1783. Adam Varner's son John Varner was living on Adam's former farm in 1785, according to the tax records for that year for Randolph County. Another white male between 21 and 50 was also living there. Undoubtedly, this was Adam's son Jacob Varner.[3]

---

[1]--Randolph County, NC, Tax Digest, 1779.

[2]--North Carolina Land Entry # 2658. "Kenigha Unda Bowers enters 50 acres of land in Rowan on the waters of Uwharrie beginning at the county line adjoining the Widow Varner including a field. Sept. 23, 1783."

[3]--List of Taxable Property of Capt. Clark's and Capt. Gray's Dists. Randolph County, NC. Taken Aug. 12, 1785.

(continued...)

What were the names of Adam Varner's wife and children? This author found no record of Adam's wife's name. Some evidence was located that suggests who his children were. Records clearly prove that Adam Varner had sons named **Jacob Varner** and **John Varner**. Others who might have been his children include **Henry Varner, Frederick Varner,** and **George Varner**. There were likely daughters also, but extant records do not confirm this.[1] Henry later moved to Tennessee. Frederick and George moved to Georgia. More information about John, Jacob, Frederick, George, and Henry is included in following sections of this chapter and in later chapters of this book.

John Varner of Rowan Co, NC

John Varner, probably a younger brother of Adam Varner, settled on the Yadkin River in Rowan County, NC

---

[3](...continued)
"John Varner, 2 white poles, and 289 acres." Two white poles means that two white males between the ages of 21 and 60 lived on that property. It gives no clues about females of any age or males under 21 or over 60.

[1]--It is more difficult to identify daughters from early American records than it is sons. It is particularly difficult in North Carolina because there are no extant records for many early marriages in that state.

Under North Carolina laws people who were married in churches were not required to purchase marriage licenses. Those who chose secular marriages were required to buy a license, which cost $15. This law existed until 1868.

Prior to 1868, about two-thirds of the couples were married in churches and one third through civil marriages. Civil authorities maintained records of secular marriages, but generally no records of early church weddings exist today.

before or during the Revolutionary War. (The land where he settled became a part of Davidson County when it was formed in 1822. The 400-acre claim is on the Northeast bank of the Yadkin River less than a mile upstream from where U.S. Highway 49 crosses the river today. The property line follows the river bank for nearly a mile.) John probably moved into North Carolina with his brother Adam in 1763 or soon thereafter. He entered a land claim in 1778[1]. He probably had been a squatter[2] on that land some years earlier[3] and delayed filing his claim

---

[1]--From Rowan County, NC, Deed Book 28 -- Page 351.

Land Grant # 2622. For the sum of 50 schillings for every 100 acres of land the State of North Carolina have given and granted to John Varner a tract of land containing 400 acres being in Rowan County on the east side of the Yadkin River, beginning at a pine standing on the east bank of the river, on Robert Shipton's and Henley's lines, east 55 chains to a white oak thence south 14 chains to a hickory thence east 43 chains to a post oak thence south 42 chains to a small post oak thence west 56 chains to a birch, locust and sprouts standing on the aforesaid river bank thence up the aforesaid river as it meanders to the beginning.

Entered the 9th day of Feb., 1778.

[2]--People who moved onto and farmed unclaimed land without first purchasing it or filing for a land grant from the government were called "squatters." This was a common practice on the American frontier, at that time and place and later elsewhere as the Frontier moved ever westward.

[3]--Affidavits filed by Matthew Varner, one of John Varner's sons, when he applied for a Revolutionary War pension, attested that the John Varner family lived on the family farm on the Yadkin River in Rowan Co, NC, when the Revolutionary War
(continued...)

until 1778.[1] Being younger than his brother Adam, he might have lived with or adjacent to him for awhile after moving to North Carolina. Or he might have lived near Baltimore in Maryland for a few years while on his journey from Pennsylvania to North Carolina. His son Matthew Varner was born "four miles from Baltimore, Maryland."[2]

John Varner's name appears on the Rowan County Tax List of 1778. He lived in Capt. Cox' District.[3] John Varner was bondsman for his son John Varner's wedding to Rebecca Davis, 4 May 1784, Rowan County, NC.[4]

John Varner died in Rowan County, NC, after 1800, leaving no will and no estate record. The latest discovered record about him was in connection with the sale of his land by his son John Varner, Jr., in 1800.[5] The fact that

---

[3](...continued)
broke out (1775).

[1]--The North Carolina government passed a law in 1778 that required "squatters" to file claims for their land not later than 1779 or risk losing it. Consequently, hundreds of people entered land claims in 1778 and 1779.

[2]--In his application for a pension for his Revolutionary War military service, made in 1832, Matthew Varner attested that he was born "four miles from Baltimore, MD." Revolutionary War Record # S 7787.

[3]--Rowan County, NC, Tax List for 1778.

[4]--Rowan County, NC. Marriage Records.

[5]--Rowan County Deed Book 17, Page 486. "John Varner to Michael Fisher.
"This indenture made the 3rd day of November, 1800,
(continued...)

his son transacted business for him indicates but does not prove that John Varner the father was failing in health either because of advancing age or illness.

What sons and daughters did John Varner have? There is positive proof for three: **John Varner, Jr.**[1], **Jacob Varner**[2] and **Matthew Varner**[3]. George Varner was

---

[5](...continued)
between John Varner, Jr. for and on behalf of his father John Varner, of the county of Rowan and state of North Carolina ...(sells to) Michael Fisher, Esquire, of the County of Rowan and state aforesaid ... in consideration of the sum of 200 pounds current and lawful money ... sell to Michael Fisher ... that tract or parcel of land situated ... in the county of Rowan on the Northeast side of the Yadkin River beginning at a pine standing on the east bank of the river to Robert Shipton's corner in Adderton line and runs thence with Shipton's and Henley's line east 55 chains to a white oak and then south 14 chains to a hickory then east 43 chains to a post oak, thence south 42 chains to a small post oak, thence west 56 chains to a bunch locust sprouts standing on the aforesaid river bank thence up the aforesaid river as it meanders to the beginning. (Originally) Entered the 9th day of January, 1778, containing 400 acres ... for John Varner and myself. Signed John Varner, Jr., his mark." Witnesses: Christopher Stokes, Daniel Soflin, his mark. Deed was duly proved in open court and ordered to be registered, Nov. 6, 1800."

[1]--The sale of John Varner, Sr.'s land by John Varner, Jr., is the most firm evidence of a father-son relationship. There is additional evidence also, including tax, land, and census records.

[2]..Jacob Varner left a will and other records. See Appendix IV-D at the end of this chapter.

[3]--John Varner of Rowan County is identified as the father (continued...)

probably John's son also. Frederick and Henry may have been, but no firm proof of this was found. John Varner probably had daughters also, but no records about daughters were found.

Who Were Adam and John's Parents?

The author believes but has not proven that Adam Varner and John Varner's parents were Hans Adam Werner (Warner) and Katharina Werner. The Werner family[1] arrived in Philadelphia, PA, in 1732, on the Galley Johnson.

Werner passengers on the ship's roster included **Hans Adam Werner**, **Katharina** (believed to be Hans' wife), **Adam** (a boy under 14, believed to be Hans and Katharina's son), and **Katharina** (a girl under 14, believed to be Hans and Katharina's daughter). According to the ship's log, these passengers came from the Palatinate, which was a region along the Rhine River on the western edge of Germany.

Hans Adam Werner wrote his will in 1770. He mentioned his wife Catherana and the following children: John Adam, Catherana, Fronaney, George, Jacob,

---

[3](...continued)
of Matthew Varner several times in Matthew's application for a Revolutionary War pension, op. cit.

[1]..Information on the Hans Adam Werner family's trip to America and other research material about the Werners was sent to the author by Lowell Varner Hammer, Potomac, MD. Mr. Hammer is a descendant of Hans Adam Werner and Catherana Werner's son Christophel (Christopher).

Christopher, and John.[2] The will was probated in 1775 in York County, PA.

The author believes that Hans Adam and Catherana Werner's son Adam was the Adam Varner who settled on the Uwharrie River in Rowan County, NC. The author also believes that their son John Varner was the John Varner who settled on the Yadkin River in Rowan County, NC, during the 1770's. Additional research on early North Carolina records would likely confirm these relationships.[2]

If it is true that Adam and John Varner were sons of Hans Adam and Catharana Werner, they apparently lived in Maryland for awhile after they left Pennsylvania and before they settled in North Carolina.

Two of the children of Adam and/or John Varner said they were born in or near Baltimore, MD when they applied for Revolutionary War pensions[3]. One of these children was Matthew Varner, a known son of John Varner. The other was Henry Varner, who is believed to have been a son of Adam Varner.

---

[1]..This information submitted by Lowell V. Hammer, op. cit.

[2]..Janet K. Pease, Arvada, CO, said that her research has confirmed that John Adam Varner and Catherine Varner Fouts, two of Hans Adam Werner and Catharana Werner's children, settled on the Uwharrie River in Rowan Co, NC. This information was sent to the author by Lowell V. Hammer of Potomac, MD, op. cit.

[3]--Matthew Varner, Revolutionary War record # S 7787, and Henry Varner, Revolutionary War record # S 4701.

John Varner, Son of Adam Varner

The name of **John Varner**, who was a son of Adam Varner, appears in the Randolph County, NC, records frequently from 1785 until his death in 1829. As noted above, he paid taxes on his late father's land in 1785. At the time of the 1790 Federal Census, John Varner was living in the Hillsborough District of Randolph Co, NC, adjacent to his brother Jacob Varner. He served on the Randolph Co, NC, Superior Court jury for the Oct 1807 term.[1]

Apparently, John Varner, son of Adam Varner, did not serve in the military during the Revolutionary War because no service records were located. He may not have been old enough to serve during the war. But he did serve in the North Carolina militia in 1788 and possibly other years.[2] Throughout his entire adult life, John Varner lived on and farmed part of the land on the Richland Fork of the Uwharrie River where his family settled in the early 1760's.[3] This land adjoined the land of his brother Jacob Varner.

---

[1]--Court of Pleas and Quarter Sessions, Randolph Co, NC.

[2]--John Varner's name appears along with his brother Jacob's name in Ebenezer Snow's militia company in 1788. Members of the company, including these Varner brothers, expressed their support for the new United States Constitution to the North Carolina General Assembly while it was considering ratification of the Constitution.

[3]--John Varner paid taxes on 300 acres in 1803 and 223 acres in 1815, 1817, 1819, 1820, and 1827. These are years for which tax records are extant.

Randolph County tax records suggest that John Varner was born between 1753 and 1765.[4] He died shortly after he wrote his will, which was dated 20 Jan 1829. He was between 65 and 77 years of age. John Varner's wife and children were named in his will.[2] His wife's name was Clovis. His children were **William Varner, Andrew Varner, Catherine Varner Garron, Millie Varner West, Molly Varner, and Susannah Varner.**

Jacob Varner, Son of Adam Varner

Jacob Varner, son of Adam Varner, lived in Randolph County, NC, throughout his adult life. His land was adjacent to that of his brother John Varner's and might have included part of his father Adam Varner's original land grant on the Richland Fork of the Uwharrie River[3], which was acquired in 1763. Like his brother John Varner, Jacob was probably born between 1753 and 1765.[4]

---

[1]--Every white male between the ages of 21 and 50 were required to pay a white pole tax. John Varner paid a white pole tax in 1803 but did not in 1815. Thus John Varner must have reached the age of 50 during that 12 year period, meaning that he would have been born after 1753 but before 1765. No tax records for years between 1803 and 1815 were discovered.

[2]--See Appendix I-A for a copy of the Will of John Varner of Randolph Co, NC.

[3]--John Varner of Randolph Co, NC, sold 126 acres on the waters of the Uwharrie in Randolph to Jacob Varner of Randolph Co, NC, 14 Aug 1798. Randolph Co, NC, Deed Book 5, page 64.

[4]--Jacob Varner, son of Adam Varner, was between 21 and 50 years of age in 1803 and over 50 in 1815, according to the
(continued...)

Perhaps Jacob Varner was too young to have fought in the Revolutionary War as no record of service was located. But he did serve in the Randolph Co Militia with his brother John in 1788[1]. Jacob Varner served on the Randolph Co, NC, jury for the Feb 1797 term[2]. He and his family were listed in the 1790 and 1800 federal census reports for Randolph County. He paid taxes on 215 acres of land and one stud horse in 1803 and on 257 acres valued at $770 in 1815.

Jacob Varner died in 1816, at the approximate age of 52 to 64. He left no will. However, estate and land records identify his wife and children. His wife **Mary Magdeline Varner** was administratix of his estate[3]. Jacob and Mary's children were **David Varner, Elizabeth Varner Hawkins,**

---

[4](...continued)
tax records for those years. See endnote above regarding pole taxes.

[1]--See footnote above regarding militia service by John Varner of Randolph Co.

[2]--Minutes of the Randolph Co, NC, Court of Pleas and Quarter Sessions.

[3]--Mary M. Varner of Randolph Co, NC, administratix of Jacob Varner's estate, appointed Phillip Copple of Rowan Co, NC, as her attorney to represent her in handling the affairs of Jacob Varner's estate. Randolph Co, NC, <u>Deed Book 13</u>, page 144.

Mary Varner Pugh, Nancy Varner, and Jacob Varner, Jr.[4] (Nancy Varner was a minor).

Jacob Varner's Estate

Shortly before his death, Jacob Varner gave one parcel of land to his son David Varner "for the natural love and affection which he has and bears for the said David Varner, his son."[2] Soon after his death, Jacob Varner's home place was divided into four parts, with his widow Mary M. Varner and three of his children (Elizabeth, Nancy and Jacob) each receiving about 40 acres. The portion for Jacob's widow Mary included all the buildings and improvements, including the house where Jacob Varner lived.[3] The remaining land that belonged to the Jacob Varner estate, consisting of 180 acres on both sides of the Richland Prong of the Uwharrie River, were sold in 1818 for $606.25.[4]

In addition to his land, Jacob Varner, son of Adam Varner, left an estate that included two Negro slaves: Poll and her son Franklin. They were "hired out" in 1817 and earned the estate $81. They were sold in 1820, Poll for $410 and Franklin for $200. Other property--a list four

---

[1]--Jacob Varner's wife and children are identified in several extant records, including: (1) the estate record on file at the NC Archives in Raleigh, (2) Randolph Co, NC, Deed Book 13, pages 144 and 353, and (3) Randolph Co, NC, Deed Book 16, page 16.

[2]--Rowan Co, NC, Deed Book 23, page 632. This land was located in Rowan Co, NC, on Hembes Creek, a branch of the Uwharrie River.

[3]--Randolph Co, NC, Deed Book 13, page 353.

[4]--Randolph Co, NC, Deed Book 16, page 16.

pages long--was sold for a total of $414.18.[1] Deed records indicate that on 25 March 1813, Jacob Varner purchased for $240 two other slaves--one Negro man by the name of Caesar about 60 years old and a Negro woman by the name of Jane about the age of 50.[2]

John Varner, Son of John Varner

As noted above, **John Varner**, brother of Adam Varner, settled on the Yadkin River, in what is now the southern part of Davidson Co, NC, before the Revolutionary War. The elder John Varner was the known father of Matthew Varner, Jacob Varner, and John Varner. In addition, he was probably the father of George Varner and possibly the father of Frederick Varner and Henry Varner and an unknown number of daughters. As explained elsewhere in this chapter, two of the elder John Varner's sons--John and Jacob--lived their entire adult lives in Rowan (now Davidson) Co, NC. The others moved to Georgia and Tennessee.

Several records concerning John Varner, son of John Varner, are extant, including his will. He sold the original John Varner home place, which had been recorded with the state in 1778, for and on behalf of his father John Varner, Sr. Consisting of 400 acres and improvements located on the Yadkin River in what is now the southern end of Davidson County, this property was sold to Michael

---

[1]--This and much more information is included in the Jacob Varner Estate Folder on file at the NC State Archives in Raleigh, NC.

[2]--No reference to Caesar or Jane was found in the estate records.

Fisher for 200 pounds 3 Nov 1800.[1] The name of the younger John Varner also appears in several other deed records and in extant Rowan County tax records.[2]

John Varner was probably not old enough to fight in the Revolutionary War; no service record was located. He married Rebecca Davis 4 May 1784 in Rowan Co, NC[3]. Based on John's will, estate records, and land holdings, he was a successful farmer.

John Varner of Rowan County wrote his will[4] 16 Feb 1826. His son William Varner, as one of the executors of the estate, held the estate sale 18 Oct 1827[5]. Final probate action on the will was taken in 1828.[6]

John and Rebecca Varner were parents of eight known children: **Matthew Varner, Nancy Varner, Thomas**

---

[1]--Rowan County, NC, <u>Deed Book 17</u>, page 486. These two John Varners are referred to as John Varner, Sr., and John Varner, Jr., in this deed transaction. However, in most extant records, each of them is referred to as John Varner, as are most of the other countless John Varners in 18th and 19th century records.

[2]--Rowan Co, NC, research by the author.

[3]--John Varner was bondsman and Ad Osborn was witness. Rowan Co, NC, marriage records.

[4]--See <u>Appendix I-B</u> for a copy of the Will of John Varner of Davidson Co, NC.

[5]--See <u>Appendix I-C</u> for more information about the estate sale of John Varner of Davidson, Co, NC.

[6]--John Varner's will and estate papers are on file at the NC Archives in Raleigh, NC.

Varner, John Varner, Lucy Varner, Polly Varner, William Varner, and Eli Varner.[7]

Jacob Varner, Son of John Varner

As explained earlier, **Jacob Varner** was one of three known sons of John Varner, who settled on the Yadkin River in Rowan Co (now Davidson Co), NC, prior to the Revolutionary War. Like the other Varners in Rowan and Randolph counties, Jacob was a farmer. He mentioned his plantation in his will. Jacob Varner also identified his wife and children in his will:[2] **Charity Varner**, his wife and executor of his estate; **Kathryn Varner** (married to a Huffman), **Barbara Varner, Margaret Varner, Polly Varner, John Varner, Jacob Varner,** unidentified daughter married to Philip Hoover, and unidentified daughter married to Jacob Hoover.

Henry Varner: Son of Adam Varner?

The name of **Henry Varner** appeared in Rowan Co, NC, records as early as 1778. At that time his name was on a list of people who had refused or neglected to sign an oath of allegiance to North Carolina or to appear in court and render an excuse for having not done so.[3] Later, however, he professed his allegiance to the United States

---

[1]--Identified from John Varner's will and other extant records.

[2]--See Appendix I-D for a copy of the will of Jacob Varner of Rowan Co, NC.

[3]--Rowan Co, NC, Minutes of the Court of Pleas and Quarter Sessions.

by fighting for it against the British in the Revolutionary War.[1]

Henry Varner married **Claranhappy Tucker** 22 Mar 1786 in Randolph Co, NC.[2] In 1793, Henry Varner purchased 300 acres of land from George Varner, who had moved to Wilkes Co, GA. He resold that tract to John Johnston on the same day.[3] The latest record found of Henry Varner in North Carolina was a summons to serve on the Randolph County jury, 13 Jun 1795.[4]

Henry Varner migrated to Tennessee, probably soon after 1795. He was living in Greene Co, TN, at the time of the 1830 census and in 1832 when he applied for a Revolutionary War pension. The 1830 Federal census shows him as a resident of Greene Co, TN, and reports him as being over 60 and under 70 years of age.[5] In his application for a Revolutionary War pension[6], made in 1833, Henry Varner claims to have been born in 1741 and he said he was 92. One of these sources is obviously in error.

---

[1]--Henry Varner's name is listed in the Index to Revolutionary War Accounts, North Carolina, located at the NC Archives in Raleigh. Henry also described his military service in his application for a pension. Federal military record # S 4701.

[2]--Randolph Co, NC, marriage records.

[3]--Rowan Co, NC, Deed Book 15, pages 470 and 481.

[4]--Randolph Co, NC, Minutes of the Court of Pleas and Quarter Sessions.

[5]--A woman of 60 and under 70 and a male of 10 and under 15 are also enumerated with Henry Varner in the 1830 census.

[6]--Federal military record # S 4701.

Records for Henry Varner were also found in Sullivan and Maury counties in Tennessee. In Sullivan Co, TN, he acquired land in 1799 and paid taxes there in 1812.[1] In Maury Co, TN, Henry Varner was assigned to work on a road crew in 1813 and 1814 and he purchased land in Nov 1814. He joined the Rock Creek Baptist Church by letter 8 Feb 1823, was licensed to preach in April 1823, and was dismissed by letter in Sep 1823.[2] He paid taxes on 87 acres in 1815. There is no known proof that the Henry Varner of Sullivan and Maury counties, TN, was the Henry Varner from Rowan or Randolph Co, NC.

Names of Henry Varner's children, if any, are unknown. However, **William Varner** was a resident of Greene Co, TN, in 1830 and 1840, suggesting that he was Henry Varner's son.[3]

Frederick Varner: Son of Adam Varner?

Frederick Varner settled adjacent to George Varner and Matthew Varner in Wilkes Co (now Oglethorpe), GA,

---

[1]--First Land Owners of Sullivan Co, TN, p. 91., and Early Tennessee Tax Lists.

[2]--Maury County, TN, Genealogical Abstract of Minute Books 1 and 2, by Carol Wells. Ericson Books, Nacogdoches, TX.

[3]--William was between 20 and 30 years old in 1830. Enumerated with him was a female of 20 and under 30, (probably his wife), a male under 5, 2 females under 5, and a female of 5 and under 10. In 1840 William and his wife were between 40 and 50. Their children: a male under 5, a male of 15 and under 20, a female of 5 and under 10, and a female of 10 and under 15.

a few years after the Revolutionary War ended[4]. Other Varner researchers have concluded that George, Frederick, and Matthew Varner were brothers, primarily because they went into Georgia at about the same time and settled in the same vicinity. Extant records prove that Matthew Varner and George Varner had both lived in Rowan and/or Randolph Co, NC, during the Revolutionary War and for a few years thereafter. Frederick Varner probably lived in Randolph or Rowan County, NC, before moving to Georgia also. Only one record was located that supports that claim, however. In 1779, he was listed in the Randolph Co, NC, Minutes of the Court of Pleas and Quarter Sessions for failing to return an inventory of his taxable property.[2] The fact that Frederick Varner was a resident of Randolph County suggests, but does not prove, that he was a son of Adam Varner rather than of John Varner.

Matthew Varner, Son of John Varner

The application by **Matthew Varner** for a Revolutionary War pension proves beyond doubt that his father was John Varner of Rowan County, NC.[3] That record also proves that Matthew Varner was a substitute

---

[1]..Most of the fighting ended in 1781; the Treaty of Paris, which officially ended the war, was signed in 1783.

[2]--Randolph Co, Tax List for 1779. William Cole's District: Frederick Verner was on the list of those refusing to return inventories of taxable property.

Frederick Verner: 3 horses, 8 cattle, 8 shillings on hand. Total value: 380 pounds and 8 shillings.

[3]--Matthew Varner's Revolutionary War service record # S 7787. Op. cit.

for George Varner. The relationship of Matthew to George is not stated. However, one of the affidavits submitted with the application by a person who had lived near the John Varner family during the war said she remembered that Matthew and his brothers were away from home for long periods of time during the war. She believed then, and still did when she wrote the testimonial, that Matthew and his brothers were fighting in the war. The brothers were not named. Nevertheless, this suggests, but does not prove, that George and possibly Henry and/or Frederick were Matthews' brothers. No specific record was located to prove whether Frederick Varner fought in the Revolutionary War.

Records of Matthew Varner while he was a resident of Rowan County, NC, consist of his marriage and his testimony as a witness to a legal document. He married Susannah Henley, 17 Aug 1787, in Rowan Co, NC. Darby Henley, believed to have been Susannah's father, was bondsman and John Macey was witness.[1] On 27 Oct 1786, Matthew Varner was witness to the transfer of land from William Lambert to Mighi Dillow.[2]

George Varner, Son of John or Adam Varner

George Varner was a soldier in the Revolutionary War. His name is entered twice in the Index to Revolutionary Army Accounts, North Carolina, which is located at the NC Archives in Raleigh. One entry is dated 13 Aug 1782. Matthew Varner swore under oath that he

---

[1]--Rowan Co, NC, marriage records.

[2]--Rowan Co, NC, Minutes of Court of Pleas and Quarter Sessions.

was a substitute for George Varner.[3] In Georgia, George Varner, resident of Oglethorpe Co, GA, was eligible to participate in the 1827 Land Lottery because he was a veteran of the Revolutionary War.[2] Even though this evidence strongly supports the fact that George Varner did fight for the American cause in the Revolutionary War, the National Archives apparently has no record of it and no one has joined the Daughters or Sons of the American Revolution on George Varner's service record.

George Varner Gets Land Grant

In addition to his military service record, George Varner left other evidence of having been a resident of Rowan and/or Randolph County, NC. On 25 Oct 1786, he acquired a land grant of 300 acres on Beaverdam Creek in Rowan County, NC, from the State of North Carolina. He may have already moved to Wilkes Co, GA, by the time the grant was acquired and the records are not clear as to whether he ever lived on the land. But he could have been a "squatter" on it before the grant was formalized. The

---

[1]--Matthew Varner's Revolutionary War Record, # S 7787.

[2]--Authentic Lists of All Land Lottery Grants Made to Veterans of the Revolutionary War by the State of Georgia, taken from official state records in the Surveyor General Department, located in the Georgia Department of Archives and History. Compiled by Alex M. Hitz. By authority of the Secretary of State of Georgia, Atlanta, 1955.

Page 71. George Varner, Oglethorpe County, in 1827, drew land lot # 28 in district 3 of Troop County. It was claimed on January 28, 1833.

(Revolutionary veterans did not receive preference in the land lotteries of 1805, 1807, and 1821, but they did in 1827 and 1832.)

acreage is located in the southern part of what is now Davidson County, about 10 or 15 miles northeast of where John Varner settled prior to the Revolutionary War. It is about 10 to 15 miles southwest of where Adam Varner settled in the early 1760's. George Varner sold his 300 acres in Rowan Co, NC, in two transactions. The major part of it, 275 acres, was sold to Henry Varner, as reported above, after George had moved to Georgia.

As explained more fully in paragraphs above, George Varner was probably a son of John Varner and a brother of Matthew Varner, but as indicated, he could have been a son of Adam Varner instead.

Appendix I-A
Will of John Varner[1] of Randolph Co, NC
<u>Will of John Varner</u>, Randolph County, NC, 1829.

I John Varner of the County of Randolph and State of North Carolina being in low state of health but being of sound mind and memory do this date make this my last will and testament, in the following manner, to wit:

First, my will is that all of my just debts be paid out of my property.

Second, I give and bequeath to my son William Varner the plantation whereon he now lives together with 14 acres lying and being in the county of Davidson.

Third, I give and bequeath to my son Andrew Varner the plantation whereon I now live.

Fourth, I give and bequeath to my beloved wife Covis? Varner during her natural life all my stock of hogs and one bay horse, two cows, three calves, one wagon, and

---

[1]--This John Varner was a son of Adam Varner of Randolph County, NC.

guns?, and bed and furniture, one dresser and furniture, one iron pot, that the above named William Varner and Andrew Varner shall maintain the said Clovis Varner during her life out of the above willed tracts of land.

Fifth, I give and bequeath to my daughter Molly Varner one farm and working ? (one line of copy torn off and missing).

Sixth, that all my personal estate not mentioned above be sold and the proceeds be equally divided among my four daughters, namely Catherine Garron, Millie West, Molly Varner, and Susannah Varner.

I do nominate and appoint my true and worthy friends William Varner and Andrew Varner to be my executors to this my last will and testament.

In witness whereof, I have hereunto set my hand and affixed my seal this 20th of January, 1829.

Signed John Varner, his mark.

Sealed and signed in the presence of Joseph Hoover and Benjamin Hawkins.

Proved in open court, Court of Pleas and Quarter Sessions, Randolph County, February term 1829. John Harper, Clerk.

Appendix I-B
Will of John Varner[1] of Davidson Co, NC

Davidson County, NC. <u>Will of John Varner, Sr.</u>

In the name of God, Amen. I John Varner Sr. of the County of Davidson, State of North Carolina, being

---

[1]--This John Varner was a son of John Varner of Rowan County, NC, and a first cousin of the John Varner whose will appears immediately preceding this one. This John Varner was a brother of Matthew Varner.

gathering in years but perfect in mind and memory thanks be to God for his mercies and calling to mind that all mankind has wont to die do make this my last will and testament in like manner following:

First of all, I will my soul to God who gives thereof and that my surviving managers that I will hereinafter name pay all my just debts and due to my body be decently buried in a Christian like manner and funeral expenses honorably paid and as to my worldly properties that God hath been pleased to bless me with I will as follows:

I will to my children or these lawful heirs that I shall now name $1.00 each and no more than what they have already received, naming this Nancy, Thomas, John, Lucy Smith, Polly, Harrison, son William, Eli, Betsy Ward and Rebecca Cooper are truly to receive the above $1.00 from my surviving manager of this my last will. And as to the property that I am now blessed with I also will as follows. I will to my beloved wife Rebecca all and singular these properties, all the land that I now own, namely 200 acres in the old tract and 130 in the other tract lying on the Big Branch, all my horses, cattle, hogs, sheep, and still and necessaries therein to belonging and wagon.

I will that at or near my decease that the horses, wagon, still, and necessaries thereto belonging be equally divided between William and Mathew and at the decease of my wife the remaining part of the stock go to the use of Mathew or his lawful heirs and as to the house, household and kitchen furniture after the decease of my wife, Mathew or his heirs are to have that property and now turn over and divide the land.

The division of my lands after the death of my wife Rebecca, the first tract, called the old tract, is to be divided as follows: beginning at Nichols' line on the creek and running with the meanders of the creek to the mouth of Thorny Branch and beginning at the mouth of the Pond Branch and then up that to the line and the North end of this tract I will to my son William or his lawful heirs. The other I will to my son Mathew and his lawful heirs together with the houses thereon.

And as to the other tract of 130 acres, lying on the Big Branch, I will as follows, if that is for William and Mathew to have an equal number of acres to be divided by a line east and west and for William to also have the north end of said tract, Mathew the other south end. And as for the performance of the above within instrument, I fully put my whole trust in my beloved wife Rebecca and my son William to execute the same...as I acknowledge the same to be my entire last will and testament before God and these subscribing witnesses.

In testimony I hereunto set my hand and seal this 16th day of February in the year of our Lord one thousand eight hundred and twenty-six.

Signed John Varner his mark.
Witness L. McDaniel and John Redwine.

Appendix I-C
Estate Sale of John Varner, Davidson Co, NC

Estate Sale of John Varner (NC Archives, Raleigh, NC).

List indicates that $1 was paid to John Varner, $1 to Eli Varner. Lists other distributions as expenses. Total estate sale brought in $116.53.

"The amount of the property of John Varner, deceased, and the amount of what said property sold at on the 18th of October last agreeable to letter of administration certified by Mr. William Varner, manager of said estate, the 12th of December, 1827.

Purchases at estate sale:

Rebecca Varner, the widow, five hogs, $15; William Varner, 1 cow, $7.57; the widow, 1 cow, $7.25; the widow, 10 lots of hogs, $3.50; the widow, 3 sheep, $1.60; Thomas Davis, 2 sheep, $2.13; Thomas Adderton, 2 sheep, $1.90; William Cox, 3 sheep, $2.06; Mathew Varner, 1 little bull, $3.25; John Varner, 1 little steer, $3.00.

Steven Miller, 1 sorrel mare, $21; Benjamin Cooper, 1 sorrel colt, $18.35; Lew Adderton, lot of hogs, $2.51; the widow, 7 shoats, $10.35; Johnathon Ward, 1 hog, $1.00; Mathew Varner, 1 black colt, $13.01; widow, 2 bee hives, 50 cents; widow, 4 head geese, 50 cents; Eli Varner, 4 geese, 56 cents; and the widow, 1 beef hide, $1.55.

Total: $116.53.

"I fully believe this is the true bill of sale sold the day above mentioned."   Signed William Varner

Appendix I-D
Will of Jacob Varner[1] of Rowan Co, NC

Rowan County, NC. Original Will of Jacob Varner. (Rowan County Will Book G, Page 328, Nov. 1814.)

Duly proven in open court by Jacob Hoover.

In the name of God, Amen. I Jacob Varner of Rowan County in the State of North Carolina being weak in body but in perfect and sound mind and memory this 20th day of September, 1814, do make and publish this my last will and testament in the following manner, to wit:

First, I give and bequeath to my beloved wife Charity Varner my land and plantation where I now live, also stock of all kinds, household and kitchen furniture,

---

[1]--Jacob Varner was a son of John Varner of Rowan County, NC, and a brother to Matthew Varner.

plantation utensils to enjoy during her natural life and if she Charity my beloved wife sees cause for her better support to sell the said plantation and land together with all the rest of the property it is my will that she should do so and live upon the money during her natural life.

At the decease of my beloved wife I give and bequeath to my beloved daughter Katherine Huffman $20 to be paid out of my estate.

Item. I give and bequeath to my beloved children Barbara, Margaret, Polly, John, and Jacob each five shillings to be paid to each of them out of my estate after the death of my wife.

Then my will is that Philip Hoover, Jacob Hoover, and Katherine Huffman have and receive all the balance of my estate to be equally divided among them as their right and property.

I do hereby appoint my beloved wife Charity Varner executrix of this my last will and testament.

In witness hereof I have hereunto set my hand and seal the year and date above written. Signed and published in the presence of us: W. Self and Jacob Hoover, his mark. Signed Jacob Varner, his mark.

Appendix I-E
George Varner Land Grant in NC

Land Grant to George Varner. Rowan County Deeds, Vol. 9, page 664. North Carolina Land Grant # 1232.

"To all who shall come, Greeting: Know ye that we for and in consideration of the sum of 50 shillings for every 100 acres hereby granted paid into our treasury by George Varner have given and granted and by these presents do give and grant unto the said George Varner a tract of land containing 300 acres being and lying in our county of Rowan on the waters of Beaverdam Creek beginning at a pine and runs east 75 chains to a stone in a bed of rocks thence south 40 chains to a stone thence west 75 chains to a pine thence north to the beginning as by the plat hereunto annexed doeth appear together with all woods, waters, mines, minerals hereditaments and appurtenances belonging or appertaining to hold to the said George Varner his heirs and assigns forever yielding and paying to us such sums of money yearly or otherwise as our general assembly may from time to time direct. Provided always that the said George Varner shall cause this grant to be registered in the register's office of our said county of Rowan within 12 months from the date hereof, otherwise the same shall be void and of no effect.

In testimony whereof we have caused these our letters to be made patent and our great seal to be hereunto affixed. Witness Richard Caswell, Esquire, Governor, Captain General and Commander-in-Chief, at Kingston, the 25th day of October in the 11th year of our independence and in the year of our Lord one thousand seven hundred and eighty six.

Seal Caswel # 1232 by his excellency commander J. Glasgow, Secretary.

George Varner 300 acres, Rowan County. Recorded in the secretary's office. W. Williams, secretary.

Chapter II
George Varner of Oglethorpe Co, GA

For more information about George Varner, his parents and grandparents, and other relatives, see Chapter I.

George Varner was born in Pennsylvania or Maryland in about 1755. He moved to Rowan County, NC, with his parents, probably during his early childhood years. He fought with American forces during the Revolutionary War. He moved to Wilkes Co, GA, soon after the end of that war. He became a prosperous planter, acquiring extensive holdings of land and Negro slaves. He died in Oglethorpe Co, GA, in 1827. George and his wife Elizabeth "Betsy", raised a large family. Their children moved to other communities in Georgia, Alabama, and Louisiana.

George Varner moved to Georgia from Rowan or Randolph Co, NC, during the 1780's, shortly after the Revolutionary War ended. He was a resident of Wilkes Co (Oglethorpe Co after 1794), GA, as early as 1785, when he and John Henley, Sr., both residents of Wilkes Co, GA, sold 200 acres of land[1], part of a 400 acre tract located on

---

[1]--Wilkes Co, GA, <u>Deed Book EE</u>, p. 89. George Varner and John Henley Sr. both residents of Wilkes County, State of Georgia, sold 200 acres on Falling Creek in Washington County, Georgia, to Barnaba Dunn, resident of Montgomery County, State of North Carolina for 500 pounds sterling on the 5th day of July 1785. The 200 acres is part of a 400 acre tract belonging to George Varner. Witnesses: F. Sims and John Henley.

(continued...)

Falling Creek in Washington Co, GA, to Barnaba Dunn, 5 Jul 1785. Tax records also place George Varner in Wilkes County as early as the late 1780's.[1]

In 1788, George Varner was granted 200 acres on Dry Fork of Long Branch in Wilkes Co (Oglethorpe Co after 1794), GA.[2] On 2 Jun 1791, he purchased an additional 300 acres on Long Branch.[3] He built his plantation home on one of these acreages, and as the years passed he added to his land holdings. He owned over 1700 acres at the time of his death in 1827. Most of his land holdings were located on Dry Fork of Long Branch, near his plantation home. Unfortunately, no records that describe the plantation buildings have been found.

George Varner's land holdings on Dry Fork of Long Branch were located in Wilkes Co, GA, until Oglethorpe

---

[1](...continued)
Signed George Varner and John Henley

[1]--1790 Census for Wilkes County, Georgia. Prepared from tax records. Compiled by Frank Parker, 1978. Copyrighted 1988. Reprint Co., Spartanburg, SC. Page 75.

George Varner resided in Wilkes County and paid taxes in 1787 and 1791. The area where he lived became part of Capt. Duke's District when Oglethorpe County was formed in 1794.

Frederick Varner and Matthew Varner paid taxes in Wilkes County in 1791. Therefore, they are assumed to have been residents of Wilkes County in 1790. They too were placed in Oglethorpe County, Capt. Duke's District, when Oglethorpe County was created in 1794.

[2]--Wilkes Co, GA, Deed Book P, p. 382.

[3]--See Appendix II-A at the end of this chapter for the deed abstract of George Varner's land purchase in Wilkes Co, GA in 1791.

County was created in 1794, at which time the George Varner plantation home became a part of Oglethorpe County. It was located in what is now the Northeast corner of Oglethorpe County, near the County Line Baptist Church.

George Varner Marries Elizabeth Henley

George and Elizabeth "Betsy" Varner married while they were residents of North Carolina although no record of their marriage has been located. This conclusion is based on the fact that their son John Varner was born in North Carolina in 1783.[1] Based on the order in which George and Betsy's children were listed in George Varner's will, John Varner is believed to have been their oldest son.

Elizabeth "Betsy" Varner is believed to have been Elizabeth Henley before her marriage. She was probably the daughter of John Henley and sister of Susannah Henley, who married Matthew Varner. Several Varner researchers have reached this conclusion, based partly on the fact that George and Betsy named one of their sons Henley. Also the name has been used many times by later generations of George and Betsy's descendants.

George Varner's wife's name was discovered by searching land deed records. George Varner and his wife Elizabeth "Betsy" Varner sold land on three occasions.[2]

---

[1]--Grave marker for John Varner, located in Providence Cemetery, Coosa County, AL, federal census records for 1850 and 1860, and other extant records in GA and AL.

[2]--See Appendix II-B at the end of this chapter for deed abstracts that recorded the sale of three parcels of land by
(continued...)

Apparently, Elizabeth "Betsy" Varner died before George Varner wrote his will, in 1825. She is not mentioned in the will.

George and Elizabeth Varner lived on land which was adjacent to Frederick Varner's plantation. Frederick is believed to have been George Varner's brother or cousin. Matthew Varner also lived near George and Frederick for a few years after the three of them settled in Georgia. Matthew is also believed to have been George Varner's brother or cousin. George and Frederick lived adjacent to one another until their deaths during the 1820's. In about 1800, Matthew moved about 12 miles Northeast of George and Frederick, to farm land located on Falling Creek, also in Oglethorpe County.

For more information about the probable relationship of George, Frederick, and Matthew Varner, see Chapter I.

George Varner, Planter

Eventually, George Varner undoubtedly became a major producer of cotton. But during his early years in Georgia, he probably grew more tobacco and grain than cotton. Cotton gradually became a significant crop after the invention of the cotton gin in 1793, but it did not become the major crop in Oglethorpe County until about 1815.[1] Tobacco was the major crop prior to then, but corn,

----

[2](...continued)
George and Betsy Varner during the 1790's.

[1]--<u>Oglethorpe County, GA, During the Formative Years 1773-1830</u>, Clarence Lee Mohr, Master's Thesis, Univ of Ga, (continued...)

wheat, oats, rye, barley, and flax were also grown. Livestock included sheep, cattle, horses, swine, and, in a few cases, mules. Much of the grain went into domestic liquor production, although it was also used for grain and flour. In 1810 the county produced 34,455 gallons of spirits worth $27,564.[1] George Varner's estate appraisal listed three stills, suggesting that his plantation produced some of the domestic liquor.[2] Economic statistics for Wilkes County, which was adjacent to Oglethorpe County, reflect a similar dominant agrarian pattern.[3]

---

[1](...continued)
1970, p. 93.

[1]--Ibid., pp. 89, 94, and 95.

[2]--Oglethorpe County Ordinary's Office, Book B, Appraisals 1828-1837, pp. 91-93, located at the Oglethorpe Co, GA, Courthouse.

[3]--An Historical and Editorial Study of the Washington, Georgia, News Reporter. By Parks Smythe Newsome. Thesis. University of Georgia. Written in 1954 and published in 1966.
Economic Development (Page 8)
"The economy of Wilkes county was sustained by extensive agricultural development. When men returned from fighting (in the Revolutionary War) to plant crops of corn, flax, and indigo as well as large crops of tobacco of which the county exported 3,000 hogsheads in 1790, cotton was grown in amounts sufficient only for family clothing needs prior to 1793. But Eli Whitney's invention of the cotton gin caused an abrupt turn from tobacco to cotton growing as the basic money crop of the county.
"Production figures are not available for Wilkes county, but the state production of cotton indicates the rapid changeover
(continued...)

Based on extant property records, George Varner was more prosperous than Frederick Varner and Matthew Varner and the brothers and cousins they left behind in North Carolina. He acquired his wealth through the use of slave labor combined with sound management and, most likely, hard work. Oglethorpe Co, GA, tax records and George Varner's will show gradual, steady growth in both his land and slave holdings.

George Varner Builds Slave Holdings

In 1796, the first year for which complete tax records were located, George Varner owned 9 slaves and 160 acres of land. He paid taxes of $3.96 3/4. The land had an estimated value of $94.05; the tax records do not give an estimated value for slaves. In just nine years--from 1796 to 1805--George had increased his slave ownership to 25 and his land holdings to 1136 acres. His tax bill for that year was $9.54 1/2. After another ten years, in 1815, he owned 36 Negro slaves and 1679 acres of land, all on Long Branch. In 1825 he had 42 Negro slaves and 1820 acres and paid $15.26 1/2 in taxes.[1] For several years in the

---

[3](...continued)
and the direct influence of Whitney's invention. In 1790 the state had produced only 1,000 bales of cotton. This figure was increased to 20,000 bales in 1801, to 90,000 in 1821, and soared to 561,472 bales in 1859. The cotton gin alone did not account for the tremendous increase. The great success of cotton as a cash crop led to the introduction of slave labor. In 1802 there were 5,039 slaves in Wilkes county. By 1857 this number had increased to 7,587."

[1]<u>Tax Records</u>, Oglethorpe Co, GA, 1795-1829. The original records are at the Oglethorpe Co Courthouse, Lexington, GA.

(continued...)

1810's and early 1820's, George also reported ownership of a "2-wheel gigg," apparently a "Cadillac" means of transportation for that day and time. The county, or state, levied an annual "luxury" tax on it of 50 cents!

George Varner needed a good means of transportation because he lived about 15 miles from Lexington, the Oglethorpe Co seat of government, where he had to travel frequently to engage in such endeavors as serve on juries[1], which he did many times[2], and transact business. His property holdings placed him in the wealthiest 100

---

[1](...continued)

1796--George Varner had 160 acres of #3 oak and hickory land on Dry Fork of Long Creek and 9 slaves. His land was valued at $54.05, and adjoined Ellis. Taxes: $3.96 3/4.

1805--George Varner had 1136 acres on Dry Fork of Long Creek and 25 Negro slaves. He paid $9.54 1/2 in taxes.

1815--George Varner had 1160 acres of #3 oak and hickory land on Dry Fork of Long Creek, 200 acres of #3 oak and hickory land on Long Creek, and 319 acres of #2 oak and hickory land on Long Branch, and 36 Negro slaves. He paid $14.50 1/4 in taxes. In addition, he paid 50 cents taxes on a two wheel carriage.

1825--George Varner, Sr. had 1620 acres on Dry Fork of Long Creek, 200 acres on Dry Fork, and 42 Negro slaves. He paid $15.96 1/2 in taxes.

[1]--Oglethorpe Co Superior Court Minutes list George Varner as being called to serve on the grand jury in 1803, 1805, 1807, 1813, and 1817 and on the petit jury a few other times. It was common for planters and other members of the ruling class to serve regularly on juries. During the early years of the Republic, ordinary people were not considered qualified.

[2]--See Appendix II-C at the end of this chapter for a record of George Varner's service on Oglethorpe Co, GA, juries.

families in Oglethorpe County, which was at the center of Georgia's thriving agricultural industry of that day. From time to time he probably also traveled to the bustling commerce centers of Augusta and Athens, each a distance of 40 to 50 miles from his plantation. Augusta was to the northeast and Athens was to the southwest of George's plantation home . He lived close to a major road that led to Augusta in one direction and Lexington and Athens in the other direction. Putnam County, where George's sons Henley and William lived during the last 15 years of George's life, was some 30 miles southeast of George's plantation.

The Oglethorpe County, GA, Superior Court was a familiar scene to George Varner because he served on its juries several times during the last 30 years of his life, as noted above. He also knew the Superior Court as a defendant in one known law suit. On 11 Feb 1822, Littleberry Jackson brought suit against George Varner seeking payment of $300 which he said George owed him.[1] Jackson claimed that George Varner, on 20 Dec 1820, employed him as an overseer[2] on George's plantation for the year 1821. The rate of pay was to be $300 for the year. He said he reported for duty 1 Jan 1821 and served until 4 Jan 1822. He said he worked in the capacity of an overseer and attended to the plantation business. He told the Court that George Varner had refused to pay him the $300 promised and that he attempted to defraud him out

---

[1]--Oglethorpe County, GA, Superior Court Minutes 1821-1825, pages 294-297.

[2]..An overseer on a plantation was the manager, or boss, of slaves. An overseer frequently performed additional management duties also. It depended on the wishes and needs of the plantation owner.

of it. The jury found in favor of Littleberry Jackson and ordered George Varner to pay him $300 plus interest from 1 Jan 1822. George was also directed to pay court costs. Records that were located did not include an argument from George Varner as to why he had refused to pay Jackson.

George Varner Writes His Will

George Varner wrote his will in 1825. His executors filed it for probate in 1827. The will and subsequent estate proceedings reflect George's substantial capital holdings.[1] According to his will, he had already given large sums of money to each of his children, all but one of whom had reached adulthood. Even after making those gifts, his personal estate was appraised[2] at over $16,000, a substantial sum for that period in U.S. history, and he still owned about 1800 acres of land. (The appraisal lists 52 Negro slaves by name. This suggests that he may not have declared all of them for tax records or on the 1820 U.S. census return, which reported him as having only 40 slaves.)

It is obvious that George Varner was financially able to and actually did give his children a good start toward accumulating their own estates. And the records show that some of them prospered, although it appears that none of them fared as well in an economic sense as George did. At least three of George and Betsy's children-- William, Henley, and John--served the public in important government positions in their respective communities.

---

[1]--See Appendix II-D at the end of this chapter for a copy of George Varner's Last Will and Testament.

[2]--Oglethorpe Co, GA, Book B, Appraisals 1828-1837.

The inventory of the property of George Varner, which was made by the probate office after his death, suggests that his plantation was producing a variety of products, many of which were likely being consumed by residents of the plantation, including his slaves and other workers, family members, and animals. In addition to the 52 Negro slaves and 3 liquor distilleries already mentioned, the inventory included the following items: 300 barrels of corn, 30 bushels of wheat, 27 head of cattle, 13 horses, 2 yoke of oxen and 1 work steer, 100 head hogs, 35 geese, 45 sheep, 27 turkeys, a wide assortment of farm tools and equipment, and miscellaneous household furnishings.[1]

George and Betsy Did Not Attend Local Church

Apparently, George and Betsy Varner did not attend the nearby County Line Baptist Church. This conclusion is based on a careful examination of the original copy of the Church minutes[2]. George Varner's name is mentioned

---

[1] --See Appendix II-E at the end of this chapter for a record of the appraised value of the property in George Varner's estate.

[2] --County Line Baptist Church Minutes, Oglethorpe County, GA.
(County Line Baptist Church is located 14 miles Southeast of Lexington. It was organized in 1797. Original minutes, dating from 1807, are in the possession of the clerk of the church.) Entries that refer to Mr. George Varner and his slaves follow:
"Saturday, July 3, 1813. The church met in conference, Bro. Robertson moderator. A door was opened for the reception of members whereupon Bro. William Calloway and a black woman by the name of Rhoda belonging to Mr. George Varner
(continued...)

only in reference to two of his slaves who joined the church. He was referred to in the minutes as Mr. George Varner. Had he been a member, he would have been referred to as Bro. George Varner. Betsy Varner's name does not appear in the minutes.[1] George and Betsy's plantation was near the church, so attendance there would have been convenient for them. George's brother (or cousin) Frederick and his wife Judah were members. George and Betsy's plantation adjoined Frederick and Judah's. There were other churches in the area that George and Betsy might have attended, including a Methodist one, but early day minutes for them were not located.[2]

George and Betsy Varner's Children

George and Betsy had nine children: **William, John, George, Jr., Henley, Frederick, Susannah, Elizabeth, Sarah and Emily Sophronia.**

---

[2](...continued)
came forward and related their experiences upon which they were received into fellowship."

"Saturday, July 2, 1814. The church met in conference, Bro. Thomas Rhoades, moderator... Mr. George Varner's Letta came forward and related her experience upon which she was received into fellowship."

[1]--The minutes for the earliest years of the church (1797-1808) have been lost. Betsy Varner might have joined the church during those years.

[2]--See Chapter III for more information on this topic.

VARNER FAMILIES OF THE SOUTH--II

For information about George and Elizabeth Varner's children, their families, and descendants, see chapters that follow.

Appendix II-A
George Varner Land Purchase in Wilkes Co, GA

Wilkes Co, GA, Deed Book KK, p. 94.

State of Georgia. This indenture made the 2nd day of June in the year of our Lord 1791 and in the 15th year of the independence of the United States of America between Jeremiah Morgan and Mary his wife of the county of Wilkes and state aforesaid of the one part and George Verner of the state aforesaid and County of Wilkes on the other part witnesseth that the said Jeremiah Morgan and Mary his wife for and in consideration of the sum of 100 pounds sterling lawful money of the said state...sold...to the said George Verner ...that tract or parcel of land containing three hundred acres...situated in the county of Wilkes on the waters of Long Creek bounding northwardly by Glenn Owens land, westwardly by McNeil's land, and southwardly by the heirs of Poentley and eastwardly by Lane's land having such form and shape natural and artificial as appears by a plat of the same and annexed to a grant granted to the said Jeremiah Morgan.

Jeremiah Morgan (his mark) Molly Morgan (her mark)

Sealed and delivered in the presence of Biney Elrod, Haner Elrod, James Elrod. Executed before me by Jeremiah Morgan. (Signed) Josiah Cole, J.P.

Appendix II-B
George and Betsy Varner Land Sales in GA

Oglethorpe County Deed Book B 1796-1798. Page 170.
July 26, 1796. Between George Varner and his wife Elizabeth of the county of Oglethorpe on the one part and James Taylor of the same county. George and Elizabeth Varner in consideration of the sum of 100 pounds sterling to them in hand paid doeth sell to James Taylor a certain parcel or tract of land being part of a tract granted to Peter Smith containing 500 acres lying on a branch of the Dry Fork of Long Creek...in the county of Oglethorpe bounded as follows:

Beginning at a stake on Bankson's old tract now Daniel Jackson, thence 41 chains to a pine thence nearly east 64 chains to a white oak corner on a branch thence north 53 1/2 chains to a dividing line agreed on between Talbert and Lowden thence west on a line 32 chains to a hickory on Bankson's old line then south to a post oak and then west to the beginning of the said tract of land containing 312 acres more or less together with all the appurtenances thereunto. Acknowledged before me, Chadwick Wyman, J.P.

Signed George Varner and Elizabeth Varner

Wilkes County, GA, Deed Book E, Page 414.

April 5, 1791. George Varner of Wilkes County and Joseph Price of Greene County. George Varner sold for 80 pounds good and lawful money of Georgia a tract of land lying in the county of Greene on the waters of the Oconee on the branch of Falling Creek 280 acres of land. Said George Varner and Elizabeth Varner his wife relinquish this land. Signed by George Varner, Elizabeth Varner, her mark. Witness: John Lumpkin, J. P.

Oglethorpe County, GA, Deed Book A, Page 95.

Feb. 7, 1794 between George Varner of the County of Oglethorpe and Betsy his wife of the one part and William Ellis of said county on the other part. Said George Varner and Betsy his wife for the sum of six pounds hereby sell to William Ellis all that tract or parcel of land being in the county aforesaid containing 34 acres joining Radford Ellis' land beginning at a post oak corner thence north 45 east 9 chains 5 links to a black jack thence north 58 west 36 to a red oak thence south 45 west 9 chains to a hickory thence to the beginning and surveyed Feb. 3, 1794 by William Graves. Signed George Varner

Witness: George Swain, J. P.

Appendix II-C
George Varner Serves on Juries

Minutes of the Superior Court, Wilkes County, Georgia, 1787-1792. (Entries not dated.) George Varner was one of 52 jurors called to serve on the Petit Jury. Nearby entry dated July, 1791.

Minutes 1800-1808, Oglethorpe County. George Varner was summoned to serve on the grand jury Mar. 21, 1800. He was one of 23 sworn in to serve on the grand jury, Sept. 15, 1800. As a member of Special Jury # 1, he was one of 12 members who found for the respondent on appeal for $385.15 in case of Joshua Glass vs Daniel Stocker, respondent.

George Varner was one of 30 men chosen to serve on the grand jury for the Sept. term, 1803. He was one of 19 sworn in Sept. 19, 1803.

George Varner being one of 18 grand jury members who signed the indictment, the grand jury in the September term of 1803 made the following charges:

"Being drunk and engaging in profane swearing: Fleming Jordan, Esquire, Big John Johnson, Richard Moore, and Daniel Hottesfield.

"Engaging in profane swearing: Joseph Gill, Henry Beasley, John Gwinnel, Andrew McIlroy, Samuel Bell, and William Reason.

"Breach of the Sabbath: Richard Hargraves.

"Keeping a disorderly house: Thomas Stone.

"We warn men to attend general muster.

"We charge as a guidance that the patrol law is not now generally enforced.

"We present as a guidance that the clerk of the Inferior Court has not been more particular in punishing the different surveyors of the roads with orders and a list of hands liable to work on the roads.

"And we present Jones Orders of the road for not keeping that part assigned to him in proper repairs.

"And we express our thanks to his honor Judge Griffin for the strict attention he has given the duties of his office during the present term."

March 1805, George Varner's name was again chosen to serve on the grand jury. However, he was one of 11 of the 30 who were called who was not sworn in.

George Varner was one of 30 whose names were drawn to serve on the grand jury for the March term 1807. He was one of 21 sworn in to serve, on March 9, 1807. He served on three special juries during that term.

Minutes of Superior Court 1812-1819. George Varner was one of 48 persons whose names were drawn to serve on the grand jury for the March term, 1813.

Minutes of Superior Court 1812-1819. George Varner was sworn in as a member of a 23-member grand jury on March 8, 1813.

George Varner was one of 36 people whose names were drawn to serve on the grand jury for the March term of 1817.

Appendix II-D
George Varner's Last Will and Testament

Oglethorpe Co, GA, Will Book C, pp. 28-30.

The Last Will and Testament of George Varner, Sr.
IN THE NAME OF GOD AMEN.

I George Varner, Sr. of the County of Oglethorpe and State of Georgia being weak in body but I hope of sound mind and memory but calling to mind the mortality of my body believing as I do that all men have to die, shall dispose of my worldly estate in manner and form following (to wit)

Item lst. I give and bequeath to my beloved daughter Elmiry Sophrony Varner, ten Negroes (to wit) one Negro woman Sall, Lucy, Caroline, Addeline, Burwell, Abram, Clary, Cheny, Caroline (the younger) and Eaify, which ten Negroes above named with their increase my said daughter is to have full possession of when she marries or becomes of age, together with all my household and furniture of every description, and well selected saddle horse suitable for her, worth one hundred and fifty dollars, a good saddle and bridle, equivalent to be educated as well as the nature of the case will admit of out of my estate exclusive of her specific legacy.

Item 2nd. It is my will and desire that all the rest and residue of my estate both real & personal not already disposed of between the whole of my children except James Neal my son-in-law. He is fully represented by his two daughters Martha A. Neal and Susan V. Neal, my grand daughters, who are to draw one good bed and

GEORGE VARNER OF OGLETHORPE CO, GA

furniture each in the first place and then to draw an equal share or part of the residue with my children already named and to be hereinafter named except my son George Varner who is also to receive one good bed and furniture out of my household furniture already specifically given to my daughter Almiry Sophronia Varner, and then to draw an equal share or part of the residue with the whole already mentioned and to be mentioned (to wit) Almiry Sophrony Varner my sons John Varner, William Varner, Frederick Varner, George Varner, Henly Varner, Elizabeth Neal, and Sarah Whitfield after deducting from each legacy the amount received by each child they equally divide the balance of my estate--

First my son John Varner has already received one thousand nine hundred dollars.

William Varner has received one thousand six hundred dollars.

Frederick Varner has received one thousand two hundred dollars.

George Varner Jr. has received one thousand one hundred and fifty dollars.

Henly Varner has received two thousand three hundred and fifty dollars.

Thomas Neal has received seven hundred dollars.

George Whitfield has received one thousand dollars.

Now after deducting the aforesaid several sums, all sums annexed to each legatees named, then add the two grand daughters above named as two legatees; then and not until then, they proceed to divide by nine share and share alike till all is equally divided.

Lastly, I nominate and appoint my two sons, William Varner and Henly Varner and my son-in-law George Whitfield my lawful executors to this my last will and testament, allowing all and whatsoever they may lawfully do in the aforesaid premises, revoking all former wills by

me heretofore made. In testimony whereof I have hereunto set my hand and affixed my seal this 13th day of January, 1825. George Varner, Sr. (Seal)
Signed...in the presence of John H. Gresham, Talbot May, Valentine Brown, J. W. Lumpkin.

State of Georgia, Oglethorpe County
 In vacation Sept 17th, 1827. You John Gresham, J. W. Lumpkin, and Valentine Brown do solemnly swear that you saw the within named George Varner Sr. sign seal publish and declare the within instrument of writing to be his last will and testament and at the time of so doing he was of sound mind and memory to the best of your knowledge and belief and also saw Talbert May subscribe the same as a witness. So help us God.
 Sworn and subscribed the 17th Sept. 1827. John H. Gresham, J. W. Lumpkin and Valentine Brown.

Oct. 3rd, 1827. Adjourned term of ordinary for said county. The within will was exhibited in court and Wm Varner one of the executors to said will was sworn in as witness and the will ordered to be recorded in full.
Charles V. Collier DCCO

Appendix II-E
Appraisal of George Varner's Estate
Recorded 9 Jan 1828, the appraisal record is in Oglethorpe Co, GA, <u>Book B, Appraisals</u> 1828-1837, pp. 91-93.
 <u>An Inventory of the Appraisement of the Property of George Varner, Senior, Deceased</u>
 90 Mobby Stands, $45.00; 3 Stills (60 gallons, 40 gallons, 30 gallons), 65.00; 4 Cow hides 4.50; 14 tight casks 14.00; 2 Cans 1.00; 2 Pr Stillgards 2.00; 10 Cotton

GEORGE VARNER OF OGLETHORPE CO, GA

wheels 10.00; 1 Carding machine 20.00; 1 Loom 2.00; 5 slays 5.00; 1 Shot gun 5.00; 9 Demijons? 12.00; 4 Jugs 2.00; 1 Gallon hot gut pot & funnel 1.00; 4 tight casks 1.50; 3 Sides harness leather 6.00;

6 Black bottles .75; 1 Gig & harness 150.00; 3 Small Casks .50; 7 Mattocks 7.00; 23 Weeding hoes 11.00; 13 Club axes 15.00; 2 Broad axes 1.50; 6 Iron wedges 1.50; 4 Spades 2.00; 1 Whiss saw 3.00; 1 Crow Bar 1.00; 6 Scythes & Cradles 9.00; 1 Ox cart 25.00; 14 Plow Stocks & Singletrees 14.00; 6 Plow molds 6.00; 2 Dagon Plows 20.00; 9 Coulters & Stocks 5.00; 1 Lot plows 5.00; 1 Lot Augers, Chisels & Square 2.00; 10 Pair plow gears 12.00.

1 Lot old Waggon tyre 6.00; 1 Lot Black Smith tools 45.00; 1 Grind stone 2.00; 1 Road Waggon & harness 80.00; 1 Wheat fan 16.00; 20 Bushels Rye 10.00; 30 Bushels Wheat 15.00; 1 Cotton Gin 75.00; 1 Old Cotton gin 1.00; 1 Threshing Machine 10.00; 1 Road Waggon & harness 100.00; 1 Ox Cart 20.00; 1 Old Wheat fan 8.00; 1 Cutting knife & Box 1.00; Old cutting knife .50;

9 Bushels Barley 6.50; 100 Head Hogs 200.00; 45 Sheep 50.00; 35 Geese 10.00; 1 Bay horse Tom 20.00; 1 Horse Boneyparte 75.00; 1 Horse Potomac 75.00; 1 Horse Royalist 25.00; 1 Mare Merandy 50.00; 1 Gray Lumpkin filly 200.00; 1 Boneypart filly 30.00; 1 Boneypart filly 30.00; 1 Colt Sir Andrew 40.00; 1 Colt Flag 140.00; 1 mare Georgian 60.00; 1 Black mare 75.00; 1 cato mare 60.00; 300 Barrels Corn 600.00; 1 Cross Cut Saw 2.00; 1 Yoke oxen 40.00; 1 Yoke Oxen 40.00; 1 Work Steer 15.00; 20 Head Cattle 120.00; 7 Cows & Calves 70.00; 1 Bull 12.00;

1 Negro man Rob 125.00; 1 Negro woman Milly 75.00; 1 Negro man Primos 200.00; 1 Negro man Ben 200.00; 1 Negro man Harry 300.00; 1 Negro woman Rhody 150; 1 Negro woman Sarah 80; 1 Negro man Dick 280.00; 1 Negro man Jim $300; 1 Negro man John 350; 1 Negro

man Charles 425; 1 Negro man young Harry 500; 1 Negro man Newton 450; 1 Negro man Major 500.00; 1 Negro man Robin 500.00; 1 Negro man Randol 500.00; 1 Negro man Henry 480.00; 1 Negro man Nathan 400.00;

1 Negro man Giles 400.00; 1 Negro man Jacob 350.00; 1 Negro man Warren 375.00; 1 Negro man James 300.00; 1 Negro man Butler 250; 1 Negro man Simon 150; 1 Negro man Wat 150; 1 Negro man Frank 120; 1 Negro woman Tilly 250; 1 Negro child Milly 100; 1 Negro girl Telvira 200; 1 Negro child Tabby 200; 1 Negro child Ciller 280; 1 Negro child Charity 300.00; 1 Negro child Fillis 280; 1 Negro girl Elinder 260; 1 Negro woman Amy 125; 1 Negro girl Janett 200; 1 Negro woman Sarah 240; 1 Negro woman Avey 500;

1 Negro woman Aram 500; 1 Negro woman Mary 300; 1 Negro Child Sally 100; 1 Negro child Cherry 140; 1 Negro child Caroline 120; 1 Negro child Dick 100; 1 Negro woman Adaline 300; 1 Negro child Charles 100; 1 Negro child 300; 1 Negro child Daniel 100; 1 Negro child Nehley 100; 1 Negro Woman Edify 300; 1 Negro child Reuben 100; 1 Negro Boy Burrel 250;

1 Desk 25.00; 1 Clock and Case 80; 1 Side Board 30; 1 Lot Glass Ware 3.50; 1 Lot China 15.00; 1 Lot Earthen Ware 8.00; 1 Cupboard 15.00; 1 Folding table 10.00; 2 Pine tables 2.00; 1 Slab 6.00; 7 Beds bedsteads & furniture 181.00; 1 Pine Cupboard 3.00; 2 Lots knives & forks 2.00; 1 Coffee mill 1.50; 2 Lot Candle Sticks 3.50; 4 Looking Glasses 4.00; 1 profile looking glass .50; 9 Windsor Chairs 9.00; 14 Split bottom chairs 7.00; 1 Small Walnut Table 2.00; 2 Pair fire tongs .50; 1 Shovel & tongs 1.50; 1 Family Bible 8.00; 2 Stone jars 1.00; 5 Pewter Basins 2.00; 3.00; 5 Pots 8.00; 3 Ovens 4.00; 2 Spiders 1.00; 2 Brass kettles 3.00; 2 Grid irons .25; 3 Washing Tubs 3.00; 3 Smoothing Irons 1.50; 27 Turkeys 12.00.

 TOTAL APPRAISED VALUE: $16,223.50

GEORGE VARNER OF OGLETHORPE CO, GA

Georgia, Oglethorpe County

We do hereby certify that the within is a true inventory & appraisement of the goods and chattels of George Varner, Senior, deceased, so far as was shown to us by the executor William Varner & to the best of our understanding.

Given under our hands and seals on the above day and date. John Lumpkin, John H. Gresham, Elisha Ogden, & Thomas Davis.

Recorded the 9th day of December 1828. Isaac Hardeman, Clerk.

Chapter III
Frederick Varner
Of Oglethorpe Co, GA

For more information about Frederick Varner, his parents and grandparents, and other relatives, see Chapters I and II.

Frederick Varner was born in Pennsylvania or Maryland in about 1750 to 1760. He moved to Rowan County, NC, probably with his parents during his childhood years. Later, he moved to Wilkes Co, GA, in about 1790. He settled adjacent to George Varner, believed to have been his brother or cousin, and Matthew Varner, with whom he was also likely related. Like George and Matthew Varner, Frederick was a planter. He owned large acerages of land and several slaves. He and his wife Judah (or Judy) raised a large family. He is believed to have died between 1826 and 1830, probably in Oglethorpe Co, GA.

As noted in Chapter I, Frederick Varner is believed to have been a son of either Adam Varner, of Randolph Co, NC, or John Varner, of Rowan Co, NC. However, he left less evidence of having lived in North Carolina (see Chapter I) than either George or Matthew did. But the fact that he settled and lived adjacent to George and Matthew in Georgia strongly suggests a family relationship with them.

Apparently, Frederick Varner did not fight in the Revolutionary War. No record of service could be located in North Carolina or Georgia or at the National Archives.

Frederick Varner in Georgia

The earliest known positive proof that Frederick Varner was a resident of Georgia is the 1791 tax record for Wilkes County.[1] Other early records show that he was appointed Constable of Capt. McIlroy's District in Oglethorpe Co, GA, in 1796 and that he served on the Oglethorpe County jury in 1797.[2] Also in 1796, he signed a bond[3] in support of Samuel Clay, an orphan child.

In addition to jury duty in 1797, Frederick was called and served on Oglethorpe County juries at least four additional times: in 1808, 1818, 1820, and 1823.[4] In 1803,

---

[1] --1790 Census for Wilkes County, Georgia. Prepared from tax records. Compiled by Frank Parker, 1978. Copyrighted 1988. Reprint Co., Spartanburg, SC. Page 75.

Frederick Varner...paid taxes in Wilkes County in 1791. Therefore, he is assumed to have been a resident of Wilkes County in 1790. He was placed in Oglethorpe County, Capt. Duke's District, in 1794, when Oglethorpe County was created.

[2] --Inferior Court Minutes 1794-1808, Oglethorpe County, page 56.

[3] --Inferior Court Petitions 1794-1802, Oglethorpe County. Page 25. Jesse Clay, Frederick Varner, and Henry Haynes pledged $1500 to be paid to the governor or his successors if Jesse Clay failed to live up to promised conditions as guardian of Samuel Clay, minor, orphan, and son of Abbie Clay, deceased. Action took place Nov. 29, 1796.

[4] --See Appendix III-A at the end of this chapter for a record of Frederick's service on Oglethorpe County, GA, juries.

Frederick Varner successfully brought suit in the court to collect money owed him on a promissory note.[5]

Frederick Varner gradually acquired acreages and Negro slaves but at a slower pace than his brother (or cousin) George Varner. The Oglethorpe County tax records reflect this growth. In 1795, Frederick had no slaves and only 130 acres of land.[2] He first reported ownership of slaves in 1797, at which time he had two.[3] By 1805, his land holdings had grown to 620 acres and he had eight slaves.[4] By 1815 his land holdings had dropped slightly, to 530 acres, and his slave ownership had inched

---

[1]--Minutes Superior Court 1800-1803. Page 369.

Frederick Varner vs. Roland Hudson and F. John Beasley. Frederick petitioned for $180, which he said Hudson and Beasley owed on a promissory note, which was signed Jan. 1, 1803. They used as security a Negro boy named Ellis. Varner said the note had not been paid as promised and he asked the court to intercede. The case was tried before a jury, which rendered a decision in favor of Varner. Defendants were given the option of paying money or turning the Negro boy over to Varner and pay court costs. Sept. 21, 1803.

[2]--Oglethorpe County Tax Records, 1795. Frederick Varner had 130 acres of oak and hickory land (3rd grade), one pole and no Negro slaves. Value of all property: 9 pounds, 15 shillings. Tax: 2 shillings, 6 pence.

[3]--Oglethorpe Co, GA, Tax Records 1797.

Frederick Varner had 130 acres of #3 oak and hickory land worth $40.20 and 2 Negro slaves under the age of 60.

[4]--Oglethorpe County, GA, Tax Records, 1805.

Frederick Varner had 620 acres on Long Creek and 6 Negro slaves. He paid $2.96 1/2 in taxes.

up to 11.[5] In 1825, he had raised his Oglethorpe County land ownership to 720 acres and his slave population to 16.[2]

Compared with the average Oglethorpe County resident, Frederick Varner was a wealthy man in 1825 even though his property was worth only about one-third as much as George Varner's. In an economic sense, both Frederick and George were leading citizens in their community and county, in 1825. And they had occupied that high status for several years. But both were soon to lose their wealth. George died two years later and his wealth passed on to this children.

Frederick's property was already being seized by the Court and Sheriff because Frederick had co-signed promissory notes in an attempt to avert an impending bankruptcy by his land-speculating son, Edward Varner. This disaster would not only topple Frederick in an economic sense, but it also indirectly caused him to be removed from membership in the County Line Baptist Church, where he had become an active deacon.

Frederick Varner Suffers Losses

Frederick Varner's economic world came tumbling down in 1825 and 1826. His son Edward Varner seems to have been the cause of it. Edward was a land speculator

---

[1]--Oglethorpe County, GA, Tax Records, 1815.
Frederick Varner had 522 acres on Long Creek and 11 Negro slaves. He paid $4.52 1/2 in taxes. His land was adjacent to John Ragan. It was originally granted to Mathew Talbert.

[2]--Oglethorpe County Tax Records, 1825.
Frederick Varner had 715 acres on Long Creek...and 16 Negro slaves. He paid $6.46 in taxes.

and business man residing in Eatonton, Putnam Co, GA. He had acquired land holdings in several Georgia counties. He even purchased town lots in Old Washington, Rhea Co, TN, and Chattanooga, TN[1]. Putnam Co, GA, tax records show that Edward Varner was the wealthiest man in Putnam County in the late 1810's and early 1820's. He served as sheriff in Putnam Co, GA, for several years during that time. But Edward's properties were heavily mortgaged and he became unable to meet his financial obligations. He was forced into bankruptcy and much of his property was seized and sold at auction in 1824.

Frederick had signed several promissory notes to his son Edward Varner in 1822 and 1823 in an effort to ward off Edward's bankruptcy. Edward used those notes as collateral to raise some needed funds. When Edward was unable to redeem the notes that Frederick had signed, holders of the notes went to court to force Frederick to make good on the payments.

In several jury cases,[2] the Oglethorpe County Superior Court ruled that Frederick Varner was liable for the notes he signed and ordered the sheriff to seize and sell his property to satisfy Edward's creditors. Frederick was so upset by the decisions that he promptly appealed them and just as quickly lost the appeals. Those decisions, including the appeals, were made by juries whose members were Oglethorpe County property owners.

---

[1]..The author happened onto these items while researching East Tennessee records for information about his GG grandparents David Verner, Jr., and Judy Priddy. Edward Varner lost those Tennessee land holdings at the same time he was having such severe financial problems in Georgia.

[2]--See Appendix III-B for a list and brief description of these law cases.

Frederick most likely knew many of them well personally. He probably had served on juries with some of them. When the sheriff showed up to seize and sell his property, Frederick behaved toward the sheriff in such an "unChristianlike" manner that Frederick's church, where he was then serving as deacon, summarily expelled him[1] from fellowship in the church. The court cases occurred in 1825; Frederick Varner's land was sold by the sheriff[2] in 1826.

---

[1]--County Line Baptist Church Minutes, op. cit.
Saturday, March 4, 1826. There being evil reports against Bro. Frederick Varner whereupon Thomas Davis, Valentine Brown, and Aaron Jones were appointed to cite Bro. Varner to the next conference.
Saturday, April 1, 1826. The item in the minutes of the previous conference reporting the conduct of Frederick Varner was read. Brother Brown reported that they had cited Bro. Varner and he promised to attend but has failed to do so. A proposition was then made that Bro. Brittain Stamps should relate the circumstance which related to Bro. Varner's case and he did so. And after hearing the circumstances it appears that Bro. Varner is guilty of fabricating and falsifying to defraud good honest citizens out of their property by withholding his property and resisting a lawful process and abusing the sheriff in a very unChristianlike manner and many other things too trifling to enumerate and for said causes he is hereby excluded from all fellowship with the church.
(NOTE: Brittain Stamps was the sheriff who seized and sold Frederick Varner's property.)

[2]--See Appendix III-C at the end of this chapter for deed summaries about the sheriff's sales of Frederick Varner's land in Oglethorpe Co, GA.

Frederick Varner Becomes Church Deacon

Frederick Varner was a long-time, active member of the County Line Baptist Church although his relationship with the church was not always a smooth one. Frederick and his wife Judah (or Judy) probably joined the County Line Baptist Church between 1797, when it was founded, and 1807. Minutes for those years have been lost; consequently, the date they joined cannot be determined. Frederick Varner's name appears in the minutes often from 1807 through 1826; Judah Varner's name appears only once, in 1830 at which time she asked for a letter of dismissal[1] so that she could join another church.

In 1807, the church worked out a compromise between Frederick Varner and David Caldwell concerning a business disagreement.[2]

Two years later, Bro. F. Varner was investigated by the church on an accusation of "doing violence" or attempting to do violence to a female member. The matter was discussed at three sessions of the church, during which Frederick Varner expressed penance for his wrong doings and asked forgiveness. The church accepted his apologies and continued him in fellowship on condition he

---

[1]--County Line Baptist Church, Minutes.
Saturday, Dec. 4, 1830. Sister Judah Varner applied to the clerk for a letter of dismission, which was ordered.

[2]--County Line Baptist Church Minutes, Feb. 28, 1807.
There was a problem involving Frederick Varner and David Caldwell on a business matter. Three men were appointed to try to work out a compromise. (Copy torn and some missing.)

Apr. 4, 1807. In the case involving F. Varner and David Caldwell, a compromise was worked out between Bro. Varner and Mr. Caldwell. "Everybody was happy about the settlement." (Page torn and some words missing.)

obtain forgiveness from Sister May, the apparent offended female member. At a subsequent session, Polly May pleaded guilty to committing adultery and voluntarily withdrew from the church.[1]

Between 1809 and 1825, Frederick Varner's name appears in the minutes frequently for various, mostly routine, reasons.[2] He was chosen deacon of the church in May of 1822 and served in that role until he was expelled from the church in 1826. The final entries that include Frederick Varner's name occurred in the minutes for 1826, cited above, following the sheriff's seizure and sale of Frederick's property.

Frederick Varner Leaves No Will

Frederick Varner is believed to have died between 1826 and 1830. He must have been an angry or bitter person. There is evidence of that in the County Line Baptist Church minutes and in the court records. It seems that his anger should have been directed toward his son Edward Varner, but the evidence is not conclusive on this. He could have blamed others, or the economic conditions of the region or country, for Edward's bankruptcy. Or he simply could have been angry or frustrated at himself for having signed the promissory notes for his son. In any event, he died and left no will. No estate papers were

---

[1]--See Appendix III-C at the end of this chapter for County Line Church Minutes that tell about Frederick Varner being charged with sexual misconduct.

[2]--See Appendix III-D at the end of this chapter for miscellaneous entries in County Line Baptist Church Minutes about Frederick Varner, Mark Varner, other Varners, and their slaves.

located in Oglethorpe County records. In 1830, Judah Varner was listed in the federal census as residing with a white male (probably a son) between 30 and 40 years of age in Coweta Co, GA. She also applied for a letter of dismissal from the County Line Baptist Church in Oglethorpe County in 1830.

Descendants of Frederick and Judah Varner have been studied by other Varner researchers. The <u>Varner Collection of Family Papers</u> contain extensive data on Edward Varner and his descendants. These papers are in possession of the Georgia Historical Society, Savannah, Georgia. Copies are also on microfilm (6 rolls) at the Georgia State Archives in Atlanta. Birdie Varner Sanders, long-time Georgia school teacher, contributed much of the material contained in these papers.

Margaret Wallis Haile[1] also researched the Frederick Varner family along with her study of Matthew and George Varner. Her unpublished manuscript, which was kindly provided to the author by Jane Ellis Rogers of Highland City, FL, furnished invaluable clues to the author of this book in the early phases of his work on this project.

Since Frederick Varner left no will and no estate papers, an accurate list of the names of Frederick and Judah Varner's children is impossible to compile. Many Varners were married in Oglethorpe County, GA, between 1800 and 1830. One could assume that the ones who were married there during that time were Frederick and Judah's children except for the ones who were identified as children of George Varner and Matthew Varner in their

---

[1]..<u>Varners of Oglethorpe County, GA.</u> Compiled by Margaret Wallis Haile, Del Mar, CA, 1980. Unpublished manuscript.

wills and estate records. Such assumption might not hold true in all cases because of the multiple use of the same name in two or more families. Commonly, each Varner family named one son John, another one George, another one William, and another one Frederick. And seldom did these children use a middle initial or other identifying factors while signing records.

Children of Frederick and Judah Varner

Frederick and Judah are believed to have been the parents of the following: **Edward, George, Marcus "Mark," William, Mary "Polly," Cassandra, Onia and Cynthia.**[1]

Edward Varner was born 4 Nov 1789 in Wilkes Co, GA. He died 19 Feb 1869 at Milledgeville, Baldwin Co, GA[2]. Edward is the son whose over-extended business dealing and land speculating led to Frederick Varner's financial collapse. (See preceding pages in this chapter). Other Varner researchers[3] have devoted more attention to Edward Varner and his descendants.

George Varner. Frederick deeded land in Morgan Co, GA on 22 Jan 1808 "...for the good will and affection he

---

[1]--These were listed as Frederick and Judah's children in Varners of Oglethorpe County, GA and the Varner Family Papers, op. cit.

[2]--Varner Family Papers, op. cit., state that Edward Varner died on this date while a patient at the State Lunatic Asylum at Milledgeville, GA.

[3]..The Varner Family Papers and Varners of Oglethorpe County, Georgia, op. cit, also include additional material about Edward Varner.

owed to his said son, George."[4] The author of this book uncovered no additional information about this George Varner.

Marcus "Mark" Varner. Mark became a member of the County Line Baptist Church 31 Mar 1810.[2] He had lost interest in the church by 1814 and confessed that he was gambling. For those reasons, the church excluded him from membership.[3] Mark was listed as a taxpayer in Putnam Co, GA, during the 1820's and his name appears in the census reports in other Georgia counties in subsequent years. These and other references to Mark

---

[1]--Varners of Oglethorpe Co, GA. Compiled by Margaret Wallis Haile, Del Mar, CA, 1980. Unpublished Manuscript.

[2]--County Line Baptist Church, Minutes.
March 31, 1810. A door was opened for the reception of members whereupon George Stowell, Peggy Rhodes, Mark Varner, David Owen, Jane Martin, Moses Bates, and a Negro man Pompey severally related their experiences and were received into fellowship. Wilson Lumpkin, clerk.

[3]--County Line Baptist Church, Minutes.
Saturday, July 2, 1814. The church met in conference, Bro. Thomas Rhoades, moderator. Bro. F. Varner was appointed to notify Bro. Mark Varner to attend the next conference and render his reasons for neglecting conference meetings, also to answer reports that are in circulation against him.

Aug. 6, 1814. The case of Bro. Mark Varner was laid over until next conference. The brothers Lamby and L. Beales requested to labor with him and report to next conference.

Sept. 3, 1814. The case of Mark Varner was taken up. He was charged with gambling, which he confessed. He also declared his unfellowship with the church. The message was sent as he refused to attend the conference for all of which conduct he is hereby excluded all fellowship from the church.

Varner appear in other sections of this book on Putnam Co, GA, tax records and Census records for Georgia.

William Varner[1] marr on 6 Feb 1828 **Mary A. Kinnebrew,** (dau of A.L. Kinnebrew).

Molly "Polly" Varner marr in May, 1807 at Oglethorpe Co, GA, to **John Moore.**

Cassandra Varner marr 26 Apr 1813 at Oglethorpe Co, GA to **Edward Sutherlin.**

Onia "Onie" Varner marr at Oglethorpe Co, GA on 6 Dec 1818 to **Major Blackwell.**

Cynthia Varner (b. abt 1800, d. abt 1859 Fayette Co, GA) marr at Oglethorpe Co, GA on 4 Jan 1822 to **Allen Jennings.**

This author did no research from primary sources on Molly, Cassandra, Onia, or Cynthia Varner.

Appendix III-A
Frederick Varner's Service on Juries

Inferior Court Minutes 1794-1808, Oglethorpe County. P. 257.

Frederick Varner one of 48 chosen to serve on the jury. For January term, 1808.

Minutes Superior Court 1812-1829. (Pages not numbered).

Frederick Varner was selected to serve on the petit jury for the March term 1818.

---

[1]..This William Varner might have been William Varner, son of George Varner of Oglethorpe Co, GA, rather than a son of Frederick Varner. Indeed, this author questions whether Frederick and Judy had a son named William. See Chapter V, Children of George Varner.

Frederick Varner was one of 36 whose names were drawn to serve on the grand jury for the March term 1820.
Superior Court Minutes 1820-1823. Page 1.
Frederick Varner was one of 23 persons sworn in to serve on the Grand Jury. April 17, 1820.
Minutes Inferior Court 1822-1832. Pages not numbered.
Frederick Varner was one of 39 who were chosen to serve on the jury for the June term, 1823.

Appendix III-B
Sheriff Sells Frederick Varner's Land

Oglethorpe County, GA, Deed Book L. Page 345. March 23, 1826.

Between Brittain Stamps, Sheriff of the County of Oglethorpe, and Francis M. Barnett.

"Witnesseth, that whereas an execution issued from the honorable the Superior Court of Oglethorpe County bearing date the 17th day of January, 1826, against Frederick Varner in favor of William Varner and by virtue of said execution was levied on 300 acres of land more or less adjoining Daniel Morgan and others and on the waters of Long Creek which land was advertised in the Georgia Journal for sale on the first Tuesday in March and on said day was sold between the usual hours of sale to the highest bidder at the courthouse door in the town of Lexington and the county aforesaid and Francis M. Barnett being the highest bidder for the same was knocked off to him at the sum of $433 and I Brittain Stamps, sheriff of the county aforesaid do covenant and agree insofar as the law authorizes me as sheriff and no further to bear out the right and title of the said premises aforesaid from the claim or claims of all and every other person or persons whatsoever unto the said Francis M. Barnett his heirs and assigns forever.

In witness whereof I have hereunto set my hand and affixed my seal this 23rd day of March, 1826.
        Brittain Stamps, Sheriff
Signed, sealed and acknowledged in presence of William B. Raney and William W. Baldwin.

 Recorded April 8, 1826. Charles B. Collier, Clerk."

Oglethorpe County, GA, <u>Deed Book M</u>. Pages 49-50.

March 9, 1826, between Brittain Stamps, sheriff of Oglethorpe County and John Rupert of the same county. On order from Superior Court in judgment obtained in said court in the October term 1825 and in favor of Dryer Hillyer vs. Frederick Varner and in favor of Squire Hillyer vs Frederick Varner, execution was levied on 400 acres of land lying on the waters of Little River adjoining George Varner and others lived on as the property of Frederick Varner and in his possession and the same was advertised according to law in the Georgia Journal and was on the first Tuesday of this instant offered for sale at the Courthouse in Oglethorpe County. John Rupert was the high bidder and same was knocked down to him for the sum of $870.

 Witnesses: Present Robertson and Robert Jones.
 Recorded July 5, 1827. Charles V. Collier, Clerk.
  Signed Brittain Stamps, Sheriff

Appendix III-C
Frederick Varner Accused of Misconduct
County Line Baptist Church Minutes.

Feb. 6, 1809. It being reported to the church that there was a report in circulation that Bro. Varner had been guilty of offering or attempting violence to a female who is a member of this church, the brethren R. Rhodes, William Walker, and J. Ragan were appointed "to inquire into said report and notify Bro. Varner to attend the next conference." Signed Wilson Lumpkin, clerk.

Mar. 4, 1809. "The committee appointed to inquire into the prevailing reports against Bro. F. Varner reported that they had performed the duty assigned them. And that there appeared to be a matter of penance in said brother and not knowing the cause of attending the conference in person, the hearing was laid over until the next conference." Wilson Lumpkin, clerk.

Apr. 1, 1809. The case of Bro. Varner taken up and after discussion agreed to defer the same to the next conference in order that Sister May and Bro. Varner may have further opportunity to get reconciled to each other. Wilson Lumpkin, clerk.

May 6, 1809. "The case of Bro. Varner being taken up. And a relation of the whole matter on both sides being rehearsed. Bro. Varner related by a penance and hope of forgiveness for his crimes. And made such acknowledgements as the church feels to get along with and continue him in fellowship upon his procuring Sister May's satisfaction." And the Bro. R. Rhoades and Bro. Thromby were appointed to go with said brother for the purpose of endeavoring to aid in a reconciliation, upon attaining which Bro. Varner is to be restored to his former privileges upon the brother moderator giving him a suitable rebuke and admonition for his crimes.

June 30, 1809. Polly May is hereby excluded fellowship in this church at her own request and for living in the sin of adultery acknowledged by herself.

Appendix III-D
Church Minutes Concerning Frederick Varner, Mark Varner, Other Varners and Their Slaves

County Line Baptist Church <u>Minutes</u>.

Saturday evening, June 12, 1812. For the accommodation of the black people, leave was obtained from the church and a door opened for the reception of members, a number of brethren being present, whereupon Isaac, Jim, and Sophia, belonging to Young Stokes, Millie and Haggar, belonging to Glen Owen, Easter, belonging to Lincoln Walker, Betsy, belonging to William McIlroy, Hannah, belonging to Frederick Varner, severally came forward and related their experiences upon which they were received into fellowship. Wilson Lumpkin, clerk.

Feb. 6, 1813. The church met in conference, Bro. Thomas Rhoades, moderator...There being various charges against Bro. Graham, to wit that of drunkenness, abusing his family, swearing of the brethren E. Beal, William Walker, F. Varner, and Wilson Lumpkin were appointed to collect testimony and gather further information respecting said reports. Signed Lester Lacy.

Saturday, July 2, 1814. The church met in conference, Bro. Thomas Rhoades, moderator. Bro. F. Varner was appointed to notify Bro. Mark Varner[1] to attend the next conference and render his reasons for

---

[1]..Mark Varner was Frederick and Judy Varner's son.

neglecting conference meetings, also to answer reports that are in circulation against him...

Sept. 3, 1814. The case of Mark Varner was taken up. He was charged with gambling, which he confessed. He also declared his unfellowship with the church. The message was sent as he refused to attend the conference for all of which conduct he is hereby excluded all fellowship from the church.

Aug. 31, 1816. Church met in conference, Bro. Rhoades moderator. Bro. Thomas Rhoades informed the church there were certain matters of difference and conflict between him and Bro. Ellis Bell who is of another church and after giving a relation of the case the church proceeded to appoint brethren Lumpkin, Stokes, Fromby, Varner, and Ragan to accompany Bro. Rhoades in meeting Bro. Bell and the like number of brethren from the church to which he belonged to consider with and adjust and settle said matters of difference, to meet at the house of Wilson Lumpkin, Jr., Friday before the first Sunday in October next and the clerk of the church is directed to communicate this arrangement to brethren in the other church and to request their concurrence. The clerk was appointed to write the letter to the opposition. Signed Wilson Lumpkin.

Saturday, May 31, 1817...Bro. Francis Everett and Bro. James Mickleborough applied by Bro. Varner for letters of dismission, which were ordered.

Saturday, Dec. 4, 1819. Bro. John Ragan charged with having a fray with his brother Mark. Bro. Varner and Bro. James Rhoades appointed to cite Bro. Ragan to our next conference. Bro. Thomas Rhoades applied for a letter of dismission, which was ordered.

Feb. 5, 1820. The following brethren were appointed, to wit, James McHoover, Frederick Varner, Danish Morgan, and Anthony Cdmong to draw up the particulars of our conference on the 6th and 8th of November, 1819, for the inspection of our next meeting.

May 4, 1822. Met in conference, Bro. Gibson moderator. The case of Sister Porter taken up and after some deliberations on the same Sister Porter made such acknowledgements as to give satisfaction to the church, then proceeded to the choice of a deacon. Bro. Varner was the choice of the church. The church then resolved to call the aid of Bro. Watley to our next conference to aid us in ordaining Bro. Varner to the office of a deacon. Bro. Morgan appointed to bear a letter to Bro. Watley, Bro. James Rhoades to witness the same.

June 1, 1822. Met in conference. Bro. Varner ordained to the office of a deacon.

Aug. 31, 1822. Bro. Frederick Varner and Bro. Daniel Morgan were appointed delegates to the association in place of fallen Bro. E. Jackson.

Nov. 2, 1822. Met in conference, Bro. Gibson moderator. A door was opened for the reception of members whereupon James Edison and Harry a man of color belonging to M. B. Ragan came forward and related their experiences and were received into fellowship. There being evil reports against Jack L. Prudence members of this church Bro. Morgan and Bro. Varner were appointed to cite them to our next conference.

Saturday, May 3, 1823. The difficulty against Peter a man of color belonging to Bartley Johnson was taken up and after due determination the church found him living in a state of adultery. He is therefore no more a member of this church. Church appointed the following brethren, to wit, Bro. Frederick Varner, John Arnold, Daniel Morgan, Bradford Green, Benjamin Holmes, Owen Jackson, and Davis Owen to settle with Bro. Ephriam Jackson for the work that he did on the meeting house and also to have the side of the meeting next to the spring recovered. John Arnold, clerk.

Saturday, Sept. 4, 1824. Met in conference, Bro. Gibson moderator. The brethren Radford Gunn and John Arnold were nominated and appointed to represent this church in the ensuing association and Bro. Frederick Varner in case of the failure of either of them.

Saturday, Jan. 1, 1825. Bro. F. Varner rendered a satisfactory excuse for his absence at the last conference.

Saturday, Apr. 2, 1825. Met in conference, Bro. Gibson moderator. The brethren F. Varner, Thomas Davis, James Arnold, George Huddleston, and John Moore absent.

Saturday, Apr. 30, 1825. Met in conference, Bro. Gibson moderator. The brethren F. Varner, L. B. Jackson, Thomas Davis, James Hemmet are excused for their absence at the last conference.

Saturday, Oct. 1, 1825. The case of Bro. E. Jackson and Daniel Jackson was taken up whereupon a committee was appointed to settle said difficulty. The committee appointed is the brethren Glenn Owen, Frederick Varner, David Owen, James West, and Valentine Brown.

Saturday, Nov. 5, 1825. F. Varner was appointed to correspond with Centre Church. (He was one of several people appointed to correspond with other churches.)

Saturday, Dec. 3, 1825. Jack and Juda, the property of John Ragan, applied for letters of dismission which were granted. Taken up the case of the two brothers Jackson. Three brethren appointed to go to see Daniel Jackson and cite him to attend the next conference. Appointed were R. Gunn, F. Varner, and I. Arnold. S. Gibson selected as preacher for the next year. John Arnold, clerk.

Chapter IV
Matthew Varner of Oglethorpe Co, GA

For more information about Matthew Varner, his parents and grandparents, and other relatives, see Chapters I and II.

Matthew Varner was born in Maryland in about 1760. He moved to Rowan County, NC, with his parents during his early childhood years. He fought there with American forces during the Revolutionary War. Shortly after the war, he married Susannah Henley. The two of them then moved to Wilkes County (later Oglethorpe), GA, where they settled adjacent to George Varner, believed to have been Matthew's brother, and Frederick Varner, who was probably Matthew's cousin or brother.

Matthew Varner, a known son of John Varner of Rowan County, NC, was born about four miles from Baltimore, Maryland.[1] His year of birth is unknown.[2] But since he fought in 1780-1781 with the American Army during the Revolutionary War, he is believed to have been born about 1760. Matthew Varner died 29 July 1847 in Oglethorpe Co, GA.[3]

---

[1].--Matthew Varner said he was born in Maryland about four miles from Baltimore when he applied for a Revolutionary War pension. His Revolutionary War record # is 7787.

[2].--In his pension application, op. cit., Matthew Varner said he did not "recollect the year he was born."

[3].--<u>Varners of Oglethorpe County, Georgia</u>. Unpublished manuscript compiled by Margaret Wallis Haile, 13439 Portofino Drive, Del Mar, CA 92014. 1980. Ms. Haile cites a letter written
(continued...)

Matthew Varner fought with American forces in the Revolutionary War. His service record is well documented and many of his descendants have joined the DAR (Daughters of the American Revolution) and the SAR (Sons of the American Revolution) on his record. According to information he submitted with his claims for a war service pension, he said that while he was a resident of Rowan County, NC, he served with the American Army for 18 months[1], in both North Carolina and South Carolina.

Matthew Varner married Susannah Henley[2], in Rowan Co, NC on 17 Aug 1787. Matthew and Susannah moved to Wilkes County (later Oglethorpe), GA, between 1787, when they were married, and 1791, when Matthew was listed as a taxpayer in Wilkes County, GA.[3]

Matthew and Susannah Varner Move to Georgia

Matthew and Susannah Varner settled in the Southeast corner of present day Oglethorpe County, GA near George and Betsy Varner and Frederick and Judy Varner. (That area was part of Wilkes County until Oglethorpe County was created in 1794.) However, after

---

[3](...continued)
to a relative by Matthew Varner, Jr., giving 8:00 p.m. 29 Jul 1847 as the time of death of his father.

[1]--Revolutionary War Record # 7787, op. cit.

[2]--From marriage records of North Carolina: Matthew Varner and Susannah Henley, 17 Aug 1787, Rowan Co, NC. Darby Henly, bondsman; John Macey, witness.

[3]--<u>1790 Census for Wilkes Co, GA</u>, op. cit., p. 75.

a few years, Matthew and Susannah moved some 15 to 20 miles southwest of the original settlement.

Matthew, George, and Frederick Varner paid taxes in Wilkes County, GA, in 1791. They lived near one another at that time. The area where all three lived then became part of Capt. Duke's militia district in Oglethorpe County when that county was formed in 1794. The three were also neighbors, living in the same militia district, in 1795 and 1796. But by 1800, Matthew Varner had relocated to acreage on Falling Creek, in the southwest corner of Oglethorpe County.[1] George Varner and Frederick Varner continued to live adjacent to one another until 1826 when Frederick lost his land because of his son Edward Varner's bankruptcy. (See Chapter III). As noted in Chapter II, George Varner died in 1827.

Although he bought and sold land from time to time, Matthew Varner continued to live in the same home place, on Falling Creek in Oglethorpe Co, GA, for about 50 years, until his death in 1847. His property, both land and slave holdings, increased at a slow rate in the early years of the 1800's and then accelerated about 20 years later. In 1800, he owned only 140 acres of land and one Negro slave.[2] In 1803, he had 200 acres and two slaves. In

---

[1]--Matthew Varner's grandson, John William Varner, said that Matthew Varner's plantation home place was "on the old Scull Shoals and Hermon and Maxey wagon road about 10 miles from Scull Shoals...three miles from Hermon...and five miles from Maxey Station on the Georgia Railroad." This is reported by Ms. Haile, <u>Varners of Oglethorpe County, Georgia</u>, op. cit., p. 22.

[2]--Land and slave holdings mentioned in this paragraph were taken from official Oglethorpe County tax records located
(continued...)

1813, his land ownership had increased to 350 acres and his slave holdings to seven. By 1819 he had 605 acres and 13 slaves. Then in 1826, Matthew paid taxes on over 1400 acres of land and he had 26 slaves. His property holdings then remained at about the same level until at or near the time of his death.[1]

Like his brothers and\or cousins, George Varner and Frederick Varner, Matthew Varner served on Oglethorpe County juries from time to time. Minutes of the Inferior Court report that he served on juries in 1794, 1799, and 1808.[2] The minutes are not indexed, thus there may have been additional times that a quick review of the minutes did not reveal.

Matthew and Susannah Varner may have attended the County Line Baptist Church in its very early years, when they lived nearby. Church minutes for the years prior to 1807 were not located.[3] This family had moved about 15 to 20 miles away from where the church is located before 1807 and their names do not appear in the

---

[2](...continued)
in the county courthouse in Lexington, GA.

[1]--In 1839, the last year for which tax records were checked, Matthew Varner owned 730 acres on Falling Creek in Oglethorpe County and 27 Negro slaves. He also owned over 700 acres of land in two other Georgia counties.

[2]--<u>Inferior Court Minutes</u> 1794-1808, Oglethorpe County, pages 2, 7, 104, and 270.

[3]--As noted in Chapters 2 and 3, County Line Baptist Church minutes for the years after 1807 are in the possession of the Church Clerk. They are also available on microfilm at the Georgia State Archives in Atlanta.

minutes for the years after 1807. They may have attended a church closer to their plantation on Falling Creek.

Will Fails To Include Some Children

Matthew Varner wrote his will[1] 30 Oct 1845, nearly two years before his death. It was submitted for probate in September 1847. Matthew did not choose to divide his property equally among his children, leaving some of them nothing. Consequently, those who were not granted equal shares contested the will. They claimed that Matthew Varner "was not of sound mind and disposing memory at the time of the making of the said pretended will...that (he was) very aged and infirm, (and that) undue influence was exercised and fraudulent representations made by the legatees mentioned in said will to cause the said Matthew Varner to disinherit the caveators...(and that) the said Matthew Varner was very aged and possessed of feeble mind and no recollection" at the time he made the will.[2]

Apparently, the dispute was settled out of court because the children who had brought action against the will withdrew their suit. Matthew Varner, Jr., was then confirmed by the court as executor of the will. Subsequently, the property was appraised and the estate was settled.

The date of death of Matthew Varner's wife, Susannah Henley Varner is unknown. She died prior to the time in 1845 when Matthew wrote his will because she is not mentioned in the will nor in the estate proceedings.

---

[1]--Matthew Varner's Will and Testament is printed in Appendix IV-A at the end of this chapter.

[2]--See Appendix IV-B at the end of this chapter for probate court records on the challenge to Matthew Varner's will.

Children of Matthew and Susannah Varner

Matthew and Susannah had seven known children: **Elizabeth, Olive, Mahalia, John Henly, William, Sarah W. and Matthew**.[1] All were identified in Matthew Varner's will and/or in the probate proceedings.

Elizabeth Varner married **John Christopher** in Oglethorpe Co, GA on 3 Mar 1812.[2] Elizabeth was living when Matthew Varner wrote his will in 1845. She received a share of the estate.

Olive Varner (b. 7 Dec 1797[3] Oglethorpe Co, GA) married **James Ellis** in Oglethorpe Co, GA 11 Mar 1816.[4] James Ellis was named one of the executors of Matthew Varner's will, but Olive was excluded from receiving any of the benefits from it.

Mahalia Varner (b. 7 Dec 1797 Oglethorpe Co, GA, d. 23 Dec 1876 Campbell, TX) married **Wiley J. Sorrells** in Oglethorpe Co, GA, 9 Jan 1817. Mahalia and Olive were twins.[5] Mahalia was named in her father's will to indirectly receive the benefits of a thousand dollars in gold if she applied for it.

John Henley Varner (b. ca. 1799 Oglethorpe Co, GA, d. 27 Apr 1836 Palmetto, Fulton Co, GA) married **Mary**

---

[1]--According to Ms. Haile in Varners in Oglethorpe County, GA, op. cit.

[2]--Oglethorpe Co, GA marriage records.

[3]--Research of Eleanor Duke, El Paso, TX.

[4]--Oglethorpe Co, GA marriage records.

[5]--Varners of Oglethorpe County, GA, op. cit., p. 9.

Campbell in Oglethorpe Co, GA on 27 July 1824.[6] John Varner, who lived near Matthew Varner, paid pole tax[2] for the first time in 1819. This means that he had reached the age of 21. The heirs of John Varner were granted a share of Matthew Varner's estate in his will.

William Varner (b. ca. 1800 Oglethorpe Co, GA, d. 1846) married **Ann Catherine Watson** in Green Co, GA, 31 Jan 1825. William was named in his father Matthew Varner's will to receive a share of the estate, but he preceded his father in death. William and Ann Varner's three sons--**Joseph Varner, Felix Varner and Alonzo Varner**--took the slaves they inherited from their father and migrated to Arkansas. There, they founded the town of Varner, Lincoln County, Arkansas.[3]

Sarah W. Varner (b. 1805) married first **William R. Johnson** in Oglethorpe Co, GA on 10 May 1825. She married 2nd **Dr. Alfred D. Reese**.[4] Sarah was not named in her father's will to receive a share of the estate.

Matthew Varner, Jr. (b. ca. 1808 Oglethorpe Co, GA, d. ca. 1865-1866 Cobb Co, GA) married **Sarah Georgia Lumpkin** in Oglethorpe Co, GA, 4 May 1833.[5] Matthew paid a pole tax for the first time in 1829[6], which proves that he had reached the age of 21.

---

[1]--Research of Eleanor Duke, El Paso, TX.

[2]--Tax records of Oglethorpe County, GA.

[3]--<u>Varners of Oglethorpe County, GA</u>, op. cit., p. 10.

[4]--<u>Varners of Oglethorpe County, GA</u>, op. cit., p. 9.

[5]--<u>Varners of Oglethorpe County, Georgia</u>, op. cit., p. 11.

[6]--Tax records of Oglethorpe County, GA.

Appendix IV-A
Will of Matthew Varner

Oglethorpe County, GA, Will Book D, page 218.

The Last Will and Testament of Matthew Varner
Georgia, Oglethorpe County. IN THE NAME OF GOD AMEN. I, Matthew Varner, Sr., of the County and State aforesaid, being of sound mind and disposing memory, do constitute and ordain this my last Will and Testament in the words following, to wit:

Item 1st. I give to my two sons William Varner and Matthew Varner and my daughter Elizabeth Christopher and the lawful heirs of my son John Varner, five Negroes named Crawford, a man, Robert, a man, Jim, a boy, Henry, a boy, and Green, a boy, and also any money that I may have on hand to be equally divided between them at my death.

Item 2nd. I give to my two sons William Varner and Matthew Varner, one thousand dollars in gold, which they are to apply as agents for the use and benefit of my daughter Mahalia Sorrells, to be faithfully applied provided she applies for it, but if she should not apply for it, then they are to give it to the heirs of her body.

Item 3rd. It is my desire that my household stuff, horses, oxen, wagon, barouch should belong to whichever one of my children I may be living with at the time of my death.

Item 4th. I appoint my son-in-law James Ellis and my son Matthew Varner to execute this my last Will and Testament.

In testimony whereof I have hereunto set my hand and seal, this the 30th day of October one thousand eight hundred and forty five.

Witnesses: Andrew Campbell and Bradley Berry.
Matthew Varner (his mark) (SEAL).

Appendix IV-B
Matthew Varner's Will Challenged

Oglethorpe County, GA, Minutes Court of Ordinary 1845-1851. Pages 147-148. Sept. term 1847. "And now at this term a paper writing purporting to be the last will and testament of Matthew Varner, Sr., being offered in court for probate and record, comes John Ellis and his wife Susan, formerly Susan Varner, Edmond Luther and his wife Cassandra, formerly Cassandra Varner, Wiley Sorrell and his wife Mahalia, formerly Mahalia Varner, Alfred B. Reese and his wife Sarah W., formerly Sarah Varner, and enter this caveat against same on the following grounds, to wit, because that the said Matthew Varner, Sr. was not of sound mind and disposing memory at the time of the making of the said pretended will, second for that the said Matthew Varner being very aged and infirm, undue influence was exercised and fraudulent representations made by the legatees mentioned in said will to cause the said Matthew Varner to disinherit the caveators, third, because the said Matthew Varner was very aged and possessed of feeble mind and no recollection and said will was presented by the legatees therein named. Signed Thomas R. R. Cobb and Dawson and McHenry, attorneys for Caveators.

Oglethorpe County, Georgia, Minutes Court of Ordinary. Page 186. May term 1848. Mathew Varner propounded will vs. Alfred B. Reese and other caveators. Judgment of this court overruling the caveat in this case and ordering the will propounded to be admitted to probate and recorded and appeal to the superior court. It appearing to the court that the appellants in the above case by the consent of Mathew Varner did at the last term of the superior court of this county withdraw said appeal. Wherefore it is ordered by the court that the paper bearing date 30th of October 1845 and tested by Andrew Campbell and Brawley Berry propounded as the last will and testament of Matthew Varner, Sr. deceased, be and the same is hereby declared to be once more the last will and testament of said deceased and that the record and probate heretofore made be ratified and confirmed.

Oglethorpe County, GA, <u>Minutes of the Court of Ordinary</u>, page 188. May term 1848. Matthew Varner Jr. Esquire, having been appointed executor by the last will and testament of Matthew Varner, Sr. late of Oglethorpe County deceased, but now qualified to the same prays the court to appoint appraisers to appraise said estate, wherefore it is ordered that Andrew Campbell, Franklin C. Campbell, Joseph E. Smith, William I. Paris, and William Ellis, Esquires, be and they are hereby appointed commissioners to appraise said estate according to law.

Page 203. November term 1848. The petition of Matthew Varner, Jr., executor of the last will and testament of Matthew Varner, Sr. deceased, shows to the court that he has given the due and legal notice of the intention to apply to this court for leave to sell all the Negroes belonging to the estate of said deceased. And no objection having been made to the same, it is therefore ordered by this court that leave be and leave is hereby granted to Matthew Varner, Jr. executor aforesaid of Mathew Varner, Sr. deceased, to sell all the Negroes belonging to the estate of said deceased by complying with the statute in such cases made and provided.

Appendix IV-C
Matthew Varner Land Purchases and Sales

Oglethorpe County, GA, <u>Deed Book D,</u> Page 401.

    Matthew Varner of Oglethorpe County purchased 200 acres from Edward Maxwell of Pendleton County, State of South Carolina. Feb. 1, 1795. Varner paid 50 pounds sterling. This land was in county of Greene in the State of Georgia on the waters of Falling Creek.

Oglethorpe Co, GA, <u>Deed Book I</u>, Page 423.

    Matthew Varner, Sr. purchased 100 acres from the University of Georgia, Lot # 21 from a tract of 5,000 acres. Located on Falling Creek. Paid $700. May 16, 1816.

Oglethorpe Co, GA, <u>Deed Book I</u>, Page 425.

    Matthew Varner, Sr. purchased 100 acres from the University of Georgia, Lot # 3, located on Falling Creek. Paid $256. May 17, 1816.

Oglethorpe Co, GA, <u>Deed Book I</u>, Page 426.

    Matthew Varner, Sr. purchased 140 acres from Frederick Varner for $1000. Nov. 21, 1817. Gives description but does not give location.

        Signed by Frederick Varner

In presence of William Ellis, Jr. and William Varner. Attested to by John Hale, J. P.

Oglethorpe Co, GA, <u>Deed Book N,</u> Pages 628-629.

    Matthew Varner of Oglethorpe County sold to Edward G. Brooks, for $5, Falling Creek Academy lots # 6 and # 9 (includes buildings). Jan. 2, 1834. Mathew C. Hale and Matthew Varner, Jr. were witnesses.

        Signed Matthew Varner, Sr., his mark.

Chapter V
Children of George Varner[1]

For information about George and Betsy Varner, see Chapter II.

George Varner, who grew up in Rowan County, NC, and lived most of his adult life in Oglethorpe County, GA, identified nine children in his will: **John Varner, William Varner, Frederick Varner, George Varner, Jr., Henley Varner, Susannah (Varner) Neal[2], Elizabeth (Varner) Neal, Sarah (Varner) Whitfield, and Emily Sophronia Varner**. All are assumed to have been the children of Elizabeth "Betsy" Henley Varner as well, but there is no known extant record to prove this. Betsy is not mentioned in George's will. Almost certainly, this means that she was no longer living when he wrote his will.

Most of the remainder of this book is concerned with John Varner and Nancy Powell and their descendants. But since this researcher unearthed information about several other children of George and Betsy, some attention is given to them in this chapter.

John Varner, Son of George Varner

John Varner is believed to have been the oldest of George and Betsy Varner's sons, and perhaps the oldest of their children as well. There is little proof of the dates of

---

[1]--George Varner was a son of John Varner of Rowan Co, NC, or Adam Varner of Randolph Co, NC. See Chapters I and II.

[2]--Susannah was deceased at the time George wrote his will. Her children, Martha A. Neal and Susan V. Neal, were left shares of the estate. See <u>Appendix II-D</u> at the end of Chapter II for a copy of George Varner's Will.

birth of John's sisters. John Varner was born in North Carolina, in 1783, according to later census records and his grave marker.[1] He moved to Wilkes (later Oglethorpe) Co, GA, with his parents at a very young age. He married Nancy Powell in Oglethorpe County, GA, in 1808. With financial help from his father, he became a planter in Oglethorpe County, GA, and prospered there for several years, before relocating to a frontier settlement in Alabama.

John and Nancy sold their Georgia land in 1819. They took their slaves and settled on the Alabama River in what was then Montgomery County (later Lowndes), AL. When Lowndes County was formed, in 1830, John Varner was elected Clerk of the County Court and served in that capacity for 12 years. He continued to manage his plantation during that time. In the mid-1840's, he moved to Coosa County, AL, where he established one of the pioneer plantations there. Nancy Powell Varner died sometime during the 1840's. John then married Amanda Mulkey[2], in Chambers Co, AL, 20 Mar 1850. With the help of his younger sons, Hardaway and Esselman, John continued to manage his plantation until or near the time of his death.

John Varner and Nancy Powell are treated in more depth in Chapter VI. Their children and other descendants are covered in chapters VI, VII, VIII, IX, X, XI, and XII.

---

[1]--John Varner is buried in Providence Cemetery, Coosa County, AL. He died in 1869, according to the grave marker.

[2]..Chambers Co, AL, marriage records.

William Varner, Son of George Varner

William Varner was born about 1785[1], in Wilkes Co, GA, or Rowan or Randolph Co, NC. He died Oct 1831[2], in Houston Co, GA). He married 6 Feb 1828 **Mary L. Kinnabrew** in Putnam Co, GA.[3]

William lived for many years in Putnam Co, GA, near two brothers (Henley and George), three sisters (Susannah, Sarah, and Emily Sophronia), and two cousins (Edward Varner and Marcus Varner). Like his brother Henley and cousin Edward, William was a land speculator and businessman. He was also a politician, serving as Putnam Co sheriff and representative to the Georgia Legislature. He also owned and operated a plantation. His

---

[1]..William is believed to have been the second oldest of George Varner's sons, primarily because he was listed second in George's will. John Varner, named first in the will, was born in 1783, according to his grave marker in Providence Cemetery, Coosa Co, AL.

[2]--William Varner's brother Henley Varner notified their brother John Varner by letter dated 27 Nov 1831 of William's death. The letter is with the Lowndes Co, AL, estate records-- filed under John Varner--at the AL Archives in Montgomery. It is reprinted as an appendix at the end of Chapter VI.

[3]--The William Varner who married Mary Kinnebrew is believed to have been George Varner, Sr.'s son, but there is no known positive proof of it. If this is true, and if John F. Varner and David N. Varner were William's sons, as concluded in paragraphs that follow, this would have been a second marriage for William Varner. No record of an earlier marriage was located.

tax records reflect ownership of several Negro slaves, and he had extensive land holdings.

Although William Varner owned less property than his cousin Edward Varner (see preceding chapter), he was nevertheless one of the largest property holders in Putnam Co, as reflected in tax records for 1817, 1820, 1824, 1826, 1827, 1828, and 1830. For example, in 1827 he owned 202 acres and two town lots in Putnam Co, 250 acres in Early Co, 490 acres in Appling Co, 170 acres in Monroe Co, 250 acres in Walton Co, and 80 acres in Clark Co. He paid taxes of $19.10.[1] In 1828, as resident of Putnam Co, he also paid taxes on his father George Varner, Sr.'s estate.[2] He was administrator of that estate. This is the record that proves that the Putnam Co William

---

[1]--Tax Digest for Putnam Co, GA, 1827.

[2]--Putnam County, GA, Tax Records for 1828.
William Varner, 28 poles. 250 acres in Early County in 19th District, 202 1/2 acres in DeKalb County, 490 acres in Appling County, 202 1/2 acres in Houston County, 202 1/2 acres in Troop County, town lots in Eatonton with estimated value of $1600. Paid tax of $15.51 3/4. Resided in Capt. Jesse Bledsoe's District.

William Varner, as executor of George Varner's estate, deceased, 46 poles, 1600 acres of land in Oglethorpe County on Dry Fork of Long Creek adjacent to Gresham, 200 acres in Oglethorpe County on Dry Fork adjacent to Wynn, 202 1/2 acres in Houston County in 8th District, 1 2-wheel carriage. Tax of $18.63 1/2.

(Note: "Poles" were males between the ages of 21 and 60. Most of the 28 poles that William reported for himself and the 46 that he reported for his father George Varner's estate were probably male slaves in that age range. Some early tax records differentiate between "white" and "black" poles, but the Putnam Co, GA, records did not report that information.)

Varner was the son of George Varner, Sr., and not of Frederick Varner as some other Varner researchers have incorrectly concluded.[1]

William Varner, Sheriff and Legislator

William Varner was sheriff of Putnam Co, GA, from 1809 to 1811, 1818-1819, and 1824-1825.[2] As sheriff, he sold two pieces of court-seized property to his land-speculating cousin Edward Varner for trifling sums.[3] In 1812, after William was elected to the Georgia House of Representatives, Edward Varner succeeded him as sheriff of Putnam County. As sheriff, Edward also sold seized

---

[1] --The author of Varners of Oglethorpe County, GA, op. cit., concluded that the William Varner who left many "tracks" in Putnam County was a son of Frederick and Judah Varner. This false conclusion was probably based primarily on the fact that William and Edward were big business operatives and took turns being sheriff of Putnam County. Thus Ms. Haile assumed that William and Edward were brothers, when in fact they were cousins. Birdie Varner Sanders, who compiled the White-Varner papers which are in the possession of the Georgia Genealogical Society, Charleston, SC, also incorrectly assumed that William was a son of Frederick.

[2] --Putnam County, GA Deed Records. William Varner sold town lots and farm acreages while he was sheriff of Putnam County, GA, in 1809, 1810, 1811, 1818, 1819, 1824, and 1825. The property had been seized by the courts from land owners who had failed to pay debts and/or taxes.

[3] --One was a lot in Eatonton which he sold to Edward Varner for $1.00, the other was a 1/2 acre lot which he sold for $5.00. Putnam Co, GA, Deed Book B, p. 224.

property to relatives. On 2 Jun 1812, he sold 202 acres to his father Frederick Varner for $50.[4]

William Varner served two terms (1812 and 1827) from Putnam Co in the Georgia House of Representatives. His voting record can be examined in the Journal of the Georgia House of Representatives.[2] The record for the 1812 session shows that he voted for several bills that would have alleviated the problems of debtors. Those bills failed. He voted against a bill that amended a law passed in 1809 that outlawed dueling. He voted for a bill that passed allowing local authorities to impose penalties against persons who wantonly abused or killed domestic animals or maliciously beat, wounded, or abused slaves where the damage sustained did not exceed $30. He voted for a bill that passed that encouraged the breeding of sheep in Georgia.

During the 1827 session, William Varner voted against inviting a preacher of the gospel to open daily sessions of the Georgia House with a prayer.[3] That measure passed anyway with 82 yes and 47 no votes. He

---

[1]--Putnam Co, GA, Deed Book C, p. 44.

[2]--The Journal of the House of Representatives is located at the GA Dept. of Archives.

[3]--The second Great Awakening was causing a wave of religious enthusiasm to sweep across America. Methodists, Baptists, and other evangelical sects were growing rapidly, particularly in frontier communities. It was probably this influence that prompted the Georgia House to begin opening its sessions with a prayer from a minister of the gospel. The fact that William Varner voted against prayers in the House suggests that perhaps this line of Varners, or at least William himself, had not become a participant in this religious fervor.

voted with the majority to table a measure petitioning the U.S. government to speed up its acquisition of Cherokee lands in Georgia. He voted with a small minority that opposed extending civil jurisdiction of the state over territory then in possession of the Cherokee Indians. The measure passed 100 to 14. He voted for only two of eight bills that would have granted divorces.[1] Six of the requested divorces were approved by the House and two were rejected. Varner did not vote on roll call votes between Nov. 26 and Dec. 11, 1827. Probably, he was absent because of the death of his father, George Varner, of Oglethorpe Co, GA.[2]

William Varner was a captain in the Georgia Militia and commanded a cavalry company that marched against the Cherokee Indians during the War of 1812. Two letters that he wrote to the governor of Georgia concerning that duty are on file at the Georgia Dept. of Archives and History in Atlanta.[3]

William was one of the administrators of his father's estate but had not completely settled its affairs before he died. He sold three large parcels of land in Oglethorpe Co, including the acreage where George's plantation home was

---

[1]--During that period of American history, it was common for an act of the state legislature to be needed for a couple to get a divorce. Frequently, such divorce requests were denied.

[2]--Journal of the Georgia House of Representatives for 1827. Several entries from Nov. 15 to Dec. 13.

[3]--The letters are reprinted as Appendix V-A at the end of this chapter.

located.[4] The final steps of closing the estate were handled by his brother-in-law, George B. Whitfield, who was married to William's sister Sarah.[2]

William Varner may have moved from Putnam County, GA, to Houston County, GA, shortly before his death. He was a resident of Putnam Co at the time of the 1830 census. He is known to have died in Houston County in Oct 1831[3]. He had purchased land in Houston County, in Dec 1828[4]. Known records do not indicate whether

---

[1]--The 1120-acre tract where George Varner, Sr. lived was sold 4 Nov 1828. Oglethorpe Co, GA, Deed Book M, pp. 445-446. Other land sale records are recorded in Deed Book N, p. 174 and Deed Book P, p. 6.

[2]--Oglethorpe Co Court of Ordinary on 20 Jan 1832 noted that William Varner, previously approved as administrator of George Varner, Sr.'s estate, had since died. The Court then ordered that George B. Whitfield, the other administrator named in the will, be authorized to handle the affairs of the estate. Minutes, 1830-1838, p. 68. Subsequently, the Court authorized the sale of the remaining unsold real estate belonging to the estate of George Varner, Sr. Minutes, p. 81.

[3]--William Varner's death was announced by his brother Henley Varner in a letter to their brother John Varner of Lowndes County, AL. The letter is printed as an appendix at the end of Chapter VI. A fourth brother, Frederick Varner, is mentioned in the letter.

[4]--Houston County, GA, Deed Book D. Pages 23-24.
Land in Houston County was purchased by William Varner, of the County of Putnam, State of Georgia. Bought from James Cummings of Forsyth County, for $355. In 8th District of Houston County, known by lot # 138, containing 202 1/2 acres. Witnesses Larkin Barnett and Charles Collins. Dec. 15, 1828.

William Varner was living in Houston Co at the time he died or whether he was there for some other reason. He might have been tending to business related to the land he owned there.

Children of William Varner

William Varner left three known orphans: **John F. Varner, David N. Varner, and Susan Varner.** The three were mentioned by name by their uncle Henley Varner in a letter which he wrote to his brother John Varner informing John of the death of their brother William Varner. The letter, which is on file at the Alabama Archives in Montgomery, is printed as an appendix at the end of Chapter VI.

William Varner's orphans, who resided in Stewart's District, Warren Co, at the time, drew land in the 1832 Cherokee Land Lottery[1].

John F. Varner, who lived in Henry County, GA, for many years and died there in 1862, and **David N. Varner**, who died in Pike County, GA, in 1851, were sons of William Varner. David N. Varner identified John F. Varner as his brother in his will.[2] John F. Varner identified Henley Varner as his uncle in his will.[3] Further

---

[1]--1832 Cherokee Land Lottery, by James F. Smith, Milledgeville, GA, 1838. Printed by Harper and Brothers, NY.
Page 178. 25th district, 2nd section Cherokee 316, William Varner's orphans. They lived in Stewart's District in Warren Co, in 1832, at the time of the Cherokee Lottery.

[2]--David N. Varner's will is recorded in Pike Co, GA, Will Book C, p. 85.

[3]--Henry County, Georgia, the Mother of Counties, Vessie
(continued...)

CHILDREN OF GEORGE VARNER

evidence that John F. and David N. were sons of William Varner is the fact that David N. Varner willed three lots of land in the Cherokee part of the state to his brother John F. Varner. As noted above, William Varner's orphans had won land in the Cherokee part of the state in the 1832 Georgia Land Lottery.

John F. Varner was born in 1820 and died in 1862. He married Martha Callaway (b. 1827, d. 1906) in McDonough, Henry Co, GA. According to Henry County, Mother of Counties[1], John F. and Martha were parents of three children: **Eliza, Carrie, and Henley J.**

Eliza Varner (b. 1848, d. 1927) married **George Campbell Crookshanks**. This couple left no heirs. **Carrie Varner** (b. 1852, d. 1923) married **James C. Daniel**. Their children included Henley Daniel and Robert Henley Daniel, Jr. **Henley J. Varner** married **Arpie Price**. Descendants of this couple live in McDonough today.[2]

John F. Varner wrote his will 11 Jan 1862[3]. It was filed for probate 18 Mar 1862. In addition to Eliza, Carrie, and Henley, mentioned above, John F. Varner named a fourth child: **William D. Varner.**

Soon after John F. Varner's death, the property left in his estate was appraised. The list is extensive and

---

[3](...continued)
Thrasher Rainer, 1971. No publisher listed, p. 120. John F. Varner's will was probated 15 Mar 1862.

[1]--Henry County, Georgia, the Mother of Counties, op. cit.

[2]--Information on John F. Varner and his descendants taken from Mother of Counties, op. cit., p. 120.

[3]--John F. Varner's will is reprinted as Appendix V-B at the end of this chapter.

interesting. In the middle of hundreds of farm and household items, five slaves were named along with an estimated value for each: **Alsey,** worth $400; **Jerry,** worth $300; **Billy,** worth $1400; **Georgia,** worth $800; and **Margaret,** worth $800.[1]

David N. Varner's will was filed for probate 1 Sep 1851. He left his daughter Minerva J. Waller his land and improvements and each of her four children (William Waller, John Waller, Martha Waller, and Ella Waller, an infant) each $1,000. He left his uncle **John Neal** $600, a buggy, and the Negro **Glasco**. In addition to the land mentioned above, David N. left his brother John F. Varner Negroes **Frank and Jerry**. He left his niece Elizabeth Thomas[2] $800 and one-half of his household furniture.[3]

George Varner, Jr., Son of George Varner

George Varner, Jr., was born in about 1787 in Rowan or Randolph Co, NC, or Wilkes County, GA. He married **Patience Jackson** in Oglethorpe Co, GA, 17 Dec 1805. George is believed to have lived near his brothers William and Henley in Putnam Co, GA, in 1817 and 1820. His name appeared on the tax lists there for those years. He was listed in the tax records for Oglethorpe Co in 1823,

---

[1]--See Appendix V-C at the end of this chapter for notes on the appraisal of John F. Varner's estate.

[2]--See the section on Henley Varner that follows for more information on Elizabeth Thomas.

[3]--As noted above, David N. Varner's will is recorded in Pike Co, GA, Will Book C, page 85.

1824, 1825, 1826, and 1827, suggesting that he was a resident of that county during those years.[4]

Patience Varner, resident of Oglethorpe Co, entered the 1827 Georgia Land Lottery, basing her eligibility on a declaration that her husband had been absent for three years. However, her successful draw, for land in Monroe Co, was ruled fraudulent, and thus invalid, by the governor.[2] Presumably, her husband had not been absent three years, as she had claimed.

Patience Varner was received by experience in the County Line Baptist Church in Oglethorpe Co, GA, 4 Jan 1812 and dismissed by letter 4 Mar 1837.[3] Patience was a resident of Harris Co, GA, in 1839, when the estate of her father Daniel Jackson, deceased, was probated.[4]

---

[1]--The George Varner who was in these Putnam County, GA, records might have been Frederick Varner's son George rather than George Varner's son George.

[2]--Georgia Black Book, by Robert Scott Davis, Jr., p. 43.

[3]--Original minutes of the County Line Baptist Church, op. cit.

[4]--Oglethorpe Co, GA, Deed Book P, p. 251.

Henley Varner, Son of George Varner

Henley Varner[1] was born 15 Aug 1790[2] in Wilkes Co, GA. He died 11 Dec 1868[3], in McDonough, Henry Co, GA. He married **Martha Caroline Napier** in Eatonton, Putnam Co, GA on 9 Nov 1819. Martha was born 10 Jan 1803 and died 5 Jan 1871, Henry Co, GA. She was a daughter of **Thomas Napier**, a native of VA.[4]

Henley lived in Eatonton, Putnam Co, GA, from about 1818 until 1824 or later. He was in the Georgia Militia reserves from 1808 to 1829, serving as a lieutenant in Putnam Co in 1818 and a captain in Putnam Co in 1821.[5] He was listed as owning a town lot in Eatonton in the 1820 tax records for Putnam County. He was also listed as a resident of Putnam County when he was a successful drawer of land in the 1820 Georgia Land Lottery. The land was located in Appling County. Apparently, he did not choose to live on that land.[6] He was still a resident of

---

[1]--Henley was spelled Hendley is a few sources and Henly in a few others. This author arbitrarily chose to use the Henley spelling except in a few cases where source references are quoted directly.

[2]--<u>Henry County, Georgia, The Mother of Counties</u>, Vessie Thrasher Rainer, 1971. No publisher listed. p. 119.

[3]--Ibid.

[4]--Martha's birth date, death date and name of father obtained from <u>Mother of Counties</u>, op. cit., p. 119.

[5]--<u>Miscellaneous Files</u>, GA Dept of Archives.

[6]--<u>The Third, or 1820 Land Lottery of Georgia</u>. By Silas Lucas, Jr. Page 338. Henley Varner of Putnam County, Oslins
(continued...)

Putnam Co at the time of the 1824 Georgia State Census. His brothers William and George, Jr., his sisters Susannah Neal and Sarah Whitfield, and cousins Edward and Mark Varner also lived in Putnam Co all or most of those years.

By 1828 Henley Varner had moved to McDonough, Henry Co, GA. He became a high ranking leader in both the economic and political communities there. He is remembered prominently in two histories of Henry Co. One of those books includes a photograph of the home where he and his wife Martha lived for the last several years of their lives.[1] Like so many of his Varner relatives, Henley speculated in real estate, buying and then reselling many of the finer homes in McDonough.[2] Henley was also a slave owner, reporting that he had 3 slaves in 1820 and 28 in 1830. But his slave ownership had dropped to four by 1840, suggesting that he was directing his financial interests away from agriculture and more toward real estate and/or other business interests.[3]

---

[6](...continued)
Militia District, won Lot 107, Section 7, in Appling County.

[1]--Henry Co, GA, Landmark Houses, by Dr. R. A. Ranier, PO Box 597, McDonough, GA 30253. See pages 86, 87, 101, and 254. The other book is Henry County, Georgia, the Mother of Counties, by Vessie Thrasher Ranier, 1970, p. 119-120. No publisher listed.

[2]--Ibid.

[3]--1850 and 1860 slave schedules were not checked for Henley Varner.

Henley Varner, Community Leader

In politics, Henley Varner was commissioned a Justice of Inferior Court for Henry Co, 14 Jan 1829.[1] Henley was a member of the Georgia House of Representatives from Henry Co in 1832, 1833, 1834, and 1841. He was a Georgia State Senator from Henry Co in 1828, 1829, 1830, 1836, 1837, 1838, and 1839.[2] On measures voted on by the Georgia Senate during the 1837 session--the only session record reviewed by the author--Henley cast votes as follows:

He voted against a motion to table a bill asking for the speedy removal of the Cherokee Indians from the State of Georgia; the motion to table[3] passed 46 to 29. Henley voted for a resolution instructing Georgia's representatives and senators in Congress to oppose the establishment of a 2nd national bank.[4] In other landmark legislation, the 1837 Georgia Senate voted to establish a

---

[1]--Mother of Counties, op. cit., p. 119.

[2]--Records are at the GA Dept of Archives.

[3]--A motion to table asks that action be postponed; in effect, it frequently means the proposed action is killed. However, this bill was probably taken off the table and passed later because the Cherokees were removed to west of the Mississippi River the following year. About one-fourth of the Indians died during the forced march. This was the infamous "Trail of Tears."

[4]--This was one of the hottest national political issues of that era. The Democratic Party opposed a national bank while the Whig party was for it. The U.S. entered a depression in 1837, probably the most severe one experienced up to that time.

general system of public education. Henley Varner and 53 other senators voted for it while only 20 voted nay.[5]

Henley and Martha Varner were parents of one child, **LeRoy Monroe Varner**, who died young, in 1837.[2] Henley, Martha, and LeRoy are all buried in Griffin Cemetery in McDonough.[3]

Henley cared for a sick sister[4] in his home prior to her death in 1838. Henley and Martha then reared the deceased sister's child, Elizabeth Rust Thomas, who was three years old at the time of her mother's death. Elizabeth Thomas married 16 Nov 1851 Joseph A. Thrasher, who was a young attorney in McDonough.[5] Records that would identify which of Henley's sisters died in his home in 1838 were not located.

An interesting personal letter, written in 1831, from Henley Varner of McDonough, GA, to his brother John Varner, Hayneville, AL, has been preserved. It is in

---

[1]--Journal of the Georgia Senate for 1837, available at the GA Dept. of Archives.

[2]--Mother of Counties, op. cit., p. 119.

[3]--Ibid.

[4]--Henry County, Georgia, Cemeteries. Compiled by Vessie Thrasher Rainer. Page 16. From Henry County Weekly, Aug. 31, 1894: "In 1838, a sister of Mr. Henley Varner and wife of Dr. George Thomas died at Mr. Varner's and was buried in an unmarked grave in McDonough, leaving a three-year old daughter. Mr. Varner reared the child. The child, Elizabeth Thomas, married a young lawyer, Joseph Armstrong Thrasher, here."

[5]--Mother of Counties, op. cit. p. 119.

Henley's handwriting, of course, and it contains a wealth of family news.[1]

Frederick Varner, Son of George Varner

Frederick Varner was born in about 1789 in Wilkes Co, GA. He died in 1855 in Caldwell Parish, LA. He married **Sarah "Sally" Graves** in Oglethorpe Co, GA on 27 Jun 1808. Like so many others in his family, Frederick Varner was a planter. His first farm was in Oglethorpe Co, GA, near his father George Varner.

In 1819, Frederick acquired land on the Alabama River, in Montgomery Co (Lowndes Co after 1830). His brother John Varner settled there at the same time. John's land was about one mile downriver from Frederick's.

During the early 1840's Frederick and most of his children left Lowndes Co, AL, and relocated to the east bank of the Quachita River in Caldwell Parish, LA. He prospered there as well.

Frederick and Sarah had eight children: **Thomas Jefferson, Amarantha L., Elizabeth, William Graves, George W., Frederick, Jr., John F., and Francis M.**[2]

See Chapter XIII for information about Frederick Varner, his wife Sarah Graves, and their descendants.

---

[1]--It is located in the AL Dept of Archives filed with the Lowndes Co, AL, estate papers under the name John Varner. It is printed as an appendix in Chapter VI of this book.

[2]--Much of the information about Frederick and Sarah's children and grandchildren was obtained from Frederick's will and estate papers, which are located in the Caldwell Par, LA, Courthouse.

Susannah Varner, Daughter of George Varner

Susannah Varner, daughter of George Varner and Betsy Henley, was born in about 1791 in Wilkes Co, GA. She married **James Neal** in Oglethorpe Co, GA on 29 Nov 1810. Susannah died before George Varner wrote his will in 1825. Her children, Martha A. Neal and Susan V. Neal, are named in their grandfather George Varner's will.

Susannah and James are believed to have lived in Putnam Co, GA, as early as 1810 and possibly as late as 1824. James Neal completed real estate transactions there in 1810, 1814, and 1824. Susannah's brothers William, Henley, and George, Jr., and her cousins Edward and Marcus Varner were living in Putnam County during most or all of those years.

Elizabeth Varner, Daughter of George Varner

Elizabeth Varner, daughter of George Varner and Betsy Henley, was born about 1793 in Wilkes Co, GA. She married **Thomas Neal** in Oglethorpe Co, GA on 16 Mar 1812.

Sarah Varner, Daughter of George Varner

Sarah Varner, daughter of George Varner and Betsy Henley, was born about 1800 in Oglethorpe Co, GA. She married **George B. Whitfield** in Oglethorpe Co, GA on 4 Oct 1820. George died in 1838 or 1839 in Lowndes Co, AL).[1]

---

[1]--Lowndes Co, AL, Circuit Court records reveal that George B. Whitfield died between its spring term 1838 and its spring term 1839.

This was probably a second marriage for George B. Whitfield and he was probably several years older than Sarah.[1] Whitfield was a planter in Putnam Co, GA. His 1824 tax record, in Putnam Co, indicates that he owned a large number of slaves, perhaps as many as 70, and his land holdings totaled over 1300 acres.[2]

By 1831, however, Whitfield had apparently lost most of his wealth. Sarah's brother, Henley Varner, in a personal letter to their brother John Varner, expressed concern about Whitfield's financial worth. Henley said he was concerned about economic support for Sarah and her children after George's death. Henley also mentioned that Whitfield was "drinking." The letter strongly infers that George was getting old or was in failing health for some other reason.[3]

George B. Whitfield was one of the administrators of the estate of George Varner, Sr. He took over that roll alone after the death of William Varner, the other active administrator.

Between 1831 and 1836, George and Sarah and their children moved to Lowndes Co, AL, where Sarah's brothers John Varner and Frederick Varner lived. George B. Whitfield was sued in Circuit Court there several times

---

[1]--Sarah's brother Henley expressed a fear that George would die leaving Sarah to raise her children with little or no financial resources. This concern was expressed in a letter that Henley wrote in 1831 to his and Sarah's brother John Varner, in Alabama. The original letter is in the AL Archives. A transcribed copy of it appears as an appendix in Chapter VI of this book.

[2]--<u>Putnam Co, GA, Tax Records for 1824</u>.

[3]--Henley Varner letter, op. cit.

between 1836 and 1839 for failing to meet his financial obligations.[1] George B. Whitfield's death was reported to the Court at its spring term in 1839. The sheriff was instructed to search for property that belonged to the estate that could be used to pay the obligations. A notation from the sheriff said: "Sold house and lot in Hayneville lately occupied by George B. Whitfield for $155 on Jan. 6, 1840. Money was applied to an earlier execution." A. Harrison, Sheriff.[2]

The 1840 census for Lowndes Co, AL, lists Sarah Whitfield as head of household with 1 male 5 to 10, 2 males 10-15, 1 male 15-20, 1 female under 5, 1 female 5-10, 1 female 30 to 40, and 4 slaves. Three of the 11 residents were engaged in agriculture.

Sarah was not listed in the 1850 Lowndes Co census.

Emily S. Varner, Daughter of George Varner

Emily Sophronia Varner was born in about 1807 in Oglethorpe Co, GA. She married **Bryant Manghan** in Eatonton, Putnam Co, GA on 23 Dec 1827. Emily was a minor in 1825 when her father wrote his will.

---

[1]--Lowndes Co, AL, Circuit Court Records, 1834-1837, p. 611, and 1838-1841, pp. 15, 157, 159, 205, 228 and Execution Docket, 1838-1841, pp. 38 and 111.

[2]--Execution Docket, op. cit., p. 111.

Appendix V-A
William Varner Letters

Letter From William Varner
To David B. Mitchell, Esquire, Milledgeville, GA.
Eatonton, Aug. 3, 1813
David B. Mitchell, Esquire, Sir:

These few lines is (sic) dropped by way of tendering to you my services together with a volunteer troop of horse under my command to march at any time called on in case we can be accepted to go against the Indians in the present expected expedition. If we can be accepted be so good as to inform me by Lt. Richardson or if not you will please say whether a volunteer company of militia would be accepted for the same expedition or if my troop of horse cannot be accepted I wish to go and can raise a volunteer militia company. I am bound to you sir, your most obedient servant,   William Varner

----

Received 23 Aug. 1813,

From His Excellency, David B. Mitchell, Governor of Georgia, 28 horsemen's swords, scabbards, for the use of my troop of light dragoons in Putnam County ordered into service by general orders dated the 18th instant, which with the 50 delivered to me on the first of July, ultimo?, as per my receipt then given, makes 78 for the use of my said troop now ordered into service.

William Varner, Captain, Commander

Appendix V-B
Will of John F. Varner

Henry County Wills Book A. Page 306.
Notes on Will of John F. Varner[1] of Henry County, GA.

Wills that son William D. Varner and daughter Eliza R. Varner having realized a legacy by bequest from and out of the estate of their uncle David N. Varner, late of Pike County, deceased, of a considerable amount and my daughter Carry Varner and my son Henley Varner and my wife Martha A. Varner not having participated in those legacies and bequests of said David N. Varner, deceased and being desirous that my wife Martha A. Varner and my daughter Carry Varner and my son Henley Varner should own and possess and enjoy an equal estate in form, evaluation and amount to that owned and possessed by my son William D. Varner and my daughter Eliza R. Varner bequeathed to them aforesaid provided my uncle Henley Varner should bequeath to my daughter Carry Varner and my son Henley Varner one thousand dollars each which amount if bequeathed to them shall be considered so much towards making up their portion equal to the amount left to William D. Varner and Eliza R. Varner, I therefore bequeath that at my death all of my estate both real and personal be reduced to money, the house and lot in the town of McDonough and the land adjoining, whereon I now live, and the household and kitchen furniture excepted. And out of the said sum I give and bequeath to my wife Martha A. Varner and my daughter Carry Varner and my son Henley Varner a special legacy arising from the sale of my property equal

---

[1]..John F. Varner was a son of William Varner, who was a prominent citizen of Putnam Co, GA, and a grandson of George Varner of Oglethorpe Co, GA.

and as the same amount including the principal and interest of that legacy bequeathed to my son William D. Varner and daughter Eliza R. Varner by the said David N. Varner, deceased, less the amount to be left by my uncle Henley Varner to my daughter Carry Varner and my son Henley Varner.

I desire and direct the balance remaining be divided equally between my four children, William D. Varner, Eliza R. Varner, Carry Varner, and Henley Varner, and my wife Martha A. Varner.

I leave my house and lot in the town of McDonough to my wife Martha A. Varner, also all my family books and household and kitchen furniture for her use during her lifetime. Provided my executors hereinafter named think it best to sell said property or a part thereof and invest the proceeds in other property of the same description and at her death the same to be sold according to the laws of the state and the money arising therefrom shall be equally divided between my four children.

Named David Knott and Martha A. Varner, executors of the estate.

Witnesses Lewis M. Tye, James B. Crabb, and Henley Varner.

Signed by John Varner, Jan. 11, 1862.

Executors came into court on March 18, 1862, along with witnesses including Henley Varner, and asked that the will be probated.

Appendix V-C
Appraisal of John F. Varner's Estate

Appraisement Book D, Henry County, GA. Pages 64 to 66.

The following is a partial list of the property belonging to the John F. Varner estate, with the appraised value of selected items: 4 bottles Jaynes hair dye -- appraised at $2.67; 21 bottles of Moffits Bitters -- $14.66; 6 boxes of Ague pills -- $4.00; Variety of cows and calves and one bull (11 total); a bay horse; a mule; a few hogs; a boar; two sows; some plows, including a subsoil plow; Harrow, single trees, 19 plow hoes.

One buggy and harness -- $75; one saddle, one hand saw, two squares, one draw knife; one compass, one foot adze, three augers; three pair plow gear and traces; two long tables; one scythe and cradle; three bedsteads.

Three bales of cotton, one wheel barrow; six axes, one spade and shovel, three hoes; one crow bar, one grubbing hoe, one briar hook; two iron wedges, one two-horse wagon and harness -- $60; one one-horse wagon and harness -- $10; one grind stone and crank -- 75 cents.

One slave Alsey -- $400; one slave -- Jerry $300; one slave -- Billy $1400; one slave -- Georgia $800; one slave -- Margaret $800.

77 boxes of Jaynes pills -- 16 cents each -- $12.82 total; 1 shot gun -- $10; 1 case and bottle, two silver watches -- $40; 26 bottles of Jaynes Expectorant -- $17.33; 30 bottles of Jaynes Alleralia -- $20; 28 bottles of ??? Balsam -- $8; brass kettle, 1 lot cooking utensils, two trays and sifter; one set candle molds, one lot tinware; one spinning wheel, one hair card, three kitchen tables.

Three sod irons, 5 tables, 1 boiler, 1 rake; one lot crooking ware, silverware jars, 8 candlesticks; one cupboard, two small tables, one saw case, 12 chairs; six chairs, 1 coffee mill and strainer, 1 small table; three water buckets, a churn, foot tub, one sausage grinder; four bedsteads and furniture -- $200; one bedstead and furniture -- $25; one bedstead and furniture -- $30; three bedsteads and furniture -- $60; six mattresses, two tables, four looking glasses.

Two bowls and pitchers, one fender, 18 coverlets; one holster and two pillows; 19 sheets, 37 towels, 2 table clothes, 30 slips; one water stand, two trunks, two chests, five parlor chairs; two rocking chairs, one candle stand, one sofa, two lamps; one wardrobe, 1 pair ??? andirons, 4 pairs common andirons; one wardrobe, one toilet, one clock, two shovels, 3 tongs; one small table, one lot of books -- $5.00; one trunk.

Appraisers: Henley Varner, A. C. Sloan, A. R. Brown.
Submitted to Court of Ordinary, March 22, 1862.

Chapter VI
John Varner, Son of George Varner

John Varner, son of **George Varner and Betsy Henley** of Oglethorpe County, GA, (b. 10 Sep 1783 Rowan Co or Randolph Co, NC, d. 31 Dec 1869[1] Coosa Co, AL; bur Providence Ch Cem, Coosa Co, AL) marr in Oglethorpe Co, GA on 10 Jan 1807 to **Nancy Powell**, dau of **Edward Powell and Mary**, (b. ca. 1790, d. betw 1840 and 1850[2] in AL).

The Powell family moved from Virginia to Wilkes Co, GA (later Oglethorpe Co) at about the same time that the Varners moved there from North Carolina. Edward and Mary Powell lived on Long Creek near George Varner's plantation. Edward died between 1801, when he wrote his will[3], and 1805, when his minor children (Polly, Lucy, Nancy, and Rebecca) were listed as eligible drawers in the 1805 Georgia land lottery.[4] John Powell, Thomas Powell, and Edward W. Powell were guardians of Nancy Powell, a minor, at the time of her marriage to John Varner in Jan 1807.[5]

---

[1]--Birth date and place and death date taken from John Varner's grave marker in Providence Cemetery, Coosa Co, AL.

[2]--Nancy Powell was living at the time of the 1840 census but she was not enumerated in the 1850 census.

[3]--Edward Powell's will is recorded in Oglethorpe Co, GA, Will Book A, p. 107.

[4]--The Georgia Researcher, Allstate Research, Murray, UT, Vol. 1, No. 4, p. 34.

[5]--Oglethorpe Co, GA, Bonds for 1804-1807, p. 71.

John Varner Becomes a Planter

John Varner was a planter; first, in Oglethorpe Co, GA, from 1810 to 1819; second, in Montgomery Co (Lowndes Co after 1830), AL, from 1820 to about 1843; and third, in Coosa Co, AL, from about 1843 until his death in 1869. He also found time to serve 12 years as Clerk of the County Court in Lowndes Co, AL. Like so many of his other relatives--father, uncles, brothers, and cousins--he used slave labor to build his capital holdings and support his family.

John purchased two parcels of land in 1810 in Oglethorpe Co, GA, near his father's plantation. The parcels were adjacent to one another, on Syls Fork of Little River. One was 417 acres[1] in size and the other one was 239 acres.[2]. In 1813, the earliest year for which his tax records were located, John Varner listed 9 Negro slaves in his possession. By 1819, the last year he farmed in GA, the number of his slaves had grown to 13.[3]

John's wife Nancy was a member of the County Line Baptist Church, Oglethorpe Co, GA. She "related her experience and was accepted into fellowship" 2 Jun 1810. She applied for a letter of dismission, which was granted, 6 Nov 1819.[4] According to the records, John Varner did not join the church. He was referred to as Mr. John

---

[1].See Appendix # VI-A at the end of this chapter for a copy of the deed that recorded this land purchase.

[2].See Appendix # VI-B at the end of this chapter for a copy of the deed that recorded this land purchase.

[3]..Oglethorpe Co, GA, Tax Records, op. cit.

[4]..County Line Baptist Church Minutes, op. cit., 2 Jun 1810 and 6 Nov 1819.

Varner, not as Bro. John Varner, in the minutes for 31 Oct 1818, which state: "Mr. John Varner's Negro woman Millie came to the church and related her experiences and was received into fellowship."[1]

John and Nancy Varner Move to Alabama

John Varner and Nancy Powell sold their Oglethorpe County land holdings in 1816[2] and 1819[3]. They then took their five young children and their slaves and moved to the frontier wilderness in Alabama. They were joined in this trek by John's brother Frederick and his family, and probably other relatives and friends. They settled on the Alabama River in what was then Montgomery County (Lowndes Co after 1830). Drury Powell, Hudson Powell, Thomas Powell, and Seymour Powell, who also moved from Oglethorpe Co, GA, and settled near John and Frederick Varner in 1818 and 1819, are believed to have been related to John Varner's wife, Nancy Powell.

John Varner's first Alabama plantation[4] was about 1 mile south of the Alabama River and one-half mile west of Cypress Creek, between the villages of St. Clair and

---

[1]..County Line Church Minutes, op. cit.

[2]..Oglethorpe Co, GA, Deed Book I, p. 212.
Mar. 11, 1816, John Varner of County of Oglethorpe sold 242 1/2 acres on Syls Fork of Little River to Mathew Phillips for $1200. Signed by John Varner.

[3]..Oglethorpe County, GA, Deed Book J, p. 222.
Nov. 2, 1819, John and Nancy Varner sold 414 acres on Little River to William Hatchet for $1800. Signed by both John and Nancy Varner.

[4]..He purchased his first Alabama land, 80 acres, from the Federal Government 20 Oct 1819. Lowndes Tract Book, p. 151.

Whitehall.[1] The neighborhood where he settled was apparently called Old Town in the early days because some correspondence was addressed to John Varner, Old Town, AL. One letter was simply addressed to John Varner, Alabama. He received it, so John Varner must have been a well known person in the young state. (Or perhaps the sender merely sent the letter with someone he knew who was traveling to the settlement where John Varner lived.)

John Varner Elected Clerk of County Court

John Varner was elected the first clerk of the Lowndes County Court when that county was created in 1830. He served in that county wide office for 12 years. He was responsible for maintaining land, marriage, probate, and miscellaneous other official county records. Hundreds of books of his records can be found in the Lowndes County Courthouse in Hayneville today and used by interested researchers. Those records contributed much of the material concerning the Varners in Lowndes County that is included in this book.[2]

John Varner relocated his plantation to Big Swamp Creek, less than a mile Southwest of the county seat of Hayneville, after he was elected Clerk of the Court. His farm there was on the Southeast side of AL Hwy 21 where it crosses Big Swamp Creek. This location, close to the

---

[1]..John Varner's first AL plantation was on the north side of present day AL HWY 40 where the spur road leaves HWY 40 to lead to the state park. It was planted to cotton in 1988, 1989, and 1991 when the author of this book visited there.

[2]..This author spent about 12 days going through Lowndes County records, many of which had been kept by John Varner, Clerk of the County Court.

JOHN VARNER, SON OF GEORGE VARNER

Courthouse, enabled John to manage his plantation while he also kept the records of the County Court. At that time, serving as court clerk was probably a part time endeavor, with much of his pay coming from fees rather than a salary.[1] After John moved to Coosa Co, John and Nancy's son Azariah Varner remained in Lowndes Co and continued to farm the acreage on Big Swamp Creek until Azariah's death in 1856. Then John and Amanda Varner (John's second wife), of Coosa Co, AL, sold the land where Azariah lived and died.[2]

As noted elsewhere (primarily in Chapter V), John Varner and Frederick Varner were not the only children of George and Betsy Varner who moved to Lowndes County, AL. John and Frederick's sister Sarah Varner and her family moved there between 1831 and 1836. Sarah's husband George B. Whitfield died there in 1838 or 1839. Sarah and her seven children resided in Lowndes County at the time of the 1840 census.[3]

When John Varner finished his work as Clerk of the County Court in Lowndes County, he inadvertently left behind a folder of personal papers. That folder of papers included 41 items, such as receipts for bill payments and correspondence, both personal and business. The folder of papers ended up filed with the Lowndes County estate

---

[1]..Many extant records at the Lowndes Co Courthouse and the AL Archives refer to payment of such fees to "John Varner, Esq." Typically, they were paid for such tasks as recording land deed transactions, issuing marriage licenses, and recording probate proceedings.

[2]..Lowndes Co, AL, <u>Deed Book E</u>, p. 11.

[3]..This researcher made no effort to trace the Whitfield family beyond 1840.

papers. The papers are now stored at the Alabama State Archives in Montgomery. The item of greatest genealogical value was a personal letter to John Varner from his brother Henley Varner of McDonough, Henry County, GA. Written in 1831, it told of the death of John and Henley's brother, William Varner, as well as other news of family interest.[1]

John Varner Moves to Coosa County, AL

In about 1844 John Varner moved from Lowndes County, AL, to Coosa County, AL, a distance of about 100 miles northeast of Lowndes County. All of his children except George H., Susan Eliza, William F., and Azariah also moved to Coosa County. Son George H. had moved to Franklin Co, MS, six years earlier. Susan Eliza, Azariah, and William F. and their families remained in Lowndes County. John took his slaves also, except for those that he put in trusts to support his son Azariah's children and his daughter Susan Eliza.

At about the time John Varner moved to Coosa County, AL, John Varner's brother Frederick Varner and all of his children except William G. Varner moved to Caldwell Parish, LA, a distance of some 300 miles west of Lowndes County, AL. William G. Varner was married to John's daughter Susan Eliza. That family was one of only three Varner families that remained in Lowndes County. The other ones were the Azariah and Mary L. Varner family and the William F. and Margaret Varner family. Interestingly, Azariah's family remained on the former John Varner property and farmed it while the William G.

---

[1]..See Appendix # VI-C at the end of this chapter for a copy of Henley Varner's letter to his brother John Varner.

and Susan Varner family remained on the former Frederick Varner land and farmed it.

Why Did Varner Families Separate?

Why did the John Varner and Frederick Varner families move to separate locations so far removed from one another after having been neighbors for so many years--in both Oglethorpe County, GA, and Lowndes County, AL? They had moved together twice previously: (1) from Oglethorpe Co, GA, to land near the Alabama River in what was then Montgomery Co, in 1819 and (2) from those farms to land near Hayneville in the center of the newly created Lowndes County in the early 1830's.

Extant records suggest, but do not prove, possible reasons. During the late 1830's and early 1840's, the following events involving the John Varner and Frederick Varner families occurred[1]:

1. John Varner's wife Nancy Powell Varner died (between 1840 and 1850).

2. In Franklin County, MS, Circuit Court, William G. Varner, Frederick's son, entered and won a law suit against George H. Varner, John's son. (See Chapter X).

3. George W. Varner, believed to have been a son of Frederick Varner, was convicted of fraud and attempting to extort property in Lowndes County Chancery Court. He died shortly thereafter. His estate was insolvent. (See Chapter V).

4. George B. Whitfield, who was married to Sarah Varner, one of John Varner's and Frederick Varner's sisters, died in Lowndes Co, AL. He left insufficient funds to pay his debts.

---

[1]..These events are covered and documented elsewhere in this and other chapters of this book.

5. William G. Varner, husband of Susan Eliza Varner and son of Frederick Varner, began to drink to excess. (See Chapter XII).

6. Azariah Varner, John Varner's son, experienced serious difficulties in meeting his financial obligations--whether from drinking, naturally poor health or illness, or simply poor management skills--is uncertain.

7. Thomas Jefferson Varner, Frederick Varner's son, died. His widow died soon thereafter, leaving four orphans. (See Chapter XII).

9. Amaziah Varner, John Varner's son, was arrested and convicted of "retailing" (moonshining). Convicted with him was his cousin George W. Varner. This was not long before the latter died. (See section on Amaziah Varner in Chapter VII).

It would be presumptuous to conclude that any or all of these events were responsible for John Varner's move to Coosa County, AL, and\or Frederick Varner's move to Caldwell Parish, LA. There is no evidence strong enough to prove it. But one or more of these happenings might have been part or all of the reason.

Families May Have Parted Friends

It is possible that John and Frederick and their children had no quarrel of significance. They may have parted on good terms. They could have been merely seeking a healthier climate, new lands to clear and farm, or simply new experiences or "more elbow room" on the frontier.

John Varner continued to add to his slave holdings after moving to Alabama, reporting ownership of 18 in

1830, 15 in 1840, 28 in 1850, and 33 in 1860[1]. He also reported that his plantation in Coosa Co had 8 slave houses in 1860. Earlier censuses had not asked for that information. The 1850 and 1860 slave schedules gave the sex and ages of slaves but no names for them. John Varner had reduced his slave holdings somewwhat by giving some to trusts which he set up to help support his daughter Susan and her children and the children of his son Azariah.[2] He set up the trusts rather than make outright gifts to protect the property (slaves) from becoming liable to pay the debts of William G. Varner (Susan's husband) and Azariah Varner. Nevertheless, creditors attempted but failed to seize the slaves which John Varner had put in both trusts. A record of the trusts and those lengthy Chancery Court cases are on file at the Lowndes Co, AL, Courthouse in Hayneville.[3]

---

[1]..U.S. census records for 1830 and 1840 and Slave Schedules for 1850 and 1860.

[2]..John Varner probably gave his other children a few slaves also as that practice seems to have been common by the Varners who had large slave-holdings. In addition to Azariah and Susan, John's children George H., William F., Edward P., and John W. all owned a few slaves early in their adulthood. It is unlikely that they could have acquired them without financial help from their father. John Varner's gifts of slaves to his other children are not recorded in public documents because John did not set up trusts when he gifted them. He trusted those children to be successful managers of their property.

[3]..Chancery Court Cases # 414 and # 387. The cases are summarized in <u>Chancery Court Records</u>, Bk. 10. Original records of the trials were located in a Lowndes Co warehouse behind the jail in Hayneville, AL. The records for one of the
(continued...)

VARNER FAMILIES OF THE SOUTH--VI

John and Nancy Varner Face Problems

Outwardly, it appears that John Varner and Nancy Powell were successful Alabama planters during their years in Lowndes County and that John was a respected member of the ruling class, serving honorably as Clerk of the Lowndes County Court. But surface looks can be deceiving. There are only minor clues that John had to struggle to meet his financial obligations, but there are clear signs that some of his children and other relatives had major financial[1] and health problems.[2] Many close

---

[3](...continued)
suits include an affidavit submitted by John Varner wherein he admits that he knew that his son-in-law William G. Varner was "dissipating" when he set up the trust (in 1842). The papers of the other case include testimony by Azariah Varner admitting that he "is insolvent...and that he is diseased and sickly and cannot work..."

[1]..In dozens of Lowndes Co Circuit Court cases, Varners were sued for failing to pay promissory notes and take care of other financial agreements. John's son Azariah and son-in-law William G. Varner were the most frequent targets of such litigations. But suits were also brought against John's sons William F. Varner and Amaziah Varner, John's nephew George W. Varner, and John's brother-in-law George B. Whitfield.

[2]..Varners who appear to have had health problems included John's son Azariah, who had health problems over a period of years (possibly alcoholic); John's son-in-law William G. Varner (almost certainly alcoholic); John's son Amaziah (possibly alcoholic); John's brother George W. Varner (probably an alcoholic); and John's brother-in-law George Whitfield (alcoholic).

JOHN VARNER, SON OF GEORGE VARNER

relatives died[3] over a short span of years, many of them while they were very young. Several of those who died during the 1850's might have been victims of the yellow fever epidemic which hit the southern costal area.[2] John seems to have had good health, but he was reported in the 1860 census to be blind.

No evidence was found to explain when or why he lost his sight. He must have had good eyesight when he recorded the thousands of documents that comprise the early day official records of the Lowndes County Court.

John lost his wife Nancy Powell to death sometime during the 1840's. Records show that he was married to a woman whose first name was Amanda[3] during the 1850's and 1860's when he lived in Coosa County. John and Amanda's Coosa County plantation was located about

---

[1]..John Varner's relatives who died in Alabama and Louisiana between about 1840 and 1860 included John's first wife Nancy Powell; John's sons Amaziah, Azariah, and William F.; John's nephews William G., George W., Francis M., and Thomas J.; John's nieces Amarantha and Elizabeth; John's brother-in-law George B. Whitfield; and several of John and Nancy's grandchildren. William G., George W., Francis M., Thomas J., Amarantha, and Elizabeth were children of Frederick Varner, John Varner's brother.

[2]..Hardy Vickers Whooten, who was a doctor in Lowndesborough, Lowndes Co, AL, during the 1840's and 1850's, kept a diary. Several times he talked about yellow fever spreading from New Orleans, Mobile, and Montgomery. The diary is in the AL Archives.

[3]..Marriage records of Chambers Co, AL, show that John Varner married Mandy Mulkey there 20 Mar 1850. This is believed to be John Varner of Coosa Co, previously Lowndes Co, AL and Oglethorpe Co, GA.

one mile north of Providence Church, in the Southwest corner of Coosa County[1]. It was on the west side of AL Hwy 27 about halfway between Providence Church and the junction of Hwy 27 and Hwy 22.

John Varner Loses Most of His Wealth

At the outbreak of the Civil War in 1861, John Varner was a wealthy man. The 1860 census reported that he owned personal property (mostly slaves) worth $46,000 and real estate worth $3,500. He owned 33 slaves[2] and 640 acres of land. The Agricultural Census also suggested that John Varner was prospering. In addition to the land and slaves, John Varner owned livestock that was worth $1500. The farm produced corn, cotton, and a variety of other grains and vegetables.[3]

---

[1]..John Varner purchased the following described land in Coosa County (240 acres) from the Federal government on Feb. 16, 1843: NE 1/4 and the E 1/2 of the SE 1/4 of T 21N, R17E, S 16. Coosa County Tract Book, pages 272-273.

[2]..1860 Slave Schedule for Coosa County, AL. John Varner owned 14 male slaves and 19 female slaves. Ages of the males: 55, 51, 35, 34, 35, 26, 14, 4, 14, 10, 8, 3, 3, and 5. Ages of the females: 68, 47, 47, 25, 38, 27, 26, 23, 13, 12, 12, 12, 10, 9, 7, 2, 5, 1, and 23. He had eight slave houses. The Schedule did not include names of slaves.

[3]..1860 AGRICULTURAL CENSUS, COOSA COUNTY

John Varner: 400 acres improved land, 240 acres unimproved land. Value of farm land: $4,000. Value of farm equipment and tools: $375.

Livestock owned at time of census: 3 horses, 4 mules and asses, 15 milch cows, 2 working oxen, 12 other cattle, 5 sheep, 30 swine.

(continued...)

JOHN VARNER, SON OF GEORGE VARNER

Like slave holders throughout the South, John Varner lost most of his wealth when his slaves were freed. When he died in 1869, four years after the Civil War ended, John Varner was able to leave only $100 to each of his children[1]. In contrast, John's father had left each of his children about $5,000 when he died in 1827. John's brother Frederick Varner, who died in 1855, six years before the Civil War began, left each of his children about $3,000. Extant records indicate that John Varner had been somewhat more wealthy than his brother Frederick. But the loss of his slave property left John Varner little more than his land, livestock, and farm products along with some farm equipment and tools.

John Varner wrote his will shortly before his death in 1869. He died on New Year's Eve that December. He identified his children in the will even though four of

---

[3](...continued)
Value of livestock: $1550.

Crop production during past twelve months: 800 bushels Indian corn, 10 bushels of oats, 20 bales of ginned cotton, 10 pounds of wool, 70 bushels of peas and beans, 2 bushels of Irish potatoes, 20 pounds of butter.

Value of manufactured goods made in the home: $20.

Value of livestock slaughtered: $50.

[1]..John Varner was able to be a little more generous to his two youngest sons, who were living with him and managing his farm at the time of his death. He left $400 to his son Esselman and his farm land and buildings to his son Hardaway.

them had preceded him in death.[2] The estate sale followed a few weeks after John Varner's death.[3]

John and Nancy Varner had ten children: **Amaziah, Azariah, Susan Eliza, George H., Edward P., William F., John W., Hardaway, Esselman and Lucy A.**

See Chapter VII for information about John and Nancy Varner's children.

See Chapter VIII for additional information about Azariah Varner and his descendants.

See Chapter IX for additional information about Susan Eliza Varner and her descendants.

See Chapter X for additional information about George H. Varner and his descendants.

See Chapter XI for additional information about John W. Varner and his descendants.

See Chapter XII for additional information about Esselman Varner and his descendants.

---

[1]..See Appendix # VI-D at the end of this chapter for a copy of John Varner's will.

[2]..See Appendix # VI-E at the end of this chapter for a record of John Varner's estate sale.

Appendix VI-A
John Varner Purchases 417 Acres of Land

Oglethorpe County, GA, <u>Deed Book G</u>, page 188.
JOHN VARNER BUYS 417 ACRES OF LAND.

This indenture made this twelfth day of October in the year of our Lord one thousand and eight hundred and ten between Robert Owen of the County of Randolph and State of Georgia of the one part and John Varner of the County of Oglethorpe and State aforesaid of the other part, Witnesseth, that for the consideration of eight hundred and thirty-four dollars...the said Robert Owen, hath...sold...to the said John Varner...that tract or parcel of land...in the County of Oglethorpe and State aforesaid containing four hundred and seventeen acres...Beginning at a sweet gum corner on McNeals line and running with this line N. 45 East eighty eight chains and fifty links to a hickory corner thence on Jonathan Ragans line South forty five degrees East fifty four chains to a black gum corner, thence on Bullocks line South forty five degrees West, Twenty nine chain seventy five links to a hickory corner, thence of J. Ragan Jr.'s? line, South seventy one degrees West forty three chain and fifty links to a hickory corner, South ten West twenty three chains to a Stake corner in the field, Thence North forty five degrees West forty eight chain and fifty links to the beginning...In witness whereof the said Robert Owen hath hereunto set his hand and affixed his seal the day and date first above written.

Robert Owen (Seal)

Signed, sealed and delivered in the presence of: Jacob Owen, Littleberry Kennibrew, and Jonathan Ragan, Jr.

Appendix VI-B
John Varner Purchases 239 Acres of Land
Oglethorpe County, GA, Deed Book G, page 189.
 JOHN VARNER BUYS 239 ACRES OF LAND
 This indenture made the 12th day of October, 1810 between Robert Owen of the county of Randolph, State of Georgia, and John Varner of Oglethorpe County of the other part. Witnesseth: that the said Robert Owen for and in consideration of $600 of good and lawful money of the said state to him in hand paid by the said John Varner...hath...sold...to the said John Varner...a certain tract or parcel of land containing 239 acres...in the county of Oglethorpe...on both sides of Syls Fork of Little River and bounded as follows, viz, beginning at a pine corner, thence north 45.10 36 chains to a pine corner thence south 70.10 18 chains and 50 links on Stallings baseline to a dogwood corner thence north 10.21 chains to a hickory corner thence south 75.10 20 chains to a post oak thence south 25 west 22 chains to a red oak thence south 22 east 10 chains to a post oak corner thence east 22 chains west to a red oak corner thence south 10 east 22 chains on Littleberry Kinnebrew's line to a white oak corner thence on said Kinnebrew's line south 86 east 36 chains to a red oak thence on said Thorneberry line north 30 east? 22 chains and 50 links to the beginning corner...In witness whereof the said Robert Owen hath hereunto set his hand and affixed his seal the day and date fixed above. Written, signed, sealed, and delivered in presence of Jacob Owen, Littleberry Kennebrew, and Johnathan Ragan.
 Signed Robert Owen.

Appendix VI-C
Henley Varner Letter to Brother John Varner

Letter from Henley Varner to John Varner
Return address: McDonough, GA, Nov. 29.
  Postage: 18 3/4 written in upper right hand corner of envelop. Addressed to:
  Mr. John Varner, Lowndes County, Alabama.
Text of letter:
McDonough 27th Nov. 1831
Dear Brother,
  It becomes me at this time, though Painful, to inform you of the Death of our Bro. William Varner. He is no more. He Died about the Twentieth of last month in Houston County and has left the business of Father's Estate unsettled, and all that he collected is gone, and no one can tell when nor how he has made way with it. He has left nothing for his own children and no person will administer on his Estate for they can't without becoming the Administrator on father's Estate, and it all is in such a deranged state that it would in all probability involve the person in a loss that would undertake it. George Whitfield says he will be qualified and get what he can and says he has received nothing on his part since the death of father. But Brother William told me that Whitfield had received more than his share, or that he had paid for him more than was coming to him. So it rests, for I know nothing about it myself. Brother (William) is gone and the matter stands unsettled and perhaps will so remain.
  I was down at Whitfields a few days back and they are all well. But I am sorry to inform you that I fear that our Sister Sarah Whitfield will be left in this world with several children and nothing to support them on, for Whitfield does Drink and does not appear to make any

progress towards making or providing for them. And all of his property is gone except what he has belonging to his son William and daughter[1]. And if they should take them[2] away, he and his family will be in a deplorable situation. And it will devolve on Sister's Brothers and Sisters to help her. As for me, I am willing to do my part and I hope all the rest will help her for she is our sister. And if she has been unfortunate it is not her fault but her misfortune. Whitfield often talks of moving here and settling by me, which will be gratifying to his wife and me and my wife but it is not certain that he will move here yet.

I did expect to come out to see you and Bro. Frederick, but I guess I will not be able to come as I have Susan Varner[3] with us. She has been with us ever since last February. David and John Varner[4] are with John Neal[5] in Zebulon.

---

[1]..These were probably Whitfield's children from an earlier marriage.

[2]..The word "them" probably refers to slaves. Henley is suggesting that Whitfield's slaves might be seized and sold to pay Whitfield's debts. Events that took place later in Lowndes County, AL, suggest that the slaves were sold for that purpose. See Chapter V.

[3]..Susan Varner was probably William Varner's daughter and Henley Varner's niece.

[4]..David and John Varner were William Varner's orphan sons. See Chapter V.

[5]..The identity of John Neal is unclear. He might have been Thomas Neal, who married Elizabeth Varner, daughter of George Varner of Oglethorpe Co, GA. Or he could have been
(continued...)

We have fine crops in this state this year.

Bro. William was only sick five or six days and was up the evening before he died. (He died) that night about one o'clock. I hope he is better off than he was here, but he left no evidence of that, and perhaps was not knowledgeable that death was so near. We ought to be always ready for we know not when our death may come.

You will please show this to Bro. Frederick and write me as soon as you can. You have my love to you and all the family and Bro. F. Also my wife sends her love to you all. We are all well. We would be glad to see you all. Come in if you can.

I have nothing more to write you at this time. Will try and write you oftener than I have and hope you will do the same. You must excuse me for not informing you sooner of the death of Brother.

I remain your Dear Brother,

Henley Varner.

Appendix VI-D
John Varner's Will

Coosa County, AL. **WILL OF JOHN VARNER**

I, John Varner, Sr., at the County of Coosa and State of Alabama, considering the uncertainty of this life and being of sound mind and memory do make and publish this my last will and testament.

First, I direct that my funeral expenses be paid.

2. I give and bequeath unto my beloved wife Amanda one thousand dollars in gold, the bed, bedstead, and

---

[5](...continued)
James Neal, who married George Varner's daughter Sarah. Zebulon is in Pike Co, GA.

furniture that we usually lie upon, one horse bridle and saddle to be worth one hundred and twenty-five dollars and, provided she relinquish right of dower and receives the above as her full portion of my estate.

3. I give and bequeath unto my great granddaughter Iwanna Garnett one hundred dollars to be paid to her by my Executors when she becomes of age or when she marries. The above is the amount that my son Amaziah Varner (deceased) is entitled to.

4. I give and bequeath unto my granddaughter Sarah Varner, daughter of my son Azariah Varner (deceased), fifty dollars, and my grandson John Varner, Jr., fifty dollars, it being a fair share of their father Azariah Varner (deceased).

5. I give and bequeath unto the children of my son William Varner (deceased) one hundred dollars to be equally divided between them.

6. I give and bequeath unto my daughter Susan Eliza Dacus, fifty dollars, and fifty dollars unto her son John Varner.

7. I give and bequeath unto my son George H. Varner one hundred dollars.

8. I give and bequeath unto my son E. P. Varner one hundred dollars.

9. I give and bequeath unto my granddaughter Sarah Varner, daughter of John Varner (deceased), one hundred dollars.

10. I give and bequeath unto my son Hardaway Varner all my land that I live upon containing in all five hundred and sixty acres and one hundred dollars in money.

11. I give and bequeath unto my son Esselman Varner four hundred dollars and my silver watch.

JOHN VARNER, SON OF GEORGE VARNER

12. I give and bequeath unto my granddaughter Amanda Wilson one hundred dollars to be paid her by my Executor when she becomes of age or marries.

13. I give and bequeath unto Nancy, my old colored cook, ten dollars in gold to be paid by my Executor.

14. I direct that after my death that my interest in the mill known as Varner Mill, including land and gin, my stock of every kind, house hold and kitchen furniture, wagons, farming utensils, tools of every description, and my library be sold by my executors on credit of six months secured by note and Security.

15. I direct that my beloved Amanda, my sons and daughters, receive the amounts specified in this instrument out of the money that may be on hand, if any, at my death.

16. I direct that if any of my grand or great grandchildren that is included in this instrument should die before they become of full age the amounts that I have given to them in this will shall be reverted back to my children that may be living.

17. I direct that all moneys accruing from sales and the collection of outstanding debts and all moneys that may be on hand after my wife Amanda, my sons and daughters, receive the amount as directed in the fifteenth be equally divided between my wife Amanda and living children. And I do hereby make and ordain my beloved wife Amanda, E. P. Varner, and Hardaway Varner Executrix and Executors of this last will and testament in witness whereof I, John Varner, the Testator have to this my last will set my hand and Seal this the 12th day of October in the year of our Lord one thousand eight hundred and sixty nine.

JOHN VARNER (L.S.)

Signed and sealed and delivered in presence of us who have subscribed in presence of each other. F. A. Gulledge, Elias Kelly.

Wills and Orphans Records, Old Series, Vol. 2 (1843-1888), P. 229, Coosa County, AL.

E. P. Varner, Hardaway Varner, and Amanda Varner, executors of the last will & testament of John Varner, took out a bond for $3,000, Feb. 19, 1870. They paid a stamp fee of $1.00 in U.S. Revenue. Signed by Thomas H. Fargason, Judge of Probate. Bondsmen in security: Thomas Hull, James Hull, Esselman Varner, and B. F. Higgins. Coosa County Bonds, Vol. C, p 83.

Appendix VI-E
John Varner Estate Sale

Estate of John Varner, Deceased.
Probate Court, in Vacation. March 21, 1870.

1 piece sole leather, sold to Bob Varner for 65 cents; 3 raw hides, sold to E. Kelly for $2.50; 1 lot harness, John H. Lewis, 2.25; 1 lot plows, T. Jones, 4.00; 2 lots plows, E. Varner, 2.75; 1 lot of plows, E. P. Varner, 1.10; 1 lot of plows, W. H. Curlee, 1.00; 1 set ?, W. H. Curlee, 1.15; 2 single trees & pair hanes, H. W. Pence, 85 cents; 1 jr. tr. chunes, W. H. Curlee, 55 cents.

1 log chain, E. Varner, 4.00; 1 log chain, H. Norrell, 75 cents; 2 sod iron, R. Wilson, 2.10; 2 Gars, Bob Varner, 25 cents; 1 Jurs?, J. C. Traywick, 1.00; 1 lot of jugs, A. Turrell, 50 cents; 1 jar, Bob Varner, 1.05; 1 jug & vinegar, James Hilyer, 80 cents; 1 jug & vinegar, J. Knight, 95 cents; 1 jug & vinegar, J. P. Thornton, 1.00; 1 spinning wheel, Hardy Varner, 4.00; 1 lot & hand saw, E. Varner, 2.25; 1 bell, Amanda Varner, 10 cents.

JOHN VARNER, SON OF GEORGE VARNER

1 wheel, James Guy, 50 cents; 1 Broad ax, B. F. Higgins, 3.00; 1 fros?, B. F. Higgins, 75 cents; 1 Screw plate, A. B. Blocker, 4.50; 1 cross cut saw, E. Kelly, 4.20; 1 fifth chain, E. E. Estes, 3.00; 1 washing tub, J. R. Knight, 1.00; 1 Waffle irons, E. Varner, 75 cents; 1 Oven, A. B. Blocker, 1.70; 1 Spider & Lid, Florence Smith, 1.80; 1 Oven & lid, B. F. Higgens, 1.50; 1 Oven, Nancy Thomas, 15 cents; 1 Kettle, E. R. Mastin, 1.30; 1 Pot, A. B. Wilson, 80 cents.

1 Cradle Scythe, E. E. Estes, 1.00; 1 Sythe & Cradle, B. F. Higgins, 4.00; 1 Tray & Tub, H. Varner, 60 cents; 2 Raw hides, E. Kelly, 4.00; 1/4 Interest in fish traps, John Talin, 15.25.; 1 Tub, E. P. Varner, 30 cents; 2 Decanters, E. Varner, 2.25; 1 Coffee pot, J. B. Lanier, 75 cents; 1 set of Plates, J. Calloway, 95 cents.

1 Basket & Contents, E. E. Estes, 65 cents; 1 Pair of cards, E. Varner, 1.40; 1 Churn, B. F. Higgins, 80 cents; Cups & Saucers, T. Jones, 80 cents; 2 Preserves cups, E. Varner, 2.00; 2 Pitchers, J. J. Thornton, 1.40; 1 Lot of Articles, E. Varner, 1.00; 1 Lot of knives & forks, J. Calloway, 2.00; 1 morter? & Pitcher, J. B. Larsen, 1.75; 1 Bottle Soua?, B. F. Higgins, 65 cents; 8 fine plates, B. F. Higgins, 75 cents; 8 fine plates, T. Miller, 75 cents.

1 Lot of Articles, J. Calloway, 1.55; 1 Lot of Articles, T. Jones, 1.75; 1 Water & Glasses, E. Varner, 2.45; 1 Roler & Bottles, E. Varner, 25 cents; 2 Slays, W. A. Gulledge, 1.50; 2 Slays, E. E. Estes, 1.00; 2 Slays, Bob Varner, 1.25; 1 Table & Box, John Varner, 1.75; 1 Table & Clothes, Bob Varner, 3.30; 1 Table, D. E. Harder, 1.58; 1 Bucket & Looking Glass, D. E. Harder, 1.25.

1 Library of Books & Table, Ed Glenn, 50.00; 1 Bed & Bedding, E. Varner, 120.00; 1 Looking Glass, E. Varner, 4.00; 1 bed & bedding, E. Varner, 120.00; 1 overhead, T. Jones, 8.50; 1 Counter pan, T. Jones, 4.00; 1 Counter pan, H. Norrell, 2.00; 1 Folding Table, Jack Thompson, 5.50; 1

side board, John Varner, 9.00; 1 Beoura?, J. J. Thornton, 10.00; 1 Looking Glass, E. P. Varner, 55 cents.

1 Clock, J. J. Thornton, 10.00; 1 Shot Gun, E. Kelly, 20.00; 1 Bed & Bedding, S. E. Dacus[1], 105.00; 1 Bed & Bedding, H. Varner, 32.00; 1 Cupboard, Bob Varner, 8.10; 2 bee hives, No. 1 & 2, T. J. Hull, 6.00; 2 bee hives, No. 3 & 4, J. M. Wyatt, 4.50; 2 bee hives, No. 5 & 6, E. P. Varner, 8.50; 2 bee hives, No. 7 & 8, W. A. J. Gulledge, 8.25; 2 bee hives, No. 9 & 10, E. B. Glenn, 7.75.

2 bee hives, No. 11 & 12, E. P. Varner, 9.00; 2 bee hives, No. 13 & 14, R. Wilson, 8.50; 2 bee hives, No. 15 & 16, H. Varner, 9.50; 4 bee hives, E. P. Varner, 12.00; 4 bee hives, John Wyatt, 1.05; 2 bee gums, John Wyatt, 55 cents; 1 Cy? Waggon & Dou??????, John Ingram, 50.05; 1 Yoke of Oxen, J. T. Pritchett, 80.00; 2 Chairs, J. T. Lanier, 1.75; 2 Chairs, E. Kelly, 3.00; 2 Chairs, D. E. Harden, 3.10; 2 Chairs, John Lewis, 1.50.

1 Chair, T. Jones, 1.25; 3 Chairs, J. C. Traywick, 2.00; 2 Chairs, Tobe? Bryant, 1.00; 2 Benches, Bob Varner, 50 cents; 1 Kettle, J. H. Lewis, 5.00; 1 Pot, Bob Varner, 6.00; 1 Loom, R. J. Allen, 1.25; 1/2 Interest in Varner Mill & Gin, T. J. Hull, 400.00.

1 Set of Blacksmith Tools, B. F. Higgins, 25.00; 1 Brindle Cow, J. H. Lewis, 22.00; 1 Red Cow, E. Varner, 30.00; 1 Red Cow, B. F. Higgins, 29.00; 1 Buff Head Steer, T. J. Traywick, 19.00; 1 Steer, R. Wilson, 20.55; 1 Yoke Young Oxen, J. B. Lanier, 27.30; 1 White Cow, Albert Overton, 15.25; 1 Spotted Cow, W. T. Watson, 18.25; 1 Yellow Cow, Richard Pond, 21.25; 1 Dry Cow, John Kelly,

---

[1]..S. E. Dacus was Susan Eliza Varner Dacus, daughter of John Varner, and widow of William G. Varner of Lowndes County, AL.

9.00; 1 Bull Cow, Noah Foshee, 12.75; 1 heifer, B. F. Higgins, 13.50; 2 heifers, B. F. Higgins, 19.00.

Sold at Private Sale to Hardaway Varner the following (to wit):

1 Gray horse, three mules, 150 bushels of corn, 500 bundles fodder, Amounting to $657.50.

Sold to E. P. Varner at private sale, one sow at $20.00.

(Recorded in Coosa County, Alabama, Probate Minutes, Book 13, Pages 337-340.)

Chapter VII
Children of John and Nancy Varner

Five of John Varner and Nancy Powell's children, their wives, and their descendants are covered in this chapter. Separate chapters are devoted to the others.

Amaziah, Edward P., William F., John W., Hardaway, and Lucy A. are treated in this chapter. The others are covered in separate chapters as follows:

--Azariah Varner: Chapter VIII.
--Susan Eliza Varner: Chapter IX.
--George H. Varner: Chapter X.
--John W. Varner: Chapter XI.
--Esselman Varner: Chapter XII.

Amaziah Varner and Martha Pickering

Amaziah Varner, son of **John Varner and Nancy Powell**, was born in Oglethorpe Co, GA, in about 1812. He died 5 Nov 1856 at his home in Coosa Co, AL. He married **Martha Pickering** at Lowndes Co, AL on 7 Feb 1833. Amaziah and his brother Azariah are believed to have been twins[1] even though Amaziah gave his age as 38 in the 1850 census and his brother Azariah gave his as 37.

Amaziah Varner was Deputy Clerk of the County Court of Lowndes Co, AL, for a year or two during the 1830's, assisting his father John Varner, who was the Clerk. His name and title of deputy clerk are entered on many of the records for that period.

As a young man, Amaziah had several run-ins with the law. In 1832, at the age of 20 or 21, he was arrested and later convicted of illegal gambling, along with Robert

---

[1]..This conclusion is based on unusual, similar names, the closeness of their ages, and the fact that they married sisters.

CHILDREN OF JOHN AND NANCY VARNER

Blanks, who was married to Amaziah's cousin Elizabeth Varner[1], and two other men. They were charged that they did "with force and arms play cards in a Store House for the retailing of Spirituous liquors" in violation of a state law. Amaziah's father John Varner bailed his son out of jail pending trial. The jury found the four men guilty as charged and fined each defendant $21 plus court costs. The judge ordered them to be held in jail until the fines were paid.[2]

A year later, Amaziah was charged with and found guilty of finding and expending for his own use promissory notes that did not belong to him.[3]

Twice, in 1842 and 1849, Amaziah was indicted by grand juries for "retailing" Spirituous liquors without a license and for playing cards in a public place "against the peace and dignity of the State of Alabama." The jury found Amaziah and four others who were charged with him innocent of the indictment reached in 1849. No disposition of the other case was located.[4]

Amaziah was the defendant in two suits claiming that he had failed to make payment on promissory notes. In

---

[1]..Elizabeth Varner Blanks was a daughter of Frederick Varner and granddaughter of George Varner or Oglethorpe Co, GA.

[2]..Lowndes Co, AL, Circuit Court Records 1830-1834, pp. 333-335.

[3]..Ibid. pp. 360-361.

[4]..Circuit Court Minutes 1842-1848, p. 63 and Circuit Court Record 1847-1849, p. 314.

both cases, in 1839 and 1850, he was ordered to redeem the notes and pay court costs.[5]

Amaziah Varner joined the Masons in Lowndes Co, AL, 3 Feb 1838, and soon passed the membership exam and then attained the rank of Master Mason. For a time, he served Lowndes County Lodge # 33 as Junior Warden, the third highest ranking lodge officer.[2]

Amaziah Varner joined the U.S. Army in Mobile, AL, 26 May 1846, for service in the Mexican War. He served in Co G, 1st AL Reg.[3] He joined at the same time and served in the same outfit as his brothers, Azariah Varner and Edward P. Varner.

The only information found about Martha Pickering was her wedding to Amaziah Varner. She probably died between 1843 and 1850. She gave birth to Mary S. Varner, the only known child born to her and Amaziah, in 1843. She was not enumerated with the family in the 1850 census. In 1850, Amaziah, age 38, and Mary, age 7, were living in Coosa County with Amaziah's father and stepmother, John and Amanda Varner.

Amaziah Varner died at his home in Coosa Co--probably at the John Varner plantation--5 Nov 1856, according to an item in the Dispatch[4]. He left no will and no estate papers were located.

---

[1]..Execution Docket 1837-1839, p. 350 and Circuit Court Minutes 1848-1854, p. 141.

[2]..Records of the Grand Lodge of Masons, Montgomery, AL.

[3]..Military records on microfilm at AL Archives.

[4]..Amasiah Varner died Nov. 5, 1856, in Coosa County at his residence of consumption. From Dispatch, Nov. 28, 1856. On microfilm at Alabama Archives.

CHILDREN OF JOHN AND NANCY VARNER

Amaziah Varner and Martha Pickering were parents of one known child: **Mary S. Varner.**

A. **Mary S. Varner**, dau of Amaziah Varner and Martha Pickering, (b. 1843, Lowndes Co, AL, d. betw 1860 and 1862[1], prob Coosa Co, AL) marr 18 Sep 1856, Coosa Co, AL, **William F. Garnett**, son of **Nelson Garnett** of Lincoln Co, GA, (b. 1831, GA, d. Dec 1862[2], Coosa Co, AL).

William Garnett was a physician in Rockford, Coosa Co. He kept a diary for the year 1857, in which he told about several visits by him and Mary to the Varners. The diary is in the possession of the Coosa Co Historical Society.

Mary and William were parents of one known child: **Mary Iwanna Garnett.**

1. **Mary Iwanna Garnett**, dau of **Mary S. Varner and William F. Garnett**, (b. 1857, Coosa Co, AL.) marr 22 Nov 1876, Coosa Co, AL, **W. R. Thompson**. Mary was orphaned when she was 5 and was raised by John W. Garnett, who was probably her uncle.[3] Mary Iwanna was named in her great grandfather John Varner's will to

---

[1]..Mary was listed in the 1860 census. She was no longer living when her husband William F. Garnett's estate was probated in 1862.

[2]..William F. Garnett's estate papers are on record at the Coosa County, AL, courthouse.

[3]..Information on the Garnetts taken from several sources in Coosa County, AL, including Orphans Court Minutes, the William Garnett Diary, and issues of Coosa Heritage, published by the Coosa County Historical Society.

receive the $100 that John's son Amaziah (deceased) was entitled to.[1]

Edward P. Varner and His Descendants

Edward P. Varner was a son of John Varner and Nancy Powell. Edward was born in Oct 1819 in Oglethorpe Co, GA. He died 4 Feb 1906 in Coosa Co, AL, and is buried in the Providence Church Cemetery in Coosa Co, AL. Edward P. married 1st in Coosa Co, AL, on 13 Dec 1847, **Jane Knight** (b. 1834, AL, d. 13 Jun 1857, Coosa Co, AL)[2].

Edward P. Varner was an infant when his family moved with their slaves from Oglethorpe Co, GA, to the frontier settlement on the Alabama River some 15-miles downstream from the town of Montgomery. He grew up on his parents' plantations, his first 11 years on the farm near the river. He spent his teen years on the plantation near the village of Hayneville, the seat of government for Lowndes County. His father John Varner was clerk of the Lowndes County Court at that time. Edward was about 25 when he moved with his father and other family members to Coosa County, AL.

Edward was a farmer in Coosa Co, AL. His farm was adjacent to his father John Varner's plantation.[3] Like his

---

[1]..John Varner's will is recorded in Coosa Co, AL, Wills and Orphans Records, Old Series, Vol 2 (1843-1888), p. 229.

[2]..Diary of William F. Garnett for the year 1857, which is in the possession of the Coosa Co, AL, Historical Society.

[3]..E. P. Varner purchased 40 acres (NW 1/4 of SE 1/4 of T 21N, R 17E, S 27) from the Federal government Jan. 19, 1855.

(continued...)

CHILDREN OF JOHN AND NANCY VARNER

brothers and uncles, Edward was a slave owner, reporting that he owned five in 1850 and 10, with 3 slave houses, in 1860.[1]

The 1860 agricultural census indicates that Edward was a prosperous farmer. He had 240 acres of land valued at $1500; his livestock was also worth $1500.[2] His personal property, consisting primarily of slaves, was worth $15,000.[3]

Edward P. Varner, pvt, fought in the Mexican War alongside his brothers Amaziah and Azariah, in Co. G, 1st AL Regiment. They enlisted in Mobile, AL, 26 May 1846.[4] Edward received a tax credit of $1.00 in Coosa County in 1863 because he was a veteran of the Mexican War.[5]

Edward P. Varner was a sergeant, Co C, 24th Battalion, Alabama Calvary, in the Civil War. He enlisted in Coosa Co, AL, 3 Aug 1863 for the duration of the war. He was paroled at Montgomery, AL, in May 1865.[6]

---

[3] (...continued)
Coosa Tract Book. (Certificate # 168).

[1] ..Coosa County, AL, Slave Schedules for 1850 and 1860.

[2] ..See Appendix # VII-A at the end of this chapter.

[3] ..U. S. Census for Coosa Co, AL, for 1860.

[4] ..From microfilm of Federal military records, a copy of which is located at the LDS Family History Library, Salt Lake City, UT.

[5] ..E. Varner was granted a tax credit of $1.00 for having been a soldier in the Mexican War. Sept. 7, 1863. Minutes Commissioners Court, Vol. 8, pp 401-413, Coosa County, AL.

[6] ..From Confederate Service Records, AL Archives.

E. P. Varner applied for a confederate veteran's pension March 14, 1878, stating that he had served as a private in Co. C, 53rd Regiment. His wife Senora Varner also signed the application. A pension of $1.50 was granted.[1]

Edward P. Varner was an active member of the Grand Lodge Free & Accepted Masons of Alabama. He was initiated in Coosa County Lodge # 242 Dec. 25, 1858. He passed the membership exam Jan. 22, 1859 and was raised to Master Mason Feb. 26, 1859. (Lodge # 242 was located at Buyck, which is now in Elmore County.) Edward P. Varner was demitted Dec. 8, 1900, so that he could help organize a new lodge, Brockton # 571. J. D. Barrett's store, Sykes Mill, in Coosa County, was the meeting place of the Lodge. This Lodge received a charter on Jan. 1, 1901. Edward P. Varner's son Emmett was also a charter member of this new lodge.[2]

Even though he lived near Providence Baptist Church, Edward P. Varner did not profess his faith and join the church until the waning years of his life, according to the writings of Rev. J. D. Hughes, who was a pastor of the church for 39 years.[3] Rev. Hughes gave an emotional description of his successful efforts to convert the aging

---

[1]..Confederate Pension Records, Alabama Archives, Montgomery.

[2]..Masonic information obtained from records at the offices of the Grand Lodge Free & Accepted Masons of Alabama, located at 3033 Vaughn Road, Montgomery, Alabama.

[3]..Life and Experiences of a Pioneer Preacher, by Rev. J. D. Hughes. Undated. Clanton Press, Clanton, AL.

Edward P. Varner to his version of Evangelical Christianity.[4]

Edward named his second wife, Senora, and his children who were living at the time, in his will, which he wrote in 1888.[2]

Edward P. Varner and Jane Knight were parents of three children: **Eula, Emmett B., and Rachel Ella.**

Children of E. P. Varner and Jane Knight

A. **Eula (or Eulia) Varner** (b. 1849, Coosa Co, AL, d. after 1888[3]) marr 18 Oct 1866, Coosa Co, AL, Jacob A. Florney.

B. **Emmett B. Varner** (b. 22 Jan 1852, Coosa Co, AL, d. 17 Sep 1947[4]) marr 1891[5] **Faithie Balzorah** (b. 24 Aug 1857, d. 12 Aug 1952). Emmett and his wife Faithie are buried in the City Cemetery, Sylacauga, AL.

In contrast to his father Edward P. Varner, Emmett was a long time active worshiper at the Providence Baptist Church, which was located near the homes of both Edward and Emmett in Coosa Co, AL. This is based on

---

[1]..See Appendix # VII-B at the end of this chapter.

[2]..See Appendix VII-C at the end of this chapter for a copy of Edward P. Varner's will.

[3]..Eulia Varner Florney was living in 1888 when her father wrote his will.

[4]..Grave markers in the Marble Valley City Cemetery, in Sylacauga, Talladega Co, AL. give birth and death dates for Emmett B. Varner and Fathie Balzorah Varner.

[5]..The 1900 census reported that Emmett and Faithie Varner had been married nine years.

information provided by Rev. J. D. Hughes, who was a pastor at Providence for 39 years.[1]

Emmett B. Varner and Faithie Balzorah were parents of one child, who died young.[2]

C. Rachel Ella Varner (b. 24 Aug 1854, d. 26 May 1927)[3] marr 24 Dec 1871, Coosa Co, AL, **John M. Wyatt**.[4]

---

[1]..Life and Experiences of a Pioneer Preacher, by Rev. J. D. Hughes. Undated. Clanton Press, Clanton, AL. Page 18. "I preached at Providence one Saturday from 1st Corinthians 4:21--'What will ye? Shall I come unto you with a rod, or in love, and in the spirit of meekness?' We had a real revival. Bro. Emmett Varner got happy, and shouted all around, but it wasn't anything uncommon to see Bro. Varner get happy. He and his wife were faithful to their church.

"I told them in my sermon, perhaps sometimes I come to you with a rod, but this time I come to you in love. I always thought we should give the flowers while we live. I went on to explain what each member had meant to me the long years I had been their pastor. I mentioned a number of them who were present. Not only did Uncle Emmett get happy, but most of the congregation."

On page 44, there is a full page testimonial letter to Rev. Hughes written by Mr. and Mrs. E. B. Varner.

[2]..The 1900 census reported that Balzorah was the mother of one child, who was not living at that time.

[3]..Grave marker at Providence Cemetery, Coosa Co, AL, gives birth and death dates of Rachel Ella Varner.

[4]..Birth and death dates and husband's name appear on grave marker in Providence Cemetery, Coosa Co, AL.

Children of E. P. Varner and Senora Bonnet

Edward P. Varner, fifth child of John Varner and Nancy Powell marr 2nd, 8 Dec 1859, Coosa Co, AL, **Senora Bonnet** (b. 19 May 1840 in SC, d. 22 Apr 1913[1], Coosa Co, AL).

Edward and Senora were parents of eight known children[2]: **Nina, Annie, Bell, Lucy D., Hattie, Jeff D., Alice, and Minnie.**

A. **Nina Varner** (b. 1860, Coosa Co, AL, d. bef 1888[3]).

B. **Ann "Annie" E. Varner** (b. 1861, Coosa Co, AL, d. after 1888[4]) marr, 2 Oct 1879, Coosa Co, AL, **Wash Hilyer.**

C. **Mary Bell Varner** (b. 1863, Coosa Co, AL, d. after 1888[5]), marr 23 Dec 1882, Coosa Co, AL, **J. W. Hull.**

D. **Lucy D. Varner** (b. 24 Sep 1866, Coosa Co, AL[6], d.

---

[1]..Senora Bonnet Varner's birth and death dates appear on a grave marker in the Providence Cemetery, Lowndes Co, AL.

[2]..The 1910 census reported that Senora was the mother of 10 children and that nine were then living.

[3]..Listed in the 1860 and 1870 censuses for Coosa County. Not mentioned in her father's will, written in 1888.

[4]..Living in 1888, the year that her father wrote his will.

[5]..Living when her father wrote his will, in 1888.

[6]..Listed in the 1870 and 1880 censuses for Coosa Co, AL.

6 Jun 1886[7]), marr 30 Dec 1884, Coosa Co, AL, **G. W. Hughen**[2].

   E. Hattie (or Hettie) J. Varner (b. 1869, Coosa Co, AL, d. after 1888[3]), marr 15 Nov 1886, Coosa Co, AL, M. N. Ward.

   F. Jeff D. Varner (b. 30 Apr 1872, Coosa Co, AL[4], d. 28 Jan 1893, Coosa Co, AL[5]).

   G. Alice B. Varner (b. 1875, Coosa Co, AL, d. after 1888[6]).

   H. Minnie S. Varner (b. 1877, Coosa Co, AL[7]).

William F. Varner and Margaret F. Bonham

William F. Varner, was the sixth child of John Varner and Nancy Powell, and the first one born after their move to Alabama. William F. was born 5 Jul 1823, Montgomery Co, AL. He died 26 Oct 1860 Lowndes Co, AL, and is

---

[1]..Birth and death dates appear on grave marker in Providence Cemetery, Coosa Co, AL.

[2]..Note from E. P. Varner stated that he gave his permission for his daughter Lucy, who was under age, to marry Mr. G. Hughen.

[3]..Living in 1888, the year that her father wrote his will.

[4]..Listed in the 1880 census for Coosa Co, AL.

[5]..His grave marker in Providence Cemetery, Coosa Co, AL, reads: "J. D. Varner, son of E. P. & S. Varner, 30 Apr 1872-28 Jan 1893."

[6]..Identified as a minor in her father's will, written in 1888.

[7]..Identified as a minor in her father's will, written in 1888.

CHILDREN OF JOHN AND NANCY VARNER

buried in the Bonham Cemetery in Montgomery Co, AL[8]. He married in Montgomery Co, AL, 12 Nov 1845, **Margaret F. Bonham** (b. 20 Sep 1824, d. 13 Feb 1900[2], Montgomery Co, AL).

William F. Varner was a farmer in Lowndes Co, AL. Records suggest that he was a competent manager of his financial affairs although he generally owned less property than most of his brothers and uncles. He paid taxes on two slaves in 1853[3] and reported ownership of three slaves in 1860, at which time his personal estate value was given as $5,775. Court records attest that he paid his bills in a timely fashion.

William F. Varner served on the Lowndes County Circuit Court grand jury at the spring term in 1854.[4]

---

[1]..His grave marker reads: "Wm. F. Varner (son of John & Nancy Varner). Died Oct. 26, 1860 -- aged 37 years, 3 months, 22 days."

[2]..Margaret Varner's birth and death dates appear on her grave marker in the Bonham Cemetery, Montgomery Co, AL.

[3]..<u>Taxes on Personal Property</u>, 1853, Lowndes Co, AL. William F. Varner paid personal taxes as follows:
    1 white male age 21-45 -- 50 cents.
    1 clock -- 25 cents.
    2 slaves aged 15 to 30 at $1.10 each -- $2.20.
    Fund for slaves executed--2 slaves age 10 to 50 at
        2 cents each -- 4 cents.
    Tax on money -- 50 cents.
    TOTAL TAXES -- $2.99.

[4]..William F. Varner, planter from Hayneville, was summoned to serve on the Circuit Court Grand Jury for the spring term of 1854. He responded and served. (<u>Circuit Court</u> (continued...)

After his brother Azariah Varner died, William F. Varner agreed to become trustee of property that John Varner donated to Azariah's children. This was on the condition that the property--consisting of slaves--could be sold and the proceeds distributed to the children. The Lowndes County Chancery Court approved a plan to sell the slaves. But before it could be carried out, William F. Varner also died. Apparently, the slaves were never sold.[1]

The middle decades of the 1800's were wrought with deaths of an unusually large number of young people in Lowndes County, Alabama. The William F. and Margaret Varner family suffered more than its share of such tragedies. A detailed account showing causes of death cannot be recreated, but records that are available tell a heart-rending story.

William F. Varner died 26 Oct 1860 at the age of 47. He left no will. On 16 Nov 1860, Margaret F. Varner, his widow, asked the Probate Court to appoint her administratrix of the estate, which was adjudged to be

---

[4](...continued)
Minutes 1848-1854, p 266.)

[1]..This was Chancery Court Case # 414, William F. Varner v Rufus W. Dacus. See Chapter VIII for more information about it.

CHILDREN OF JOHN AND NANCY VARNER

worth about $4,000.[2] The record of the estate sale gives an insight concerning William F. Varner's property.[1]

William F. Varner's funeral expenses came to $90.[3]

William F. Varner and Margaret F. Bonham were parents of several children, most of whom appear to have died young. The order of birth can only partially be determined from records that were located. Cemetery, census, and court records indicate that the following were children of William F. Varner and Margaret F. Bonham.

A. **Pormelia Varner** (b. and d. Oct 1846[4]).

---

[1]..Notes on William F. Varner's Estate.

Margaret F. Varner appeared before the Probate Court in Lowndes County on 16 Nov 1860. She said that William F. Varner had been dead more than 15 days and that he left no will. She was appointed administratrix. (Minutes of Probate Court, Lowndes County, page 736). Nov. 17, 1860, Margaret F. Varner posted bond of $8,000, double the value of the estate. (Page 737). Nov. 17, 1860, Margaret F. Varner was ordered by the court to inventory the estate. (Page 738). Nov. 30, 1860, Margaret F. Varner was granted permission to hire the slaves of William F. Varner's estate for 1861. She was also given permission to sell the perishable property (stock, plantation tools, and farm produce) belonging to the estate. (Page 760).

[2]..See Appendix # VII-D at the end of this chapter for notes on William F. Varner's estate sale.

[3]..Funeral Expenses for William F. Varner.
   Statement from Williams & Waldron
   1860 Oct. 26 -- 1 Burial Case and box for same -- $80.00
   --Use of hearse 1 day --   10.00
                         TOTAL $90.00
From William F. Varner Estate Papers, Alabama Archives.

[4]..Grave marker in Bonham Cemetery notes: "Pormelia
(continued...)

Varner Families of the South--VII

    B. **James Madison Varner** (b. 1848, Montgomery Co, AL, d. 28 Sep 1853, Montgomery Co, AL[1]).
    C. **Henley Varner**[2].
    D. **(Unnamed son) Varner**[3]
    E. **William W. Varner**[4] (b. 1852, Lowndes Co, AL).
    F. **Benjamin J. Varner**[5] (b. 1854, Lowndes Co, AL).
    G. **George H. Varner**[6] (b. 1856, Lowndes Co, AL, d. after 1900).
    H. **Mulbrina Tatnell Varner** (b. 1858, d. 26 Oct 1860[7]).

---

[4](...continued)
Varner, infant daughter of W. F. & M. Varner, Died Oct 1846."

[1]..James M. Varner was listed in the 1850 census. His death date appears on his grave marker in the Bonham Cemetery, Montgomery Co, AL.

[2]..Grave marker adjacent to Margaret Varner's gives the name but no dates for birth or death. Henley Varner is not listed in any censuses.

[3]..Grave marker indicates son of William and Margaret Varner, but no name or dates given.

[4]..Enumerated in the 1860 census for Lowndes Co, AL.

[5]..Enumerated in the 1860 census for Lowndes Co, AL, and the 1870 census for Montgomery Co, AL.

[6]..Enumerated in the 1860 census for Lowndes Co, AL, and the 1870 and 1900 censuses for Montgomery Co, AL. He was "living alone" in 1900.

[7]..Her grave marker in the Bonham Cemetery gives her age at death as 1 year and six months.

CHILDREN OF JOHN AND NANCY VARNER

I. **Molvin F. Varner** (d. in Mar 1860, age 1 yr.[8]).
J. **Wallis Varner**[2]
K. **Bethel Varner**[3]

Hardaway Varner and Caroline Glenn

Hardaway Varner was the eighth child of **John Varner and Nancy Powell**. He was born 1 Jan 1829 in Montgomery Co, AL. He died 22 Apr 1903, in Coosa Co, AL[4]. Hardaway married 5 Dec 1888, Coosa Co, AL, **Caroline Glenn** (b. 1850).

Hardaway spent his childhood years in Lowndes County, AL, while his father John Varner was Clerk of the County Court there. In his early adulthood, Hardaway lived with his sister Susan Eliza Varner and her husband William G. Varner in Lowndes County for a few years. He

---

[1]..This information taken from the U.S. Mortality Census for 1860. It reported that Molvin F. Varner, William F. Varner's child, was a 1-year old female and that she died from scrofula after being ill for 180 days. It is unclear whether Molvin was the same person as Mulbrina. They could have been twins.

[2]..Wallis Varner and Bethel Varner were identified as minor heirs of William Varner, deceased, entitled to receive money from their grandfather John Varner's estate in an entry dated 5 Feb. 1875 in Coosa County Accounts, Vol. O, pp 20-21. In his will, John Varner had left $100 to the orphans of his son William F. Varner, deceased.

[3]..Ibid.

[4]..Hardaway Varner's birth and death dates appear on a grave marker at Providence Cemetery, Coosa Co, AL.

was enumerated with them in the 1850 census. His stay there was also mentioned by one of the witnesses in Lowndes County Chancery Court Case # 414, Susan E. Varner v John M. Cole. Witness Allen Davis stated that Hardaway and his brother John W. Varner "cropped" with William G. Varner and managed his slaves for a few years.[1]

In 1870, Hardaway was living in Coosa Co, AL, with his stepmother Amanda Varner and managing his deceased father's (John Varner) former farm. This was shortly after John Varner's death on 31 Dec 1869. Enumerated in the same household as Hardaway Varner and Amanda Varner were Agnez Varner, age 45, and Joseph Varner, age 7. Agnez and Joseph were mulattos. Hardaway was single and a farmer in Coosa Co, AL, in 1880. Enumerated with him was a child (Hard Dayton, 9) whose relationship, if any, to Hardaway is unknown.

Hardaway lived in Louisiana near or with his brother George H. Varner for a few years in the 1860's. He purchased 40 acres of land there 17 Oct 1861 and sold it to his brother George H. Varner 15 Jun 1871.[2]

Hardaway and Caroline Varner[3] were parents of no children. Hardaway is not known to have had any other marriages. He had no children at the time of his death, according to probate proceedings in Coosa Co, AL.

---

[1]..See Chapter XIX, "Susan Eliza and William G. Varner," for more information about this testimony and Chancery Court Case # 414.

[2]..Franklin Parish, LA, Deed Book C, pages 402 and 403.

[3]..The 1900 census reported that Caroline was a mother of no children.

Lucy A. Varner and John A. Wilson

Lucy A. Varner[1] was the tenth child of **John Varner** and **Nancy Powell.** She was born in 1842 in Lowndes Co, AL. She married in Coosa Co, AL on 3 Feb 1861, **John A. Wilson.**

Appendix VII-A
Edward P. Varner's Farm Production
1860 AGRICULTURAL CENSUS, COOSA COUNTY
    E. P. Varner

    120 acres improved land, 120 acres unimproved land
Cash value of farm: $1500

    Value of farm equipment and tools: $75

    Livestock owned at time of census: 7 horses, 8 milch cows, 4 working oxen, 16 other cattle, 16 swine. Value of livestock owned: $1500

    Crop production during past twelve months: 700 bushels of Indian corn, 30 bushels of oats, 5 bushels of peas and beans, 14 bales of ginned cotton, 10 bushels of Irish potatoes, 100 bushels of sweet potatoes, 10 pounds of beeswax, 200 pounds of honey.

    Value of manufactured goods made in the home: $50
Value of livestock slaughtered: $125

---

[1]..This author made no effort to locate information about Lucy Varner Wilson beyond these few facts.

Appendix # VII-B
Notes From a Pioneer Preacher

Notes taken from <u>Life and Experiences of a Pioneer Preacher</u>, by Rev. J. D. Hughes. Undated. Clanton Press. Hughes served as pastor of Providence Baptist Church for 39 years--from about 1890 to about 1930.

Page 14. "I was informed by one of the members of Providence church of the illness of Mr. Ed Varner[1], so I went that afternoon with one of the brethren to see him and found him in bed. He was lamenting over his neglect of duty in not joining the church. He said that he would not have the opportunity any more for he was going to die. He had an experience of grace for 30 years. I told him that I believed that if he would promise God that he would discharge his duty, and unite with the church, the Lord would raise him up.

"He said that he had promised the Lord so many times and had failed Him that he didn't feel like He would give him another chance. I told him if he would pray, and I would pray for him, that I believed the Lord would restore him and he would have another opportunity. He promised me he would.

"One month later as I filled my appointment I inquired as to how Mr. Varner was, and they said he was able to be up. I went back to see him and I asked him if he were still resolved to carry out his promises. He said that he was. So another month passed, and shortly after I reached the church I looked and saw him coming down the hill. Then I knew that the Lord had answered our prayers and gave him another chance. He came right straight to me and asked me not to wait until after the

---

[1]..Ed Varner was Edward P. Varner, son of John Varner and Nancy Powell.

conference to open the doors of the church, but to do so at the close of the sermon. His reason was, he was weak and might have to lie down. So I opened the doors of the church at the close of my sermon and he came forward and joined the church, then told his experience that he had been telling for thirty years. A month later his good wife, who was a member of the Methodist church, joined also."

Appendix VII-C
Edward P. Varner's Will

From Will Book, Vol. 3, pp 149-150, Coosa County, AL.
EDWARD P. VARNER WILL
The State of Alabama, Coosa County

Know all men by these presents that I E. P. Varner do by this my last will and testament do will and bequeath to my beloved wife Senora Varner all of my real and personal property as long as she may live and to use the same any way that necessity may direct for the welfare or sustaining of her and family except the three youngest of my beloved children, (whose) names are as follows: J. D. Varner, which when he becomes of age is to have a horse worth $75.00 or that amount in money; and Alice B. Varner and Minnie S. Varner when of age or married each to have a bed and bedding or $50 extra of the part of my other beloved children, and I furthermore will after the death of my wife Senora Varner that the property both real and personal that remain the same to be equally divided among my beloved children; names are as follows: Eulia Flourney, E. B. Varner, Rachael E. Wyatt and Ann E. Hilyer, Mary B. Hull, Hattie Ward and J. D. Varner, Alice B. Varner and Minnie S. Varner and I hereby appoint J. W. Hull and E. B. Varner as executors of my

will to see that the same be carried out according to the discretion of the same and pay all just claims that come against the same in witness whereof I hereunto set my hand and affix my seal this the 8 day of May 1888.
Attest: J. B. Barnett, W. C. Harris.   E. P. Varner.

The State of Alabama, Coosa County

Know all men by these presents that I, E. P. Varner that after making the above will and I more due consideration do in the connection of the above will do will and bequeath that Joseph B. Barnett my step son at my death and the death of my wife have an equal share of all the property that remain with the rest of my children in witness my hand and seal this the 30 day of January 1893.   E. P. Varner

----

Attest: W. C. Harris, J. V. Harris

The State of Alabama, Coosa County

I, J. A. Crawford, Judge of the Court of Probate, in and for said county, do hereby certify, that the within and forgoing instruments of writing has this day, in said Court and before me, as the judge thereof, been duly proved to be the genuine will and testament and codicil of E. P. Varner deceased, and that said will and codicil together with the proof hereof have been recorded in my office in Book of Wills, Vol. 3, page 149 and in witness whereof I have hereunder set my hand and seal of said Court this the 2nd day of April 1906.   J. A. Crawford, Judge.

Appendix VII-D
William F. Varner Estate Sale

Bill of Sale of the Estate of William F. Varner, Deceased.

Margaret F. Varner -- one cow and calf --	$6.00
B. J. Bonham -- one cow and calf --	6.00
W. D. Higgins -- one yearling calf--	3.00
Margaret F. Varner -- one bay horse --	100.00
Margaret F. Varner -- 500 lbs. of fodder --	5.00
Margaret F. Varner -- one grind stone --	.50
Margaret F. Varner -- one buggy and harness --	25.00
W. D. Higgins -- one scythe blade --	1.00
Margaret F. Varner -- three single trees --	1.00
B. J. Bonham -- one lot of plows --	.50
Margaret F. Varner -- six bee hives --	6.00
B. J. Bonham -- two grubbing hoes --	.25
B. F. Dean -- two iron wedges --	.60
TOTAL	$156.60

Feb. 21, 1861   (Signed)   M. F. Varner
R. H. Cook, Probate Judge

(Inventory Book--Probate Court 1859-1866, page 34, Lowndes County, Alabama).

Chapter VIII
Azariah Varner, Son of John Varner

Azariah Varner was a son of **John Varner and Nancy Powell**. He was born in about 1812 in Oglethorpe Co, GA. He died in May 1855 on his family farm in Lowndes Co, AL. He married **Mary L. Pickering** (d. 1858[1]) at Lowndes Co, AL on 13 Dec 1832. Mary was probably a sister of Martha Pickering who married Azariah's brother Amaziah. Although there is no known proof, Azariah and Amaziah probably were twins.

Azariah was a planter in Lowndes Co, AL. He took over and managed the plantation that his father John Varner operated before he moved to Coosa Co, AL, in about 1843. Azariah farmed it until his death in 1857. In 1858, John Varner and his second wife Amanda Varner sold the land, including the house where Azariah lived and died.[2] They had previously sold part of the plantation land to their son William F. Varner.[3]

---

[1]..Mary L. Pickering Varner's death was announced to the Lowndes Co, AL, Chancery Court as part of the proceedings in Case # 432, <u>John P. Streety vs Mary Varner, et al</u>, recorded in <u>Chancery Court Minutes</u>, Book 11, pages 196-215. The announcement was made after 30 Nov 1857 but the exact date of death is not given.

[2].See Appendix # VIII-A at the end of this chapter for the deed record on the sale of the land where Azariah Varner died.

[3]..Lowndes County, AL, <u>Deed Book C</u>, page 695.
Jan. 16, 1856, John and Amanda Varner his wife of Coosa County, AL, sold two parcels of land in Lowndes County to William F. Varner for $300. (Part of the West 1/2 of the SW 1/4 of S 9 containing 54 and 1/3 acres and part of the East 1/2 of the SE 1/4 of S 8 it being the North part of T 14, R 15.)

Like his brothers, father, uncles, and other male relatives, Azariah was a slave owner. He reported having 14 slaves in 1840 and 5 in 1850, in the U.S. censuses for those years. In 1853, he paid state taxes on 13 slaves.[1] Azariah Varner's younger brother John W. Varner was enumerated with the Azariah Varner family for the 1850 census. He was probably overseeing the slaves and assisting Azariah with other management duties.

Azariah Has Health, Financial Problems

Azariah was in failing health the last several years of his life. He had trouble meeting his financial obligations. He was the target of many lawsuits in Lowndes County Circuit Court for failing to pay his bills. The first of these occurred in 1836, four years after his marriage, and continued periodically until his death in 1857.[2]

Azariah's father, John Varner, set up a trust[3] to help maintain and educate Azariah's children. He assigned the

---

[1].See Appendix # VIII-B at the end of this chapter for the record of taxes paid by Azariah Varner in 1853.

[2]..See Appendix VIII-C at the end of this chapter for court records relating to suits against Azariah Varner for non payment of debts.

[3]..See Appendix # VIII-D at the end of this chapter for a copy of the trust that John Varner set up to support Azariah Varner's children.

following slaves[4] to the trust: **Priss**, a woman, **Lindy**, a girl, **Edefy**, a girl, and **Simon**, a boy. The purpose of the trust, of course, was to prevent creditors from seizing the slaves to pay Azariah's debts.

In addition to the above mentioned Circuit Court law suits, Azariah Varner and his debts were targets of two suits[2] in Chancery Court, a higher level legal jurisdiction. In both cases, the plaintiffs attempted to collect on Azariah's debts by having the Court seize and sell the slaves that John Varner had deeded to a trust to support Azariah's children. Both attempts failed.

Teacher Seeks Payment of Tuition

One of the Chancery Court cases was brought against Azariah by Jonathan P. Judge, a teacher and the principal of the Hayneville Female Academy. Judge said that he had taught two of Azariah's daughters--Eliza and Harriet--part of the 1849 school year and four of his daughters--Eliza, Harriet, Martha, and Sarah--for five months in 1850. He

---

[1]..The following additional description of these slaves was given to the Lowndes County, AL, Chancery Court in proceedings of Case # 387, Jonathan J. Judge v Azariah Varner. It notes: "One...is a woman who breeds, to Wit, Priss, that the others are young, comparatively, unable to do much work, that another, a young woman about 17 years of age, also breeds at this time..."

[2]..The attempts to seize the slaves were made in Chancery Court, Case # 387 and Case # 432. They are summarized in Chancery Court Minutes, Bk. 10, pp. 342 and 746 and Bk. 11, pp. 196-215. The original Chancery Court records were discovered by the author in a Lowndes County warehouse in Hayneville. The complete records contain detailed information and give more insight into the cases than do the summaries.

claimed that Azariah had paid only $34 of the $94.42 that he owed for tuition and books for the children's schooling.

Judge noted that he had obtained a judgment against Azariah Varner in a Circuit Court suit in 1854 but that he had been unable to collect the money allowed by that court. He said the sheriff reported "no property found" and that Azariah Varner "is and has been ever since said services were rendered utterly insolvent and unable to pay the same." Judge asked the Court to pay this debt from proceeds earned by the slaves that John Varner donated to the trust that he set up to support Azariah's children.

Azariah's reply to the charges was prepared by his attorneys. In it, Azariah Varner claimed that the proceeds from the trust were hardly sufficient to pay for the provisions and clothing necessary for the children's support. He said he had no land but a poor non productive tract to work the slaves on and that it would not yield a support for them. He said he was insolvent and unable to buy land and that he "is diseased and sickly and cannot work himself"[1]. The Court records note that Azariah Varner was too sick to sign his name to this affidavit and that Judge's attorneys agreed to let the Court receive it without Azariah's signature. This acceptance was dated 13 March 1855.

The Court was informed of Azariah's death at its June term in 1855. The Court dismissed this cause on a motion by Judge's attorneys at its May term in 1856. Judge, the complainant, was ordered to pay court costs.

---

[1]..Lowndes County, AL, Chancery Court Case # 387, op. cit.

Merchant Seeks Payment for Goods

The other Chancery Court case, filed 8 May 1857, involved a larger sum of money. In it, too, the complainant was unsuccessful in attempting to obtain payment of Azariah Varner's debt from the trust that John Varner had set up. John P. Streety, a long time Hayneville merchant, brought suit against Mary Varner, Azariah Varner's widow. He said he sold various articles of goods, wares, and merchandise during the years 1851, 1852, 1853, and 1854 for the maintenance of Azariah Varner's children. The goods were sold on credit, and most of them had not been paid for, Streety claimed. He said the amount due, including interest to 1 Jan 1857, was $743.45. The complainant noted that Azariah Varner had died in May 1855. He also said that Azariah Varner was "utterly insolvent and without means or credit to provide an adequate means of support and maintenance for his family..."

Mary Varner admitted to the court that Azariah Varner had been insolvent and was possessed with but small visible means or property to support his family but that he had some. She also admitted that Azariah Varner was careless and inattentive to business and improvident. She claimed that John P. Streety, the merchant and complainant, knew this about Azariah. Therefore, he should not have sold some of the expensive and unnecessary goods to the children on credit.

While this matter was pending before the Court, the announcement was made (30 Nov 1857) that Harriet Varner, one of Azariah and Mary Varner's daughters, married Rufus W. Dacus. A short time later (date not entered on the record), the Court was informed that Harriet Dacus had died. (Rufus W. Dacus married Harriet's aunt, Susan Eliza Varner, soon thereafter.)

Mary Varner's Death Announced

At a subsequent session, date again not entered on the record, the court was told of the death of both Mary Varner, Azariah's widow, and Martha Varner, one of Azariah and Mary's daughters.

The record then notes that the issue was settled out of court and that the complainant Streety was ordered to pay Court costs. It was further ordered that the final record stand as if dismissed for want of prosecution.[1] The terms of the out-of-court settlement[2] were revealed in a later Chancery Court case[3] involving the trust that John Varner set up for the children of Azariah Varner. In that case, William F. Varner, who had been appointed trustee of the trust, asked the Court for permission to sell the slaves. The slaves made up all of the property that was in the trust. William F. Varner was one of Azariah Varner's younger brothers.

The William F. Varner v Rufus W. Dacus et al case provides much information about Azariah's children and

---

[1]..Lowndes County, AL, Chancery Court Case # 432, John P. Streety v Mary Varner et al.

[2]..To reach an out-of-court settlement, William F. Varner gave John B. Streety a promissory note for $250 with one-half payable 1 Jan 1860 and one-half payable 1 Jan 1861.

[3]..Lowndes County, AL, Chancery Court Case # 486, William F. Varner v Rufus W. Dacus et al. A summary of this case is recorded in Chancery Court Minutes, Book 11, pages 194, 202, 214, 219, and 225. The complete Court record was found in a Lowndes County warehouse located behind the jail in Hayneville. That complete record gives details about family members and the slaves that made up the property in the trust.

the slaves that John Varner had placed in the trust to support the children. Court records in the case confirmed the fact that Mrs. Mary Varner, the widow of Azariah Varner, died in 1858, that Azariah's daughter Martha Varner died in the summer of 1858, and that Azariah's daughter Harriet Varner married Rufus W. Dacus sometime in 1857 and died sometime in 1858.

Court Learns Where Children Live

The Court record also told where Azariah's surviving children were living in 1859 and gave other information about them when the suit was filed with the Court. The record shows:

- A. **Sarah Varner,** aged about 20 years, was residing with her cousin Mary I. Garnett[1] and her husband William F. Garnett in Coosa County, Alabama.
- B. **Eliza Varner Cook,** age not mentioned, was living with her husband Isaac C. Cook in Lowndes County, Alabama.
- C. **James Varner,** a minor over 14 years of age, was residing with his sister Eliza Cook and her husband in Lowndes County, AL.
- D. **Charles Varner,** a minor under 14 years of age, was residing with Alfred Pickering[2] at Perryville, Perry County, Alabama.

---

[1]..Mary I. Garnett was Amaziah Varner's daughter and Sarah's first cousin.

[2]..Alfred Pickering most likely was related to Mary Pickering Varner, Charles' mother. He was probably Charles' grandfather or uncle.

- E. **John Varner,** a minor under 14 years of age, was residing with his grandfather John Varner in Coosa County, AL.
- F. **Azariah Varner,** a minor under 14 years of age, was residing with his sister Eliza Cook and her husband in Lowndes County, AL.

Court Records Identify Slaves

The William F. Varner v R. W. Dacus et al Chancery Court case also provides an unusual abundance of information about the slaves who made up the property in the trust that John Varner set up to support Azariah's children. It also identified the children of the slaves who were born after the trust was established.[1]

Following are their names and a summary of declarations made regarding each of them:
- A. **Lindy,** one of the slaves named in the trust deed, died sometime in the summer of 1856.
- B. **Priss,** a woman about 40 years of age, was "diseased and disabled with chronic rheumatism...(and) is decreasing in value and is not worth for hire more than her victuals and clothes." One witness said she was a cripple and would probably bring $100 on the market.
- C. **Edify,** "a girl about 30 years, is likely worth about $1500 and will hire for $125 per annum." One witness said she was about 25 and "sound and healthy."

---

[1]..Records refer to children of female slaves as "their increase." Of the slaves covered by the trust, Charlotte and Jackson made up "their increase" because they were born after the trust was set up in 1848.

D. **Charlotte,** a girl aged about eight years, is worth about $15 or $20 a year for hire and $700 or $800 on the market.
E. **Simon,** a boy aged about twelve years, is likely worth about $15 or $20 a year for hire and $700 or $800 on the market. One witness said that Simon "was not a likely boy."
F. **Jackson,** a boy aged about three years, is worth $350. One witness described Jackson as "a very likely boy about four years old worth $600."

As mentioned above, William F. Varner sought permission of the Court to sell the slaves belonging to the trust. The suit was filed in the fall of 1859. At its May term in 1860, the Court gave its permission for the sale and directed that it take place on the first Monday in January, 1861. However, William F. Varner died before the date set for the sale. Whereupon, the Court canceled its approval for the sale. At about that time, the Civil War commenced. No record could be located that would clarify what happened with the trust or the slaves that constituted its property. After the Civil War ended and slaves were freed, the Court declared this case abated.[1]

Court testimony in many of these cases makes it clear that Azariah was an incompetent manager and that he was persistently insolvent, although an explanation as to why is not clear. Was he an alcoholic? Could he have had a prolonged physical illness? Did he lack the mental faculties needed to successfully manage a plantation? Whatever the reason or reasons, Azariah Varner seems to

---

[1].. All of this information is included in the records of Lowndes County, AL, Chancery Court Case # 486, op. cit.

have been a failure in life, economically speaking, despite receiving substantial assistance from his father, John Varner.

Descendants of Azariah and Mary Varner

Azariah Varner and Mary L. Pickering were parents of eight children: **Martha C. Varner, Sarah Varner, Eliza Varner, Harriet Varner, James Varner, Charles Varner, John Varner, and Azariah Varner.**

A. Martha C. Varner, dau of Azariah Varner and Mary L. Pickering, (b. 1835, Lowndes Co, AL, died in the summer of 1858, Lowndes Co, AL[1]). In 1849 and 1850, Martha attended school at Hayneville Female Academy[2], taught by Jonathan P. Judge.[3]

B. Sarah Varner, dau of Azariah Varner and Mary L. Pickering, (b. 1836, Lowndes Co, AL). Sarah attended

---

[1]..Martha Varner's death was announced to Chancery Court during proceedings of Case # 486, op. cit.

[2]..Lowndes Court House, by Mildred Brewer. 1951. The Paragon Press, Montgomery, AL. pp. 28-29.

[3]..This was reported to Lowndes County Chancery Court during proceedings in Case # 387, Jonathan P. Judge v Azariah Varner, which is recorded in Chancery Court Records, Bk 10, pages 342 and 746. Plaintiff Judge was unsuccessful in his efforts to seize slaves from the defendant as compensation for tuition which Azariah Varner had not paid for sending his four daughters to Judge's school. The slaves had been donated by John Varner, Azariah's father, to a trust which he set up, to provide maintenance and education for Azariah's children.

school at Hayneville Academy[4] during 1849 and 1850.[5] Sarah Varner was residing with her cousin Mary S. Varner Garnett and her husband William F. Garnett in Coosa County, AL, in 1859.[3]

Sarah Varner was named by her grandfather John Varner to receive $50, which was half of Azariah Varner's share of John Varner's estate. The other half went to Sarah's brother, John Varner, Jr. Sarah and John were the two orphans of Azariah and Mary Varner who went to live with relatives in Coosa County after Azariah and Mary died.

C. Eliza Varner, dau of Azariah Varner and Mary L. Pickering, (b. 1838, Lowndes Co, AL) marr **Issac C. Cook** 30 Dec 1858, Lowndes Co, AL. Eliza attended Hayneville Female Academy[4] in 1849 and 1850.[5]

D. Harriet Varner, dau of Azariah Varner and Mary L. Pickering, (b. 1840, Lowndes Co, AL, d. 1858[6]) marr 14

---

[1]..Lowndes Court House, op. cit.

[2]..Reported in Chancery Court Case # 387, op. cit.

[3]..This residence was reported in proceedings of the Lowndes County Chancery Court, Case # 486, op. cit.

[4]..Lowndes Court House, op. cit.

[5]..Reported in Chancery Court Case # 387, op. cit.

[6]..Harriet Dacus' death was announced to the Lowndes County Chancery Court during the trial of Case # 432, op. cit. The announcement was made after 30 Nov 1857 but the exact date of death is not given.

May 1857, Lowndes Co, AL,[7] **Rufus W. Dacus** (b. 1818, SC, d. 30 Jun 1873, Lowndes Co, AL). Harriet attended Hayneville Female Academy[2] in 1849 and 1850.[3]

Rufus was 22 years older than his bride; he was 39 and she was 17. Harriet died less than a year after her marriage. The cause of death was not discovered in extant records. Rufus Wiley Dacus then married Harriet's aunt, Susan Eliza Varner, widow of William Graves Varner. Susan was the same age as Rufus.

E. James Varner, son of Azariah Varner and Mary L. Pickering, (b. 1838, Lowndes Co, AL, d. 18 Jul 1864, on a Civil War battlefield in Virginia). James was residing with his sister Eliza Varner Cook and her husband Issac C. Cook in 1859, after his parents died.[4]

James enlisted in the Confederate Army, 16 May 1861, in Montgomery, AL. Apparently, he fought along side his brother Charles as they were in the same company. Both were privates in Co M (formerly Co E), 6th Alabama Infantry. James also served in Co K of the 5th Alabama Infantry. He was killed in battle 18 Jul 1864

---

[1]..This wedding is recorded in the official Lowndes County marriage records. It was also announced to the Chancery Court as part of the proceedings of Case # 432, op. cit.

[2]..<u>Lowndes Courthouse</u>, op. cit.

[3]..Reported in Chancery Court Case # 387, op. cit.

[4]..Reported to Lowndes County Chancery Court during its proceedings in Case # 486, op. cit.

in the Valley of Virginia.[5] His name appears on a monument, located on the courthouse square in Hayneville, to Lowndes County soldiers who lost their lives fighting for the Confederacy.

F. Charles Allen Varner, son of Azariah Varner and Mary L. Pickering, was born in 1844 in Lowndes Co, AL, and died between 1875 and 1880[2]. He marr 1 May 1870, Lowndes Co, AL, **Amelia Jane Thomas,** (b. 1856, died 1921[3]). Charles was living with Alfred Pickering (probably his mother's brother or father) in Perryville, Perry Co, AL, in 1859, after his parents died.[4]

Like his older brother James, Charles was a private in Co M (formerly Co E) of the 6th Alabama Infantry, Confederate States Army. He enlisted in Montgomery, AL, 8 Apr 1862.[5]

Charles and Amelia were parents of two known children: **Sam M. and Charles Allen Varner II.**

---

[1]..Civil War service records located at the Alabama State Archives in Montgomery.

[2]..Charles A. Varner was not listed in the 1880 census for Lowndes Co, AL. Amelia J. Varner and her sons Sam M. and Charles A. (age 5) were residing with Mary Thomas, Amelia's mother, at that time.

[3]..Amelia Jane Thomas Varner's grave marker, in the Steep Creek Baptist Cemetery, Lowndes Co, AL, gives her birth and death years as 1854 and 1921 respectively.

[4]..Reported to Lowndes County, AL, Chancery Court during its proceedings in Case # 486, op. cit.

[5]..Confederate Service Records, op. cit.

AZARIAH VARNER, SON OF JOHN VARNER

1. **Sam M. Varner**, son of Charles Varner and Amelia Thomas (b. 1872, d. 1899, Lowndes Co, AL[1]). Sam M. Varner was listed as 8 years old at the time of the 1880 census. Sam Varner was named by Mildred Brewer as one of her classmates in the late 1880's.[2] S. M. Varner was appointed Justice of the Peace and Notary Public in Lowndes Co, AL, in 1895 and 1896.[3]
2. **Charles Allen Varner II**, son of Charles Allen Varner and Amelia Thomas, (b. 19 Mar 1875, Lowndes Co, AL, d. 22 Nov 1922[4]), marr **Mary**

---

[1]..The S. M. Varner estate was settled 28 Sep 1899. It was valued at $5,233.70. Lowndes Co, AL, Appraisement Record, p. 178.

[2]..Lowndes Court House 1830-1900, A Chronicle of Hayneville, an Alabama Black Belt Village, by Mildred Brewer, 1951. The Paragon Press, Montgomery, AL.

[3]..From a file on local public officials at the Alabama Archives.

[4]..Charles Varner, 25, was listed as a widower and farmer in Lowndes Co, AL, in 1900. Enumerated with him were his mother Amelia Varner, 48, mother of 3, 1 living; his aunt Jennie Thomas, 35; his sister-in-law Eula Varner, 24; his niece Isabelle Varner, 5; and nephew Sammie Varner, 3. Charles' birth and death dates appear on his grave marker at the Steep Creek Baptist Cemetery, Lowndes Co, AL.

Belle _____ (b. 5 Aug 1876, d. 19 Jul 1898,[5] in Lowndes Co, AL).

Charles and Mary Belle were parents of one known child: **Charles A. Varner, Jr.**, who was born 8 Jul 1898 and died 13 Jul 1898.[2] The fact that Mary Belle wrote her will shortly before the birth of her child and that she died a very short time after the birth suggests that the cause of her death was related to childbirth.

2. **Charles Allen Varner II**, marr 2nd 14 Jul 1905, Lowndes Co, AL, **Daisy May Judge**.

G. John Varner, son of Azariah Varner and Mary L. Pickering, (b. 1848, Lowndes Co, AL, d. between 1876 and 1880, Coosa Co, AL) marr 30 Aug 1868, Coosa Co, AL, **Matilda W. Wyatt** (b. 1852 in GA).

After John's parents died--in 1857 and 1858--John Varner went to live with his grandfather (John Varner) in Coosa County, AL. He was enumerated as a member of the John and Amanda Varner household in Coosa County at the time of the 1860 census. A legal notice from the Lowndes County, AL, Chancery Court, to John Varner, son of the late Azariah Varner and of the late Mary

---

[1]..Mary Belle's grave marker in Steep Creek Baptist Cemetery, Lowndes Co, AL, gives her dates of birth and death. Her will is recorded in Lowndes Co <u>Will Book C</u>, page 492. She left all earthly possessions to her husband Charley Allen Varner. The will is dated 28 Jun 1898.

[2]..Charles A. Varner, Jr.'s birth and death dates are recorded on his grave marker in the Steep Creek Baptist Cemetery, Lowndes Co, AL.

AZARIAH VARNER, SON OF JOHN VARNER

Varner, was delivered to John Varner, Sr., in Coosa County 7 Apr 1860.[3]

At the age of 16, John enlisted in the Confederate Army, 25 Apr 1864, just a year before fighting ended. He gave his occupation as a farmer at Rockford, AL. He served in Co H, 13th Regiment, Alabama Infantry. He fought in several battles in Virginia, including Wilderness, May 6, 1864, Davis Farm, 18 Aug 1864, and Petersburg, 31 Dec 1864. He spent some time in the hospital, probably due to injuries, from 31 Aug to 1 Oct 1864. He was with General Robert E. Lee's troops when they surrendered at Appomattox Courthouse, Virginia, to General Ulysses S. Grant, 9 Apr 1865.[2]

John was named by his grandfather, John Varner, in his will to receive $50, which was half of Azariah Varner's share of the estate. The other half went to John's sister Sarah Varner. John and Sarah were the two orphans of Azariah and Mary Varner who went to live with relatives in Coosa County after Azariah and Mary died.

John Varner, his wife Matilda Wyatt and their son Charles Varner were residents of Coosa County at the time of the 1870 census. The last known extant record of John Varner was a Circuit Court case involving him in

---

[1]..Lowndes County Chancery Court Case # 486, William F. Varner vs R. W. Dacus, et al, is recorded in Chancery Court Minutes, Vol. 12, pages 194, 202, 214, 219, and 225. The complete record of the proceedings in the case was discovered in a little used warehouse maintained by Lowndes County officials.

[2]..Confederate Service Records, located at the Alabama State Archives, Montgomery, AL.

Coosa County, AL, in 1872.[3] Matilda Varner was a widow living in Coosa Co, AL, with her five children at the time of the 1880 census. John Varner and Matilda's youngest child was born in 1877.

John Varner and Matilda Wyatt were parents of five known children: **Charles T. Varner, Amanda Varner, Mary J. Varner, John A. Varner, and Emma Varner**. All were listed in the 1880 census.
1. **Charles T. Varner** (b. 1869, Coosa Co, AL).
2. **Amanda Varner** (b. 1871, Coosa Co, AL).
3. **Mary J. Varner** (b. 1873, Coosa Co, AL).
4. **John A. Varner** (b. 1875, Coosa Co, AL).
5. **Emma Varner** (b. 20 ov 1878, Coosa Co, AL, d. 12 Jul 1953, Phenix City, AL) marr 24 May 1896, **William C. Jowers**.

H. **Azariah Varner**, son of Azariah Varner and Mary L. Pickering, (b. 1854, Lowndes Co, AL, d. after 1920), marr 11 Feb 1877, Lowndes Co, AL, Margaret (Maggie) Folmar (b. 1854, d. after 1920).

Azariah was living with his sister Eliza Varner Cook and her husband Issac C. Cook in 1859, after his parents died.[2]

---

[1]..John Varner was charged by the State with Assault and Battery. The jury found him guilty and fined him $1.00 and court costs. His uncles Esselman Varner and Hardaway Varner paid the fine and costs, which totaled $27.61. Recorded in Coosa County, AL, Trial Docket (for 1872), pages 45, 58, and 381.

[2]..Reported to Lowndes County Chancery Court during its proceedings in Case # 486, op. cit.

Azariah and Margaret were parents of two known children[3]: **J. L. Varner and Maggie Varner**.
1. **J. L. Varner** (b. 1880, Lowndes Co, AL).
2. **Maggie P. Varner** (b. 1901).

Appendix VIII-A
Sale of Land Where Azariah Varner Died

Lowndes County, AL, Deed Book C, p. 11.
STATE OF ALABAMA, COOSA COUNTY
Know all men by these presents that for and in consideration of the sum of sixteen hundred dollars in hand paid to us we John Varner and Amanda his wife of Said State and County do hereby bargain, sell, enfeoff and confirm unto Geo. S. Cox and George C. Freeman of the County of Lowndes in said State the following named & described piece or parcel of land situated and lying in said County of Lowndes and State of Alabama. Viz the South East quarter of Section nineteen, Township fourteen, Range fifteen, which said lands lie on Big Swamp and adjacent thereto, and it is hereby expressly intended to convey to them that quarter section of land upon which Azariah Varner lately resided, and upon which he died in said County of Lowndes...

This sale is not to effect any right which either of us may have in a suit now pending in Lowndes Circuit Court against Caswell Garrett & others for a trespass to said lands & which suit is instituted by said John Varner.

In witness our hands this the 30th day of Nov., 1858.
    (Signed)   John Varner and Amanda Varner
Test: W. F. Varner, B. J. Bonham.

---

[1]..These two children were named in the 1880 and 1900 federal censuses.

Appendix VIII-B
1853 Tax Record for Azariah Varner
Azariah Varner's Taxes on Personal Property in 1853.
   Tax of 50 cents on one white male age 21-45 -- 50 cents.
   Tax of 25 cents on one clock kept for use -- 25 cents.
   Tax on slaves:
      6 slaves under 5 years of age at 25 cents each.
      2 slaves from 5 to 10 years of age at 45 cents each.
      2 slaves from 10 to 15 years of age at 80 cents each.
      1 slave from 15 to 30 years of age at $1.10.
      2 slaves from 30 to 40 years of age at 80 cents.
   Fund for slaves executed:
      8 slaves under 10 at 1 cent tax each.
      5 slaves from 10 to 50 at 2 cents tax each.
   Gross amount of tax on slaves -- $6.70
   Tax on money ($100 at 50 cents per hundred) --   50 cents.
   TOTAL TAX ON PERSONAL PROPERTY -- $7.63.
(Taxes on Personal Property, Lowndes County, Alabama. Recorded in a ledger which was discovered in a Lowndes County warehouse in Hayneville, AL.)

Appendix VIII-C
Law Suits Against Azariah Varner
   Documentation for law suits brought against Azariah Varner in Lowndes County Circuit Court for failing to pay his debts:

P. B. Walton Co v Azariah Varner. Fall Term 1840. Walton awarded $216.22 plus costs. (Records, Circuit Court 1830-1834, p 271).

Alexander M. Luckie v Azariah Varner. Spring Term 1836. Luckie awarded $83.62 plus costs. (Records, Circuit Court 1834-1837, p 552).

A. M. Luckie v Azariah Varner. 1837. Luckie awarded $56.25 and costs.
(Records, Circuit Court 1834-1837).

Chambliss & Mundy v Azariah Varner. 17 Apr 1841. Varner ordered to pay $309.20 plus costs on a promissory note made in Benton, AL. (Final Record 1843-1847, p 270).

Glover & Fairchild v Azariah Varner. Fall term 1844. Defendant came not but made default. Glover & Farichild awarded $655.30 plus costs. (Circuit Court Minutes 1842-1848, p 163).

Chambliss & Mundy v Azariah Varner. Fall term 1847. Chambliss & Mundy awarded $309.20 plus costs. (Circuit Court Minutes 1842-1848, p. 365).

Glover & Fairchild v Azariah Varner. 14 Apr 1847. Grover & Fairchild were seeking to get from John Varner (Azariah Varner's father), garnishee, the $654.30 that the court awarded them from Azariah Varner at the 1844 spring term. They claimed that John Varner owed Azariah Varner that amount. But the court refused to collect the money from John Varner. (Final Record 1843-1846, p 209).

Jones & Smith & Co v Azariah Varner. Fall term 1848. Jones & Smith awarded $100.46 plus costs. (Circuit Court Minutes 1848-1854, p 8).

Baker Williams & Co v Azariah Varner. 21 Oct 1851. Baker Williams & Co was awarded damages of $132.49 plus costs of $6.50. Sheriff was instructed to enforce payment 5 Nov 1851. On 15 Apr 1852, the sheriff replied: "No property found." A. Harrison, Sheriff.

On 15 Oct 1852, the sheriff reported: "Levied on three bales cotton and bond given for the trial of the right of property as the statute requires." A. Harrison, Sheriff. (Execution Docket 1851-1855, p 5 and p 25. Also in Circuit Court Minutes 1848-1854, p 171).

J. J. Judge v Azariah Varner. 30 Oct 1851. Cause is submitted to the arbitration of I. B. Stone and G. S. Cox, Esquires, with the power to call in an umpire if they cannot agree. (Circuit Court Minutes 1848-1854, p 182).

P. B. Walton Co v Azariah Varner. Fall Term 1840. P. B. Walton awarded $216.22 plus costs. (Circuit Court Records 1830-1834, p 271).

Jonathan Judge v Azariah Varner. Spring 1854. Jury found for Jonathan Judge and awarded damages of $57.73 plus costs. (Circuit Court Minutes 1848-1854, p 294).

The State v Azariah Varner. 5 May 1854. The jury found the defendant not guilty. (Charges not stated.) (Circuit Court Minutes 1848-1854, p 298).

Appendix VIII-D
Trust To Support Azariah Varner's Children
Lowndes County, AL, Circuit Court Records.
TRUST FOR AZARIAH VARNER'S CHILDREN
The State of Alabama, Lowndes County

Know all men by these presents, That I, John Varner, senior of the County of Coosa and state aforesaid, in consideration of the natural love and affection which I have and do bear to my grandchildren Martha C. Varner, Sarah Varner, Eliza Varner, Harriet Varner, James Varner, Charles Varner, children of my son Azariah Varner of the County of Lowndes and state aforesaid, and

Azariah Varner, Son of John Varner

for the further consideration of five dollars to me in hand paid by my said son Azariah Varner, I have bargained, sold, and delivered, and by these presents do bargain, sell and deliver to the said Azariah Varner the following Negro slaves, to wit: Priss a woman, Lindy a girl, Edefy a girl, Simon a boy, to have and to hold the said slaves and their future increase In Trust, to and for the sole and separate use of the said Martha C. Varner, Sarah Varner, Eliza Varner, Harriet Varner, James Varner, and Charles Varner, and the said Negro slaves together with their future increase shall remain in the possession of the said Trustee until the youngest child, to wit, Charles Varner, becomes of age, then the said Negro slaves, with all their future increase shall be divided equally between the said Martha C. Varner, Sarah Varner, Eliza Varner, Harriet Varner, James Varner, and Charles Varner share and share alike. The labor and profits of said slaves shall be strictly applied by said Trustee to the maintenance and education of said children.

In testimony whereof I have hereunto set my hand and seal this 26th day of October, A. D. 1848.

(Signed) John Varner

Chapter IX
Susan Eliza Varner, Daughter of John Varner

Susan Eliza Varner, daughter of **John Varner and Nancy Powell**, was born in 1818 in Oglethorpe Co, GA. She died after 1900[1] in Lowndes Co, AL. She married in Lowndes Co, AL, 21 Dec 1837, **William Graves Varner**, son of **Frederick Varner and Sally Graves**. William was born 8 Jan 1816, Oglethorpe Co, GA; he died 12 Jan 1858, Lowndes Co, AL. Susan Eliza Varner and her husband William Graves Varner were first cousins. Their fathers, John Varner and Frederick Varner, were brothers.

William was a planter in Lowndes Co, AL, near Hayneville. He took over his father Frederick's Lowndes Co land after Frederick moved to LA. He and Susan lived on it and farmed it until his death. He had only 3 slaves in 1840 but his slave ownership grew to 15 by the time of the 1855 AL State census. He wrote his will 22 Dec 1857; it was submitted for probate 2 Mar 1858. He left his entire estate to his widow Susan Eliza Varner.[2]

John Varner Gives Slaves to Susan

Based on Lowndes Co, AL, Circuit and Chancery Court records, William G. Varner was not a responsible manager of his financial affairs. He drank excessively over a period of years and failed to pay his debts in a timely

---

[1]..Susan E. Dacus, 82, was living with her son, John F. Varner, in Hayneville, Lowndes Co, AL, at the time of the 1900 census.

[2]..*Minutes of the Probate Court*, Book L, pp. 211-213, Lowndes Co, AL. William G. Varner's estate papers are at the AL Archives.

manner. Because of William's inability to provide adequately for the needs of his family, his wife's father, John Varner--who was also William's uncle--helped support Susan and her children. In 1842, John Varner deeded three slaves to Susan Eliza Varner as her separate property. He included a provision in the deed to prohibit William G. Varner from selling them and to protect the slaves so that William's creditors could not seize them. The slaves he deeded to Susan were **Butler**, a man about 23 years old, **Sidna**, a girl about 16, and **Milly**, the infant child of Sidna.[1] William G. Varner gave his permission for his wife to accept the slaves as her separate property.[2]

Slave Child Seized and Sold

In June of 1846, in violation of the deed made in 1842, a constable seized one of the slaves, the child Milly[3], and sold her at public auction. The constable was authorized to sell the slave by a justice of the peace at the

---

[1] ..See Appendix # IX-A at the end of this chapter for a copy of the deed of trust in which John Varner gave slaves to his daughter Susan Varner.

[2] ..See Appendix # IX-B at the end of this chapter for William G. Varner's statement approving John Varner's gift of slaves to Susan Eliza Varner as her separate property.

[3] ..Milly was an infant in 1842 when John Varner deeded her to his daughter Susan Eliza Varner. Milly was four to six years of age when she was seized by a sheriff's deputy and sold for $100 to cover some of William G. Varner's debts. She was 14 to 16 years of age when the Court ordered that she be returned to the ownership of Susan Eliza Varner.

request of one of William G. Varner's creditors. John M. Cole purchased the slave Milly for $100.[4]

Seeking to reclaim the slave, Susan Eliza Varner twice filed suit against John M. Cole. The first case was initiated in the Lowndes County, AL, Circuit Court in 1851. The Court ruled that the deed of gift of the slave issued by John Varner in 1842 was equitable but not legal. Therefore, the Circuit Court refused to intercede on Susan Varner's behalf.[2]

Subsequently, in 1856, Susan E. Varner went before the Lowndes County Chancery Court in her continuing effort to regain possession of the slave. She again asked that the slave Milly be returned to her. She also sought damages from Cole for seizing property that rightfully belonged to her. This time she was successful. Susan Varner won the case and Cole was ordered to return the slave and make appropriate payments to Susan Varner for loss of her property, plus costs and interest.[3] Cole appealed the decision to the Alabama Supreme Court, which upheld the Chancery Court decision. The Court

---

[1]..See Appendix # IX-C at the end of this chapter for court testimony on the seizure and sale of the slave Milly.

[2]..This information is included in the affidavit filed by Susan Varner in Chancery Court Case # 414, Susan E. Varner v John M. Cole.

[3]..See Appendix IX-D at the end of this chapter for the court ruling and record of costs regarding Chancery Court Case # 414.

testimony in this case provides interesting insights about William G. Varner and his family.[4]

Witnesses Describe Drinking Problem

Witness Allen Davis, who had known William G. Varner for 32 years, said that Varner began drinking to excess in about 1841 and that he kept doing so for several years afterwards.[2] Another witness, McDaniel Atchison, who lived near him at the time, said that William G. Varner "commenced drinking very hard in 1841 or 1842."[3]

Witness William A. Rice said he had frequently seen William G. Varner intoxicated but that he did not know when he started drinking heavily but thinks he kept it up several years. Rice added that, in about 1841, 1842, or 1843, W. G. Varner told him that he (Varner) was considerably dissipated and despondent.[4]

John Varner, William's uncle and Susan's father, testified that when he set up the deed of trust he knew that William G. Varner had been dissipating for some time

---

[1]..Lowndes Co Chancery Court Case # 414 is summarized in <u>Chancery Court Minutes</u>, Bk. 11, pp. 371-389. The author found the original records, which include testimony of witnesses, in a storage warehouse located behind the jail in Hayneville, Lowndes Co, AL. The testimony of witnesses quoted in this chapter was part of the record found in the warehouse.

[2]..See Appendix # IX-E at the end of this chapter for notes on the testimony of witness Allen Davis.

[3]..See Appendix # IX-F at the end of this chapter for notes on the testimony of witness McDaniel Atchison.

[4]..See Appendix # IX-G at the end of this chapter for notes on the testimony of witness William A. Rice.

and admitted that the purpose of establishing the trust, rather than making an outright gift, was to protect the property (slaves) from becoming liable for William's debts.[1]

Five years later, in 1847, John Varner donated four additional slaves to Susan Eliza Varner to use as her separate property to provide support for her and the children. This time, he set up a trust and assigned the slaves to it, rather than issue a deed. He probably believed this would provide stronger protection for them against William G. Varner's creditors. The slaves donated to this trust were **Aggy** a woman about twenty-seven years of age, and her children: **Oney** a girl about seven years of age, **Mose** a boy about five years of age, and **Joe** a boy about one year old.[2]

Other records prove that William G. Varner was a success in some respects. He was summoned and served on Circuit Court juries at least three times.[3] Tax records,

---

[1]..See Appendix # IX-H at the end of this chapter for notes on the testimony of witness John Varner. John Varner was Susan E. Varner's father and the person who deeded the slave Milly to Susan E. Varner.

[2]..See Appendix # IX-I at the end of this chapter for a copy of the trust that John Varner set up to assist his daughter Susan E. Varner.

[3]..William G. Varner served as foreman of the jury in a civil case during the fall term of the Circuit Court in 1849. (Circuit Court Minutes 1848-1854, p 77).

William G. Varner was summoned to Circuit Court jury duty on March 7, 1841. He responded and served. (Record, Circuit Court, pp 296-297).

William G. Varner, planter from Hayneville, was called to
(continued...)

which were located for one year during the 1850's, suggest that he owned a significant amount of property, primarily slaves.[1] After William's death, Susan E. Varner, executrix of his estate, was able to pay all of her deceased husband's debts and reported a balance in the estate of $3,200.[2]

William G. Varner named his wife Susan E. Varner as the executrix of his will and sole heir of his estate. Susan filed the will for probate 30 Jan 1858, which was 18 days after his death.[3] One of William's bills that Susan paid in settling the estate was the doctor's charges for attending to William the two days before he died. The doctor

---

[3](...continued)
serve on the jury for a special session of the Circuit Court held Oct. 10, 1853. (Circuit Court Minutes 1848-1854, p 246).

[1]..See Appendix # IX-J at the end of this chapter for one year's tax record for William G. Varner, Susan E. Varner's husband.

[2]..The Probate Court approved the final settlement of the estate of William G. Varner on Feb. 17, 1860. The entire estate, valued at $3,200, went to Susan E. Varner, the widow, as specified in the will. (Minutes of Probate Court Book 12, p. 539.)

[3]..Susan E. Varner, widow of William G. Varner, deceased, submitted the last will of the deceased to the Lowndes County Probate Court 30 Jan 1858. She said that William left the following children, all under 14: William L. Varner, Mary E. Varner, Amaziah Varner, Samuel Varner, and John F. Varner. The will was accepted by the court and Susan Varner was ordered to inventory the estate. (Minutes of the Probate Court Book L, pp. 211-213.)

charged $3 each for two visits to William G. Varner,[4] apparently in his home. Another bill paid from his estate was for his funeral expenses,[2] which totaled $85.

William G. and Susan Eliza Varner were parents of six known children: **Amerentha L., William L., Amaziah, Elizabeth, Martha M. and John F.**

Children of Susan and William Varner

A. **Amerentha L. Varner**, daughter of William G. and Susan Eliza Varner, (b. 1844, Lowndes Co, AL, d. betw 1850-1857[3]).

---

[1]..Statement to W. G. Varner. From Drs. Pritchett and McCall:
    1858 Jan. 10 Visit self   3.00
           "   11 Visit self   3.00
(Jan. 7, 1859 -- Received payment -- Pritchett & McCall)
(From William G. Varner estate papers in Alabama Archives.)

[2]..Funeral Expenses for William G. Varner.
From Williams & Waldrone -- 1858
    Jan. 12 -- 75 inch Rose Wood metallic Burial Case -- $75.00
                    Box & plank --   4.00
                    Use of Hearse --   6.00
                                    $85.00
Nov. 18 -- Received payment of Mrs. S. E. Varner
                      Williams & Waldrone
(From William G. Varner Estate Papers at the Alabama Archives.)

[3]..Amarentha L. Varner was enumerated in the 1850 census but was not living at the time her father died, in 1857.

B. **William F. Varner**, son of William G. and Susan Eliza Varner, (b. 1846, Lowndes Co, AL, d. between 1860 and 1877[4]).

C. **Amaziah Varner**, son of William G. and Susan Eliza Varner, (b. Dec 1848, Lowndes Co, AL, d. 26 Jun 1909, Lowndes Co, AL, bur Hayneville Cem, Lowndes Co, AL) marr 29 Oct 1873, Lowndes Co, AL, **Harriet Virginia Tucker** (b. 30 Jun 1854, d. 29 Sep 1915, Lowndes Co, AL[2]).

Amaziah and Harriet were parents of eight children, according to the 1900 census. Only five were living in 1900. The three who were deceased in 1900 are unknown. The five known children: **Maggie Varner, William A. Varner, Mary E. Varner, Robert L. Varner, and Emma V. Varner.**

1. **Maggie Varner** (b. 1877, Lowndes Co, AL, d. after 1915[3]) marr 8 Nov 1896, Lowndes Co, AL, **W. W. West.** Maggie Varner was named by Mildred

---

[1]..William L. Varner's name appears in the 1850 and 1860 census reports and in the estate proceedings of William G. Varner, his father, in 1857. But he is not listed as a surviving heir of William G. Varner when his heirs partitioned William G. Varner's land in 1877. Lowndes County Deed Book L, p. 358.

[2]..Harriet Tucker Varner is buried in the Hayneville Cemetery, Lowndes Co, AL.

[3]..Maggie Varner West was named by her mother Harriet Virginia Tucker in her will, probated in 1915, to receive a share of the proceeds from her estate.

Brewer as one of her classmates during the late 1880's.[4]

Maggie and W. W. were parents of six known children: **Mary Lynn West, Margie West, Agaster West, William West, Herman West, and Maud West**. Mary Lynn married Wilbur Wynn; Margie married a man named Carter; and Agaster married Luther Haigler. All three of these couples had children, but their names are unknown.[2]

2. **William A. Varner** (b. May 1878, Lowndes Co, AL, d. after 1915[3]). Will Varner was named by Mildred Brewer as one of her classmates during the late 1800's.[4]

William married a woman whose last name was Clifford. They were parents of two children: **Ray Varner and Elizabeth Varner**. Elizabeth married a man whose last name was Davis. William's children lived in Birmingham, AL.[5]

---

[1]..Lowndes Court House, op. cit.

[2]..Information on Maggie and W. W. West's children was submitted by Virginia Waller Varner, Hayneville, AL.

[3]..William A. Varner was named by his mother Harriet Virginia Varner in her will to receive a share of her estate. The will was probated in 1915.

[4]..Lowndes Court House, op. cit.

[5]..Information on William A. Varner's children was submitted by Virginia Waller Varner, Hayneville, AL.

3. **Mary E. Varner** (b. July 1880, Lowndes Co, AL, d. after 1915[6]) marr 16 Dec 1900, Lowndes Co, AL, **Charlie Norris**.
Mary and Charlie Norris are buried in Ft. Deposit, AL. They had one child: **Erleen Norris**. She was adopted.[2]
4. **Robert Lafayette Varner** (b. Nov 1883, Lowndes Co, AL, d. 3 Sep 1938[3], Lowndes Co, AL), marr **Sarah Zutella Brown**. Robert L. Varner was the executor of his mother Harriet Virginia Varner's estate, which was probated in 1915.[4]

Robert L. and Sadie Varner were parents of six children: **Harvey A. Varner, Buelah Zutella Varner, John Robert Varner, Edward L. Varner, Sarah Jumelle Varner, and Nora Virginia Varner.**
   a. **Harvey Amaziah Varner** (b. 1905, d. 1932).[5]
   b. **Buelah Zutella Varner** (b. 17 Mar 1910, Lowndes Co, AL), marr **Charles Dickerson Holladay** (b. 7 Apr 1904, Lowndes Co, AL, d. 1959, Hayneville, AL), son of **Steve Holladay and Mary Pet Gardiner**. Zutella lives in Hayneville, Lowndes Co, AL, in 1993.

---

[1]..Mary E. Norris was named in her mother Harriet Virginia Varner's will to receive a share of her estate. The will was probated in 1915.

[2]..According to Virginia Waller Varner, Hayneville, AL.

[3]..Death announced in the Montgomery Advertiser.

[4]..Recorded in Lowndes County, AL, Will Book D, p. 166.

[5]..Harvey was listed in the 1910 census. His birth and death dates appear on a grave marker in the Hayneville Cemetery, Lowndes Co, AL.

Buelah and Charles were parents of two children: **Mary Charles Holladay and Robert Laslie Holladay**.

(1) **Mary Charles Holladay** (b. 29 Nov 1929, Bessemer, AL) marr **Grady H. Nichols II**.

Mary and Grady live in Mobile, AL, in 1993. They are parents of two children: **Grady Henry Nichols III, and Wayne Varner Nichols**.

(a) **Grady Henry Nichols III** (b. 5 Jun 1947) marr **Jeanne Stedman**. Grady and Jeanne are parents of one child: **Grady Henry Nichols IV** (b. 7 Dec 1978).

(b) **Wayne Varner Nichols** (b. 13 Dec 1949) marr **Brenda Timmons**. Wayne and Brenda are parents of one child: **Joshua Varner Nichols** (b. 9 Jul 1980).

(2) **Robert Laslie Holladay** (b. 24 Jan 1938, Montgomery, AL) marr in Mobile, AL, **Fay Gibbs**. Robert and Fay live in Memphis, TN, in 1993.

c. **John Robert Varner**[1] (b. 1 May 1913, Hayneville, Lowndes Co, AL), marr **Virginia Waller** (b. 14 Jul 1916, Braggs, AL), dau of **Lewis Edwin Waller and Rosa Bell Gates Waller**.

John is a retired farmer and state employee. John and Virginia live in

---

[1]..Information on the John Robert Varner family was submitted by Virginia Waller Varner of Hayneville, AL.

Hayneville, Lowndes Co, AL, in 1993. They are parents of two children: **John R. Varner, Jr., and Martha Jeannine Varner**.
(1) **John R. Varner, Jr.** (b. 13 Dec 1942, Montgomery, AL) marr 6 Jul 1968 at Homerville, GA, **Sandra Morgan**. John is an electrical engineer. John and Sandra live in Kennesaw, GA, in 1993.

John and Sandra are parents of three children: **John R. Varner III, Jason Morgan Varner, and Joseph Waller Varner**.
  (a) **John R. Varner** (b. 28 Apr 1969, Jeseys, GA).
  (b) **Jason Morgan Varner** (b. 1 Sep 1976, Marietta, GA).
  (c) **Joseph Waller Varner** (b. 21 Dec 1980, Marietta, GA).
(2) **Martha Jeannine Varner** (b. 25 June 1946, Montgomery, AL) marr 2 Aug 1970, Hayneville, AL, **Ronald Walter Disney**.

Martha Jeannine is a school teacher. She and Ronald live in Fayetteville, GA, in 1993. They have one child: **Alison Virginia Disney**.
  (a) **Alison Virginia Disney** (b. 28 Oct 1978, Jonesboro, GA).
d. **Edward Lafayette Varner** (b. 3 Oct 1916, Hayneville, Lowndes Co, AL), marr **Eloise Till** (b. 28 Apr 1921, Macedoma, AL), dau of **John Henry Till and Mary Louise Stabler Till**.

Edward and Eloise are retired and live in Hayneville, Lowndes Co, AL, in 1993. They

are parents of two children: **Edward L. Varner, Jr., and Marilyn Diane Varner.**
(1) **Edward L. Varner, Jr.,** (b. 24 Nov 1942, Greenville, AL) marr 12 Jun 1965, Greensboro, AL, **Patricia Stewart.**

Edward is an engineer. He and Patricia live in Tuscaloosa, AL, in 1993. They are parents of one child: **Edward Scott Varner.**

(a) **Edward Scott Varner,** (b. 2 Apr 1969, Jacksonville, FL.

(2) **Marilyn Diane Varner** (b. 19 Jan 1945, Montgomery, AL) marr 30 Dec 1965, Hayneville, AL, **George W. Ward, Jr.**

Marilyn and George live in Gulf Shores, AL, in 1993. They are parents of three children: **George Wilburn Ward III, Marilyn Ward, and Michael Varner Ward.**

(a) **George Wilburn Ward III** (b. 13 Sep 1967, Auburn, AL) marr 8 Aug 1992, **Brooke Libby.** George is golf superintendent in Jackson, MS, in 1993.

(b) **Marilyn Ward** (b. 22 Dec 1969, Auburn, AL).

(c) **Michael Varner Ward** (b. 9 Mar 1973, Auburn, AL, d. 8 May 1976).

e. **Sarah Jumelle Varner** (b. 31 Mar 1918, Lowndes Co, AL, d. 1936[1]).

---

[1]..Birth and death dates appear on a grave marker in the Hayneville Cemetery, Lowndes Co, AL.

f. **Nora Virginia Varner** (b. 11 Jan 1921, d. 24 Apr 1989) marr **Edward R. Crossley** (b. Jun 1918), son of **Carl Crossley and Lucy Robinson**. Nora and Edward had one child: **Karlyeen Varner Crossley.**
(1) **Karlyeen Varner Crossley** (b. 30 Sep 1955). Karlyeen was adopted.
5. **Emma V. Varner** (b. Oct 1886, Lowndes Co, AL).[1] Emma married **Tom Light**. Emma and Tom had three children: **Mytel Mason Light, Jim Light, and Virginia Light**. This family moved to Way Co, TX.[2]

D. **Mary Elizabeth Varner**, daughter of William G. and Susan Eliza Varner, (b. 1851, Lowndes Co, AL), marr **Jerre Light**.

Mary and Jerre were parents of three children: **Lyzinkie Light, Lillie Light, and Elizabeth Light**.

Lyzinkie never married; she is buried in Birmingham, AL. Lillie married Fin Barganier. Elizabeth married but her husband's name is unknown.[3]

---

[1]..In her will, Harriet Virginia Varner named Vasser Light as a daughter who was to receive one-sixth of her estate. This daughter probably was Emma V. Varner.

[2]..Information on Emma V. Varner's husband and children submitted by Virginia Waller Varner, Hayneville, AL.

[3]..Names and other information on Jerre and Mary Light's children was submitted by Virginia Waller Varner of Hayneville, AL.

E. **Martha M. Varner**, daughter of William G. and Susan Eliza Varner, (b. 1854, Lowndes Co, AL, d. after 1870[1]).

F. **John Frank Varner**, son of William G. and Susan Eliza Varner, (b. 1856, Lowndes Co, AL, d. 1 Nov 1948, Lowndes Co, AL[2]) marr 3 Apr 1885, Lowndes Co, AL, **Ella Thomas**.

A partial list of the unmarried ladies and their escorts for the leap year ball of 1884, copied from a newspaper of the time, included Miss Mary Folmar and Mr. Frank Varner.[3]

Susan E. Dacus, on Feb. 15, 1887, deeded her land[4] in Lowndes County to John F. Varner "in consideration of the love and affection which I bear for my son John F. Varner and the further consideration of his care and labor in supporting me."

Susan Eliza Varner Marries Rufus W. Dacus

Susan Eliza Varner, dau of John Varner and Nancy Powell, marr 2nd 21 Feb 1860, Montgomery Co, AL, **Rufus**

---

[1]..Listed in the 1860 and 1870 census reports.

[2]..John Frank Varner, 92, death was announced in the Montgomery Advertiser, 1 Nov 1948. He died at his home in Hayneville.

[3]..Lowndes Court House, op. cit.

[4]..(SW 1/4 of S 15 -- 51 acres off NW 1/2 of E 1/4 of S 22, all in T 14, R 15). Lowndes Co, AL, Deed Book U, page 200.

Wiley Dacus (b. 1818 in SC, d. 30 Jun 1873, at his home in Hayneville, Lowndes Co, AL[5]

Rufus was a planter in Lowndes County, AL. In 1860, he reported that his real estate was worth $9,600 and that his personal estate was worth $23,355. The personal estate primarily consisted of slaves; he reported having 20[2]. By 1870--after slaves were freed--his personal estate was worth only $1,075.

Apparently, Rufus helped Susan raise her children. Five of them resided with the Dacus' in 1860 and three were still with them in 1870. The house where Susan and Rufus and some of the children lived still stands in Hayneville, AL, in 1993.

Appendix IX-A
John Varner Deeds Slaves to His Daughter

Lowndes County Chancery Court Case # 414.

Exhibit A. DEED OF SLAVES FROM JOHN VARNER TO SUSAN ELIZA VARNER.

The State of Alabama, Lowndes County. Know all men by these presents that I John Varner of the County and Sate aforesaid for and in consideration of the love and affection which I have and bear my beloved daughter Susan Eliza Varner as well as for the consideration of one dollar to me in hand paid by said Susan Eliza Varner the receipt of which is hereby acknowledged do hereby give

---

[1]..Death announced in the <u>Greenville Advocate.</u> Copy on microfilm at the AL Archives.

[2]..Many or all of these are believed to have been the slaves "and their increase" that John Varner deeded to his daughter Susan Eliza Varner as her separate property.

bargain sell and confirm unto the said Susan Eliza Varner the following named slaves (viz) Butler a man about twenty-three years old, Sidna a girl about sixteen years old and her infant child named Milly, to have and to hold the said slaves and all their future increase to the said Susan Eliza Varner to her sole and special use free from the disposal of anyone and for and during the term and period of her natural life, and at her death to the children of her body lawfully begotten forever.

In witness whereof I have hereunto set my hand and seal the 12th day of April A.D. 1842.   John Varner (Seal)

Signed, sealed, and delivered in the presence of Thomas M. Williams, Morgan J. Hinkle, and W. A. Rice.

Appendix IX-B
William G. Varner Approves Gift of Slaves

Lowndes County Chancery Court Case # 414.

Exhibit B. WILLIAM G. VARNER'S APPROVAL FOR HIS WIFE TO ACCEPT SLAVES AS HER SEPARATE PROPERTY.

The State of Alabama, Lowndes County. Know all men by these presents that I William G. Varner of the county and state aforesaid do freely give my consent and approbation and further it is my request that John Varner the reputed father of my wife Susan Eliza Varner shall give and make over to my said wife Susan Eliza Varner and the lawful heirs of her body forever free from my control or disposal the following named slaves which the said John Varner loaned to my said wife immediately after the intermarriage of myself and the said Susan Eliza which are named in a deed made by the said John Varner bearing same date with this instrument and recorded in the county clerk's office of the county aforesaid namely Butler a Negro man slave aged about twenty-three years old, Sidna a Negro girl slave about sixteen years old and her infant child named Milly and all their future increase.

In witness whereof I have voluntarily affixed my hand and seal this twelfth day of April A.D. 1842.
William G. Varner
Testi -- Saml. P. NeSmith.

Appendix IX-C
Testimony on Seizure and Sale of Slave Milly
Lowndes County Chancery Court Case # 414.
NOTES ON TESTIMONY CONCERNING SEIZURE AND SALE OF THE SLAVE MILLY.

Sometime during 1846, the precise date not recollected, one B. B. Smith, a constable of county of Lowndes, levied upon the slave Milly under five executions issued by a Justice of the Peace of said county (whose name is unknown to complainant), one in favor of Burbrage & Jewell for use of Jacob Marshall, two in favor of said Marshall, one in favor of Wm F. Varner for the use of Englander and Brothers, and one in favor of said Englander and Brothers; all against said William G. Varner the precise date and amounts of which are unknown to complainant.

Sometime in June 1846 said constable sold said Milly to one John M. Cole, now a resident citizen of said County of Lowndes and of full age, for the sum of one hundred dollars.

Appendix IX-D
Court Rules in Favor of Susan E. Varner

Lowndes County, AL, Chancery Court Case 414, Susan E. Varner v John M. Cole.

The Court found in favor of Susan E. Varner and ordered Cole to return the slave Milly to her and pay damages and costs, as determined by a Court appointed appraiser. Following is taken from the report of the appraiser:

Value of the hire for the Negro girl Milly:

For the year 1854 is	$29.00	
Interest 2 years and 6 mo to Jul 57	5.80	$34.80
For the year 1855	33.00	
Interest for 1 1/2 years	3.96	36.96
For the year 1856	47.00	
6 mo interest to July '57	1.88	48.88
For 1857 fr Jany 1 to July 1	35.00	55.00
Amount due complainant for hire		$155.64

I report the above amount of one hundred and fifty five and 64/100 dollars as due complainant for the hire of said Negro girl. I do not think the testimony justifies a charge for hire prior to 1854.

The defendant contended that he should be allowed reasonable compensation annually for feeding and clothing the girl from the time she went into his possession to the time she became useful; and took testimony on that point, to which the complainant objected. My opinion is that under the decree of reference, I have no authority to make such allowance and have not done so.

I further report that it is admitted by complainant's solicitors that the Negro girl has been delivered up to complainant.

All of which is respectfully submitted July 8th 1857.

E. H. Herbert, Register.

Appendix IX-E
Testimony of Witness Allen Davis

Lowndes County, AL, Chancery Court Case # 414, Susan E. Varner v John M. Cole.

NOTES ON TESTIMONY FROM ALLEN DAVIS

Witness has known Susan E. Varner about 20 or 30 years and William G. Varner 32 years. They moved to near where the witness lived in 1838 or 1839. Wm G. Varner managed and controlled the said Negro upon his plantation as long as he has known her, with the exception of some two or three years when they were managed by John and Hardaway Varner[1], who were cropping with the said William G. Varner at that time.

Witness knows that William G. Varner drank a good deal and dissipated. Witness says he commenced drinking to excess in about 1841 and kept doing so for several years afterwards.

He lived three-quarters of a mile from Wm G. Varner and was on Varner's farm often. He frequently saw Wm G. Varner ordering and making the Negroes work, telling them all to do such and such things and the Negroes obeying him, Sidna among the rest. He saw no difference in the way Wm G. Varner managed Sidna and the rest. He did not see Susan E. give orders to Sidna.

Signed J. A. Pruitt, Commissioner.

---

[1]..John and Hardaway were sons of John Varner of Coosa Co, AL, brothers of Susan Eliza Varner, and cousins of William G. Varner.

Appendix IX-F
Testimony of Witness McDaniel Atchison
Lowndes County Chancery Court Case # 414.
TESTIMONY FROM McDANIEL ATCHISON.
Witness has known Wm G. and Susan Varner since 1838, when they moved near him. Does not know where or when they were married or where they lived before moving near him. Does not know whether or when Wm G. Varner contracted debts.

Witness says Wm G. Varner "commenced drinking very hard in 1841 or 42."

Wm G. Varner lived one-quarter of a mile from the witness from 1838 to 1842. During that time, he knows that Wm G. managed and controlled the slave Sidna because he (witness) has been on Varner's plantation and saw him tell her to do things, which she did. Varner managed the Negroes all alike.

Signed J. A. Pruitt, Commissioner.

Appendix IX-G
Testimony of Witness William A. Rice
Lowndes County Chancery Court Case # 414.
NOTES ON TESTIMONY FROM WILLIAM A. RICE.
William G. and Susan E. Varner lived about two miles East of Hayneville on or near a place formerly occupied by W. G. Varner's father.

William G. Varner was at one time considered as being in embarrassed circumstances. Does not recollect the time but thinks it was about 1841, 42, or 43. Does not know of his contracting many debts, or at what time. Said W. G. Varner about that time mentioned that he was considerably dissipated and despondent. Has frequently seen him intoxicated, does not know when he commenced drinking but thinks he kept it up several years.

He said that he was called upon by John Varner about April 1842 in the Clerk's office in Hayneville to witness said instrument (the deed). That he did so together with F. M. Williams and M. B. Hinkle. John Varner remarked at that time or about the time of the witnessing of said instrument "That he was making over or conveying to his daughter this property, that William G. Varner was doing badly, or managing bad, and drinking, or wasting his property, or words in substance, and he wished to secure it in this way, or other words amounting to this, that left the impression that he was fixing the property for his daughter by this deed so that Wm G. Varner could not dispose of it.

He said that it was currently reported, and believed in the neighborhood that Wm G. Varner was embarrassed by John Varner's deeding of the property to his wife, but he does not know it of his own knowledge.

He said he was never at Wm G. Varner's home as he now recollects. Witness lived in Hayneville, 2 or 3 miles away. Disposition signed by J. A. Pruitt, Commissioner.

Appendix IX-H
Testimony of Witness John Varner

Lowndes County Chancery Court Case # 414.
NOTES ON TESTIMONY OF JOHN VARNER.
Disposition of witness -- John Varner, sworn and examined the 31st day of May in the year 1856 at the house of John Varner, in Coosa County, AL, under and by virtue of a commission issued out of the Chancery Court of the State of Alabama for Lowndes County in a certain

cause therein pending, between Susan E. Varner...and John M. Cole.

"I owned said slave Sidney at the intermarriage of Susan E and Wm G Varner. I did loan said slave Sidney to Susan E. Varner in the winter of 1838. Said slave continued in possession of said Susan E. under said loan about four years and two or three months.

"I first parted with the title to the said slave Sidney and her child Milly on the 12th day of April, 1842, by a deed of gift executed to Susan E. Varner.

"Said deed was executed by me with the design of securing said slaves to the said Susan E. Varner. Wm G Varner was not in debt at that time to my knowledge. I had no intention to defraud any one or to hinder or delay any creditor of the said Wm G Varner. If he had any intention to defraud any one I was ignorant of the fact.

"I did a short time after the marriage of my Daughter with Wm G. Varner, send said slave Sidney to the home of Wm G Varner for the use of Susan E. Varner. Soon after this I sent another slave to the home of Wm G Varner for the same purpose. I had come to no definite conclusion, as to whether she should keep said slave forever or not, I had no appointed time to take it from her. After I had sent said slave Sidney home to complainant, the possession was not changed, to my knowledge.

"Said slave Sidney nor Milly never returned to my possession after they went into the possession of my Daughter as stated by me above.

"William A. Rice, and I think Thos. M. Williams and others were present when I signed the deed. It was done in the Clerk's office in the courthouse of Lowndes County. I did know at the time said deed was executed that said Wm G. Varner had been dissipating for some time. I did not know that he was running in debt, or that he was in debt at that time.

"Wm G Varner did manage and control said slaves as the separate property of his wife up to the date of said Deed. The manner of his management and control was in no way changed after the making of said deed. He did exercise the same management after the date of the deed as before."

Signed John Varner

The foregoing evidence of the witness, who is personally known to me, was taken down under oath duly administered by me. The same was correctly and audibly read over to the witness and approved by him, and subscribed at a time and place appointed by me -- Witness my hand and seal.   Joel Gulledge

(Adam Harrall and Vines Smith were the other two members of the commission appointed to take the deposition from John Varner. The address: Travellers Rest, Coosa County, Alabama, is entered on the document following the commission members names.

Appendix IX-I
John Varner Trust for Susan E. Varner

<u>Trust Set Up by John Varner to Help Susan Eliza Varner</u>.

The State of Alabama, Lowndes County. Know all men by these presents that I, John Varner senior of Coosa County in the said state, in consideration of the natural love and affection, which I have and do bear to my daughter Susan Eliza Varner, wife of William G. Varner of the County of Lowndes aforesaid, and for the further consideration of one dollar to me in hand paid by Amaziah Varner, my son, I have bargained, sold, and delivered and by these presents do bargain, sell, and deliver to the said

Amaziah Varner the following Negro slaves, to wit, Aggy a woman about twenty-seven years of age, Oney a girl about seven years of age, Mose a boy about five years of age, Joe a boy about one year old, children of the said woman Aggy, To Have and To Hold the said slaves and their future increase, In Trust, to and for the sole and separate use of the said Susan Eliza Varner, for and during the time of her natural life, and at her death the said slaves and their future increase, and all the product of their labor which may not have been expended by the said Susan Eliza Varner in her said lifetime, to descend to and be equally divided among each child or children as the said Susan Eliza Varner may leave living, share and share alike, their heirs, executors and administrators forever, and it is hereby expressly covenanted and agreed by and between the said John Varner senior and the said Amaziah Varner that the said Amaziah Varner shall suffer and permit the said Susan Eliza Varner during the term of her said natural life, to possess, manage, control and direct the said slaves and their future increase as her own separate estate and also that she, during her said natural life, shall also take and receive the value of the products, labor and services of the said slaves and apply the same to her sole and separate use the same as if she was single and unmarried, but so as neither the said slaves nor their future increase nor the labor and services of the said slaves or their future increase shall be any way liable to the debts, contracts, control, forfeitures, or encumbrances of the said William G. Varner nor any other husband with whom the said Susan Eliza Varner might hereinafter marry.

In testimony whereof I have hereunto set my hand and affixed my seal this 14th day of April, 1847.
(Signed) John Varner

I Amaziah Varner do hereby accept of the above Trust as given under my hand and seal this 14th day of April, 1847. (Signed) Amaziah Varner

----

I Morgan B. Hinkle Clerk of the County Court for Lowndes County, do hereby certify that John Varner, senior, above named did this day appear before me and acknowledged that he signed, sealed, and delivered the foregoing deed to Amaziah Varner above named for the purposes therein contained and the day and year therein set forth. (Signed) Morgan B. Hinkle, Clerk, Lowndes County Court.

Appendix IX-J
Tax Record for William G. Varner

For one year in the 1850's (exact date missing from the record), William G. Varner paid taxes as follows.

Tax on 1 gold watch -- 50 cents.

Tax on vehicle valued at $100 that is kept for use and is not exempt -- 25 cents.

Tax on 6 slaves 5 to 10 years of age -- 45 cents each.

Tax on 4 slaves 10 to 15 years of age -- 80 cents each.

Tax on 5 slaves 15 to 30 years of age -- $1.10 each.

Tax on 5 slaves 30 to 40 years of age -- 80 cents each.

TOTAL TAX ON SLAVES -- $15.40

Tax on slaves for fund for slaves executed:

Six slaves under 10 at 1 cent each -- 6 cents.

Fourteen slaves 10 to 60 at 2 cents each -- 28 cents.

TOTAL Taxes on personal property --$16.49.

(From Personal Tax Records located in a county warehouse in Lowndes County, Alabama.)

Chapter X
George H. Varner, Son of John Varner

George H. Varner was a son of John Varner and Nancy Powell. He was born 15 July 1815 in Oglethorpe Co, GA. He died at the age of 67 years, 4 months, and 13 days on 18 Nov 1882 in Richland Parish, LA[1].

George H. Varner was four years old when his family moved from a well established and prosperous farming region in Oglethorpe County, GA, to settle on the frontier in Alabama. He was 15 when his father was elected Clerk of the Lowndes County, AL, County Court and the family moved to farm land just outside the village of Hayneville, seat of the Lowndes County government.

George H. Varner Moves to Mississippi

George left his parents' plantation when he was 23, to move to Franklin County, MS, where he married and established his first farm. He was the only child of John Varner and Nancy Powell who did not settle near his/her

---

[1]..George H. Varner's birth, marriage, and death dates and places were taken from Bible records which are in possession of his descendants. The earliest records were written by George H. Varner himself in a Bible that he presented to his daughter Winford A. Varner 4 Sep 1872.

A copy of this Bible record was sent to the author by Margaret Varner Barton, Santa Anna, TX. Ms. Barton is one of George H. Varner's great granddaughters.

According to Ms. Barton, descendants of George H. Varner believe the initial "H" stands for Henley, the maiden name of Elizabeth "Betsy" Henley Varner, his grandmother. The author found no record either to substantiate or to refute this family tradition.

George H. Varner, Son of John Varner

parents in either Lowndes County or Coosa County, AL, upon reaching adulthood.[1]

Extant records give little or no insight as to why George H. Varner moved away while the others remained near their parents. Perhaps the family of Amelia Greggs, the woman he married in Mississippi, had lived in Lowndes County, Alabama. George H. Varner might have known the Greggs in Alabama and either went with them to Mississippi or followed them there.

Whatever the reason, George H. Varner moved from Lowndes County, AL, to Franklin Co, MS, in 1838. (He won a judgement in court in Lowndes County, AL, in April 1838.[2] He married **Amelia Greggs** in Franklin Co,

---

[1]..There is one partial exception to this statement. Hardaway Varner lived for a few years during the 1860's in Franklin Parish, LA, near his brother George H. Varner. Hardaway then moved back to Alabama and lived on his father's home property in Coosa County the remainder of his life.

[2]..George H. Varner v Edward Mickelborough April 1838. Judgment in favor of Plaintiff George H. Varner, $50 plus costs of $13.12 1/2. The court ordered that Mickelborough's land (NE 1/4 of NE 1/4 of S 7 and NE 1/2 of NE 1/2 of S 12 in T 12, T 12, R 15) be sold to pay the $50 judgment rendered to Varner previously in a Justice of the Peace Court. The proceeds were to be used to cover the $50 plus costs in the J.P. Court and in the Circuit Court. April 1838. (Circuit Court Record, Spring Term 1838, Execution Docket, 1837-1838, Book B, p 77, Lowndes County, AL).

MS, 17 May 1838.[3]) This was to be the first of three marriages of George H. Varner.

George H. Varner purchased his first land in Franklin Co, Mississippi 3 Nov 1838.[2] Eighteen days later, 21 Nov 1838, he mortgaged that land along with Negro slaves.[3] The 1840 census reported that George H. Varner and his wife were each between 20 and 29 years old, that they had a female child under 5 years of age, and that they had three slaves.[4]

George H. Varner Copes with Money Problems

Apparently, hard times hit George H. and Amelia Varner in the early 1840's. To raise needed cash they sold

---

[1]..<u>Franklin County, MS, Marriage Records</u>, Book 2, page 5. George H. Varner and Amelia Gregg, both of Franklin County, Mississippi. License issued May 4, 1838. Signed John P. Steward, clerk. Marriage ceremony performed May 17, 1838, by Jason M. Jones, J.P.

[2]..Franklin Co, MS, <u>Deed Book C</u>, page 476. George H. Varner purchased the SE 1/4 of S 28, T 6, R 5, containing 160 acres, from John Furniss and wife. Nov. 3, 1838.

[3]..Franklin Co, MS, <u>Deed Book C</u>, page 472. George H. Varner mortgaged land and slaves to John Furniss. Nov. 21, 1838.

[4]..The slaves were a male 10 through 24 years of age, a male from 26 through 45 years of age, and a female 10 through 24 years of age.

George H. Varner, Son of John Varner

their farm, in 1842,[5] and mortgaged a slave--a teenage male named **London**--two times, in 1842[1] and 1844.[2]

---

[1]..Franklin Co, MS, <u>Deed Book D</u>, page 14. Conveyance between George H. Varner and Amelia, his wife of Franklin County, State of Mississippi, and George Adams of the same county and state. For $200, George H. Varner and his wife sold to George Adams a parcel of land and the appurtenances thereto. SE quarter of section 28, township 6, range 5, containing 160 acres. Signed by George H. Varner, his seal, and Amelia Varner, her mark. Witnesses: S. J. McGee, James L. Wolling. Signed July 30, 1842.

[2]..Franklin Co, MS, <u>Deed Book D</u>, page 43. This indenture made the 28th day of December, 1842, between George H. Varner of the County of Franklin and State of Mississippi and Archibald Buis of the same state and county.

Varner was indebted that day for $300 to Buis. To secure the loan Varner mortgaged a Negro boy named London aged about 14 years. If Varner repaid the $300 to Buis anytime within four years from the date of the agreement, Buis agreed to return the said Negro to George H. Varner. Should Varner fail to repay to Buis the $300, Buis may sell the Negro to the highest bidder at the front door of the courthouse of said county and take the money from the proceeds. Buis was to have possession and use of the labor of said Negro until the loan was repaid.

Signed George H. Varner.

[3]..Franklin Co, MS, <u>Deed Book D</u>, page 145. This indenture made July 10, 1844, between George H. Varner of the County of Franklin and State of Mississippi and Archibald Smith of the same county and state. George H. Varner is indebted to Archibald Smith to the sum of $300 for cash advanced to him by Archibald Smith to pay a judgement in Circuit Court of Franklin County against the said George H. Varner in favor of

(continued...)

Varner Families of the South--X

Why did this young Varner family face a financial setback in its early years? The evidence is inconclusive. However, it appears that a court judgement against George H. Varner in favor of William G. Varner was at least partially responsible for it. When George H. Varner mortgaged his slave, London, in 1844, he said the reason he needed the money was to pay what he owed to William G. Varner as a result of a Franklin County, MS, Circuit Court judgement against him in favor of William G. Varner.[1]

William G. Varner was George H. Varner's first cousin and also his brother-in-law. (William G. Varner married George H. Varner's sister Susan Eliza Varner in Lowndes Co, AL, in 1838, the same year that George married Amelia Gregg in Franklin Co, MS.) No record was located to indicate why William G. had sued George H. Also, there is no known record to prove that William G. Varner ever resided in Franklin Co, MS. Perhaps the lawsuit was based on something that George H. Varner did or did not do in Alabama before he moved to Mississippi.

This law suit took place at about the same time that several Varner families of Lowndes County, AL, dispersed

---

[3](...continued)
William G. Varner. To secure the loan George H. Varner mortgages a Negro named London aged about 16 years. Should Varner not repay the loan without interest by Jan. 1, 1847, Smith may sell said property and take $300 from the proceeds thereof. Smith is to have possession of the said Negro and receive the services of his labor until the loan is repaid. Should the said Negro die prior to repayment of the loan the loss is to be sustained by Varner.   Signed by George H. Varner.

[1]..Franklin Co, MS, Deed Book D, op. cit., page 145.

George H. Varner, Son of John Varner

to other locations. John Varner, the father of George H. Varner and Susan Eliza Varner, and several of his children moved to Coosa County, AL. Frederick Varner, John Varner's brother and William G. Varner's father, and all of his children except William G. Varner moved to Caldwell Parish, LA.

It would be presumptuous to conclude that the law suit that William G. Varner brought against his cousin and brother-in-law George H. Varner was responsible for John Varner's move to Coosa County, AL, and\or Frederick Varner's move to Caldwell Parish, LA. There is not enough evidence to prove or even necessarily to suggest it. But it seems to reveal a serious family dispute and could have been a contributing factor.

George H. Varner Loses Wife and Daughter

George H. Varner and Amelia Greggs were parents of one child: **Mary Ann Greggs**. She was born 4 Mar 1839; she died 6 Sep 1842 at the age of three years, six months, and 2 days. Amelia died a few years later: 12 Mar 1849, in Franklin Co, MS.[1]

In the 1850 census, George H. Varner was enumerated with Sutton Byrd, who owned 36 slaves, and Ira Byrd, who owned 11 slaves. George H. Varner was not shown as owning slaves. He may have been working as an overseer on the Byrd plantation.[2] George H. Varner

---

[1]..These vital statistics taken from the George H. Varner Bible record, op. cit.

[2]..<u>1850 Federal Census, Franklin County, Mississippi</u>
    Dwelling # 185.
Ira E. Byrd, 34, male, farmer, born in Mississippi.

(continued...)

VARNER FAMILIES OF THE SOUTH--X

purchased farm land from Sutton Byrd in Oct 1850[1]. He sold that land in 1853[2].

---

[2](...continued)
George H. Varner, 35, male, farmer, born in Georgia.
Sutton Byrd, 48, male, born in South Carolina.
1850 Slave Schedule for Franklin County, Mississippi
Sutton Byrd--36 slaves.
Ira E. Byrd--11 slaves.
George H. Varner not listed as owning slaves.

[1]..Franklin County, MS, Deed Book D, page 438. This indenture made the 4th day of October, 1850, between Sutton Byrd and Rebecca Byrd, his wife, and George H. Varner. For the sum of $800, Sutton Byrd and Rebecca his wife sells to George H. Varner a parcel of land lying on Magen Creek and Horse Creek near their junction in the County of Franklin and the State of Mississippi. The East half of the SE 1/4 of section 32 and the SE quarter of section 29 and the west half of the SW 1/4 of section 28 and the east half of the SW 1/4 of Section 28 containing in all about 480 acres lying in township 6, range 5.

Signed by Sutton Byrd, his seal, and Rebecca Byrd, her mark.

Witnesses: James M. Jones and Edward Byrd.

[2]..Franklin Co, MS, Deed Book D, page 591. This indenture made the 12th day of February, 1853, between George H. Varner of the County of Franklin and State of Mississippi, and John F. Lee, of the same county and state.

For the consideration of the sum of $1,333 paid to Varner by Lee, Varner sells to Lee a parcel of land on Magen Creek and Horse Creek in Franklin County, MS, the East 1/2 of the SE 1/4 of Section 32, the SE 1/4 of Section 29, and the SW 1/4 of Section 28, all in township 6, range 5 East containing in the aggregate 480 acres, being the same land that was conveyed by Sutton Byrd and Rebecca his wife to George H. Varner by deed
(continued...)

George H. Varner Moves to Louisiana.

George H. Varner moved to Richland Parish, LA, sometime between 1853, when he sold his land in Franklin Co, MS, and 1857, when he married Melissa Melvina Iler (b. 1 Dec 1839, d. 22 Dec 1866) in Franklin Parish, LA, 28 Jan 1857.[1] George H. Varner bought land in Franklin Parish (later Richland), LA, in 1860 and 1861.[2]

Hardaway Varner, a younger brother of George H. Varner, lived near George in Louisiana for a few years in the 1860's.[3]

Apparently, George H. Varner never served in the armed forces for either the United States or the Confederate States. No military service record for him could be located. He was in his early thirties during the Mexican War. But there was no draft for that war and relatively few volunteers were needed. He was in his upper forties during the Civil War. The Confederate States drafted many men in that age range, especially in the latter years of the war. However, by that time the Union

---

[2](...continued)
dated Oct. 4, 1850. Signed by George H. Varner, his seal.

[1]..George H. Varner Bible record, op. cit.

[2]..Franklin Parish, LA, <u>Deed Book E</u>, page 604. George H. Varner bought land from Samuel Tillman in 1860. Page 740. George H. Varner bought land from Nancy Smith in 1861.

[3]..<u>Franklin Parish, LA, Land Records.</u>
Hardaway Varner of Franklin Parish, LA, bought 40 acres of land for $400. Oct. 17, 1861. <u>Deed Book C</u>, page 402.
George H. Varner bought 40 acres of land from Hardaway Varner for $300. June 15, 1871. <u>Deed Book C</u>, page 403.

Army had gained control of the Mississippi River and the Confederate government was unable to exercise effective control in many localities in the Western portion of the Confederate States. This may explain why George H. Varner[1] did not serve in the Confederate Army.

Descendants of George H. Varner

George H. Varner and Melissa Iler were parents of five children: **Mary Ann, Winford Annie, Josephine H., John Hardaway, and George Washington.**[2]

A. **Mary Ann Varner**, daughter of George H. Varner and Melissa Iler, (b. 5 Jun 1858, d. 1 Sep 1859).

B. **Winford "Annis" Varner,** daughter of George H. Varner and Melissa Iler, (b. 14 Apr 1860 Franklin Par, LA, d. 5 Feb 1928; bur Oakwood Cem, Waco, TX) marr 1st at Alto, Richland Par, LA, 30 Jan 1878 to **Benjamin Franklin "B.F." Newbery,** son of **William Newbery and Annie Beard,** (b. 22 Mar 1856 AL, d. 1 Apr 1915).

Annis and B.F. Newbery were parents of eight children: **Daisy Lillian, Annie Josephine, Mamie Elizabeth, Annie Varner, Benjamin Ryan, Clarence Franklin, Mildred F. and Lucile.**

---

[1]..The author is not positive that George H. Varner did not serve in the Confederate Army because he did not check for records at the Louisiana State Archives. However, no record could be found on microfilmed records at the LDS Family History Library in Salt Lake City, UT.

[2]..Information on George H. Varner's children and other descendants was submitted by Margaret Varner Barton, Santa Anna, TX.

George H. Varner, Son of John Varner

1. **Daisy Lillian Newbery** (b. 13 Dec 1880 near Alto, Richland Par, LA, bur Terrell, TX) marr at Waco, TX, 24 Dec 1905 to **R.B. Adams**. Daisy and R. B. were parents of two children: **Gladys Winford and John Quincy**.
    a. **Gladys Winford Adams** (b. 21 Sept 1906, d. 10 Jan 1978; bur Crown Hill Cem, Dallas, TX). No children.
    b. **John Quincy Adams** (b. 30 May 1908) marr to **Aida Lee**. John and Aida had one child: **J.B. Adams**.
2. **Annie Josephine Newbery** (b. 18 July 1884 in Alto, Richland Par, LA, d. 20 Aug 1886, bur Little Church Cem, Alto, LA).
3. **Mamie Elizabeth Newbery** (b. 22 July 1887 near Alto, Richland Par, LA, d. 17 Sep 1888, bur Little Church Cem, Alto, LA).
4. **Annie Varner Newbery** (b. 15 July 1889 near Alto, Richland Par, LA, d. 12 Jan 1973, Waco, TX; bur Oakwood Cem, Waco, TX) marr at Waco, TX on 16 Aug 1908 to **G.A. McCade** (d. 5 July 1969).
5. **Benjamin Ryan Newbery** (b. 10 Feb 1892 near Alto, Richland Par, LA, d. 6 Oct 1978; bur at Grove Hill Cem, Dallas, TX) marr at Ft. Worth, TX on 30 Sept 1916 to **Mary Louise Haden**. No children.
6. **Clarence Franklin Newbery** (b. 19 Dec 1894 near Alto, Richland Par, LA; bur Little Rock, AR) marr at Hot Springs, AR on 3 Dec 1916 to **Nellie Harrell**. Clarence and Nellie were parents of one child: **Frank**.
    a. **Frank Newbery** (born Little Rock, ARK) marr to **Hiawatha** _____. Frank and

Hiawatha were parents of two children: **Jane and Jim**.

7. **Lucile Rebecca Newbery** (b. 9 June 1897 near Alto, LA, d. 24 Dec 1988; bur Oakwood Cem, Waco, TX) marr at Waco, TX on 20 Sept 1915 to **B.S. Sonntag**. Lucile and B. S. were parents of two children: **Bernice Winfred and Robert Bernhard**.
   a. **Bernice Winford Sonntag** (b. 3 Jul 1916 Waco, TX) marr to **Herbert E. Webb**. Bernice and Herbert were parents of one child: **Patricia Ann** (b. 26 Jan 1945).
   b. **Robert Bernhard Sonntag** (b. 21 Aug 1921 Waco, TX, d. May, 1979, bur Grove Hill Cem, Dallas, TX). No children.
8. **Mildred F. Newbery** (b. 16 July 1900 near Alto, Richland Par, LA, d. 24 Jan 1990; bur Oakwood Cem, Waco, McLennan Co, TX) marr at Waco, TX on 27 Sep 1919 to **Marion Jack Henson, Sr.** (b. 25 Apr 1894, d. 7 Nov 1978; bur Oakwood Cem, Waco, TX). Mildred and Marion were parents of one child: **Marion Jack Henson, Jr.**
   a. **Marion Jack "M. Jack" Henson, Jr.** (b. 21 Jan 1926 Waco, TX) marr at Waco, TX on 18 Jul 1952 to **Nancy D. Tripp**, dau of **Dr. Frank Tripp and Elvira Whittaker**, (b. 29 May 1929, St. Joseph, MO). Jack is owner of Henson's, Inc. a business supply center. He and Nancy reside at Valley Mills, TX. Jack and Nancy had two children: **Marion Jack Henson, III, and Jeffery David**.
      (1) **Marion Jack Henson, III**. (b. 14 Dec 1954 Waco, TX) marr on 9 Jun 1979 to **Michelle Roach**. They had two

George H. Varner, Son of John Varner

daughters: **Amy Suzanne** (b. 21 July 1981) and **Deena Ann** (b. 26 Oct 1985).
(2) **Jeffery David Henson** (b. 5 Oct 1956 Waco, TX) marr on 10 Mar 1990 to **Sharon Decker**. They had one child: **Gregory David Henson** (b. 11 Oct 1982).

C. **Josephine H. "Josie" Varner**, daughter of George H. Varner and Melissa Iler, (b. 25 Dec 1861) marr to _____ **Cook**. They had one known child: **George**.

D. **John Hardaway Varner**, son of George H. Varner and Melissa Iler, (b. 3 Nov 1863, d. 4 Nov 1863).

E. **George Washington Varner**, son of George H. Varner and Melissa Iler, (b. 16 May 1866, Ft. Worth, TX, d. 24 Apr 1923, Elm Mott, McLennan Co, TX; bur White Rock, TX) marr at Delhi, Richland Par, LA on 18 Dec 1888 to **Sarah Janette "Nettie" Dean**, dau of **Benjamin Henley and Margaret Dean**, (b. 4 Mar 1869 Delhi, Richland Par, LA, d. 14 Dec 1937 Waco, McLennan Co, TX).

George and Sarah had four children: **Benjamin Henley, George Washington, Ernest Millar and William Ashby**.

1. **Benjamin "Ben" Henley Varner** (b. 20 Oct 1889, d. 30 Mar 1978 Waco, McLennan Co, TX) marr 1st to **Callie Abernathy** (b. 2 Oct 1894 Waco, McLennan Co, TX, d. 1942?). No children.
1. **Benjamin Henley Varner** marr 2nd **Daisy** _____ (b. 7 Sept 1922, d. 25 Jan 1961).
2. **George Washington Varner** (b. 9 Dec 1893 Alto, LA, d. 9 Oct 1957 Waco, TX, bur White Rock Cem, Ross, TX) marr on 28 Oct 1916 to **Mrs. Jewel Pauline (Matthews) Abernathy**, dau of

Andrew Jackson Mathews and Ella Smith, (b. 19 Feb 1890 England, AR, d. 5 Nov 1959 Waco, TX; bur White Rock Cem, Ross, TX).

George and Jewel had five children: **Nettie Pearl, Earl Emmett, Albert Ashby, George Washington and Janette Ruth.**

- a. **Nettie Pearl Varner** (b. and d. 24 May 1918 Waco, TX).
- b. **Earl Emmett Varner** (b. 20 Sep 1920 Elm Mott, TX) marr at Marlin, TX on 4 Nov 1944 to **Mary Christine Wilson,** dau of **John Roy Wilson and Alice Dorothy Busch,** (b. 29 Jan 1925 Waco, TX). This marriage ended in divorce, in 1980. Earl lives in Grand Prairie, TX.

  Earl and Mary had four children: **Mickey Jeanette, George Roy, Mark Wilson and Rebecca.**
  - (1) **Mickey Jeanette Varner** (b. 8 Jan 1946 Waco, TX) marr on 20 Jun 1969 to **Norman E. Davis.**
  - (2) **George Roy Varner** (b. 9 Oct 1947 Waco, TX) marr in July, 1973 to **Valerie Siler.**
  - (3) **Mark Wilson Varner** (b. 24 Apr 1956 Waco, TX).
  - (4) **Rebecca Varner** (b. 1 Jun 1957 Waco, TX).
- c. **Albert Ashby Varner** (b. 22 Nov 1922 Waco, TX) marr at Waco, TX on 7 Nov 1942 to **Evelyn Mercede Wallis,** dau of **Lamar C. Wallis and Mary Ellen Shuemate,** (b. 10 Nov 1928 Temple, TX). They live in Waco, TX. They had three children: **Lana Jo, Linda Sue and Deborah Lorraine.**

George H. Varner, Son of John Varner

(1) **Lana Jo Varner** (b. 16 Sept 1943 Waco, TX) marr in Dec, 1961 to **Donald L. Braun**.
(2) **Linda Sue Varner** (b. 16 Feb 1950 Waco, TX) marr on 10 Jun 1967 to **Gary Wicks**.
(3) **Deborah Lorraine Varner** (b. 24 Sep 1954 Waco, TX) marr at Tulsa, OK in March, 1976 to Patrick LaPrade.

d. **George Washington Varner** (b. 27 May 1925 Waco, McLennon Co, TX) marr in Waco, Falls Co, TX on 7 May 1947 to **Evelyn Margaret Upmore,** dau of **Thomas George Upmore and Caroline Magdalene Schutz** (b. 4 Jan 1930 Tours, McLennan Co, TX).

They live in Waco, TX. They had three children: **Gregory Wayne, Nancy Lea and Kathy Lynn.**

(1) **Gregory Wayne Varner** (b. 18 Apr 1948 Waco, TX) marr on 22 Mar 1976 to **Marilyn Lockridge Haley.** They live in Arlington, TX. They had four children: **Brandy Charmaine Varner** (b. 25 Dec 1975), **Bridget Margaret Varner** (b. 11 Mar 1977), **Benjamin Wayne Varner** (b. 19 Aug 1978), **and Brian Gregory Varner** (b. 26 Mar 1980).
(2) **Nancy Lea Varner** (b. 18 May 1951 Waco, TX) marr on 13 Aug 1971 to **Gary Stevens Eubanks**, son of **Jim Eubanks and Annette Richardson.** They live in Ocoee, FL. They had two children: **Kimberly Machael Eubanks** (b. 19 Dec 1974) **and Brian Jay Eubanks** (b. 15 Aug 1981).

(3) **Kathy Lynn Varner** (b. 8 Sep 1953 Waco, TX) marr 1st on 13 Jan 1973 to **Donnie Ebert Thornberry.** They had two children: **Jennifer Lynn Thornberry** (b. 15 Jun 1974) and **Kallie Doniel Thornberry** (b. 9 Dec 1978).
 (3) **Kathy (Varner) Thornberry** marr 2nd on 31 May 1986 to **Louis de Launey.** They live in Grapevine, TX.
 e. Janette "Ruth" Varner (b. 11 Apr 1929 Waco, TX) marr on 2 Apr 1943 to **Henry Carl McKinney,** son of **Jeff Garrett McKinney and Bessie E. Goodwin,** (b. 28 Apr 1923 Riesel, TX). They live in Waco, TX.

 They had five children: **Henry Wayne, Terry Paul, Steven Charles, James Glenn and Timothy Carl.**
 (1) **Henry Wayne McKinney** (b. 26 July 1944 Waco, TX) marr on 15 Mar 1975 to **Linda E. Northcutt.**
 (2) **Terry Paul McKinney** (b. 13 Jun 1947 Waco, TX) marr on 14 Sept 1974 to **Linda Birchfield.**
 (3) **Steven Charles McKinney** (b. 11 Oct 1949 Waco, TX) marr on 5 Dec 1970 to **Debra Sowders.**
 (4) **James Glenn McKinney** (b. and d. 31 Oct 1951 Waco, TX).
 (5) **Timothy Carl McKinney** (b. 6 Feb 1953 Waco, TX) marr on 7 Jan 1972 to **Marilyn Litton.**
3. Ernest Millar "E.M." Varner, Sr. (b. 2 Aug 1896, d. 13 Sep 1956) marr in Axtell, TX on 4 Mar 1913 to **Myrtle Rogers,** dau of **James Lafayette Rogers**

George H. Varner, Son of John Varner

and **Addie Eudorah Suggs** (b. 27 Nov 1893, d. 10 Sep 1984 Waco, TX).

They had four children: **Ernest Millar, Jr., Rachel Velma, Lois Mae and James Calvin**.

a. **Ernest Millar Varner, Jr.** (b. 20 May 1915) marr to **Mareta Haley** of Roby, TX. This couple lives in Oakdale, CA.

b. **Rachel Velma Varner** (b. 12 May 1920) marr to **Frederick "Fred" William Doye,** son of **Virgil Erastos Langston and Emma Mader Kittlitz,** (b. 28 Oct 1914 Waco, TX). They live in Waco, TX. Rachel and Fred had two children: **Fred Theodore and Larry William**.

  (1) **Fred Theodore Doye** (b. 11 May 1945 Waco, TX) marr 10 Jun 1985 **to Mrs. Velda W. Heath**.

  (2) **Larry William Doye** (b. 25 May 1952 Waco, TX, d. 2 Nov 1986 Temple, TX) marr 1st on 27 Nov 1970 to **Renee Gibson**.

  (2) **Larry William Doye** marr 2nd on 14 Apr 1973 to **Jan Mascarella**.

  (2) **Larry William Doye** marr 3rd on 15 Nov 1980 to **Debbie Urban**.

c. **Lois Mae Varner** (b. 11 Jan 1923) marr to **James William Heddleston** of St. Mary's, WV. They live in San Antonio, TX.

d. **James Calvin Varner** (b. 15 Oct 1924) marr 1st to **Mabel Inez Hughes** (deceased) of Mexia, TX.

d. **James Calvin Varner** marr 2nd to **Rose**. They live in Thornton, TX.

4. **William "Ashby" Varner** (b. 27 Jan 1899 Alto, Richland Par, LA, d.16 Oct 1962, Elm Mott, TX, bur White Rock Cem, Ross, McLennan Co, TX)

marr at Waco, McLennan Co, TX on 13 Jun 1921 to **Velma Pearl Beheler,** dau of **Joseph Morris Beheler and Mary Susan Marchbanks,** (b. 10 Apr 1903 McLennan Co, TX, d. 26 July 1983 Waco, McLennan Co, TX).

Ashby and Velma had three children: **Ben Henley, Evelyn Olene and Margaret Doris.**

a. **Ben Henley Varner** (b. 16 Apr 1922 Elm Mott, TX) marr 1st on 7 Oct 1944 to **Margaret Jane Ross** (b. 21 July 1922 Hebron, IL, d. 18 May 1989 Waco, TX). No children.

a. **Ben Henley Varner** marr 2nd on 15 Jun 1991 to **Mrs. Fay "Lorraine" Kuehl Howard** (b. 9 Mar 1927 Axtell, TX). They live in Waco, TX.

b. **Evelyn "Olene" Varner** (b. 18 Jan 1924 Elm Mott, TX) marr 1st to **Edwin Drewie Reed** at Waco, McLennan, TX, in 1942. This marriage ended in divorce in San Antonio, Bexar Co, TX, in 1967.

Olene and Drewie had three children: **LaQuita Dawn, Edwin Kent and Jerry Allen.**

(1) **La Quita Dawn Reed** (b. 2 Sep 1943) marr on 16 Feb 1973 to **Wayne D. "Lefty" Kalisky.** They live in San Antonio, TX. LaQuita and Wayne had two daughters: **Kristy K. Kalisky** (b. 22 July 1976) and **Ashley Dawn Kalisky** (b. 18 Jun 1978).

(2) **Edwin Kent Reed** (b. 22 Jun 1947) marr at San Antonio, TX on 24 Apr 1976 to **Myrna Jo Holland,** dau of **Floyd Franklin Holland and Hazel Velma Samples,** (b. 24 Nov 1954 San Antonio,

George H. Varner, Son of John Varner

Bexar Co, TX). They live in San Antonio, TX.

Edwin and Myrna Jo have one child: **Melissa Deane Reed** (b. 3 Sept 1983).

(3) **Jerry Allen Reed** (b. 9 Oct 1952) marr to **Kathy Lynn Kennedy** at Austin, Travis Co, TX. This marriage ended in divorce in 1990. Jerry lives in Dallas, TX.

b. Mrs. **Olene (Varner) Reed** marr 2nd on 6 July 1972 to **Edward Lee Horn,** son of **Henry Herman "Harry" Horn and Frances Marie Camp,** (b. 25 July 1912 San Antonio, Bexar Co, TX). Olene and Ed live in New Braunfels, TX.

c. **Margaret Doris Varner** (b. 21 Sep 1925 Waco, McLennan Co, TX) marr 1st at Stuttgart, AR on 31 July 1943 to **Carl Haskell Bilbrey** (b. 13 Jan 1923, Holdenville, OK, d. 2 Nov 1990 at Mansfield, Tarrant Co, TX, bur Big Valley Cem, Mills Co, TX). This marriage ended in divorce in 1968.

Margaret and Carl had four children: **Mary Kathleen, Karl Dwayne, Keith Wayne and Ben Kendall.** Karl and Keith are twins.

(1) **Mary Kathleen Bilbrey** (b. 12 Nov 1945, Waco, McLennan Co, TX). Kathy lives in Mills Co, TX.

(2) **Karl Dwayne Bilbrey** (b. 4 Dec 1947, Levelland, Hockley Co, TX) marr 1st at Andrews, TX, 1969 to **Wanda Joy Gross** (b. 23 Jan 1948, Brownfield, Terry Co, TX), dau of **William "Bill" J. Gross and Billie Eugene Bean** (b. 19 Jul 1927). This marriage ended in divorce in 1972.

Karl and Wanda are parents of two children: **Todd Dwayne and Kari Diana.**
- (a) **Todd Dwayne Bilbrey** (b. 7 Oct 1969, Fort Hood, TX) marr 12 Oct 1991, Fort Worth, Tarrant Co, TX, **Keri Desnetta Smith**. Todd and Keri are parents of one child: **Taylre Alexis Bilbrey** (b. 10 Jul 1992, Fort Worth, Tarrant Co, TX).
- (b) **Kari Diana Bilbrey** (b. 4 Nov 1971, Fort Worth, Tarrant Co, TX).

(2) **Karl Dwayne Bilbrey** marr 2nd, 1973, **Terry Smith Rogers** (b. 5 Aug 1953). No children.

(3) **Keith Wayne Bilbrey** (b. 4 Dec 1947 Levelland, Hockley Co, TX) marr 1st at Quincy, MA, on 2 Dec 1967 to **Maureen Ann Ciardi,** dau of **Edward F. Ciardi and Helen C. Lyons,** (b. 28 Jun 1949 Boston, MA). They live in Waco, TX. They had three children: **Keith Wayne, Jr., Christopher Michael, and Kelley Diana.**
- (a) **Keith Wayne Bilbrey, Jr.** (b. 1 Nov 1968 Quincy, MA) marr on 29 Feb 1992 to **Rebecca Miller.**
- (b) **Christopher Michael Bilbrey** (b. 13 July 1971 Ft. Worth, Tarrant Co, TX) marr on 9 Jun 1990, Hewitt, McLennan Co, TX, to **Kimberley Galloway.** They have one child: **Morgan Taylor Bilbrey** (b. 6 Nov 1992, Waco, McLennan, TX).
- (c) **Kelley D. Bilbrey** (b. 8 Jun 1982 Ft. Worth, TX).

George H. Varner, Son of John Varner

    (4) **Ben Kendall Bilbrey** (b. 13 Apr 1954 Lubbock, TX) marr 1st at Andrews, TX, to **Melody Deland Deaver**. No children. This marriage ended in divorce.

    (4) **Ben Kendall Bilbrey** marr 2nd at Conway, AR, 19 Dec 1981 to **RoDene Ballard,** dau of **Raymond Ballard and Orvella Kay Taylor,** (b. 9 Jan 1965 Neosho, MO). This family lives in Branson, MO.

    Ben and Ro have two children: **Elizabeth Kathleen Bilbrey** (b. 12 Oct 1985 at Odessa, Ector Co, TX) and **Bryce Kendall Bilbrey** (b. 2 May 1991 Odessa, Ector Co, TX).

  c. **Mrs. Margaret Doris (Varner) Bilbrey** marr 2nd at Gretna, Jefferson Par, LA on 23 Jun 1972 to **Billy Joe Bruce** (of Russellville, AR). This marriage ended in divorce in 1978.

  c. **Mrs. Margaret Doris (Varner) Bruce** marr 3rd at Midland, TX on 9 Jun 1984 to **Warren D. Barton** (b. 28 Sept 1918 Freeport, Brazoria Co, TX).

    This couple has lived in Santa Anna, TX, since 1985. They raise emus.

George H. Varner, son of John Varner and Nancy Powell, marr 3rd at Mobile, AL on 24 Oct 1869 to **Virginia Richardson Price,** (b. 5 Jan 1842, d. 28 Aug 1872). They had one child: **John Trice**.

  A. **John Trice Varner,** child of **George H. Varner and Virginia Richardson Price,** (b. 25 Aug 1872, d. 22 Oct 1872).

Chapter XI
John W. Varner, Son of John Varner

John W. Varner was a son of **John Varner and Nancy Powell**. He was born in 1827 in Montgomery Co (later Lowndes), AL, and died between 1867 and 1869[1]. He married **Elizabeth Wilson** in Coosa Co, AL on 22 Sep 1852.

The earliest record located for John W. Varner was the 1850 census. At that time, he was living with his brother Azariah Varner in Lowndes County, AL. He was listed as John Varner, Jr., and was 23 years old. Undoubtedly, he was helping Azariah manage the plantation. Azariah was living in his father's former home located just outside of Hayneville. Azariah was having serious health problems (perhaps alcoholism) and was experiencing severe financial difficulties.[2]

By 1852, John W. Varner had moved to Coosa County, where he married Elizabeth Wilson[3]. The wedding ceremony was performed by Elias Kelly, Justice of the Peace, on 23 Sep 1852. Elizabeth was a daughter of William A. Wilson.

---

[1]--John W. Varner's name was on a list of voters for the Hatchett Creek Precinct, Coosa Co, AL, in 1867. (His name was adjacent to those of his brothers Edward P. Varner and Esselman Varner.) John W. Varner was deceased at the time his father John Varner wrote his will in 1869.

[2]--See Chapter VIII.

[3]..Elizabeth Wilson was a sister of Sarah Wilson, who married John W. Varner's brother Esselman Varner in 1858, and John A. Wilson, who married John W. Varner's sister Lucy A. Varner in 1861.

JOHN W. VARNER, SON OF JOHN VARNER

In 1859, the Coosa County Board of Commissioners appointed John W. Varner overseer for road maintenance on the River Road from Bee Branch to House's Ferry. House's Ferry was probably on the nearby Coosa River. At the same meeting the Commission appointed John W.'s brother Edward P. Varner overseer on the River Road from the 23 Mile Post to Bee Branch.[1]

Based on 1860 census reports, John W. Varner, who was then 33 years old, had made a strong start toward becoming a prosperous planter. He owned seven slaves[2] and 120 acres of land.[3] His real estate was worth $1600 and his personal estate was worth $7,000.[4] Most of the personal estate value was in slaves. He also owned livestock and farm equipment and his plantation produced a variety of products.[5]

---

[1]..Coosa County, AL, <u>Commissioners Minutes</u>, Book 8, page 212. "Ordered by the Court that John W. Varner be and he is hereby appointed overseer on the River Road from Bee Branch to House's Ferry in place of John H. Lewis who is overage." Spring term, May 9, 1859.

[2]--<u>1860 Slave Schedule</u> for Coosa County, AL.
Varner, John--7 slaves--2 slave houses. Ages of three male slaves: 60, 4, and 3. Ages of four female slaves: 26, 17, 6, and 3/12.

[3]--<u>1860 Agricultural Census</u>, Coosa County.

[4]--<u>1860 Population Census</u> for Coosa Co, AL.

[5]--<u>1860 Agricultural Census</u> for Coosa Co, AL.
John Varner, Jr.
50 acres improved land, 70 acres unimproved land.
Cash value of farm: $1500.

(continued...)

John W. Varner Fights in Civil War

John W. Varner fought in the Civil War as a Pvt, Co K, 59th AL Infantry and in Co B, 2nd Battalion, Hilliard's Legion (Alabama Volunteers). He enlisted 5 May 1862, at Wetumpka[1], Coosa Co, AL, at the age of 37. He was 5' 6" tall, had dark hair, light complexion, and dark eyes. He was with the Confederate Army in Virginia from 1862 until the end of the war. He signed a pledge not to fight the United States again 18 May 1865 in Montgomery, AL. Elizabeth, John W. Varner's widow, applied for a Confederate service pension several times from 1886-1898. She reported that her property consisted of nothing and that her disability consisted of severe headache, rheumatism, and old age.[2]

The Coosa County tax collector granted John W. Varner a tax credit of $1.00 in 1862 because he was a soldier in the Civil War.[3]

---

[5](...continued)
Value of farm equipment and tools: $100.

Livestock owned at time of census: 1 horse, 1 mule or ass, 2 milch cows, 2 working oxen, 2 other cattle, 25 swine.

Value of livestock owned: $550.

Crop production past twelve months: 10 bushels of wheat, 150 bushels of Indian corn, 9 bales of ginned cotton, 5 bushels of peas and beans, 5 bushels of Irish potatoes.

Value of manufactured goods made in the home: $5.

[1]..Wetumpka is now in Elmore County, AL.

[2]--From the Federal Government's Alabama Confederate Soldier's Records on microfilm at the AL Archives in Montgomery.

[3]--Coosa County, AL, <u>Minutes Commissioners Court</u>, Vol.

(continued...)

JOHN W. VARNER, SON OF JOHN VARNER

John W. Varner was a voter in Coosa County, AL, in 1867. His name was entered on the list of eligible voters adjacent to the names of his brothers Edward P. Varner and Esselman Varner.[1] John W. Varner, farmer from Travelers Rest, was chosen to serve on the Petit Jury for Circuit Court for the fall term of 1867. The sheriff reported that he did not execute the order on Varner but he did not give the reason and John W. did not report for duty.[2]

John W. Varner died between 1867 and 1869. His father John Varner mentioned in his will, which was written in Oct 1869, that his son John W. Varner was deceased. John W. Varner left no will and no estate record was located. His widow Elizabeth and her children were listed in the 1870 census as comprising one household.

John W. Varner and Elizabeth Wilson were parents of four children: **Cicero, Sallie, Lucien A., and William**.

Descendants of Cicero Varner

A. **Cicero Varner**, son of John W. Varner and Elizabeth Wilson, (b. 8 Sep 1853, Coosa Co, AL, d. 17 Feb 1933, Coosa Co, AL) marr 17 Jan 1881, Coosa Co, AL, **Nancy E. Cranford** (b. 3 May 1861, d. 12 May 1928, Coosa Co, AL).[3]

---

[3](...continued)
8, page 401.

[1]--<u>1867 Voters of Coosa County, AL.</u>

[2]--Coosa County, AL, <u>Judgment Document</u>, Book I, page 570. Fall 1867.

[3]..Cicero Varner's and Nancy Cranford Varner's birth and
(continued...)

Cicero Varner and Nancy Cranford were parents of eleven children. The first nine were daughters; the latter two were sons. Names of the children: **Alice E. Varner, Lanetta Varner, Daisy A. Varner, Mattie Savina Varner, Ella Varner, Susan F. Varner, Martina Varner, Sally A. Varner, Viola Varner, Willie H. Varner, and Fonza L. Varner.**

1. **Alice E. Varner** (b. 1882, Coosa Co, AL).
2. **Lanetta Varner** (b. 1884, Coosa Co, AL).
3. **Daisy A. Varner** (b. 15 Mar 1886, Coosa Co, AL, d. 21 Jul 1911, Coosa Co, AL[1]).
4. **Mattie Savina Varner**[2] (b. 27 Aug 1888, Coosa Co, AL, d. 5 Aug 1958, buried in Old Weogufka Cem, Coosa Co, AL) marr 1 Jan 1905, Rockford, Coosa Co, AL, **Walter B. Fowler, Sr.** (b. 4 Jul 1884, Chilton Co, AL, d. 8 May 1969, Sylacauga, AL, buried in Old Weogufka Cem, Coosa Co, AL), son of George C. Fowler and Mallie Hughes Fowler. Walter was a farmer and Mattie was a housewife.

Mattie and Walter were parents of ten children: **Annie Belle Fowler, Daisy Ressie Fowler, Cora Lee Fowler, Lille Marie Fowler, Victor Dawson Fowler, Nancy Lucille Fowler,**

---

[3](...continued) death dates appear on grave markers at the Mt. Moriah Cemetery, Coosa Co, AL.

[1]--Daisy Varner's birth and death dates appear on a grave marker in Mt. Moriah Church Cemetery, Coosa Co, AL.

[2]--Information on Mattie Savina Varner, her family, and descendants was submitted by Lillie Marie Littleton of Sylacauga, AL.

Hiram Keener Fowler, Joseph Willis Fowler, Walter B. Fowler, Jr., and Ava Dean Fowler.

a. **Annie Belle Fowler** (b. 27 Jun 1908, Weogufka, Coosa Co, AL, d. 12 May 1969, Sylacauga, Talledega Co, AL) marr 28 Jul 1928, Coosa Co, AL, **Jim Wes Blankenship.** Annie was a housewife.

Annie and Jim had one child: **James Paul Edward Blankenship.**

b. **Daisy Ressie Fowler** (b. 9 Jan 1911, Weogufka, Coosa Co, AL) marr 15 Dec 1934, Coosa Co, AL, **James Edward Gardner.** Daisy is a housewife. A widow, she lives in Sylacauga, AL, in 1993.

Daisy and James had four children: **Robert Lee Gardner, Betty Lois Gardner, Roland Victor Gardner, and Judy Wynell Gardner.**

c. **Cora Lee Fowler** (b. 22 Jan 1913, Weogufka, Coosa Co, AL, d. 3 Nov 1991, Sylacauga, AL) marr 12 Aug 1938, Sylacauga, Talledega Co, AL, **Robert Otis Brand.** Cora Lee was a housewife.

Cora and Robert had two children: **Dale Huston Brand and Carolyn Ann Brand.**

d. **Lillie Marie Fowler** (b. 2 Nov 1915, Weogufka, Coosa Co, AL) marr 25 Feb 1939, Weogufka, Coosa Co, AL, **Melvin Philmore Littleton.** Lillie was a nurse's aid, now retired. She lives in Sylacauga, AL, in 1993.

Lillie and Melvin were parents of two children: **Melvin Maynard Littleton and Helen Inez Littleton.**

e. **Victor Dawson Fowler** (b. 22 Feb 1917, Weogufka, Coosa Co, AL, d. abt 1970) marr

Audrey Sawyers. Victor and Audrey were parents of two children: **Hershell Wade Fowler and Charlotte Renea Fowler.**

f. **Nancy Lucille Fowler** (b. 22 Nov 1919, Weogufka, Coosa Co, AL) marr, in 1937, **Lowell Edward Pody**). Nancy was a factory supervisor, now retired. She lives in Clay Co, AL, in 1993.

Nancy and Lowell were parents of one child: **Wilma June Pody.**

g. **Hiram Keener Fowler** (b. 24 Aug 1922, Weogufka, AL, deceased, buried in Old Weogufka Cem, Coosa Co, AL) marr, in 1947, **Irene Jones Bates**.

Hiram and Irene were parents of two children: **Wendell Kenneth Fowler** and **Sherry Fowler.**

h. **Joseph Willis Fowler** (b. 23 Nov 1924, deceased) marr 15 Aug 1946, Annie Lori Isbelle. Joseph and Annie are parents of two children: **Larry Willis Fowler** (b. 5 Feb 1957) and **Linda Jo Fowler** (b. 11 Aug 1950).

i. **Walter B. Fowler, Jr.** (b. 10 Jul 1927, d. 29 Apr 1981) marr **Lois McLain**. Walter and Lois had one child: **Richard Lane Fowler.**

j. **Ava Dean Fowler** (b. 17 Feb 1929, Weogufka, Coosa Co, AL) marr 1st **Wilbur Kelly** (b. 2 Sep 1915, d. 1968). Marr 2nd Joseph Murchison. Ava was an assistant administrator, Craddock Clinic, Sylacauga, AL, now retired.

Ava and Wilbur had two children: **Marilyn Fay Kelly and Janice Marie Kelly.**

5. **Ella Varner** (b. 1888, Coosa Co, AL) marr 28 Apr 1903, Coosa Co, AL, **J. S. Bates**.

6. **Susan F. Varner** (b. 1892, Coosa Co, AL).
7. **Martina Varner** (b. 1895, Coosa Co, AL).
8. **Sally A. Varner** (b. 1898, Coosa Co, AL).
9. **Viola E. Varner** (b. 1900, Coosa Co, AL).
10. **Willis "Willie" H. Varner** (b. 19 Mar 1903, Coosa Co, AL, d. 4 May 1936, Coosa Co, AL[1]).
11. **Fonza Varner** (b. 1906, Coosa Co, AL) marr 2 Jun 1928, Coosa Co, AL, **Gracie Hughes**.

B. **Sallie L. Varner,** daughter of John W. Varner and Elizabeth Wilson, (b. 1855, Coosa Co, AL),[2] marr 22 Dec 1872, **Alfred J. Mooney**. Sallie was named in her grandfather John Varner's will to receive the $100 to which his son John W. Varner, deceased, was entitled.

The Coosa County, AL, Probate Court, on 23 May 1870 appointed L. M. Wilson guardian of Sallie L. Varner, a minor heir of John Varner, Sr., deceased. L. M. Wilson was her natural uncle.[3]

Descendants of Lucien Varner

C. **Lucien A. Varner**, son of John W. Varner and Elizabeth Wilson, (b. Jun 1858, Coosa Co, AL, d. after

---

[1]--Willis H. Varner's birth and death dates appear on a grave marker in the Mt. Moriah Church Cemetery, Coosa Co, AL.

[2]--Listed in 1860 and 1870 census reports for Coosa Co, AL.

[3]--Coosa Co, AL, Probate Minutes, Bk. 9, p.700.

1920), marr 26 Jan 1883, Coosa Co, AL, **Cassandra Meharg** (b. 1867, d. 1895[4]).

Lucien (Lucian) Varner was a farmer in Coosa Co, AL in 1900, 1910, and 1920, according to the census records for those years.

Lucian A. Varner and Cassandra Meharg were parents of five known children: **William A. Varner, Mary E. Varner, Annie O. Varner, Laura L. Varner, and Alvie L. Varner.**

1. **William A. Varner** (b. Dec 1883, Coosa Co, AL, d. 1957[2]), marr 8 Nov 1903, Coosa Co, AL) **Rosa "Rosie" A. Honeycutt** (b. 1888).

    William A. Varner and Rosie A. Varner were farmers in Marble Valley, Coosa Co, AL, in 1910; they rented their farm land. William A. and "Rosie" Varner were parents of three known children, named in the 1910 and 1920 censuses: **Lula F. Varner, Odie Varner, Abbie M. Varner, and Rilla L. Varner.**

    a. **Lula F. Varner** (b. 1907, Coosa Co, AL).
    b. **Odie O. Varner** (b. 1911, Coosa Co, AL) marr 30 Jun 1932, Coosa Co, AL, Olga Robinson.
    c. **Abbie M. Varner** (b. 1913, Coosa Co, AL).
    d. **Rilla L. Varner** (b. 1919, Coosa Co, AL).

2. **Mary E. Varner** (b. Sep 1886, Coosa Co, AL). Living with her parents, occupation farm laborer, in 1910.

---

[1]--Cassandra may have died from complications of childbirth when Alvie L. Varner was born in May, 1895.

[2]--Birth and death dates of William A. Varner and Rosie A. Varner appear on a grave marker in the Stewartville Church of God Cemetery, Coosa Co, AL.

3. **Annie O. Varner** (b. Oct 1888, Coosa Co, AL) marr 9 Oct 1904, Coosa Co, AL, **David Deason** (b. 1885).
4. **Laura L. Varner** (b. Mar 1893, Coosa Co, AL).
5. **Alice D. Varner** (b. May 1895, Coosa Co, AL) marr 6 Oct 1912, Coosa Co, AL, **W. L. Fowler** (b. 1891).

C. **Lucien A. Varner**, son of John W. Varner and Elizabeth Wilson, marr 2nd, 12 May 1897, Coosa Co, AL, **Katie E. Morris**. There are no known children to this marriage.

Descendants of John William Varner

D. **John William Varner**, son of John W. Varner and Elizabeth Wilson, (b. 12 May 1861, Coosa Co, AL, d. 3 Mar 1903[1]) marr 16 Oct 1895, Coosa Co, AL, **Debbie Phillips**.

John W. Varner was a farmer in Coosa Co, AL, according to the 1900 census. John W. Varner and Debbie Phillips were parents of four children: **John Esmond Varner, Rushie L. Varner, Alberta Varner, and Floyd A. Varner**.

1. **John Esmond Varner** (b. 23 Jun 1897, Coosa Co, AL, d. 9 Aug 1978, Coosa Co, AL[2]) marr 26 Dec 1917, Coosa Co, AL, **Cora Matilda Burks** (b. 13 May 1898, d. 12 Jul 1976[3]).

---

[1]--William's birth and death dates appear on a grave marker in the Mt. Moriah Cemetery, Coosa Co, AL.

[2]--John Esmond Varner's birth and death dates appear on a grave marker in the Mt. Moriah Cemetery, Coosa Co, AL.

[3]--Cora Burks Varner's birth and death dates appear on a
(continued...)

John and Cora were parents of ten children[1]: **Clarence William Varner, Edna Leona Varner, Herbert Kenneth Varner, Bernon Elmo Varner, Myrtice Azarene Varner, Joyce May Varner, Johnny Goldson Varner, Gene Carlton Varner, Ronnie Augusta Varner, and Ellie Ruth Varner.**

a. **Clarence William Varner** (b. 28 Sep 1918, Coosa Co, AL).

b. **Edna Leona Varner**[2] (b. 4 Sep 1920, Coosa Co, AL) marr Dec 1941 in Coosa Co, AL, **Conrad Austin Bonnett** (b. 2 Sep 1921, Autauga Co, AL), son of Erskine J. Bonnett and Mary Emma Harris. Edna is a housewife and Conrad is a retired machinist. They live in Birmingham, AL, in 1993.

Edna and Conrad Bonnett are parents of five children: **Jeffery Dwight Bonnett, Gary Austin Bonnett, Janice Gail Bonnett, Donald Aubrey Bonnett, and Carol Ann Bonnett.**

(1) **Jeffery Dwight Bonnett** (b. 24 Aug 1943, Coosa Co, AL) marr 5 Dec 1970 in Birmingham. AL, **Virginia Mason**. Jeffery is a respiratory therapist. Jeffery and Virginia are parents of two children: **Byron Joseph Bonnett** (b. 24 Nov 1976)

---

[3](...continued)
grave marker in the Mt. Moriah Church Cemetery, Coosa Co, AL.

[1]--Information on this family provided by Ronnie Varner Zak of Montgomery, AL.

[2]--Information on this family was submitted by Edna Varner Bonnett of Birmingham, AL.

and **Benjamin Dwight Bonnett** (b. 2 Jul 1984).
- (2) **Gary Austin Bonnett** (b. 6 Sep 1945, Coosa Co, AL) marr 24 Sep 1982, **Donna Atkinson**. Gary works for Bell Telephone; he and Donna live in Odenville, St. Clair Co, AL, in 1993. Gary and Donna are parents of two children: **Autumn Rebekah Bonnett** (b. 1st Oct 1972) and **Joseph Austin Bonnett** (b. 27 Mar 1974).
- (3) **Janice Gail Bonnett** (b. 7 Feb 1947, Jefferson Co, AL). Janice is a county clerk and lives in Birmingham, AL, in 1993.
- (4) **Donald Aubrey Bonnett** (b. 26 Mar 1949, Jefferson Co, AL) marr 22 Dec 1973 in Birmingham, AL, **Madelyn Carr**. Donald is a printer; he and Madelyn live in Birmingham, AL, in 1993.
- (5) **Carol Ann Bonnett** (b. 8 Feb 1951, Birmingham, AL), marr 17 Sep 1983 in Birmingham, AL, **Michael Waid Edmondson, Sr**. Carol and Michael are parents of one child: **Michael Waid Edmondson, Jr.** (b. 1 Aug 1988). This family lives in Pinson, AL, in 1993.
- c. **Herbert Kenneth Varner** (b. 3 Feb 1922, Coosa Co, AL).
- d. **Bernon Elmo Varner** (b. 24 Nov 1923, Coosa Co, AL, d. 1 Feb 1958). Bernon Elmo died in an auto accident.

e. **Myrtice Azarene Varner**[1] (b. 9 Jan 1926, Coosa Co, AL) marr 26 Jul 1947 in Rockford, Coosa Co, AL, **Floyd M. Kelley** (b. 3 Jun 1926, Coosa Co, AL), son of **Charles R. Kelley and Nancy B. Culver**. Myrtice and Floyd live in Maylene, AL, in 1993. They are parents of three children: **Phil Randal Kelley, Travis Carlton Kelley, and Ronald Steven Kelley**.
  (1) **Phil Randal Kelley** (b. 18 Aug 1948, Fairfield, AL) marr 26 Nov 1978 in Birmingham, AL, **Dorothy Larson**. Phil is a retail manager.
  Phil and Dorothy are parents of two children: **Lindsey Blane Kelley** (f., b. 7 Nov 1983) and **Robert Randal Kelley** (m., b. 20 Feb 1986).
  (2) **Travis Carlton Kelley** (b. 18 Sep 1951, Birmingham, AL) marr 14 Aug 1971 in Hueytown, AL, **Susan McLellan**. Travis and Susan are parents of one child: **Eugenia Lorraine Kelley** (b. 3 Dec 1979). Travis is a retail manager; he and Susan live in Hueytown, AL, in 1993.
  (3) **Ronald Steven Kelley** (b. 27 Sep 1953, Birmingham, AL) marr 25 Oct 1975 in Birmingham, AL, **Deborah Holden**. Ronald is a coach-teacher; he and Deborah live in Shelby Co, AL, in 1993.
f. **Joyce May Varner** (b. 14 May 1928, Coosa Co, AL).

---

[1]--Information on this family was submitted by Myrtice A. Kelley of Maylene, AL.

g. **Johnny Goldson Varner** (b. 19 Mar 1931, Coosa Co, AL).

h. **Gene Carlton Varner** (b. 20 Feb 1933, Coosa Co, AL, d. 31 Jan 1951). Gene was killed in combat in the Korean War. He enlisted and served in the 7th Cavalry and in the 1st Infantry, Cavalry Division[1].

i. **Ronnie Augusta Varner**[2] (b. 8 Aug 1935, Coosa Co, AL) marr 15 Feb 1975 in Florida, **George Zak** (b. 6 Nov 1929, Chicago, IL). George is an electrical engineer and Ronnie is a homemaker. George and Ronnie live in Montgomery, AL, in 1993.

Ronnie has one son: **Dirk L. Swafford** (b. 23 Dec 1957). Dirk is a purchasing manager. He lives in Montgomery, AL, in 1993. Dirk has a daughter: **Alexandra "Ally" Swafford** (b. 28 Dec 1987).

j. **Ellen Ruth Varner**[3] (b. 25 Oct 1937, d. 20 Mar 1992, Birmingham, AL) marr 4 Sep 1956, Sylacauga, AL, **Clifford E. Faulkner** (b. 16 Aug 1936, Coosa Co, AL), son of Arthur and Naomi Faulkner. Clifford is a millwright with Kimberley-Clarke; he lives in Sylacauga, AL, in 1993.

---

[1]--This information submitted by Edna Varner Bonnett of Birmingham, AL.

[2]--Information on the Ronnie and George Zak family was submitted by Ronnie Zak of Montgomery, AL.

[3]--Information on the Ellen Ruth Varner Faulkner family was submitted by Laurie Faulkner of Sylacauga, AL.

Ellen and Clifford are parents of three children: **David E. Faulkner, Lisa G. Faulkner, and Laurie J. Faulkner.**
- (1) **David E. Faulkner** (b. 26 Oct 1957, Ft. Worth, TX). David is a fireman.
- (2) **Lisa G. Faulkner** (b. 25 Jun 1960, Altus, OK). Lisa is the parent of one child: **Michael Chase Etress** (b. 20 Apr 1989).
- (3) **Laurie J. Faulkner** (b. 23 Jul 1967, Sylacauga, AL). Laurie is a customer service representative. She lives in Sylacauga, AL, in 1993.

2. **Rushie L. Varner** (b. 7 Oct 1898, Coosa Co, AL, d. 5 Oct 1993, in Sylacauga, AL) married **Homer Ezekiel** (d. 26 Mar 1978). Rushie and Homer were parents of eight children: **Lodis V. Ezekiel, Earnest Ezekiel, Evelyn Ezekiel, Carolyn Ezekiel, Robert Ezekiel, A. V. Ezekiel, Curtis Ezekiel, and Lester Ezekiel.**

   a. **Lodis V. Ezekiel**[1] (b. 16 Nov 1918, Coosa Co, AL) marr 12 Nov 1938, in Coosa Co, AL, **Minnie Lowery** (b. 1 Jan 1920, Chilton Co, AL), dau of Simmie Lowery and Martha Riggins. Lodis is a retired electrician; he worked for Kimberly-Clark. He and Minnie live in Weogufka, AL, in 1993. They have lived in Coosa Co, AL, for 75 years.

   Lodis and Minnie Ezekiel are parents of five children: **Billy Floyd Ezekiel, Bobby**

---

[1]--Information on the Lodis V. Ezekiel family, his parents, children, and grandchildren was submitted by Lodis V. Ezekiel of Weogufka, AL.

JOHN W. VARNER, SON OF JOHN VARNER

Adair Ezekiel, Judy L. Ezekiel, Donna M. Ezekiel, and Timothy W. Ezekiel.

(1) **Billy Floyd Ezekiel** (b. 23 Jun 1940, Coosa Co, AL, d. 10 Dec 1942, Talladega, AL).

(2) **Bobby Adair Ezekiel** (b. 27 Jan 1941, Talladega Co, AL) marr **Jane Helm** of Stewartville, AL. This marriage ended in divorce in 1983.

Bobby and Jane are parents of four children: **Rhonda L. Ezekiel, Wanda J. Ezekiel, Wayne S. Ezekiel, and Kevin A. Ezekiel.**

Rhonda married **Kent Cooper**. They are parents of one child: **Amber Cooper.** This marriage ended in divorce. Rhonda is now married to **Pat Robbin** of Rockford, Coosa Co, AL.

Wanda married **Teddy Byrd** of Stewartville, AL. They are parents of one child: **Corey Byrd.**

Wayne married Lisa Jacks. They have one child: **Christopher Ezekiel.** This family lives in Weogufka in 1993.

Kevin married **Michelle Masery**. They have one child: **Codey Ezekiel.** This marriage ended in divorce. Kevin is now married to **Sonja Duffey**. This family lives in Sylacauga, AL, in 1993.

(2) **Bobby A. Ezekiel** marr 2nd **Ann Grimes Hewitt** of Weogufka. Ann has two children: **Leann Hewitt Murchison** of Rockford, AL, and **Charles Hewitt** of Weogufka, AL. Bobby works for

Kimberly-Clark. He and Ann live in Weogufka, AL, in 1993.

(3) **Judy L. Ezekiel** (b. 13 Apr 1946, Coosa Co, AL) marr 6 Jun 1964, in Talladega Co, AL, **Norman R. Woodard**. Judy is a housewife; she and Norman live in Orlando, FL, in 1993.

Judy and Norman Woodard are parents of two children: **Jennifer Woodard and Travis R. Woodard**.

Jennifer Woodard married Donnie Martin. Jennifer and Donnie are parents of dau **Colbey Martin** and twin sons **Colton Martin and Cameron Martin**. This family lives in Lufkin, TX, in 1993.

Travis R. Woodard married Dana White. They have one dau **Jordin Woodard**. This marriage ended in divorce.

(4) **Donna M. Ezekiel** (b. 29 Nov 1949, Coosa Co, AL) marr 18 Nov 1966 in Coosa Co, AL, **Johnny R. Helm**.

Donna and Johnny are parents of three children: **Tony R. Helm, Billie V. Helm, and Haley M. Helm**.

Tony married **Angie Wilson** of Stewartville. They have two daughters: **Toni M. Helm and Tiffany M. Helm**. Billy and Haley are not married.

(5) **Timothy W. Ezekiel** (b. 19 Aug 1951, Coosa Co, AL) marr 12 Dec 1969, in Coosa Co, AL, **Gail Culver**.

Timothy and Gail are parents of two children: **Kimberly L. Ezekiel and**

Matthew W. Ezekiel. Timothy works for Kimberly-Clark. This family lives in Weogufka, AL, in 1993.

b. **Evelyn Ezekiel**[1] (b. 26 Sep 1923, Weogufka, AL) marr **Johnnie Grover Blankenship** (b. 25 Dec 1916, d. 16 Aug 1991), son of **John Grover Blankenship and Ida Adams Blankenship**. Evelyn is retired and lives in Sylacauga, AL, in 1993.

Evelyn and Johnnie are parents of three children: **Grover Lloyd Blankenship, Patricia Ann Blankenship, and Abigail Blankenship**.

(1) **Grover Lloyd Blankenship** (b. 29 Dec 1939, Weogufka, Coosa Co, AL) marr in Phoenix City, AL, **Pam Bray**. Grover and his brother-in-law Tommy Vansandt are in the hardware business. Pam Blankenship is a teacher. Grover and Pam live in Sylacauga, AL, in 1993.

Grover and Pam are parents of two children: **Gregory Todd Blankenship** (b. 18 Mar 1962, Columbus, GA) **and Karen Lynn Blankenship** (b. 11 Oct 1964, Sylacauga, AL).

(2) **Patricia Ann Blankenship** (b. 19 Apr 1942, Weogufka, AL) marr in Weogufka, AL, **Tommy Vansandt**. Patricia and Tommy live in Sylacauga, AL, in 1993. They are parents of four children: **Mark Aaron Vansandt** (b. 12 Feb 1960),

---

[1]--Information on the Evelyn and Johnnie Blankenship family was submitted by Evelyn Ezekiel Blankenship of Sylacauga, AL.

Winston Craig Vansandt (b. 24 Jan 1961), **Byron Glenn Vansandt** (b. 18 Jan 1963), and **Cynthia Ann Vansandt** (b. 9 Mar 1965).
- (3) **Abigail Blankenship** (b. 3 Nov 1950, Goodwater, AL) marr **Ted J. Smith**. Abigail and Ted live in Covington, GA, in 1993.

    Abigail is the mother of two children: **Michael Kenyoa Bryant** (b. 25 Jan 1970) and **Jeffrey Harold Bryant** (b. 10 Oct 1974).
- c. **Earnest Ezekiel** (b. 9 Aug 1925, Coosa Co, AL) marr 20 Dec 1947 at Childersburg, AL, **Bennie Sue Lester** (b. 27 Jul 1928, Tallapoosa Co, AL), dau of **Furman Farris Lester and Dora Harris**. Earnest and Bennie live in Sylacauga, AL, in 1993.[1]

    Earnest and Bennie Ezekiel are parents of six children: **Allan Wade Ezekiel, Melissa Ruth Ezekiel, Melodie Sue Ezekiel, Dwayne Earnest Ezekiel, Myra Leigh Ezekiel, and Darrell Scot Ezekiel.**
    - (1) **Alan Wade Ezekiel** (b. 15 Jan 1949, Sylacauga, AL) marr 8 Dec 1973 at Childersburg, AL, **Joy Burton**. Allan is a Control Room Operator. He and Joy live in Sylacauga, AL, in 1993. They are parents of one child: **Brandon Wade Ezekiel.**

---

[1]--Information on the Earnest and Bennie Ezekiel family, their children, and grandchildren was submitted by Earnest Ezekiel of Sylacauga, AL.

(2) **Melissa Ruth Ezekiel** (b. 21 Aug 1952, Sylacauga, AL) marr 12 Apr 1980 at Ft. Benning, GA, **Francis Patrick McGarry**. Melissa is an elementary school teacher. She and Francis live in Kennett Square, PA, in 1993. They are parents of three children: **Francis Patrick McGarry III, Shane Michael McGarry, and Timothy James McGarry**.

(3) **Melodie Sue Ezekiel** (b. 12 Dec 1955, Sylacauga, AL) marr 8 Apr 1978 at Sylacauga, AL, **Bobby Ray Loudermilk**. Melodie is a District Supervisor. She and Bobby live in Birmingham, AL, in 1993. They are parents of two children: **Rebecca Ann Loudermilk and Adam Grant Loudermilk**.

(4) **Dwayne Earnest Ezekiel** (b. 1 Aug 1957, Sylacauga, AL) marr 2 Jul 1983 at Sylacauga, AL, **Kimberly Camp**. Dwayne is an electrician. He and Kimberly live in Weogufka, AL, in 1993. They are parents of two children: **Samantha Lynn Ezekiel and Trent Dwayne Ezekiel**.

(5) **Myra Leigh Ezekiel** (b. 5 Aug 1962, Sylacauga, AL) marr 17 Feb 1990 at Rockford, AL, **Normand Gilchrist Kirby**. Myra is a dental hygienist. She and Normand live in Sylacauga, AL, in 1993.

(6) **Darrell Scot Ezekiel** (b. 11 Feb 1967, Sylacauga, AL). He is a sales representative and lives in Sylacauga, AL, in 1993.

d. **Carolyn Ezekiel**[1] (b. 24 Jul 1935, Coosa Co, AL) marr 14 Jun 1952 **Ralph E. Pody** (b. 7 Dec 1927, Coosa Co, AL), son of **James David Pody and Ester Pody** and grandson of **George and Della Jacks Varner**. Carolyn and Ralph live in Piedmont, AL, in 1993. They are parents of four children: **Michael Ralph Pody, Cathy Denise Pody, Carlton Boyd Pody, and Regina Dawn Pody.**

  (1) **Michael Ralph Pody** (b. 23 Mar 1957, Etowah Co, AL) marr 2 Jul 1977 in Calhoun Co, AL, **Melinda Gowens**. Michael works in management. He and Melinda live in Piedmont, AL, in 1993. They are parents of one child: Michael Andrew Pody (b. 13 Nov 1982).

  (2) **Cathy Denise Pody** (b. 10 Oct 1958, Talladega Co, AL). Cathy is a laborer and lives in Piedmont, AL, in 1993. Cathy is the mother of two children: **Corey Ralph Wallace** (b. 19 Feb 1981) son of Cathy Denise Pody and Robyn Wallace, and **Cara Leigh Hogue** (b. 2 Feb 1990), dau of Cathy Denise Pody and Wade Hogue.

  (3) **Carlton Boyd Pody** (b. 14 Mar 1962, Calhoun Co, AL). Carlton lives in Piedmont, AL, in 1993.

---

[1]--Information on Ralph E. and Carolyn Ezekiel Pody and her family was submitted by Carolyn Ezekiel Pody of Piedmont, AL.

       (4) **Regina Dawn Pody** (b. 17 Dec 1964, Calhoun Co, AL). Regina lives in Center, AL, in 1993.
- e. **Robert Ezekiel.**
- f. **A. V. Ezekiel.**
- g. **Curtis Ezekiel.**
- h. **Lester Ezekiel.**
3. **Alberta "Allie" Varner** (b. 1901, Coosa Co, AL) marr **Arthur Dennis**. Alberta lives in Coosa Co, AL, in 1993.[1]
4. **Floyd Jackson Varner** (b. 31 May 1902, Coosa Co, AL, d. 12 Jul 1921).[2]

---

[1]..Ronnie and George Zak and the author visited "Aunt Allie" Dennis at her home near Mt. Moriah, in April, 1988. She proudly stated that she would be 88 years old in June. She said her father, John William "Little Bill" Varner, died of TB when she was two years old. She said that her Uncle Cicero Varner's children were all dead.

"Aunt Allie" said she doesn't know anything about her grandfather, John W. Varner. But she said that her grandmother Elizabeth Wilson Varner lived with the family of one of her children for about a year before she died. She fell while carrying wood. She might have had a stroke. "Aunt Allie" said that her Grandma Elizabeth Varner is buried in the old Crumbly Family Cemetery, which is near Mt. Moriah. (If that is true, the grave is not identified with a marker.)

[2]--Floyd Jackson Varner was killed by lightening, according to his sister "Aunt Allie" Varner Dennis, op. cit.

Chapter XII
Esselman Varner, Son of John Varner

Esselman Varner was a son of John Varner and Nancy Powell. He was born 30 Aug 1833 in Lowndes Co, AL. He died 14 May 1907[1] in Coosa Co, AL. He married 1st, Coosa Co, AL on 17 Dec 1860[2] **Sarah M. Wilson** (b. 15 Dec 1839, d. 10 Jun 1878, Coosa Co, AL).

Esselman was a teenager when his mother died and when the John Varner family moved from Lowndes Co, AL, to Coosa County, AL. He was living with his father John Varner and stepmother Amanda Varner at the time of the 1850 and 1860 federal censuses. Esselman and his brothers were probably helping their father John Varner manage the plantation during their father's old age.[3] (Amaziah Varner lived there and undoubtedly assisted his dad in running the plantation up until Amaziah's death in 1856. Esselman then moved into the top management job and held it until his father died. Hardaway Varner returned from Louisiana and managed the farm the last

---

[1]..Esselman's birth and death dates appear on a grave marker in the Providence Cemetery, Coosa Co, AL.

[2]..Esselman Varner and Sarah M. Wilson married 20 Dec 1860. The ceremony was performed Dec. 20, 1860, in Weogufka, AL. (He was born 8/30/1833 and died 5/14/1907. Sarah was born 12/15/1839 and died 6/10/1878. Information provided by Mrs. Myra V. Rushing, Montgomery, AL, in 1988. Accuracy verified from other sources as well.)

[3]..The 1860 census reported that John Varner was blind. Extant records do not indicate when he lost his sight or whether he remained blind the final ten years of his life. His advanced age was another reason he needed help in managing his plantation. He lived to the age of 86, remarkable for the 19th Century.

few years of his father's life. Hardaway took possession of the farm after his father John Varner died 31 Dec 1869.[1])

On 30 Dec 1869, the day before his father died, Esselman purchased land for his own farm.[2] In the 1870 census, he reported that his real estate was worth $1200 and that his personal property was also worth $1200. He lived in Traveler's Rest Beat, Coosa County, only a few households removed from that of his brother Hardaway and stepmother Amanda Varner.[3]

Esselman Joins Confederate Army

Esselman could have avoided military service for the Confederate States during the Civil War because he managed more than 15 slaves. Nevertheless, he served in the Confederate Army for awhile during the latter stages of fighting, when he was a private in Co. C, 9th AL Infantry. After the war ended, he signed a pledge of allegiance to the United States, May 19, 1865. Height: 5'6". Hair: dark. Complexion: dark. Eyes: dark. Private, Company C, 9th Alabama Infantry.[4]

---

[1]..See Chapter VII for more information about Amaziah Varner and Hardaway Varner, sons of John Varner and Nancy Powell.

[2]..Coosa County Deed Book N, page 231. Dec. 30, 1869, E. Varner purchased land in Coosa County (E 1/2 of S 1/2 of S 33, T 23, R 16) from W. A. Wilson for $500.

[3]..Esselman's family was number 33 in Traveler's Rest Beat while Hardaway and Amanda were family number 57.

[4]..Alabama Confederate Records. located at the Alabama Archives. Esselman Varner's record is filed under "Narner, E."

VARNER FAMILIES OF THE SOUTH--XII

During the years after the war, Esselman Varner and Sarah Wilson seemed to provide adequate food, clothing, and shelter for their family. They were not wealthy, but they fared much better than the average farm family in the South in the years after the Civil War. The 1880 Agricultural Census gave an indication of their material goods.[1] This may have been meager compared to what this family had during prewar days, but it was certainly more than share croppers and tenant farmers had.[2]

---

[1]. See Appendix # XII-B for notes on the 1880 Agricultural Census record for Esselman Varner.

[2]. In the post Civil War South, a share cropper was a farmer who shared the crops he\she produced with the land owner. If the land owner furnished the mules, farm equipment and tools used by the farmer, the share cropper usually received half of what he/she produced and the land owner received the other half. If the share cropper furnished his/her own mules, equipment and tools, the land owner received less than half. The latter were called tenant farmers. Tenant farmers usually were able to keep two-thirds of their corn crop and three-fourths of their cotton. (Cotton growing required more intensive labor.)

The share cropping tradition continued in rural areas of the South well into the 20th Century. It was common during the Great Depression while the author of this book was growing up in rural Arkansas.

Esselman Involved in Court Cases

Esselman Varner was involved in a few court cases, but he personally was never charged with wrong-doing. In 1867 he was a state's witness in a criminal case.[1] In 1872, Esselman and his brother Hardaway assisted their nephew John Varner[2] after he was arrested and charged with assault.[3] John Varner was found guilty. The fine was only $1.00 but court costs raised the total to $27.61, which Esselman and Hardaway paid.

In what was probably a more interesting case, Esselman Varner sued George M. Calloway, claiming that Calloway had not made payment of a $500 promissory note.[4] The jury ruled against Esselman but the Alabama

---

[1]..State Subpoena Docket, Coosa County, Book C, page 167. July, 1867. Esselman Varner was one of the state's witnesses in the State of Alabama v Isaac I. Adams, who was charged with Hotel Keeping.

[2]..This John Varner was a son of Azariah Varner. (See Chapter VIII). This John Varner had been raised by his grandfather John Varner after Azariah Varner and Mary Pickering, this John's parents, died in Lowndes County, AL.

[3].See Appendix XII-B at the end of this chapter for the court record on John Varner's trial for Assault and Battery.

[4]..From Coosa County Circuit Court, Final Record, Vol. O, page 86. Esselman Varner v George M. Calloway. Plaintiff claims $500 on a note from the defendant. April 1883.
From Coosa County Trial Docket, page 75. The jury rendered a verdict for the defendant and awarded $371.22 in damages. Spring term 1883.
From Trial Docket, page 109. Decision reversed by the Supreme Court and the case was remanded for a new trial.
(continued...)

Supreme Court overruled that decision and ordered a new trial. No record of the new trial was located. The parties may have settled out of court.

Esselman wrote his will[1] in 1896. He identified his living heirs in the will. He specified that his widow Betty was to have use of almost everything from his estate during her natural lifetime. He left George Varner, his youngest son, a gold watch that his father John Varner had given him. He left a shot gun that had belonged to his father to his son James Varner. He died 14 May 1907, leaving an estate under $2,000 in value.[2] His will was accepted for probate 7 June 1907. All surviving heirs were identified in the probate court proceedings.[3]

---

[4](...continued)
John A. Wilson and others gave interrogatories. Spring term 1885.

[1].See Appendix XII-C at the end of this chapter for a copy of Esselman Varner's will.

[2].. Coosa County, AL, Will Book 3. Acceptance of Will. On June 8, 1907, the court accepted the will, declared the estate to be worth no more than $2,000 and accepted a bond from the executives (James H. Varner, J. A. Varner, and W. A. Varner) in the amount of $2,000.

[3].See Appendix XII-D at the end of this chapter for a copy of the petition that challenged Esselman Varner's will.

Children of Esselman and Sarah Varner
Esselman and Sarah were parents of eight children: **Adolphus B., William A., Manton E., Nancy A., James Hardaway, John A., Mary A., and George Henley.**

A. **Adolphus B. Varner,** son of Esselman Varner and Sarah M. Wilson, (b. 1 Oct 1861, d. 1 Jan 1862, Coosa Co, AL[1]).

Descendants of William A. Varner
B. **William A. Varner,** son of Esselman Varner and Sarah Wilson, (b. 1863, Coosa Co, AL, d. after 1920) marr 31 Dec 1884, Coosa Co, AL, **Amanda C. Hughen**, dau of W. J. Hughen, (d. between 1904 and 1910[2]).

William A. Varner was listed as a farmer in the 1900 census and as a merchant in the 1910 census.

William A. Varner and Amanda C. Hughen were parents of nine children, according to the 1900 and 1910 census reports: **Dora L. Varner, Birdie A. Varner, Bell I. Varner, Beattrice Varner, Lewis E. Varner, Minnie I. Varner, Maggie M. Varner, Lillian Varner, and Hosiah "Hogy" Varner.**

1. **Dora E. Varner** (b. 1887, Coosa Co, AL).
2. **Birdie A. Varner** (b. 9 Oct 1887, Coosa Co, AL, 2 Dec 1910)[3] marr **G. W. Blankenship**.

---

[1]..Vital statistics for Adolphus B. Varner appear on a grave marker at Providence Cemetery, Coosa Co, AL.

[2]..Amanda C. Varner was 33 years old at the time of the 1900 census for Coosa Co, AL. She was not listed with the William A. Varner family in the 1910 census. She was the mother of Hosiah Varner, born in 1904.

[3]..Birth and death dates of Birdie A. Varner appear on a (continued...)

3. Bell I. Varner (b. 1890, Coosa Co, AL).
4. Beattrice Varner (b. 1892, Coosa Co, AL).
5. Lewis E. Varner (b. 1894, Coosa Co, AL).
6. Minnie I. Varner (b. 1897, Coosa Co, AL).
7. Maggie M. Varner (b. 1899, Coosa Co, AL).
8. Lillian Varner (b. 1902, Coosa Co, AL).
9. Hosiah "Hogy" Varner (b. 1904, Coosa Co, AL).

B. **William A. Varner**, son of Esselman Varner and Sarah Wilson, marr 2nd, 31 Dec 1911, Coosa Co, AL, **Liza "Lizzie" J. Thornell**.

William A. Varner and Liza Thornell were parents of three known children, named in the 1920 census: **William N. Varner, Mary H. Varner, and Martha B. Varner**.
1. William N. Varner (b. 1914, Coosa Co, AL).
2. Mary H. Varner (b. 1916, Coosa Co, AL).
3. Martha B. Varner (b. 1918, Coosa Co, AL).

Descendants of Manton E. Varner

C. **Manton Esselman Varner**, son of Esselman Varner and Sarah Wilson, (b. 5 Jun 1867, Coosa Co, AL, d. 8 May 1955, Coosa Co, AL[1]) marr 1st 8 Dec 1889, Coosa Co, AL, **Sarah E. Raines**, dau of Rev. Augustus Goodwin Raines (b. Dec 1870, d. betw 1901 and 1915).

Manton E. Varner and Sarah E. Raines were parents of six children: **Adolphus W. Varner, Roxie M. Varner,**

---

[3](...continued)
grave marker at Mt. Moriah Church Cemetery, Coosa Co, AL.

[1]..Manton E. Varner's birth and death dates appear on a grave marker at the Providence Cemetery, Coosa Co, AL.

James A. Varner, Nathan Varner, George R. Varner, William Alfred Varner.
1. **Adolphus W. Varner** (b. 1892, Coosa Co, AL) marr, abt 1910, **Alma** _____.

    Adolphus W. and Alma Varner were parents of three known children, all reported in the 1920 census: **Adelaide Varner, Esther Varner, and Evelyn Varner.**
    a. **Adelaide Varner** (b. 1912, Coosa Co, AL).
    b. **Esther Varner** (b. 1916, Coosa Co, AL).
    c. **Evelyn Varner** (b. 1919, Coosa Co, AL).
2. **Roxie M. Varner** (b. 1894, Coosa Co, AL) marr 25 Nov 1910, Coosa Co, AL, **G. H. Glenn.**
3. **James A. Varner** (b. 1895, Coosa Co, AL) marr 15 Nov 1915, Coosa Co, AL, **Lilla Logan** (b. 1897).
4. **Nathan Varner** (b. 1898, Coosa Co, AL), marr 2 Feb 1919, Coosa Co, AL, **Ella Varner** (b. 1899).
5. **George R. Varner** (b. 1899, Coosa Co, AL).
6. **William Alfred Varner** (b. 1900, Coosa Co, AL).

C. **Manton Esselman Varner**, son of Esselman Varner and Sarah Wilson, marr 2nd, **Ida L.** _____ (b. 1884).

Manton E. Varner and Ida L. _____ were parents of three known children: **Ula M. Varner, Rollie E. Varner**, and (unnamed infant) **Varner.**
1. **Ula M. Varner** (b. 1918, Coosa Co, AL).
2. **Rollie E. Varner** (b. 1919, Coosa Co, AL).
3. (Unnamed infant) **Varner** (b. & d. 1921).[1]

---

[1].. According to a grave marker in Providence Cemetery, Coosa Co, AL.

D. Nancy A. Varner, daughter of Esselman Varner and Sarah Wilson (b. 1869, Coosa Co, AL, d. after 1902[1]) marr _____ Johnson[2].

Descendants of James Hardaway Varner

E. James Hardaway Varner, son of Esselman Varner and Sarah Wilson, (b. 9 Aug 1871, Coosa Co, AL, d. 11 Sep 1947[3]) marr **Nancy G. White**.

James was a farmer in Coosa Co in 1900, 1910, and 1920, according to census reports for those years.

James H. Varner and Nancy G. White were parents of eight known children, five of whom died in early childhood[4]. The eight children's names: **Joseph E. Varner, Jeffie Varner, Althia Varner, and J. P. Varner, and four unnamed infants.**

1. **Unnamed Varner infant** (b. & d. 1897).
2. **Unnamed Varner infant** (b. & d. 1899).

---

[1]..Living in 1902 when her father wrote a codicil to his will.

[2]..Esselman Varner identified Nancy A. Johnson as one of his daughters in his will.

[3]..The *Montgomery Advertiser* on 12 Sep 1947 announced the death of James Hardaway Varner, age 76. He was buried in Mt. Hebron Cemetery. His wife was not listed as a survivor.

[4]..Five grave markers in the Old Hatchet Creek Cemetery (also known as Dollar Cemetery), Coosa Co, AL, give the dates of the birth and death of these five infants.

3. **Joseph Eggleston Varner**[1] (b. 11 Jun 1900, Coosa Co, AL, d. 14 Feb 1974[2]) marr 16 Dec 1923 **Ora Lee Bonnett,** dau of George Henry Bonnett and Maude Bee Thornton, (b. 16 Oct 1905, Coosa Co, AL).

   Joseph and Ora were parents of seven children: **Eunice Nell, Earl Hardaway, Edward Hugh, Charles Wayne, Daniel Ray, Carol Ann, and Nancy Lee.**
   a. Eunice Nell Varner.
   b. Earl Hardaway Varner.
   c. Edward Hugh Varner.
   d. **Charles Wayne Varner** (b. 28 May 1935, Chilton Co, AL) marr 25 Nov 1958 **Barbara Jean Curry,** dau of William Alfred Curry and Mattie May McGuire, (b. 29 Jan 1939, Tampa, FL). Charles and Barbara live in Tampa, FL. They are parents of four children: **Mitchell Wayne, Michael David, Tabitha Ann, and Matthew Joseph.**
   (1) **Mitchell Wayne Varner** (b. 13 Oct 1959, Ft. Wayne, IN).
   (2) **Michael David Varner** (b. 20 Oct 1969, Bamberg, Oberfranken, West Germany).
   (3) **Tabitha Ann Varner** (b. 3 Dec 1971, Tampa, FL).

---

[1]..Information on the Joseph E. Varner family and descendants was submitted by Charles Wayne Varner of Tampa, FL.

[2]..The Prattville Progress 14 Feb 1974 announced the death of Joseph E. Varner, 73. Charles Wayne Varner of Tampa, FL, was listed as a surviving son.

    (4) **Matthew Joseph Varner** (b. 12 Feb 1975, Tampa, FL).
  e. **Daniel Ray Varner.**
  f. **Carol Ann Varner.**
  g. **Nancy Lee Varner.**
4. **Unnamed Varner** infant (b. & d. 1903).
5. **Unnamed Varner** infant (b. & d. 1905).
6. **Jeffie Varner** (b. 1907, Coosa Co, AL).
7. **Althia Varner** (b. 30 Jun 1911, Coosa Co, AL, d. 4 Oct 1989) marr **Thomas Dozier** (b. 6 Mar 1912).
8. **J. P. Varner** (b. 2 Nov 1914, Coosa Co, AL, d. 25 Aug 1918, Coosa Co, AL).

Descendants of John A. Varner

F. **John A. Varner**, son of Esselman Varner and Sarah Wilson, (b. May 1873, Coosa Co, AL, d. after 1910[1]) marr 24 Dec 1898, Coosa Co, AL, **Alice Emma Gilmer Raines** (b. 1879).

John A. Varner and Emma Raines were parents of three known children, all listed in the 1910 census for Coosa Co, AL: **Olga Varner, Valat Varner, and Alfin G. Varner.**
  1. **Olga (or Olfie) Varner**, dau. (b. 1900, Coosa Co, AL) marr 26 Dec 1916, Coosa Co, AL, **Clayton Barrett** (b. 1896).
  2. **Valat "Vida" Varner**, dau. (b. 1907, Coosa Co, AL) marr 28 Oct 1928, Coosa Co, AL, **J. L. Brown** (b. 1900).

---

[1]..John A. Varner was named as a son and heir of Esselman Varner in Esselman's will, written in 1898. He was enumerated in the 1910 census for Coosa Co, AL.

3. **Alfin G. Varner**, son (b. 1909, Coosa Co, AL).
G. **Mary A. Varner**, daughter of Esselman Varner and Sarah Wilson, (b. 1875, d. after 1898[1]).

Descendants of George Henley Varner

H. **George Henley Varner**, son of Esselman Varner and Sarah Wilson, (b. 9 Jun 1877, Coosa Co, AL, d. 9 Sep 1960, Coosa Co, AL[2]) marr 1st 31 Dec 1900, Coosa Co, AL, I. **Della Jacks** (b. 16 Jun 1883, d. 31 Mar 1935, Coosa Co, AL).

George Henley Varner and Della Jacks were parents of seven children: **Ester, Mosley, Flossie, Maria, Shelton, Arval, and Freeman**.

1. **Sara Ester Varner**[3] (b. 1903, Coosa Co, AL) marr **James David Pody** (b. 14 Jul 1887, Coosa Co, AL, d. 8 Oct 1964). James Pody was a farmer. Sara and James were parents of seven children: **Sherill, Margaret, Ralph, James C., Clifford Neal, Stuart, and Kenneth**.
    a. **Sherill Pody** (b. 28 Aug 1924, Coosa Co, AL) marr **Catherine Ballard** (b 30 Mar 1928). This marriage ended in divorce. Sherill is retired.

---

[1]..Esselman Varner identified Mary A. Varner as one of his daughters when he wrote his will in 1898.

[2]..George H. Varner's birth and death dates appear on a grave marker at Mt. Moriah Cemetery, Coosa Co, AL.

[3]..Information on Sara Ester Varner and James David Pody and their descendants was submitted by Linda Varner Goswick of Weogufka, Coosa Co, AL.

Sherill and Catherine were parents of three children: **Donald E. Pody, Larry Douglas Pody, and Sheila Diane Pody.**
(1) **Donald E. Pody** (b. 20 Jan 1948, d. 14 Feb 1948).
(2) **Larry Douglas Pody** (b 1 Jun 1952, Talladega Co, AL) marr **Sara J. Holman**. Larry and Sara are parents on one child: **Jennifer Gale Pody** (b. 6 Dec 1978).
(3) **Sheila Diane Pody** (b. 9 Aug 1954) marr **Dewey Knox**. This marriage ended in divorce. Sheila and Dewey are parents of one child: **Michael Ashley Pody** (b. 18 Oct 1976).
(3) **Sheila Diane Pody** marr 2nd **David Thomas**. This marriage ended in divorce. Sheila and David are parents of one child: **Jeremy Wayne Thomas** (b. 6 Dec 1981).
(3) **Sheila Diane Pody** marr 3rd **Therald Parker**. This marriage ended in divorce. Sheila and Therald are parents of one child: **Jonathan Parker** (b. 20 Apr 1990).
b. **Bernice Louise Pody** (b. 3 Sep 1926, Coosa Co, AL) marr **Roy Gaither** (b. 30 Oct 1919, Coosa Co, AL, d. 25 Nov 1988). Bernice is a housekeeper. She lives in Sylacauga, AL, in 1994.

Bernice and Roy were parents of four children: **Juanita Gaither, Robbie Jean Gaither, Roy Gaither, and Kenneth Richard Gaither.**
(1) **Juanita Gaither** (b. 9 Jan 1947) marr **Harold Stone** (b. 15 Jul 1947). Juanita and Harold are parents of two children:

Monty Bruce Stone (b. 15 Mar 1967, marr **Jeanette Smith**) and **Keith Allen Stone** (b. 6 Jul 1970, marr **Traci Thomas**.
- (2) **Robbie Jean Gaither** (b. 10 Apr 1945) marr 16 Apr 1964, **John Turner**. Robbie and John are parents of three children: **Sharon Diane Turner, John David Turner, and Karen Ann Turner.**
    - (a) **Sharon Diane Turner** (b. 15 Jan 1965) marr **Randy Simmons**. Sharon and Randy are parents of three children: **Michael Turner** (b. 2 Nov 1981), **Tabitha Turner** (b. 20 Apr 1985) and **Lisa Turner** (b. 6 Jun 1987).
- (3) **Roy Gaither** marr **Wanda Lee**. Roy and Wanda are parents of two children: **Brandi Gaither and Crystal Gaither.**
- (4) **Kenneth Richard Gaither** marr **Mary Ann Gaither**. Kenneth and Mary are parents of one child **Matthew Richard Gaither** (b. 25 Sep 1989.

c. **Ralph E. Pody** (b. 7 Dec 1927, Coosa Co, AL), marr 14 Jun 1952 **Carolyn Ezekiel**[1] (b. 24 Jul 1935, Coosa Co, AL). Carolyn and Ralph live in Piedmont, AL, in 1993. They are parents of four children: **Michael Ralph Pody, Cathy Denise Pody, Carlton Boyd Pody, and Regina Dawn Pody.**

---

[1]--Information on Ralph E. and Carolyn Ezekiel Pody and her family was submitted by Carolyn Ezekiel Pody of Piedmont, AL.

(1) **Michael Ralph Pody** (b. 23 Mar 1957, Etowah Co, AL) marr 2 Jul 1977 in Calhoun Co, AL, **Melinda Gowens**. Michael works in management. He and Melinda live in Piedmont, AL, in 1993. They are parents of one child: **Michael Andrew Pody** (b. 13 Nov 1982).

(2) **Cathy Denise Pody** (b. 10 Oct 1958, Talladega Co, AL). Cathy is a laborer and lives in Piedmont, AL, in 1993. Cathy is the mother of two children: **Corey Ralph Wallace** (b. 19 Feb 1981) son of Cathy Denise Pody and Robyn Wallace, and **Cara Leigh Hogue** (b. 2 Feb 1990), dau of Cathy Denise Pody and Wade Hogue.

(3) **Carlton Boyd Pody** (b. 14 Mar 1962, Calhoun Co, AL). Carlton lives in Piedmont, AL, in 1993.

(4) **Regina Dawn Pody** (b. 17 Dec 1964, Calhoun Co, AL). Regina lives in Center, AL, in 1993.

d. **James Clinton Pody** (b. 20 Aug 1930, Coosa Co, AL, d. 7 Dec 1991, Coosa Co, AL) marr 4 Dec 1954, **Jean Ray** (b. 7 May 1939). Jean lives in Coosa Co, AL, in 1994. James was a heavy machinery operator.

James and Jean were parents of three children: **Terri Lynn Pody, Madonna Ann Pody, and Tara Jean Pody.**

(1) **Terri Lynn Pody** (b. 14 May 1956) marr **David Brown**.

(2) **Madonna Ann Pody** (b. 8 Mar 1959) marr **Jerrell Goodson**. Madonna and Jerrell have two children: **Mark**

Goodson, Jerrell's son and Madonna's stepson, (b. 17 Sep 1972) and **Monica Goodman** (b. 7 Jan 1991).
- (3) **Tara Jean Pody** (b. 22 Nov 1962) marr **Ted Bentley**. Tara and Ted have one child: **Erin F. Bentley** (b. 14 May 1990).
- e. **Clifford C. Pody** marr **Shirley Goswick**. Clifford and Shirley are parents of two children: **Jeff and Kevin**.
  - (1) **Jeff Pody** (b. 26 Feb 1962, Talladega Co, AL) marr 1 Aug 1986, Talladega Co, AL, **Sherry Ivey** (b. 10 Feb 1967, Talladega Co, AL). Jeff is a butcher and Sherry is a waitress. This family lives in Coosa Co, AL, in 1994.

    Jeff and Sherry are parents of one child: **Lacey Pody** (b. 18 May 1987).
  - (2) **Kevin Pody** (b. 10 Mar 1967, Talladega Co, AL) marr **Sabrina Culver** (b. in GA). Kevin is a forester. This couple lives in Talladega Co, AL, in 1994. Kevin and Sabrina are parents of one child: **Timothy Dupriest Pody** (b. 24 Feb 1987).
- f. **Stuart Pody** (b. 8 Aug 1936, Coosa Co, AL) marr 5 Feb 1959, Calhoun Co, AL, **Shirley Humphrey** (b. 3 Sep 1938, Talladega Co, AL). Stuart is a grocery executive and Shirley is a teacher. They live in Talladega Co, AL, in 1994.

  Stuart and Shirley are parents of two children: **Kelly Challice Pody** (b. 28 Feb 1960, Calhoun Co, AL) and **Leigh Ann Pody** (b. 21 Dec 1965, Talladega Co, AL).
  - (1) **Kelly Challice Pody** (b. 28 Feb 1960, Calhoun Co, AL) marr **David Freeman**.

Kelly and David are parents of two children: **Challice Ann Kelly** (b. 3 Nov 1985) and **Hannah Margaret Kelly** (b. 9 Jun 1989).
  (2) **Leigh Ann Pody** (b. 21 Dec 1965, Talladega Co, AL).
 g. **Kenneth Pody** (d. 15 Jan 1960).
2. **John Moseley Varner**[1] (b. 4 Aug 1904, Coosa Co, AL, d. 10 Feb 1974, Coosa Co, AL[2]) marr 12 Dec 1923, Coosa Co, AL, **Reba Harmon** (b. 10 Feb 1908, Coosa Co, AL, d. 9 Jan 1981, Coosa Co, AL).

John and Reba were parents of four children: **Howard H., Josephine, Bessie and Norma Lee**.
 a. **Howard Henley Varner** (b. 20 Aug 1924, Coosa Co, AL, d. 26 Apr 1977, Coosa Co, AL) marr 8 Jul 1949, Coosa Co, AL, **Alma Clarice Pody**. Howard was a heavy equipment operator. Alma is a homemaker; she lives in Coosa Co, AL, in 1994.

Howard and Alma were parents of two children: **Clarice Rebecca and Carol Howard**.
  (1) **Clarice Rebecca Varner** (b. 29 Jan 1950, Talladega Co, AL) marr 2 May 1968, Coosa Co, AL, **Thomas Jacob Harris** (b. 22 Jan 1947, Coosa Co, AL). This couple lives in Talladega Co, AL, in 1964.

---

[1]..Information on John Moseley Varner and Reba Harmon Varner and their descendants was submitted by Linda Varner Goswick, op. cit.

[2]..Birth and death dates appear on a grave marker at Mt. Moriah Church Cemetery, Coosa Co, AL.

Clarice and Thomas are parents of four children: **Wendy Leigh Harris** (b. 2 May 1977), **Henley Kay Harris** (b. 26 Mar 1982), **Lendsey Necole Harris** (b. 23 Dec 1983, Birmingham, AL, d. 27 Aug 1985, Birmingham, AL), and **Jacob Drew Harris** (b. 30 Dec 1988, Birmingham, AL).

 (2) **Carol Howard Varner** (b. 20 Sep 1952, Coosa Co, AL) marr 11 Dec 1970, Talladega Co, AL, **Thomas Bruce Liveoak** (b. 5 May 1948, Talladega Co, AL, d. 22 Jan 1986, Coosa Co, AL). Carol lives in Coosa Co, AL, in 1994.

Carol and Thomas were parents of two children: **Thomas Blake Liveoak** (b. 6 May 1974, Talladega Co, AL) and **Benjamin Kyle Liveoak** (b. 29 Jul 1983, Birmingham, AL).

b. **Josephine Varner** (b. 29 May 1926, Coosa Co, AL) marr 8 Feb 1945, Talladega Co, AL, **Marvin Henry** (b. 12 Nov 1918, Marion, KY, d. 7 Jan 1988, Coosa Co, AL).

Josephine and Marvin were parents of five children: **Mary Jo, Judy Kaye, Bonnie Jean, John Richard, and Tammy A.**

 (1) **Mary Jo Henry** (b. 21 Dec 1951, Lake Co, IN, **Everett Bagley**. Mary Jo and Everett are parents of one child: **Melissa Jo Bagley** (b. 1 Feb 1981, Lake Co, IN).

 (2) **Judy Kaye Henry** (b. 28 Nov 1952, Coosa Co, AL) marr 16 Jun 1972, Lake Co, IN, **Bruce Jirtle**. Judy Kaye and Bruce are parents of two children: **Jayne Lynn Jirtle** (b. 18 Nov 1972, Lake Co, IN) and

Nicole Ruth Jirtle (b. 22 Sep 1984, Lake Co, IN).
- (3) **Bonnie Jean Henry** (b. 18 Aug 1954, Coosa Co, AL) marr 8 Feb 1982, Coosa Co, AL, **William Booth**.
- (4) **John Richard Henry** (b. 8 Mar 1958, Lake Co, IN) marr 22 Jun 1984, Coosa Co, AL, **Angela Johnston**. John and Angela are parents of two children: **Ryan William Henry** (b. 23 Jul 1985, Coosa Co, AL) and **Iain D. Henry** (b. 9 Nov 1989, Coosa Co, AL).
- (5) **Tammy A. Henry** (b. 25 May 1968, Lake Co, IN) marr 15 Oct 1988, Coosa Co, AL, **Barry D. Bryant**. Tammy and Barry are parents of one child: **Noah Taylor Bryant** (b. 22 Oct 1993, Coosa Co, AL).

c. **Bessie Varner** (b. 30 Mar 1933, Coosa Co, AL) marr **Paul Wallace**. This marriage ended in divorce. Bessie and Paul were parents of two children: **Mark and Sheila**.
- (1) **Mark Wallace** (b. 6 Jan 1958, Talladega Co, AL) marr **Lynn Wood**.
- (2) **Sheila Wallace** (b. 7 May 1962, Talladega Co, AL) marr in Talladega Co, AL, **Alan Giddine**.

d. **Norma Lee Varner** (b. 30 Nov 1935, Coosa Co, AL) marr Nov 1958 **William Reed, Jr.** (b. 29 Apr 1934, Freemont, NE). Norma was an office manager and William was a carpenter. Both are retired and live in Equality, AL.

Norma and William are parents of two children: **Maleia and Jonja**.
- (1) **Maleia Reed** (b. 17 Jan 1963, Atlanta, GA) marr 30 May 1981, Talladega Co,

AL, **Keith Adams** (b. 21 Sep 1959). Maleia is a retail merchandiser and Keith is a printer. This family lives in Weogufka, Coosa Co, AL, in 1994.

Maleia and Keith are parents of one child: **Cameron K. Adams** (b. 28 Mar 1990, Birmingham, AL).

(2) **Jonja Reed** (b. 2 Sep 1967, Sylacauga, AL) marr 12 Nov 1988, Sylacauga, AL, **Lamar Daugherty** (b. 12 Mar 1966). Jonja is a bank head teller and Lamar is a lineman with Central Alabama Electric. This couple lives in Weogufka, Coosa Co, AL, in 1994.

3. **Flossie Varner**[1] (b. 26 Apr 1907, Coosa Co, AL) marr 31 Oct 1926, Coosa Co, AL, **Julius Palmer** (b. 22 Sep 1907, Coosa Co, AL, d. 18 Jan 1973, Birmingham, AL).

Flossie and Julius were parents of five children: **Bertha O'Neal, Arlie Alton, Albert V., Betty Jean, and Melvin Merrel.**

a. **Bertha O'Neal Palmer** (b. 29 Sep 1927, Coosa Co, AL) marr 9 Apr 1948, Coosa Co, AL, **Connie Mooney** (b. 9 Jun 1919, Coosa Co, AL). Connie is a truck driver. Bertha and Connie live in Weogufka, Coosa Co, AL, in 1994.

Bertha and Connie are parents of four children: **Jerry Lee, Paul, Cecil, and Carolyn**.

(1) **Jerry Lee Mooney** (b. 4 May 1945, Coosa Co, AL) marr 30 Jul 1982, Coosa Co, AL,

---

[1] ..Information on the Flossie Varner and Julius Palmer family was submitted by Linda Goswick, op. cit.

Ethel Perry (b. 5 Mar 1944, Talladega Co, AL). Jerry is a superintendent and Ethel works with accounts and records. This couple lives in Sylacauga, AL, in 1994.

Jerry Lee is the parent of one child: **Christy Mooney** (b. 17 Mar 1969, Talladega Co, AL) marr Nov 1992, Talladega Co, AL, **Tom Harmon**. Christy is a clerk. She and Tom live in Sylacauga, AL, in 1994.

(2) **Paul Mooney** (b. 22 Aug 1946, Coosa Co, AL) marr 10 May 1968, Talladega Co, AL, **Shirley McDaniel** (b. 8 May 1948, Clay Co, AL). Paul is a foreman and Shirley is a bus driver. This couple lives in Sycamore, AL, in 1994.

Paul and Shirley are parents of two children: **Paula Jean and Janet**.

(a) **Paula Jean Mooney** (b. 2 Jul 1970, Talladega Co, AL) marr 26 Nov 1991, Talladega Co, AL, **Robert Turgeon**. Paula is a school teacher. This couple lives in Sycamore, AL, in 1994.

(b) **Janet Mooney** (b. 3 Jan 1977, Talladega Co, AL).

(3) **James Cecil Mooney** (b. 2 Nov 1948, Sylacauga, AL) marr 27 Feb 1973 in Coosa Co, AL, **Sherry Fowler** (b. 6 Aug 1953, Sylacauga, AL. James is a forestry supervisor and Sherry is a secretary. This family lives in Weogufka, AL, in 1994.

James and Sherry are parents of two children: **James R. Mooney** (b. 6 Dec 1973, Sylacauga, AL) and **Roger D. Mooney** (b. 27 Jul 1980). James is a laborer living in VA in 1994.

(4) **Judy Diane "Carolyn" Mooney** (b. 23 Jun 1951, Sylacauga, AL) marr 14 Sep 1974, Coosa Co, AL, **Dewey Raymond "Butch" Dobbs** (b. 14 Jul 1946, Sylacauga, AL). Judy works for EBSCO Industries and Dewey is a truck driver. This family lives in Sylacauga, AL, in 1994.

Judy and Dewey are parents of two children: **Carol Elizabeth Dobbs** (b. 16 Feb 1977, Sylacauga, AL) and **Kadie Michelle Dobbs** (b. 15 Feb 1980, Sylacauga, AL).

b. **Arlie Alton Palmer** (b. 13 Nov 1932, Coosa Co, AL, d. 18 Oct 1978, Sylacauga, AL) marr **Jo Callaway**. Jo lives in Sylacauga, AL, in 1994. Arlie and Jo were parents of two sons: **Terry Palmer and Mike Palmer**.

c. **Albert V. Palmer** (b. 13 Nov 1932, Coosa Co, AL, d. 14 Feb 1960, Sylacauga, AL) marr **Dora Haisten**. Dora lives in Weogufka, Coosa Co, AL, in 1994. Albert and Dora were parents of two children: **Sherry Palmer and Albert Palmer, Jr.** Sherry married **Donnie Morris** and Albert married **Linda Coleman**.

d. **Betty Jean Palmer** (b. 21 Aug 1939, Coosa Co, AL) marr **J. C. McLain** (b. 12 Oct 1925, Greenville, AL, d. 17 Aug 1974, Sylacauga, AL). Betty is self-employed and lives in Weogufka, Coosa Co, AL, in 1994. Betty and J. C. were parents of one child: **Jimbo**

McLain (b. 31 Aug 1959, Sylacauga, AL). Jimbo is a foreman with U.S. Steel and lives in Weogufka, Coosa Co, AL, in 1994.
  e. **Melvin Palmer** (b. 2 Feb 1942, Coosa Co, AL) marr 6 Oct 1962, Weogufka, AL, **Linda Calloway** (b. 6 Dec 1942, Coosa Co, AL). Melvin is a sales manager and Linda is self-employed. This family lives in Weogufka, Coosa Co, AL, in 1994.

  Melvin and Linda are parents of two children: **Melvin M., Jr., and Michelle**.
  (1) **Melvin Merrel Palmer, Jr.** (b. 28 Jan 1964, Sylacauga, AL) marr 1 Dec 1984, Weogufka, AL, **Melinda Harmon** (b. 13 Aug 1965, in Georgia). Melvin is a printer and Melinda is a licensed practicing nurse. This family lives in Weogufka, Coosa Co, AL, in 1994.

  Melvin and Melinda are parents of two children: **Matthew Palmer** (b. 5 Aug 1988, Sylacauga, AL) and **Myles Palmer** (b. 8 Dec 1991, Birmingham, AL).
  (2) **Michelle Palmer** (b. 3 Mar 1969, Sylacauga, AL, d. 7 Feb 1984, Weogufka, Al).
4. **Arval Ready Varner** (b. 28 Jun 1910, d. 2 Sep 1910).
5. **Maria Varner**[1] (b. 9 Jun 1915, Coosa Co, AL, d. 13 Mar 1993, Elmore Co, AL) marr 24 Sep 1934, Coosa Co, AL, **Charlie Crumbley** (b. 26 Jul 1914, Coosa Co, AL, d. 4 Sep 1984).

---

[1]..Information on the Charlie Crumbley and Maria Varner family was submitted by Linda Goswick, op. cit.

Maria and Charlie were parents of two children: **Lottie and Eddie**.
- a. **Lottie Crumbley** (b. 24 Dec 1935, Coosa Co, AL) marr 18 Mar 1956, Elmore Co, AL, **Audrey Bowdoin**. Lottie and Audrey are parents of two children: **Mike Bowdoin and Tina Bowdoin**.
- b. **Eddie Crumbley** (b. 24 Dec 1935, Elmore Co, AL) marr 1 Nov 1986, Montgomery, AL, **Jean Davis**. Eddie and Jean are parents of two children: **Sarah E. Crumbley and Hillary P. Crumbley**.

6. Shelton Varner (b. 1918, Coosa Co, AL).
7. Freeman Varner[1] (b. 6 Jan 1926, Coosa Co, AL) marr 8 Sep 1947 **Sula Green**. Freeman and Sula are parents of one child: **Barbara Varner**.
   - a. **Barbara Varner** (b. 26 Oct 1948) marr 18 Apr 1969 in Tuscaloosa Co, AL, **Scott Bonner**. Barbara and Scott are parents of two children: **Todd Bonner and Robb Bonner**.
     - (1) **Todd Bonner** (b. 21 Aug 1970, Tuscaloosa Co, AL.
     - (2) **Robb Bonner** (b. 12 May 1973, Tuscaloosa Co, AL.

----

[1]..Freeman Varner of Weogufka, AL, submitted information on his family and some of the material on other descendants of George H. Varner and Della Jacks.

H. **George Henley Varner,** son of Esselman Varner and Sarah Wilson, marr 2nd **Annie Jacks**[2] (b. 14 Sep 1912, Coosa Co, AL). George Henley Varner and Annie Jacks were parents of seven children: **Wyona Varner, Lee Varner, Ambrilla Varner, Wayne Varner, Linda Varner, Huston Varner, and Judy Varner.**
1. **Wyona Varner** (b. 13 Oct 1937, Coosa C, AL) marr **Clyde D. Crockett** (b. 21 Jul 1934, Shelby Co, AL, d. 13 Mar 1993, Chilton Co, AL). Wyona is a payroll clerk for the Alabama State Board of Corrections.

    Wyona and Clyde are parents of six children: **Donna Lynn, Dawn Elaine, Christopher Thomas, Patrick Bryan, Gwendolyn Darselle, and Tanya Jolan.**
    a. **Donna Lynn Crockett** (b. 28 Jan 1958, Jefferson Co, AL) marr **Andrew Corneil.** Donna and Andrew are parents of two children: **Regan Wyona Corneil** (b. 7 May 1979) and **Aaron Crockett Corneil** (b. 9 Feb 1990). Donna is a homemaker. This family lives in Jefferson Co, AL, in 1994.
    b. **Dawn Elaine Crockett** (b. 27 May 1959, Jefferson Co, AL). Dawn is a mortgage coordinator and lives in Hall Co, GA, in 1994.
    c. **Christopher Thomas Crockett** (b. 24 Jun 1961, Jefferson Co, AL). Christopher is a design engineer and lives in Wake Forrest, NC, in 1994.

---

[1]..Except as noted otherwise, information on descendants of George Henley Varner and Della Jacks was submitted by Linda Varner Goswick of Weogufka, Coosa Co, AL.

d. **Patrick Bryan Crockett** (b. 11 May 1964, Jefferson Co, AL) marr 15 Oct 1993, Montgomery, AL, **Cindy Taylor**. Patrick is a policeman. He and Cindy live in Montgomery, AL, in 1994.
e. **Gwendolyn Darcelle Crockett** (b. 22 Apr 1963, Jefferson Co, AL) marr **Steve Traywick**. This marriage ended in divorce. This couple are the parents of one child: **Ashley Julian Traywick** (b. 29 May 1986). Gwendolyn is a secretary and lives in Austin, TX, in 1994.
f. **Tanya Jolan Crockett** (b. 16 Jan 1973, Jefferson Co, AL, d. 13 Oct 1977).

2. **Lee Varner** (b. 4 Mar 1939, Coosa Co, AL) marr 13 Aug 1980, Coosa Co, AL, **Evelyn Palmer Varner** (b. 8 Feb 1938, Coosa Co, AL. Lee is a millwright and Evelyn is a key punch operator. This couple lives in Weogufka, Coosa Co, AL, in 1994.

Lee and Evelyn are parents of three children: **Kathy Lee, Sherry Kim, and Billy Keith**.

a. **Kathy Lee Varner** (b. 5 Feb 1960, Talladega Co, AL) marr **Rusty Cross**. Kathy is a homemaker, This family lives in Shreveport, LA, in 1994.

    Kathy and Rusty are parents of two children: **Christopher Brian Cross** (b. 13 Jan 1981) and **Michael Keith Cross** (b. 7 Mar ???).

b. **Sherry Kim Varner** (b. 25 Jul 1962, Talladega, Co, AL) marr **Tim Buchannan**. Two children were born to this couple: **Ryan Matthew Buchannan** (b. 4 Feb 1992) **and Christin Nicole Buchannan**. This marriage ended in divorce. Sherry is a papermill worker and lives in Coosa Co, AL, in 1994.

    c. **Billy Keith Varner** (b. 3 Nov 1963, Talladega Co, AL) marr **Christy Davis**. Billy is a textile worker. This family lives in Coosa Co, AL, in 1994.

3. **Ambrilla Varner** (b. 17 Sep 1941, Coosa County, AL) marr **Richard Beeson** (b. 20 Jan 1932, Pittcairn, PA). Ambrilla is a health professional and Richard is a pipe fitter. They live in Ft. Worth, TX, in 1994.

    Ambrilla and Richard are parents of five children: **Michael Ray, Richard Keith, Patricia Lynn, Steven Wayne, and Pamela Denece**.

    a. **Michael Ray Beeson** (b. 12 Feb 1963, Talladega Co, AL) marr **Lisa Cherry**. This marriage resulted in the birth of two children: **Kristin Nicole** (b. 15 Dec 1984) and **Kelley Elizabeth** (b. 30 Jun 1989). This marriage ended in divorce. Michael is a police officer in Ft. Worth, TX, in 1994.

    b. **Richard Keith Beeson** (b. 27 Sep 1965, Tarrant Co, TX) marr **Ann Cobb**. One child was born to this marriage: **Britanny Ryan** (b. 14 May 1990). This marriage ended in divorce. Richard works in the computer industry in Tarrant Co, TX, in 1994.

    c. **Patricia Lynn Beeson** (b. 20 Feb 1968, Tarrant Co, TX) marr 1st **Mike Allen**. Patricia and Mike are parents of one child: **Debra Renee Allen** (b. 15 Feb 1988). This marriage ended in divorce.

    c. **Patricia Lynn Beeson** marr 2nd **Dale Thornhill**. This family lives in Weatherford, TX, in 1994.

- d. **Steven Wayne Beeson** (b. 21 Jan 1969, Tarrant Co, TX) marr **Tiffany Eddy**. One child was born to this marriage: **Ashley Nicole** (b. 31 Jul 1987). This marriage ended in divorce. Steven works in parts. He lives in Tarrant Co, TX, in 1994.
- e. **Pamela Denece Beeson** (b. 7 May 1974, Tarrant Co, TX) marr **Joel Villareal**. One child was born to this marriage: **Brenda Marie**. This marriage ended in divorce. Pamela works in sales in Tarrant Co, TX, in 1994.

4. **Wayne Varner** (b. 26 Dec 1942) marr 21 Dec 1963, Coosa Co, AL, **Edna Davis** (b. 30 Sep 1946, Talladega Co, AL). Wayne is a truck driver and Edna is a cashier in Coosa Co, AL, in 1994.

   Wayne and Edna are parents of three children: **Patty Ruth, Larry Wayne, and Lori Leighann**.
   - a. **Patty Ruth Varner** (b. 5 Jan 1965, Talladega Co, AL) marr 23 Apr 1983 in Coosa Co, AL, **Glen Moates**. Patty is a textile worker. This family lives in Coosa Co, AL, in 1994.

     Patty and Glen are parents of two children: **Jami Ruth Moates** (b. 27 Jul 1987) and **Julie Samantha Moates** (b. 13 Jun 1989).
   - b. **Larry Wayne Varner** (b. 7 Dec 1966, Talladega Co, AL) marr 26 Mar 1992, Coosa Co, AL, **Sammy Kawaski**. Larry and Sammy are parents of one child: **Heather Ashley Varner** (b. 7 May 1993). This family lives in Coosa Co, AL, in 1994.
   - c. **Lori Leighann Varner** (b. 7 Mar 1984, Talladega, Co, AL).

5. **Linda Varner** (b. 3 Jan 1946, Coosa Co, AL) marr 15 Oct 1966, Clay Co, AL, **Ralph E. Goswick** (b. 13 Mar 1945, Talladega Co, AL). Linda is a dispatcher and Ralph is a paper mill worker. This family lives in Coosa Co, AL, in 1994.

   Linda and Ralph are parents of two children: **Andrew Gilbert and Amanda Jolan**.
   a. **Andrew Gilbert Goswick** (b. 3 Jul 1975, Blount Co, AL).
   b. **Amanda Jolan Goswick** (b. 21 May 1981, Jefferson Co, AL).

6. **Huston Varner** (b. 20 Jan 1949, Coosa Co, AL) marr **Dorothy Byrd** (b. 24 Nov 1950). Huston is an alignment specialist and Dorothy is a loan secretary. Huston and Dorothy live in Talladega Co, AL, in 1994.

   Huston and Dorothy are parents of two children: **Gary Wayne Varner and Kevin Paul Varner**.
   a. **Gary Wayne Varner** (b. 26 Jan 1971, Talladega Co, AL) marr 6 Mar 1992, Talladega Co, AL, **Sonja Castleberry**. Gary and Sonja are parents on one child: **Alexander Thomas Varner** (b. 24 Jun 1992).
   b. **Kevin Paul Varner** (b. 5 Oct 1972, Talladega Co, AL) marr **Tara Stewart**. Two children were born to this marriage: **Steven Cody Varner** (b. & d. 6 Apr 1992) and **Morgan Brittany Varner** (b. 15 Feb 1993). This marriage ended in divorce. Kevin is a truck driver. He lives in Talladega Co, AL, in 1994.

7. **Judy Varner** (b. 22 Jun 1952, Coosa Co, AL) marr **Harold Hepburn**. Three children were born to this marriage: **Harold Wayne, Carol Ann, and Donald**.

a. **Harold Wayne Hepburn** (b. 5 Mar 1968, Talladega Co, AL) marr **Lara Gazaway**. Harold is a carpenter. Harold and Lara are parents of two children: **Emily Ann Hepburn** (b. 30 Jun 1990, Ft. Worth, TX) and **Anthony Wayne Hepburn** (b. 9 Nov 1992).
b. **Carol Ann Hepburn** (b. 4 Jun 1969, Wichita, KS) marr **Charlie Carns**. Carol works in public relations. This family lives in Arvada, CO, in 1994. Carol and Charlie are parents of two children: **Charles Davis Carns, Jr.** (b. 5 Jun 1991) and **Cody Dallas Carns** (b. 17 Nov 1992).
c. **Donald Hepburn** (b. 17 Aug 1973, Talladega Co, AL). Donald is a sergeant in the U.S. Army, in Colorado Springs, CO, in 1994.
7. **Judy Varner** marr 2nd **Ronald Brown** (b. 30 Sep 1950, Talladega Co, AL). This marriage ended in divorce. Judy is a machinery operator. She lives in Ft. Worth, TX, in 1994.

Judy and Ronald are parents of one child: **Angela Brown** (b. 25 Aug 1978, Chilton Co, AL).

Esselman Varner, son of John Varner and Nancy Powell, marr 2nd, 30 Jan 1879, Coosa Co, AL, **Susan Elizabeth "Betty" Glenn**.

Appendix XII-A
1880 Agricultural Census for Esselman Varner
<u>1880 Agricultural Census, Coosa County, AL</u>.
Esselman Varner, Travelers Rest Beat
    Land: 40 acres of land tilled, 250 acres woodland.
    Value of farm, including building and fences: $600.

Value of farm equipment and tools: $10.
Value of livestock: $250.
Estimated value of all farm production: $300.
Livestock owned as of 6/1/1880: 2 horses, 2 mules, 2 working oxen, 8 swine, 14 barnyard poultry, 4 other poultry.
2 calves dropped during past year.
1 cattle sold living during past year.
1 cattle died, strayed or stolen.
150 pounds of butter produced on farm.
40 dozen eggs produced in 1880.
6 acres of Indian corn produced 75 bushels.
10 acres of cotton produced 4 bales.
1/2 acre potatoes produced 25 bushels.
20 cords of wood cut.
Value of forest products sold or consumed in 1879: $40.

Appendix XII-B
John Varner Charged with Assault and Battery
THE STATE OF ALABAMA VS JOHN VARNER[1]
From Trial Docket, page 45, Coosa County Circuit Court records:

John Varner arrested and charged with Assault and Battery.

Defendant released on bond. 1871 (exact date not recorded).

From Trial Docket, page 58.

Jury found the defendant guilty and levied a fine of $1.00.

---

[1]..This John Varner was a son of Azariah Varner and Mary Pickering. See Chapter VIII.

Esselman Varner and Hardaway Varner confessed the judgment along with the defendant. Spring term 1872. From Trial Docket, page 381. State of Alabama vs. John Varner, Esselman Varner, and Hardaway Varner. Judgment October 21, 1872.

Fine	$1.00
Clerk's fees	5.65
Sheriff's fees	4.55
County tax	2.00
Solicitor's fee	15.00

Received from Esselman and Hardaway Varner $27.61 in full satisfaction of the fine and costs in this case, Jan. 2, 1873. R. H. Gulledge, Sheriff.

Appendix XII-C
Esselman Varner's Will

The State of Alabama, Coosa County

Know all men by these presents that I Esselman Varner do by this my last Will and Testament will and bequeath to my beloved wife Betty Varner all my property both real and personal so long as she may live after paying all of my just debts of which she shall have full control sufficiently to sustain and support her natural life except selling the real estate of which she is barred.

I will furthermore when my son George Varner becomes of lawful age that he be furnished or given a horse and saddle of equal value to the ones that I have given to my other sons. I also will that my son George Varner have a certain gold watch that my father owned at his death as he is my youngest son.

It is my will that my wife Betty Varner after complying with the above part of this will that she shall have full control of all of my property both real and personal so long as she may live and all the income thereof and after her death then all of the property that remain at her death shall be equally divided among all of my lawful heirs. Their names are as follows to wit: William A. Varner, Manton E. Varner, Nancy A. Johnson, James H. Varner, John A. Varner, Mary A. Varner, George H. Varner.

And furthermore it is my will that a certain double barrel shot gun that my father owned at his death, which I have in my possession at this date, first go to my son James Varner and if for any cause he should see proper to dispose of said gun that it shall be given to one of my other children and to see that this my last will be carried out strictly according to the above will I hereby appoint as executives to this my last will James H. Varner and J. A. Varner, and William A. Varner said executives to carry out said will strictly according the above directions without any cost or proceedings of any courts of said state of county in witness whereof I hereunto set my hand and affix my seal this the 8 day of August 1896. E. Varner

Attest: W. C. Harris, J. R. White

Recorded in Coosa County, AL, Will Book 3, pages 161-163.

Appendix XII-D
Petition To Probate Esselman Varner's Will
Will Book 3. Coosa County, Alabama, Probate Court

Petition of James H. Varner, J. A. Varner, and W. A. Varner for the Probate of the Will of E. Varner deceased. To the Hon. J. A. Crawford, Judge of Probate Court, Coosa County.

The petition of the undersigned James H., J. A., and W. A. Varner respectfully represents unto your Honor that

ESSELMAN VARNER, SON OF JOHN VARNER

E. Varner who was at the time of his death an inhabitant of this county departed this life at his home in Coosa County, Alabama, on or about the 14 day of May 1907 having assets in this state and leaving a last will and testament duly signed and published by him and attested by W. C. Harris, J. B. White, M. C. Glenn and A. C. Varner. That your petitioners as they verily believe are named in said will as executors and that they are sons and heirs of said E. Varner and does now herewith surrender said will to the Court, and pray that after proper proceedings and proofs, it may be probated and admitted to record as the true last will and testament of said deceased.

Your petitioner further represents that Betty Varner is the widow of said deceased, and that the names, ages, residence, and conditions of the next of kin are as follows: James H. Varner, J. A. Varner, and W. A. Varner, who are your petitioners, and Martin E. Varner, Nancy A. Johnston, wife of Fletcher Johnston, Mary A. Vance, wife of W. D. Vance, and George H. Varner all of whom are of sound mind over the age of twenty-one years and reside in Coosa County, Alabama except Mary A. Vance and her husband W. D. Vance who reside in Chilton County, Alabama.

Your petitioners would further represent that all of the said attesting witnesses reside in Coosa County, Alabama...

Felix L. Smith, Attorney for Petitioners.

Chapter XIII
Frederick Varner, Son of George Varner

Frederick Varner was a son of George Varner and Elizabeth "Betsy" Varner of Oglethorpe Co, GA. He was born in about 1789 in Wilkes Co, GA. He died 15 Oct 1855[1] in Caldwell Parish, LA. He married **Sarah "Sally" Graves** in Oglethorpe Co, GA on 27 Jun 1808. Like so many others in his family, Frederick Varner was a planter. His first farm was in Oglethorpe Co, GA, near his father George Varner. He paid taxes in Oglethorpe Co, GA, for a few years, beginning in 1813. His Georgia farm was small, only 143 acres, and he had only 3 Negro slaves while a resident of Georgia.[2]

In 1819, Frederick acquired land on the Alabama River, in Montgomery Co, AL (Lowndes Co after 1830). His brother John Varner settled there at the same time. John's land was about one mile downriver from Frederick's. Unlike his brother John, Frederick did not participate in Lowndes Co politics. But his land holdings and his slave population both grew during the 20 plus years that he farmed there. He reported ownership of 17 slaves in 1830 and 13 in 1840.

Frederick Varner Moves to Louisiana

During the early 1840's Frederick and most of his children left Lowndes Co, AL, and relocated to the east bank of the Quachita River in Caldwell Parish, LA. He prospered there as well. He left 25 slaves, named in his

---

[1]..Frederick Varner's Estate Papers. On file at the Courthouse, Caldwell Parish, Columbia, Louisiana.

[2]..Oglethorpe Co, GA, Tax Records, op. cit. for 1813-1817.

FREDERICK VARNER, SON OF GEORGE VARNER

will[1], appraised at about $10,000. In addition, his plantation, land and improvements, was appraised at $5,300. Records do not show a value for additional personal property. The appraised value of the entire estate was $18,464.93. (This total did not include gifts Frederick had previously given to his children.) Frederick's will and other estate records are located in the Courthouse in Columbia, Caldwell Parish, LA.[2]

Frederick Varner, son of George Varner of Oglethorpe Co, GA, suffered the loss of several family members during the last few years of his life. His wife Sarah, a son, Thomas Jefferson, and two daughters, Amarantha and Elizabeth, preceded him in death. These are believed to have been his three oldest children. Whether Frederick lost his wife while living in AL or after moving to LA is unknown. She preceded him in death; she is not mentioned in his will or estate records. His sons William Graves, who remained in Lowndes Co, AL, and Francis M., who moved to LA with the family, died soon after Frederick's death, before the estate was settled.

Frederick and Sarah had eight children: **Thomas Jefferson, Amarantha L., Elizabeth, William Graves, George W., Frederick, Jr., John F., and Francis M.**[3]

---

[1]..See Appendix # XIII-A at the end of this chapter for a copy of Frederick Varner's will.

[2]..The will was dated 28 Nov 1853; it was entered for probate 24 Nov 1855.

[3]..Much of the information about Frederick and Sarah's children and grandchildren was obtained from Frederick's will and estate papers, which are located in the Caldwell Par, LA, Courthouse.

Thomas Jefferson Varner and His Children

A. **Thomas Jefferson Varner**, son of Frederick Varner and Sarah Graves was born in about 1811 in Oglethorpe Co, GA. He died 28 Sept 1843[1] in Columbia, Caldwell Par, LA). He married **Nancy "Ann" L. Graves** 24 Jul 1832, in Lowndes Co, AL. Nancy L. Graves was born 4 May 1811 in Oglethorpe Co, GA; she died 8 Jul 1844, in Lowndes Co, AL. She is buried in the Graves Family Burial Ground, Lowndes Co, AL. Their orphan children were raised by John R. and Mary A. (Graves) Rogers under the supervision of the Lowndes, Co, AL, Orphans Court.[2] Mary A. Graves Rogers was a sister to Nancy L. Graves Varner. Nancy L. and Mary Graves were daughters of William Graves.[3]

Thomas was a land speculator and planter in Lowndes Co, AL, throughout the 1830's, buying and then reselling many acreages. He also expanded his slave-holdings.

---

[1]..Thomas Jefferson Varner, resident of Caldwell Parish, LA, died Thursday, 28 Sep 1843 at his home on the Quachita River. He left no will but there are extensive estate papers. His estate consisted mainly of Negroes (10), land, and stock (cattle). It was appraised at $3,377.50. Estate papers are on file in the Caldwell Parish Court House, Columbia, LA. Additional records, including many concerning his orphan children, are located at the Alabama Archives in Montgomery, AL.

[2]..Those records are in the Lowndes Co, AL, Orphans Court minutes, beginning in 1844 and ending in about 1857.

[3]..Proof that Nancy "Ann" L. Graves, wife of Thomas J. Varner, and Mary Graves, wife of John R. Rogers, were sisters can be found in William Graves' estate papers located at the AL Archives.

FREDERICK VARNER, SON OF GEORGE VARNER

Thomas joined the Masons in Lowndes County, AL, Lodge # 33, 7 Sep 1833. He passed the membership exam 2 Nov and was raised to Master Mason 7 Dec 1833.[1]

Thomas J. Varner had moved to Caldwell Parish, LA, prior to his death. After his death, his widow Nancy L. and children moved back to Lowndes County, AL, where Nancy's relatives lived. She died shortly after moving back to Alabama. The children were then raised by Nancy's relatives.

Thomas J. Varner left an estate appraised at $5,500 to support his orphans. The estate included 19 Negro slaves[2], all named in the record. They were divided among the four children.[3] That estate was monitored for each of the four children by the Lowndes Co Orphans Court until each became of age. Annual reports of the administrators give some insight regarding spending habits of the children. For example, Giles purchased tobacco regularly after about the age of 13; William purchased some tobacco, a box of cigars, a Negro whip, and several bottles of whiskey; and Louisa bought a box of snuff. Other purchases appear to be what one would normally expect for the maintenance and education of children.[4]

---

[1]..Records located at Grand Lodge Free & Accepted Masons of Alabama, 3033 Vaughn Road, Montgomery, AL.

[2]..See Appendix # XIII-B at the end of this chapter for the appraisal record of Thomas Jefferson Varner's estate.

[3]..See Appendix # XIII-C at the end of this chapter for notes on the division of the slaves owned by the estate of Thomas J. Varner.

[4]..Many of the annual reports are in the AL Dept of Archives filed with the Lowndes Co Estate Papers under
(continued...)

Thomas J. and Nancy L. were parents of four children: **Louisa, William, Mary A. and Giles T.**
1. **Louisa Varner** (b. ca. 1832, Lowndes Co, AL) marr 7 Dec 1849, Lowndes Co, AL, to **Lemuel G. Waters**.
2. **William Varner**, (b. 1834, Lowndes Co, AL).
3. **Mary A. Varner** (b. 1836, Lowndes Co, AL) marr 30 May 1856, Lowndes Co, AL, **James D. Hicks**. Mary and James were living in Autauga Co, AL, in 1855.
4. **Giles T. Varner**, (b. 1838, Lowndes Co, AL). Giles was a soldier in the Confederate Army, serving in the following units: Co F, 9th LA Inf., pvt; Co H, 1st Nelligan's LA Inf, pvt; and Co D, 1st Special Batt, Rightor's LA Inf, pvt then cpl.

B. Amarantha Varner, dau of Frederick Varner and Sarah Graves, (b. ca. 1813, Oglethorpe Co, GA, d. bef. 1855) marr 13 Jul 1829, Montgomery Co, AL, Lewis Jackson.

Children of this couple, as named in Frederick's estate papers, were **Elizabeth, Sarah, Saphronia, Susan, Virginia, Fredonia, Frederick, Martha, Emma, Amarintha, and James L.**
1. **Elizabeth Jackson**, wife of **William Ledford**.
2. **Sarah Jackson**, wife of **William C. McColluch**.
3. **Saphronia Jackson**, wife of **Clough C. McColluch**.
4. **Susan Jackson**, wife of _____ **Tanner**.
5. **Virginia Jackson**, wife of _____ **Latner**.
6. **Fredonia Jackson**.
7. **Frederick Jackson**.
8. **Martha Jackson**.
9. **Emma Jackson**.

---

[4](...continued)
Thomas J. Varner.

10. **Amarintha Jackson**.
11. **James L. Jackson**.

C. **Elizabeth Varner**, dau of Frederick Varner and Sarah Graves (b. ca. 1815, Oglethorpe Co, GA, d. bef 1855, Caldwell Par, LA) marr 29 Mar 1833, Lowndes Co, AL, **Robert A. Blanks**. Elizabeth and Robert were parents of five children, all named in the Frederick Varner estate records.
1. **Frederick A. Blanks** (b. ca. 1838, Lowndes Co, AL).
2. **John W. Blanks**, minor in 1855.
3. **Amarintha L. Blanks**, minor in 1855.
4. **Harriet E. Blanks**, minor in 1855.
5. **Josephine Blanks**, minor in 1855.

William Graves Varner and His Family

D. **William Graves Varner**, son of Frederick Varner and Sarah Graves (b. 8 Jan 1816, Oglethorpe Co, GA, d. 12 Jan 1858, Lowndes Co, AL) marr 21 Dec 1837, Lowndes Co, AL, **Susan Eliza Varner**, dau of John Varner and Nancy Powell (b. ca. 1818, Oglethorpe Co, GA, d. aft 1900, Lowndes Co, AL.) William and Susan were first cousins.

William was a planter in Lowndes Co, AL, near Hayneville. He took over his father Frederick's Lowndes Co land after Frederick moved to LA. He lived on it and farmed it until his death. He had only 3 slaves in 1840 but his slave ownership grew to 15[1] by the time of the 1855 AL State census. He wrote his will 22 Dec 1857; it was

-----

[1]..Most of these are believed to have been the slaves that John Varner deeded to his daughter Susan Eliza Varner, William G. Varner's wife, in trusts. See Chapter IX.

submitted for probate[1] 2 Mar 1858. He left his entire estate to Susan Elisa Varner, his widow.[2]

William G. Varner was a member of the Masonic Lodge # 33, Hayneville, AL.[3]

Based on Lowndes Co, AL, Circuit and Chancery Court records, William G. Varner was not a responsible manager of his financial affairs. He drank excessively over a period of years and failed to pay his debts in a timely manner. Because of William's inability to provide adequately for the needs of his family, his wife's father, John Varner--who was also William's uncle--helped support Susan and her children. In 1842, John Varner deeded three slaves[4] to Susan Eliza Varner as her separate property. He included provisions in the deed to prohibit William G. Varner from selling them and to protect the slaves so that William's creditors could not seize them. In violation of the trust, one of his creditors had a justice of

---

[1]..The Probate Court approved the final settlement of the estate of William G. Varner on Feb. 17, 1860. The entire estate, valued at $3,200, went to Susan E. Varner, the widow, as specified in the will. (Minutes of Probate Court Book 12, p. 539.)

[2]..Minutes of the Probate Court, Book L, pp. 211-213, Lowndes Co, AL. William G. Varner's estate papers are at the AL Archives, filed with Lowndes County estate papers.

[3]..Records provided by the Masons of Alabama, 3033 Vaughn Rd., Montgomery, AL. The date of William G. Varner's membership was not recorded.

[4]..For more information about the slaves--including their names, sex, and approximate ages--that John Varner "donated" as the special property of his daughter Susan Eliza Varner, see Chapter IX.

the peace seize one of the slaves (the child Milly) and sell her at public auction. The child was purchased by John M. Cole.

Susan Varner filed suit against John M. Cole in Lowndes County Chancery Court to regain possession of the slave plus damages from Cole. Susan won the case and Cole was ordered to return the slave and pay Susan for loss of her property plus costs and interest. Cole appealed the decision to the Alabama Supreme Court, which also ruled against him. The Court testimony in this case reveals a lot about William G. Varner and his family.[1]

Witness Allen Davis, who had known William G. Varner for 32 years, said that Varner began drinking to excess in about 1841 and that he kept doing so for several years afterwards. Another witness, McDaniel Atchison, who lived near him at the time, said that William G. Varner "commenced drinking very hard in 1841 or 1842." Witness William A. Rice said he had frequently seen William G. Varner intoxicated but that he did not know when he started drinking heavily but thinks he kept it up several years. Rice added that, in about 1841, 1842, or 1843, W. G. Varner told him that he (Varner) was considerably dissipated and despondent.

John Varner, William's uncle and Susan's father, testified that when he set up the trust (in 1842) he knew that William had been dissipating for some time and admitted that the purpose of establishing the trust, rather

---

[1]..This was Lowndes Co Chancery Court Case # 414, which is summarized in Chancery Court Minutes, Bk. 11, pp. 371-389.

than making an outright gift, was to protect the property (slaves) from becoming liable for William's debts.[2]

In 1847, John Varner donated four additional slaves[2] to Susan Eliza Varner to use as her separate property to provide support for her and the children. This time, he set up a trust and assigned the slaves to it, rather than issue a deed. He probably believed this would provide stronger protection for them against William G. Varner's creditors.

Other records prove that William G. Varner was a success in some respects. He was summoned and served on Circuit Court juries at least three times.[3]

Tax records suggest that he owned a significant amount of property,[4] primarily in slaves.[5] After William's

---

[1]..The information on witnesses' testimony is taken from the original Chancery Court records, which were discovered in a Lowndes County storage warehouse in Hayneville, AL, by the author.

[2]..This brought the total number of slaves that John Varner gave to his daughter in trusts to seven, plus "their increase." The term "their increase" meant any and all of their future children and grandchildren.

[3]..William G. Varner served as foreman of the jury in a civil case during the fall term of the Circuit Court in 1849. (Circuit Court Minutes 1848-1854, p 77).

William G. Varner was summoned to Circuit Court jury duty on March 7, 1841. He responded and served. (Record, Circuit Court, pp 296-297).

William G. Varner, planter from Hayneville, was called to serve on the jury for a special session of the Circuit Court held Oct. 10, 1853. (Circuit Court Minutes 1848-1854, p 246).

[4]..See Appendix # IX-J at the end of this chapter for one
(continued...)

death, Susan E. Varner, executrix of his estate, was able to pay his debts and reported a balance in the estate of $3,200.

William and Susan Varner were parents of six children: **Amerentha L., William L., Amaziah, Elizabeth, Martha M., and John F.**

For more information about William and Susan Varner and for information about their descendants, see Chapter IX.

---

[4](...continued)
year's tax record for William G. Varner, Susan E. Varner's husband.

[5]..Most of the slaves that the tax records credited to the ownership of William G. Varner were actually property of the trusts that John Varner had set up to support his daughter Susan (William's husband).

VARNER FAMILIES OF THE SOUTH--XIII

George W. Varner Found Guilty of Fraud

E. **George W. Varner**,[1] son of Frederick Varner and Sarah Graves, was born in Oglethorpe Co, GA, in about 1818, or in Montgomery Co, AL, in about 1820. He died in Lowndes Co, AL, in June 1842.

The only known records about George W. Varner were found in Lowndes Co, AL, Chancery and Circuit court records. There were several of those, however. All occurred during the final year or two of his life.

In one Circuit Court case, George W. Varner was sued for failing to construct a log cabin which he had promised to build as payment for his rent.[2] William G. Varner,

---

[1]..The author is not positive about the identity of the George W. Varner who was involved in several Lowndes County, AL, law suits from about 1840 until his death in 1842. Records strongly suggest but do not prove for certain that he was a son of Frederick Varner and Sally Graves. It seems unlikely that he could have been a son of John Varner because John Varner had a known son named George H. Varner. (See Chapter 10).

In various court records, this George W. Varner's name was associated with William G. Varner, believed to have been his brother; Robert A. Blanks, believed to have been his brother-in-law; and Amaziah Varner, believed to have been his cousin. Further evidence of this relationship is the fact that one court record mentions contacts that George W. Varner had with his Varner relatives in Caldwell Parish, LA, which is where Frederick Varner and most of his children settled after leaving Lowndes Co, AL.

[2]--William Slade v George W. Varner & William G. Varner. Spring 1842. Slade sought damages of $200 on a charge of trespassing and of not paying a promissory note. The promissory note was for $100 and was signed July 15, 1840 with a promise to pay it on Jan. 1, 1841. The note read in part:
(continued...)

believed to have been his brother, was a co-defendant in this case.

In another case, George W. Varner was sued for failing to make good on a promissory note for $50.[1] In a more interesting case, he was prosecuted by the State of Alabama for "selling Rum, Brandy, Whiskey, Gin, Tafia, and other spirituous liquors" without a license[2] to Amaziah Varner (his cousin), Samuel Gardner, and others. He was indicted by a grand jury 7 Apr 1842 and his trial was set for Sep 1842. On the appointed date for the trial, Prosecutor Nathan Cook reported the death of George W. Varner and the court declared the suit abated.[3]

---

[2](...continued)
"This note is in payment of rent on the land where I now live. I also agree to build a log cabin 16 by 18 feet with a puncheon floor and good chimney such as are usual for log cabins for Negroes, with a value of $15.00."

The defendants failed to appear in court and did not challenge the suit. The plaintiff was awarded $91.01 and costs at the fall term 1842.

Lowndes Co, AL, Circuit Court Records 1841-1842, p. 377.

[1]--John Kimball v William G. Varner and George W. Varner, Fall Term 1842. Kimball was granted the $50 he requested, plus 15 per cent interest plus costs. Judgment issued July 18, 1842. (This judgment was against William G. Varner. Other than in the title of the case, there is no mention of George W. Varner. He died before the case came to trial.) (Circuit Court Records 1841-1842, p 524, Lowndes County, AL).

[2]--Today this practice is popularly called "bootlegging." Then it was referred to as "retailing."

[3]--State of Alabama v George W. Varner, 1842.

(continued...)

In a more bizarre case, George W. Varner was accused and convicted of fraudulently acquiring promissory notes from an alcoholic planter, Ruffin E. Walton, just five days before Walton died from excessive drinking.[1] Suit against George W. Varner was brought by Drury D. Walton, brother of the deceased and administrator of his estate. Walton claimed that his brother had been drinking heavily for several days before he died and that he was too intoxicated to transact business at the time he signed the notes. The notes were dated 24 Mar 1840. But Walton claimed that the notes had been antedated; that they were actually signed 7 Jul 1841. He further attested that

---

[3](...continued)

The state charged that George W. Varner, resident of Lowndes County, "on April 5, 1842, did sell Rum, Brandy, Whiskey, Gin, Tafia, and other spirituous liquors in quantities of less than one gallon to Amaziah Varner and others without first obtaining a license from the county...against the dignity of the State of Alabama." And that he sold "Rum, Brandy, Whiskey, Gin, Tafia, and other spirituous liquors to Samuel Gardner and others in quantities of less than one quart without first obtaining a license from the county." George W. Varner was indicted by a Grand Jury on April 7, 1842, and his trial was set for the 4th Monday in September, 1842. Spring Term 1842.

Prosecutor Nathan Cook reported the death of the defendant and the court declared the suit abated. Fall Term 1842. Lowndes Co, AL, Circuit Court Minutes, 1841-1842, p. 610 and Circuit Court Minutes, 1842-1848, p. 67.

[1]--Lowndes Co, AL, Chancery Court Case # 7, filed 12 May 1842. Recorded in Chancery Court Records, Book 1, pages 249-264. The author of this book discovered the original court records, including the promissory notes with seals still intact, in a Lowndes Co, AL storage building located behind the jail in Hayneville, AL.

FREDERICK VARNER, SON OF GEORGE VARNER

George W. Varner had been out of the state on 24 Mar 1840, the date that appeared on the notes, that Ruffin Walton owed Varner nothing, and that Varner tricked him into signing the notes by claiming that if he did not do so the sheriff would seize Ruffin's property.

In his answer, George W. Varner denied all fraud whatsoever and claimed that Ruffin E. Walton was not intoxicated when he signed the notes.

Witnesses Isaac Webb, Dickson Kelley, and I. W. Blackwell substantiated the claims made by Walton.

In its ruling against Varner and in favor of Walton, the court said it agreed with all of Walton's arguments. George W. Varner died soon after 2 Jun 1842, the date he replied to the above charges. His estate, with Samuel Gardner as administrator, was directed to pay all court costs of $49.67.[1]

One final proceeding involving George W. Varner was filed with Lowndes Co, AL, Orphans Court 16 Sep 1844. Samuel Gardner, administrator of George W. Varner's estate, alleged that Varner's estate was wholly insolvent and insufficient to pay its just debts. Nobody appeared in court to contest the claim and creditors were given six months to file their claims.[2]

F. Frederick Varner, Jr., son of Frederick Varner and Sarah Graves (b. ca. 1820, Montgomery Co, AL, d. 1867, Caldwell Par, LA).

---

[1]--The author has copies, which he is willing to share with others, of all records relating to this case and many other court cases in Lowndes Co, AL, involving this line of Varners.

[2]--Lowndes Co, AL, <u>Orphans Court Records</u>, Book E, pp. 341 and 386.

Frederick Varner, Jr. was the executor of the estate of his father, Frederick Varner, Sr. Frederick Varner, Jr.'s estate was probated in 1867. Estate records for both father and son are on file in the Caldwell Parish, LA, courthouse.

G. John F. Varner, son of Frederick Varner and Sarah Graves (b. ca. 1822, Montgomery Co, AL). John was the administrator of the estate of his brother Francis M. in Caldwell Par, LA, in 1855. John F. Varner joined the LA Militia, Co H, 6th LA Volunteers, for service in the Mexican War (1846-1848).[1]

H. Francis M. Varner, son of Frederick Varner and Sarah Graves, (b. ca. 1825, Montgomery Co, AL, d. 1855, Caldwell Par, LA). His estate papers are on file at the Caldwell Parish, LA, courthouse.

Appendix XIII--A
Frederick Varner's Will

FREDERICK VARNER'S WILL--

The State of Louisiana, Parish of Caldwell. Nov. 28th, 1853. (Filed Nov. 24, 1855)

I Frederick Varner Sr. resident of the Parish of Caldwell in the State of Louisiana, remindful of the uncertainty of life and being of sound and disposing mind do ordain this my last will and testament.

1st. I give and bequeath to my son Jefferson Varner or to his four children, viz: Louisa Varner, William Varner, Jr., Mary Varner and Giles Varner, the following

---

[1]..U.S. Military Service Records, on microfilm at the LDS Family History Library, Salt Lake City.

FREDERICK VARNER, SON OF GEORGE VARNER

amount in money, viz: four hundred dollars to each of them; Jefferson Varner, the father of the above named children, has previously received $455.

2nd. I give and bequeath unto my daughter Amarantha L. Jackson the following named slaves, viz: Bob, Milly, Bill, John, and Randal, appraised at $2400. She has previously received $685.

3rd. I give and bequeath to my daughter Elizabeth Blanks or her children, the following named slaves, to wit: Elder, Judge, Mary, Major, Nancy, and George, appraised at $2525. She has previously received $680.

4th. I give and bequeath unto my son William G. Varner the following named slaves, viz: Sam, Tilda, and Phillis, appraised at $2400. He has previously received $690.

5th. I give and bequeath unto my son Frederick Varner, Jr., the following named slaves, viz: Handy, Charity, Ellen, and Cyrus, appraised at $2325. He has previously received $1580.

6th. I give and bequeath unto my son John F. Varner the following named slaves, viz: William, John, Abby, and Alabama, appraised at $2450. He has previously received $700.

7th. I give and bequeath unto my son Francis M. Varner the following named slaves, viz: Charles, Letty, and Linder, appraised at $2275. He has previously received $385.

Furthermore, I want my lands, horses, cattle, hogs, farming utensils, and blacksmith tools sold, together with my household and kitchen furniture; I want sixteen hundred dollars to be paid to the four children of Jefferson Varner as has been previously stated and designated in item 1st out of the proceeds of said sale. Also all of my just debts to be paid out of said proceeds of said sale, and the balance of the proceeds of said sale to be equally distributed among the legatees above mentioned; except the children of Jefferson Varner, who shall not receive but sixteen hundred dollars as has been previously mentioned.

Finally, I appoint my son Frederick Varner, Jr. and Lewis Jackson as executors of this my last will and testament.

In witness whereof I have caused this will to be written and read aloud in the presence of myself and the undersigned witnesses on this the 28th day of November, A. D. 1853, declaring the same to be my last will and testament. This done and signed in the Parish and State aforesaid and day aforesaid.

Frederick Varner (his mark)

Robert M. Babb, Jacob Humble, W. L. Samuels (Witnesses).

Appendix XIII-B
Appraisal of Thomas J. Varner's Estate

<u>Thomas Jefferson Varner Estate Papers</u>, Located in the Alabama Archives, filed under Lowndes County Estate Papers. The State of Alabama, Lowndes County.

"We the undersigned commissioners appointed by the judge of the County Court to value and appraise the personal property of Thomas J. Varner, deceased, have proceeded to examine and appraise the said property as follows:

Negro man Harry	$435	Negro boy Forsyth $250
" girl Caroline	300	" girl Harriet 200
" " Adeline	250	" boy Frank 175
" boy Bob	200	" girl Caty 250
" girl Jane	250	" boy Plenty 275

"	woman Cealy &		" " Andrew	225
	child Polly	500	" " Spencer	400
"	girl Dianah	450	" girl Hannah	400
"	man Suzith	400	" woman Mariah	
			& infant	450

2 bedsteads, beds and furniture 50
                TOTAL $5,550

Appraised and assigned this 28th day of December, 1844. Wm. P. Fisher, Geo. Thomas, A. J. Thomason, A. Douglass. James K. Whitman, J. P.

Presented to the Court by John R. Rogers, administrator of the estate of Thomas J. Varner, Feb. 11, 1845.

Appendix XIII-C
Division of Thomas J. Varner's Slaves

<u>Division of Slaves Owned by the Thomas J. Varner Estate</u>

The State of Alabama, Lowndes County, December 21, 1849.

Orphans Court began and held in Hayneville for said county at the court room thereof on the 21st day of December 1849. Present his Honor Edward H. Cook, Judge, presiding. This day came John R. Rogers, Administrator of the Estate of Thomas J. Varner, deceased, came into court and made application for a division of the following Negroes (to wit): Harry, Celia, Caroline, Bob, Adaline, Jane, Polly, Margaret, and one other child of Harry and Celia, name not known, Suzette, Mariah, Harriett, Forsythe, Francis, Flemming, Dinah, Andrew, Plenty, and Caty between the following named legatees and heirs at law of said deceased (to wit): Louisa Waters, wife of Lemuel G. Waters, William Varner, Mary A. Varner, and Giles W. Varner, Whereupon

It is ordered by the court that Mordicai D. Harris, Joseph H. Howard, Seymour H. Powell, James Harrison, and Thomas C. Hartwell be and they are hereby appointed commissioners to make said division among said legatees.

Ordered that said commissioners make a report of said division to this Court under the hands and seals of all their proceedings in the premises.

Ordered that Young W. Graves be and he is hereby appointed guardian Ad Litem for William Varner, Mary A. Varner and Giles W. Varner, minors, to act for them in said division, said Administrator being their Guardian proper.

(Filed with Lowndes County Estate Papers, Alabama Archives).

Chapter XIV
Varner Records in Georgia

The author collected extensive records on early day Varners in Georgia. Many of those records have been cited in footnotes and appendixes in preceding chapters. Additional records from Georgia that relate to the Varner line covered in this book are printed as supplements in this chapter.

While searching early records for the Varner line that this book is about, the author also gathered notes on several other Varner lines[1]. Records that are known to

---

[1]..For example, there were three George Varners from Georgia who fought with the American army in the Revolutionary War. One was the George Varner of Oglethorpe County who is the subject of much of this book.

A second George Varner, whose ancestors apparently came from Ireland, lived in Decatur County, GA, at the time he fought in the Revolutionary War. After the war, he moved to Pulaski County, GA. Later, this family lived in Baldwin and Monroe counties in Georgia. Two of his sons--Alexander and William--moved to Alabama, where each of them prospered and left well educated and successful children and grandchildren. Both were large slave-holders. Alexander settled in Chambers County and William built his plantation mansion in Macon County. Descendants of Alexander and William became prominent attorneys, judges, state legislators, and bankers in Macon, Montgomery, Chambers and other counties. U. S. District Judge Robert Varner of Montgomery, AL, is believed to be a descendant of the George Varner who resided in Decatur County, GA, during the Revolutionary War.

A third Revolutionary War soldier named George Varner (originally Verner) was a resident of Ninety-Six District in South Carolina during the Revolutionary War. After the war, he moved to Franklin County, GA, where he died during the 1840's. This third George Varner is believed to have come from Ireland although that belief may not be well documented. The
(continued...)

VARNER FAMILIES OF THE SOUTH--XIV

deal with Varners who were not related to the Varners covered in this book are not included.

Thus the following records pertain to the Varners--George, Frederick, and Matthew--who settled in Wilkes County, GA (later Oglethorpe) and their descendants.

Supplement XIV-A
1800 Federal Census Records
1800 CENSUS, OGLETHORPE COUNTY, GEORGIA
George Varner, Capt. McIlroy's District
    2 white males 0 through 9 years of age
    2 white males 10 through 15
    1 white male 16 through 25
    1 white male 26 through 44
    1 white male 45 and over
    2 white females 0 through 9
    1 white female 25 through 44
    20 Negro slaves

Frederick Varner, Capt. McIlroy's District
    2 white males 0 through 9 years of age
    2 white males 10 through 15
    1 white male 26 through 44
    3 white females 0 through 9
    1 white female 26 through 44
    4 Negro slaves

---

[1](...continued)
author of this book is descended from David Verner, Sr., who was one of the brothers of this George Varner. David Verner, Sr., also fought in the Revolutionary War. The author is continuing to research this line of Verners/Varners and plans to publish his findings in a second volume of <u>Varner Families of the South</u>. Publication of this second volume is planned for 1995.

Matthew Varner, Capt. Ellis' District
    2 white males 0 through 9 years of age
    1 white male 26 through 44
    4 white females 0 through 9
    1 white female 10 through 15
    1 white female 16 through 25
    1 Negro slave

Supplement XIV-B
1820 Federal Census Records

1820 FEDERAL CENSUS, OGLETHORPE CO, GA
George Varner
    1 white male 45 years of age and older
    3 white females 0 through 9
    1 white female 16 through 24
    1 white female 45 and older
    21 Negro slaves

Frederick Varner
    1 white male 26 through 44
    1 white male 45 and older
    1 white female 16 through 24
    1 white female 45 and over
    1 white female 26 through 44
    13 Negro slaves

Matthew Varner
    1 white males 0 through 9 years of age
    2 white males 16 through 25
    1 white male 45 and over
    2 white females 10 through 15
    1 white female 45 and over
    13 Negro slaves

VARNER FAMILIES OF THE SOUTH--XIV

1820 FEDERAL CENSUS, PUTNAM CO, GA
Henley Varner[1]
    1 white male 26 to 45
    1 white female 26 to 45
    1 male Negro slave under 14
    1 female Negro slave 14 to 26
    1 female Negro slave 26 to 45

Marcus Varner[2] (3 names down from Henley Varner)
    1 white male 26 to 45

George Varner[3] (next name down from Marcus).
    1 white male 26 to 45

William Varner[4] (about 20 names below George Varner)
    2 white males under 10
    1 white male 26-45
    1 white female under 10
    1 white female 26-45
    1 white female over 45
    3 male slaves under 14
    3 male slaves 14 to 26
    6 male slaves 26 to 45
    4 female slaves under 14

---

[1]..Henley Varner was a son of George Varner of Oglethorpe County, GA.

[2]..Marcus Varner was a son of Frederick Varner of Oglethorpe County, GA, and a brother of Edward Varner.

[3]..This George Varner was a son of George Varner of Oglethorpe Co, GA, or of Frederick Varner of Oglethorpe Co, GA. Each named a son George and the records are unclear as to whether this George was a son of George or a son of Frederick.

[4]..William Varner was a son of George Varner of Oglethorpe Co, GA. Some other Varner researchers have mistakenly concluded that this William was a son of Frederick. See Chapter III for proof that this William was George Varner's son.

5 female slaves 14 to 26
3 female slaves 26 to 45
1 female slave over 45
Total of 10 engaged in agriculture

Edward Varner[1] (about 100 names below William Varner)
2 white males under 10
1 white male 26 to 45
1 white female 16 to 26
2 male slaves under 14
1 male slave 14 to 26
1 male slave 26 to 45
1 female slave under 14
2 female slaves 14 to 26
3 female slaves 26 to 45
Total of 4 engaged in agriculture

Supplement XIV-C
1830 Federal Census Records
1830 FEDERAL CENSUS, OGLETHORPE COUNTY, GA
Matthew Varner
1 white male 15 to 20
1 white male 60 to 70
1 white female 40 to 50
6 male slaves under 10
3 male slaves 10 to 24
1 male slave 24 to 36
4 male slaves 36 to 55
2 male slaves 55 to 100
4 female slaves 10 to 24
4 female slaves 36 to 55
27 total inhabitants

---

[1]..Edward Varner was a son of Frederick Varner of Oglethorpe County, GA. Edward is the son whose bankruptcy brought his father Frederick Varner's financial world tumbling down with him. See Chapter III. Edward has been researched by several of his descendants.

1830 FEDERAL CENSUS, COWETA COUNTY, GA
Judy Varner[1]
 1 white male 30 to 40
 1 white female 60 to 70

1830 FEDERAL CENSUS, HENRY COUNTY, GEORGIA
Henley Varner[2]
 1 white male 30-40
 1 white female 10-15
 1 white female 20-30
 8 male slaves under 10
 1 male slave 10-20
 3 male slaves 24-36
 1 male slave 36-55
 2 male slaves 55-100
 4 female slaves under 10
 4 female slaves 10-24
 4 female slaves 24-36
 1 female slave 36-55
 31 total inhabitants

1830 FEDERAL CENSUS, JASPER COUNTY, GEORGIA
(One published census index incorrectly lists Edward Varner as a resident of Jackson County.)
Edward Varner[3]
 2 white males 5 and under
 3 white males 5 to 10
 2 white males 10 to 15
 1 white male 40 to 50
 1 white female 30 to 40
 8 male slaves under 10
 5 male slaves 10-24

---

[1]..Judy (or Judah) is believed to have been Frederick Varner's widow. The white male was probably a son.

[2]..Son of George Varner of Oglethorpe County, GA.

[3]..Son of Frederick Varner of Oglethorpe County, GA.

1 male slave 24-36
4 male slaves 36 to 55
5 female slaves under 10
3 female slaves 10-24
5 female slaves 24-36
3 female slaves 55-100
1 free colored person 10-24
44 total inhabitants

1830 FEDERAL CENSUS, MERIWETHER COUNTY, GA
Marcus Varner[1]
1 male 20 to 30
1 female 20 to 30
2 total inhabitants

1830 FEDERAL CENSUS, PUTNAM COUNTY, GA
William Varner[2]
1 white male 40-50
1 white female 10-15
1 white female 15-20
2 male slaves under 10
1 male slave 10-24
4 female slaves under 10
2 female slaves 10-24
12 total inhabitants

Supplement XIV-D
1840 Federal Census Records
1840 FEDERAL CENSUS, FAYETTE COUNTY, GA
Marcus Varner
1 male 40 to 50
1 female 30 to 40

---

[1]..If this Marcus Varner was the son of Frederick Varner of Oglethorpe County, GA, his age appears to be in error in this record.

[2]..Son of George Varner of Oglethorpe County, GA.

2 total inhabitants
1 engaged in agriculture

Edward Varner
1 male 5 to 10
1 male 10 to 15
3 males 15 to 20
1 male 20 to 30
1 male 50 to 60
1 female under 5
1 female 5 to 10
1 female 40 to 50
4 male slaves under 10
4 male slaves 10 to 24
4 male slaves 36 to 55
1 male slave 55 to 100
5 female slaves under 10
6 female slaves 10 to 24
1 female slave 24 to 36
2 female slaves 36 to 55
37 total inhabitants
10 engaged in agriculture

1840 FEDERAL CENSUS, HENRY COUNTY, GEORGIA
Henley Varner
1 male 30 to 40
1 male 40 to 50
1 female 30 to 40
2 female slaves under 10
1 female slave 10 to 24
1 female 36 to 55
7 total inhabitants
5 engaged in agriculture

1840 FEDERAL CENSUS, OGLETHORPE COUNTY, GA
Matthew Varner, Sr.
1 male 30 to 40
1 male 80 to 90
1 female 50 to 60
8 male slaves under 10
5 male slaves 10 to 24

2 male slaves 24 to 36
2 male slaves 36 to 55
3 male slaves 55 to 100
2 female slaves under 10
1 female slave 10 to 24
1 female slave 24 to 36
4 female slaves 36 to 55
31 total inhabitants
12 engaged in agriculture
2 engaged in manufactures and trades

Matthew Varner, Jr.
2 males 20 to 30
3 females under 5
1 female 20 to 30
3 male slaves under 10
3 male slaves 10 to 24
3 male slaves 24 to 36
7 female slaves under 10
2 female slaves 24 to 36
24 total inhabitants
8 engaged in agriculture
(Matthew Varner, Sr.'s name appeared on same page as Matthew Varner Jr.'s name in the census report.)

Supplement XIV-E
1850 Federal Census Records
1850 FEDERAL CENSUS[1], FAYETTE COUNTY, GA
Mark Varner[2] 59, male, farmer. Real estate value $400. Born in Georgia.

---

[1]..Slaves were enumerated on separate schedules in the 1850 and 1860 federal censuses. The author did not check those schedules for slaves owned by Varners living in Georgia during those years.

[2]..This Mark Varner is believed to have been Marcus Varner, son of Frederick Varner of Oglethorpe County, GA.

VARNER FAMILIES OF THE SOUTH--XIV

Mary Varner, 44, female, born in NC.
David Walker, 16, male, farmer, born in GA.
Mary Hancock, 17, female, born in GA.

1850 FEDERAL CENSUS, HENRY COUNTY, GEORGIA
J. F. Varner[1], 30, male, farmer. Real estate value $1,000.
Born in Georgia.
M. A. Varner, 24, female. Born in Alabama.
W. D. Varner, 5, female, born in Georgia.
E. R. Varner, 2, female, born in Georgia.

1850 FEDERAL CENSUS, JASPER COUNTY, GEORGIA
Early Varner[2], 34, male, real est. value $1800. Born in GA.
Lucy Varner, 30, female, born in GA.
Joseph Varner, 12, male, born in GA.
Elender Varner, 10, male, born in GA.
Emma Varner, 8, female, born in GA.
Martha Varner, 6, female, born in GA.
Edward Varner, 3, male, born in GA.

1850 FEDERAL CENSUS, PIKE COUNTY, GEORGIA
Henley Varner, 59, male, farmer. Real estate value $2600.
Born in Georgia.
M. C. Varner, 47, female. Born in Georgia.
Enumerated with James S. Woods family. James is 30, male, merchant. Real estate value $1800.
Born in Virginia.
Mary L. Woods, 24, female. Born in Georgia.
Carolyn T. Woods, 1, female. Born in Georgia.
H. Bartlett, 9, female. Born in Georgia.

---

[1]..This J. F. Varner was John F. Varner, a son of William Varner of Putnam County and grandson of George Varner of Oglethorpe County, GA. J. F. Varner of Henry County and David N. Varner of Pike County were brothers.

[2]..Early Varner was a son of Edward Varner of Putnam County and grandson of Frederick Varner of Oglethorpe County, GA.

C. Bartlett, 6, male. Born in Georgia.
J. L. Travis, 44, male, merchant. Born in Georgia.
E. Travis, 32, female. Born in Georgia.
W. C. Travis, 5/12, male. Born in Georgia.

(The above Hendley Varner was on page 224; the following entry was on page 213.)
Henley Varner[1], 59, farmer. Real Estate value $2400. Born in Georgia.
Martha A. Varner, 46, female, born in Georgia.
Helen Bartlett, 10, female, born in GA. Attended school past year.
Cloey Bartlett, 7, female, born in Georgia. Attended school past year.

David N. Varner[2], 39, male, no occupation. Real estate value $800. Born in Georgia. Enumerated alone.

Supplement XIV-F
Sam Varner Seeks Political Appointment
Letter[3] from Sam Dent Varner[4] to Governor of Georgia
Warrenton, GA, Oct. 1, 1859

---

[1]..The two Henley Varners enumerated for Pike County in 1850 is obviously the same person, perhaps tallied by two separate census takers. Henley Varner was a son of George Varner of Oglethorpe County, GA, as previously noted.

[2]..David N. Varner was a brother of J. F. Varner of Henry County and a grandson of George Varner of Oglethorpe County, GA.

[3]..This letter is in the rare papers collection at the Georgia Archives in Atlanta.

[4]..Samuel Dent Varner was a son of Edward Varner of Putnam County and grandson of Frederick Varner of Oglethorpe County GA.

Governor Brown, Dear Sir:
Please find enclosed letters from Col. A. E. Walker of Richmond County, Col. James M. Smythe of Augusta, and Maj. Clyde Thomasville.

You remember my speaking to you in Macon on your way up the country for the appointment of secretary to fill the vacancy caused by the death of Col. M. D. McComb.

Governor Brown, allow me to assure you sir that I would not ask this or any other appointment were I not driven to do so from recent "bad luck." My whole family of father and six brothers have always done all in our power to advance the cause of our party.

My brother, oldest?, who is now sheriff of Randolph County, exerts great influence there. My father and three brothers live in Butts County and one in Houston. I have various relatives throughout the state. Mathew Varner of Marrietta is a cousin of mine, whom you probably know.

None of our family have ever held office under the government. We have never troubled our friends but little if any in that way, and I do hope, sir, that you will give my application a favorable notice. And I pledge you my faith, sir, that should you confer the appointment on me, (neither) you nor the party shall ever have cause to complain. I will discharge my duty and my whole duty faithfully and promptly. I do honestly ask this appointment of your honor if you please and I doubt not sir that you knew my situation fully you would readily confer the place upon me.

And I have no hesitancy in saying that I believe from my extensive acquaintance through the state and the feelings of my friends that the whole party would sanction it with a "hearty good will." Col. Gartsell said to me last week that he would cheerfully write you for me asking you to give me the appointment or to recommend me to your favorable notice.

I have traveled a good deal since I saw you in Macon and I am glad to say I believe you are gaining ground. There was a Democratic meeting here yesterday. Mr. Toombs was to have spoken, but sickness prevented his being here. I have a cousin living here, a man of considerable information (Major George V. Neal) and he informs me all things are moving on well. I shall be in Atlanta as soon as I can go to Richmond County and vote and shall try to be in Milledgeville[1] in the course of a week.

I am sir your most humble servant,
Sam Dent Varner

Supplement XIV-G
Early Tax Records, Putnam County

Tax Digest, Putnam County, GA, 1817

Edward Varner[2], in Capt. Jordan Allen's District. 7 poles. Town lots in Eatonton valued at $7,000. Stock in trade estimated at $12,000. 490 acres of pine land in Warren County, 202 1/2 acres of pine land in Wilkinson County, 607 1/2 acres in Wilkinson County, and 607 1/2 acres in Putnam County. 2 2-wheel carriages. Paid tax of $62.67 1/2. (Editor's note: This was highest amount paid by anyone in Putnam County. Most ranged from 31 cents to $2 or $3. Majority were under $1.00.

William Varner[3], in Washington Rose's District. 15 poles. 140 acres of #2 land and 140 acres of #3 land in Putnam County, 80 acres in Clarke County, 26.6 acres in Putnam County on Little River, town lots in Eatonton, Putnam Co, valued at $3,500, stock in trade estimated at $1500. Total tax of $20.99 3/4.

---

[1]..Milledgeville was the capitol of Georgia at that time.

[2]..Edward Varner was a son of Frederick Varner of Oglethorpe County, GA.

[3]..William Varner was a son of George Varner of Oglethorpe County, GA.

George Varner[4], 1 pole. Stock in trade estimated at $1,000. 202 1/2 acres in Telfair County. Paid tax of $3.40 3/4. Capt. Jordan Allen's District.

Tax Digest, Putnam County, GA, 1820
William Varner, 18 poles, 140 acres of 2nd quality land, 140 acres of 3rd quality land in Putnam County on Rocky Creek; 80 acres of #2 quality land in Clarke County; agent for two town lots in Eatonton estimated at $8,000. Paid tax of $31.37 1/2. In Capt. Jesse Bledsoe's District.
Marcus Varner[2], 1 pole. Paid tax of 31 1/4 cents.
Edward Varner (3 names after Marcus Varner), 7 poles. 50 acres of #2 quality land in Putnam County on Little River; 490 acres in Wayne County on Little Branch; 202 1/2 acres in Wilkinson County, 15th district; 202 1/2 acres in Twiggs County (15th district); 535 acres of #3 quality land in Greene County; 362 acres in Greene County; town lots in Eatonton estimated at $15,000 in value; stock in trade estimated at $15,000. One 2-wheel carriage. Paid tax of $98.35 3/4. (Highest tax paid in Putnam County.) Resided in Capt. Jesse Bledsoe's District.
George Varner (down two pages from Edward Varner), 1 pole. 1 town lot estimated at $1000 value. Paid tax of $3.43 3/4. Resided in Capt. Jesse Bledsoe's District.
Henley Varner (down six pages from George Varner), 1 pole. 1 lot in Eatonton, Putnam County. Paid tax of 33 1/2 cents. Resided in Capt. Jesse Bledsoe's District.

---

[1]..Records are unclear whether George Varner was a son of George Varner of Oglethorpe County, GA, or of Frederick Varner of Oglethorpe County, GA.

[2]..Marcus Varner was a son of Frederick Varner of Oglethorpe County, GA.

Margaret Varner[3], stock in trade estimated at $3,000. Tax of $9.37 1/2.

Total tax in Putnam County for 1820: $4,489.04 1/2. Capt. Bledsoe's District total taxes was $1,441.04 1/4. This was about four times higher than any of the other districts. (Probably, the town of Eatonton made up Capt. Bledsoe's District.)

Putnam County, GA, Tax Records for 1824

George B. Whitfield[2], 79 poles[3], 711 acres in Putnam County, 405 in Houston County, 202 1/2 in Twiggs County, 5,270 fractional surveys in several counties bought at sales. Tax of $34.57. Capt. John H. Lawson's District.

Marcus Varner, 16 poles. 200 acres 2nd quality land in Jasper County on Cedar Creek. Paid tax of $5.50.

William Varner, 37 poles. 337 1/2 of # 2 land and 135 of # 3 land in Putnam County on Rocky Creek and Little River. 202 1/2 acres in DeKalb County, 490 acres in Appling County, 250 acres in Early County, agent for 80 acres in Clark County, 2 lots in Eatonton estimated at $3,500 value, 2 lots in Newman estimated at $250. Paid taxes of $24.05.

---

[1]..The identity of Margaret Varner is unclear. But she is believed to have operated a store in Eatonton. She may have been married to William Varner. In the early 18th century, it was rare for a woman to own property and operate a business unless she inherited it from a husband or father. Such might have been the case here. The author did not research this possibility.

[2]..George B. Whitfield was married to Sarah Varner, daughter of George Varner of Oglethorpe County, GA.

[3]..This number of poles suggests ownership of a large number of slaves.

Putnam County, GA, Tax Records for 1826
William Varner, 31 poles. 202 1/2 acres in Putnam County on Little River, 250 acres in Early County (19th District lot # 364), 490 acres in Appling County, 101 1/4 acres in Monroe County, 6th District. Paid tax of $22.00. Capt. Jesse Bledsoe's District.

Putnam County, GA, Tax Records for 1827
William Varner, 31 poles. 202 1/2 acres in Putnam County on Little River, 250 acres in Early County, 490 acres in Appling County, 170 acres in Monroe County, 250 acres in Walton County on Rutledge River, 80 acres in Clarke County, town lots in Eatonton with an estimated value of $2,500. Paid tax of $19.10. Capt. Jesse Bledsoe's District.

Putnam County, GA, Tax Records for 1828
William Varner, 28 poles. 250 acres in Early County in 19th District, 202 1/2 acres in DeKalb County, 490 acres in Appling County, 202 1/2 acres in Houston County, 202 1/2 acres in Troop County, town lots in Eatonton estimated at $1600. Paid tax of $15.51 3/4. Capt. Jesse Bledsoe's District.

William Varner, as executor of George Varner's estate, deceased[1]. 46 poles. 1600 acres of land in Oglethorpe County on Dry Fork of Long Creek adjacent to Gresham, 200 acres in Oglethorpe County on Dry Fork adjacent to Wynn, 202 1/2 acres in Houston County in 8th District, 1 2-wheel carriage. Tax of $18.63 1/2.

---

[1]..This is the record that proves that the William Varner who left "so many tracks" in Putnam County during the 1810's and 1820's was a son of George Varner of Oglethorpe County, GA. Several other Varner researchers have erred in concluding that this William Varner was a son of Frederick Varner of Oglethorpe County, GA.

Putnam County, GA, Tax Records for 1830
William Varner, 13 poles. 3 acres in Putnam county, 250 acres in Early County, 490 acres in Appling County, 202 1/2 acres in Coweta County, 202 1/2 acres in Decatur County, 202 1/2 acres in Houston County on Flat River, 140 acres of prime quality land in Houston County on Flat River. Taxes were $7.08 1/2. Capt. Jesse Bledsoe's District.

(Editor's note: the Putnam County tax records are not indexed. Consequently, it is possible that some Varners were overlooked by this researcher.)

Supplement XIV-H
Varner Marriages in Oglethorpe County, GA

OGLETHORPE COUNTY, GEORGIA, MARRIAGES
(From Oglethorpe County Marriage Records).
George Varner and Patience Jackson, 17 DEC 1805.
John Varner and Nancy Powell, 10 JAN 1807.
Frederick Varner, Jr. and Sally Graves, 27 JUN 1808.
Robert Varner and Martha Hudson, 11 NOV 1820.
Marcus Varner and Mary A. Bradford, 19 JAN 1823.
John Varner and Mary Campbell, 27 JUL 1824.
Mathew Varner and Elizabeth Hawkins, 30 JUN 1825.
Edward Varner and Betsy Young, 20 DEC 1807.
Polly Varner and John Moore, 30 MAR 1807.
Nancy Varner and Thomas Owen, 10 NOV 1810.
Elizabeth Varner and John Christopher, 3 MAR 1812.
Casandra Varner and Edward Sutherlin, 26 APR 1813.
Susannah Varner and James Neal, 29 NOV 1810.
Elizabeth Varner and Thomas Neal, 16 MAR 1812.
Olive Varner and James Ellis, 11 MAR 1816.
Aby Varner and Wiley J. Sorrells, 9 JAN 1817.
Syntha Varner and Booze Maxey, 20 APR 1818.
Susan Varner and John Ellis, 11 DEC 1822.
Cintha Varner and Allen Jennings, 17 JAN 1822.
Sarah W. Varner and Wm. R. Johnson, 10 MAY 1825.
Sally Varner and George Whitfield, 4 OCT 1820.
Early Varner and Lucy Callaway, 30 JAN 1838.
Mathew Varner and Sarah Lumpkin, 5 MAY 1833.

Supplement XIV-I
Approved Prices for Tavern Keeping in 1799

Inferior Court Minutes 1794-1808, Oglethorpe County. Page 110. Approved rates for tavern keeping for 1799.[1]

Jamaica rum, 18 3/4 cents per half gallon.
West India rum, 18 3/4 cents per half gallon.
Northward rum, 12 1/2 cents per half gallon.
Cognac brandy, 18 3/4 cents per half gallon.
Apple brandy, 12 1/2 cents per half gallon.
Peach brandy, 12 1/2 cents per half gallon.
Good whiskey, 12 1/2 cents per half gallon.
Madeira wine, one dollar per quart.
Tenereff wine, 75 cents per quart.
Charilly, 50 cents per quart.
Mallaga wine, 75 cents per quart.
Port wine, 50 cents per quart.
Porter, 50 cents per bottle.
Sherry wine, 75 cents per quart.
Dinner, if warm, 37 1/2 cents.
Breakfast, 25 cents.
Supper, 18 3/4 cents.
Lodging, 6 1/4 cents.
Stable and horse feed for 24 hours, 50 cents.
Corn, per gallon, 12 1/2 cents.
Oats, per gallon, 6 1/4 cents.
Fodder, 2 cents per bundle.

---

[1]..This list of approved charges for food and drink in taverns in 1799 is included to help give the reader an idea of how much a dollar was worth in purchasing power at that time.

Supplement XIV-J
Sale of Land in George Varner's Estate

Sales Made by William Varner While He Was Executor
Oglethorpe County, GA, Deed Book M. Pages 445-446. Nov. 4, 1828.

William Varner, executor of the estate of George Varner, Sr., late of Oglethorpe County, deceased, and John Moore, of Oglethorpe County. William Varner having been authorized by the Inferior Court while sitting for ordinary purposes to sell all the real estate of the said George Varner, Sr., deceased. All that parcel or tract of land on which the deceased lived at the time of his death lying in said county on one of the head branches of the Dry Fork of Long Creek containing about 1120 acres and composed of different and distinct tracts of land purchased by the deceased during his lifetime and included and bounded by lands belonging to the following persons: Thomas Davis, said John Moore, Elijah Ogden, heirs of Isaac Callaway, deceased, John Ruppert, the said John Moore, the Walker tract of land purchased at the same time and in the same manner as the tract hereby conveyed, Valentine Brown, and John H. Gresham and the said John Moore having cried out the highest bid of $100 the said William Varner, executor as aforesaid, doeth sell unto the said John Moore all that tract or parcel of land in Oglethorpe County on one of the head branches of Dry Fork of Long Creek in which George Varner, deceased, died and which is made up of several different and distinct tracts purchased by the said deceased during his lifetime and containing in all about 1120 acres. Purchase price $100.

Witnesses: John S. Lewis, Thomas W. Cobb.

Signed William Varner, executor of George Varner, deceased.

Oglethorpe County, GA, Deed Book N. Page 174-175. Nov. 4, 1828. Between William Varner, executor of the estate of George Varner, Sr., late of Oglethorpe county, deceased and John Moore, also of Oglethorpe County. William Varner, having been authorized by the Inferior

VARNER FAMILIES OF THE SOUTH--XIV

Court of Oglethorpe County to sell all the real estate belonging to the estate of the said deceased. Varner sold to John Moore 520 acres commonly called Walker's Tract for $500. Moore made the highest and best bid. Walker's Tract is situated in Oglethorpe County on the waters of Dry Fork of Long Creek granted to Randolph Ramsey and Jacob Webster, beginning at a hickory corner on a line of other lands which belonged to said George Varner, Sr. deceased. ...running south to southeast 50 chains to a red oak...on a line that was not long since Frederick Varner's thence to a hickory on Ragan's Line, thence to a white oak corner on the road on the line of land that belonged to McIlroy...thence north 58 west 39.50 to a black jack corner, thence north 58 west 39 chains to a red oak...thence north 58 west 10 chains to a hickory thence south 32 west 56 chains to the beginning having such marks and shapes form as appears by a plat of the same.

Witnesses: George H. Young, Lewis L. Dupree, J. P.

Signed William Varner, executor for George Varner, Sr., deceased.

Recorded Oct. 8, 1830. John Landrum, Clerk.

Oglethorpe County, GA, Deed Book P. Page 6. William Varner, executor, of George Varner, Sr. deceased, and John Wynne of Oglethorpe County. Varner sold to Wynne 200 acres previously owned by George Varner, Sr., lying in the county of Oglethorpe, bounded as follows: on the east by Jesse H. Head, on the south by Valentine Brown, on the west by the said Brown, and on the north by the said John Wynne lying on the waters of Dry Fork of Long Creek known and distinguished by the name of Flatwood's tract of land formerly owned by John Echolls and others. Varner exposed said tract of land on Nov. 4, 1828 in the town of Lexington. John Wynne was the highest and best bidder at $60. Given under my hand and seal March 10, 1830.

Witnesses: John Callahan, Valentine Brown.
Signed William Varner.
Recorded Sept. 19, 1837. J. M. Davenport, Clerk.

Oglethorpe County, Minutes, Court of Ordinary 1830-1838, page 68. January term, 1832. Jan. 20, 1832. At a called court this day their honors John Banks and Edward Cease. Last will and testament of George Varner, which had been heretofore proven and one of the executors therein named having been qualified but since dead, it is therefore ordered that George Whitfield one of the executors in the said will named be forthwith qualified and that letter testamentary be granted. Signed John Banks. William H. Smith, Clerk.

Oglethorpe County, Minutes, Court of Ordinary, page 81. July term, 1832. On the application of George B. Whitfield, executor of George Varner, deceased, for leave to sell all real estate of said deceased, and the exhibit of satisfactory evidence that the legal notice of such application has been made and the court being further satisfied that the same will be for the benefit of the heirs and creditors of the said deceased it is therefore ordered that the said George B. Whitfield, executor as aforesaid have leave to sell all of the real estate remaining unsold of said deceased.

Supplement XIV-K
Varner Family Papers

The <u>Varner Collection of Family Papers</u> are in possession of the Georgia Historical Society, Savannah, Georgia. They are also on microfilm (6 rolls) at the Georgia Archives in Atlanta. Birdie Varner Sanders, former school teacher in Georgia, a known descendant of Frederick Varner of Oglethorpe County, GA, contributed much of the material. These papers appear to have provided much of the material used by other Varner family researchers about this line of Varners.

The file contains family correspondence, miscellaneous archival records, genealogical data from entries in family Bibles, Birdie Varner Sanders' <u>Scrapbook</u>, and a variety of other material.

VARNER FAMILIES OF THE SOUTH--XIV

Much of the Varner Family Papers material deals with Edward Varner and his descendants. Edward was born Nov. 4, 1789, in Wilkes County, Georgia, and died Feb. 19, 1869, in Butts County, Georgia. His father was Frederick Varner. Edward was a planter until 1850, first in Putnam County and then in Jasper County. In 1849 he purchased the Indian Springs Hotel (later called the Varner House) in Butts County. At one time he was sheriff in Putnam County. He also operated a store in Eatonton, in Putnam County.

Edward and his first wife, Emma Dent, had four children: **Early Varner** (1816-?), **Ann Eliza Varner** (1817-1818), **Samuel Dent Varner** (1820-1868), and **Frederick Augustus Varner** (1822-?).

Chapter XV
Varner Records in Lowndes Co, AL

John Varner, son of George Varner of Oglethorpe County, GA, and John's wife Nancy Powell and their young children settled in what was then a part of Montgomery County, AL, in 1819, the year that Alabama became a state.

John Varner's brother Frederick Varner and his wife Sally Graves and their young children also settled in that area that year. Unknown numbers of relatives and friends of those two brothers and their wives joined them at that time and/or later.

The area of Montgomery County where those people settled became a part of the new county of Lowndes when it was created in 1830. The John and Frederick Varner farms were within a mile of one another and very close to the Alabama River, about 15 miles downriver from the city of Montgomery.

As explained more fully in earlier chapters, these Varners and their children and grandchildren left many "tracks" in the Lowndes County records. The records printed in this chapter are some of the more interesting ones.

Supplement XV-A
Census Records for Lowndes County, AL
1830 CENSUS, LOWNDES COUNTY, ALABAMA
Varner, John

2 males 0-5	1 male slave under 10
2 males 5-10	4 male slaves 10-23
1 male 10-15	2 male slaves 24-39
2 males 15-20	2 male slaves 36-54
1 male 40-50	2 female slaves under 10
1 female 10-15	3 female slaves 10-23
1 female 30-40	1 female slave 24-35
	2 female slaves 36-54
	1 female slave 55-99
	18 total slaves

Varner Families of the South--XV

Varner, Frederick
- 1 male 0-5
- 1 male 5-10
- 2 males 10-15
- 1 male 15-20
- 1 male 40-50
- 1 female 15-20
- 1 female 40-50
- 3 male slaves under 10
- 2 male slaves 10-23
- 1 male slave 24-39
- 1 male slave 36-64
- 4 female slaves under 10
- 1 female slave 10-23
- 4 female slaves 24-35
- 1 female slave 55-99
- 17 total slaves

1840 CENSUS, LOWNDES COUNTY, ALABAMA

Varner, W. G.[1]
- 1 male 20-30
- 1 female 20-30
- 1 male slave 10-24
- 2 female slaves 10-24
- 5 total residents, 4 engaged in agriculture

Varner, Frederick[2]
- 1 male 10-15
- 1 male 15-20
- 1 male 50-60
- 1 female 20-30
- 1 female 40-50
- 1 male slave under 10
- 4 male slaves 10-24
- 2 female slaves under 10
- 2 female slaves 10-23
- 3 female slaves 24-35
- 1 female slave 55-100
- 17 total residents, 6 engaged in agriculture

----

[1]..This was William Graves Varner, son of Frederick Varner of Lowndes County, AL. William's wife was Susan Eliza Varner, daughter of John Varner of Lowndes County, AL.

[2]..Frederick Varner was a son of George Varner of Oglethorpe County, GA. He moved to Caldwell Parish, LA, in the early 1840's.

Varner Records in Lowndes County, AL

Varner, Azariah[3]
   1 male 20-30   6 males slaves 10-24
   3 females under 5 1 male slave 25-35
   1 female 5-10   2 female slaves under 10
   1 female 20-30   2 female slaves 10-24
                             3 female slaves 24-35
   20 total, 9 engaged in agriculture

Varner, John[2]
   3 males 5-10   3 male slaves under 10
   1 male 10-15   1 male slave 10-20
   1 male 15-20   1 male slave 55-100
   2 males 20-30   6 female slaves under 10
   1 male 50-60   1 female slave 10-20
   1 female 5-10   2 female slaves 24-36
   1 female 20-30   1 female slave 36-55
   1 female 40-50
   26 total residents, 4 engaged in agriculture

Whitfield, Sarah[3]
   1 male 5-10   1 male slave under 10
   2 males 10-15   2 male slaves 10-24
   1 male 15-20   1 female slave 24-35
   1 female under 5   11 total residents
   1 female 5-10   3 engaged in agriculture
   1 female 30-40

---

[1]..Azariah Varner was a son of John Varner of Lowndes County, AL, and grandson of George Varner of Oglethorpe County, GA.

[2]..John Varner was a son of George Varner of Oglethorpe County, GA. He moved to Coosa County, AL, during the mid-1840's.

[3]..Sarah Whitfield was a daughter of George Varner of Oglethorpe County, GA, and sister of John Varner and Frederick Varner of Lowndes County, AL. Sarah's husband, George B. Whitfield, died in Lowndes County in 1838.

1850 CENSUS, LOWNDES COUNTY, ALABAMA

Varner, Azariah[1], 37, male, planter, born in GA. Value of real estate: $1200.
    Varner, Mary L., 36, female, born in SC.
    Varner, Martha, 15, female, born in AL. Attended school the past year.
    Varner, Sarah, 14, female, born in AL. Attended school the past year.
    Varner, Eliza, 12, female, born in AL. Attended school the past year.
    Varner, Harriet, 10, female, born in AL. Attended school the past year.
    Varner, James, 8, male, born in AL. Attended school.
    Varner, Charles, 6, born in AL.
    Varner, John, 3, male, born in AL.
    Varner, John, Jr.[2], 23, male, born in AL.
Lowndes District, Family # 32. Enumerated 9/19/1850.

Varner, W. G.[3], 34, male, born in Georgia, planter, real estate value: $1200.
    Varner, Susan E.[4], 32, female, born in GA.
    Varner, Amarentha L., 6, female, born in AL.
    Varner, William L., 4, male, born in AL.
    Varner, Amaziah, 1, male, born in AL.
    Varner, Hardaway[5], 21, male, born in AL. Planter.
Lowndes District, Family # 382.

---

[1]..Azariah was a son of John Varner of Coosa Co, AL.

[2]..This was John W. Varner, son of John Varner of Coosa Co, AL.

[3]..This was William G. Varner, son of Frederick Varner and grandson of George Varner of Oglethorpe Co, GA.

[4]..Susan was a daughter of John Varner of Coosa Co, AL, and granddaughter of George Varner of Oglethorpe Co, GA.

[5]..Hardaway was a son of John Varner of Coosa Co, AL, and grandson of George Varner of Oglethorpe Co, GA.

SLAVE SCHEDULES, 1850, LOWNDES COUNTY, AL
Varner, Azariah
Slaves owned: 1 female, age 34; 1 female, 17; 1 female, 12; 1 male, 14; 1 male, 3. Total: 5 slaves.

Varner, W. G.
Slaves owned: 1 male, 28; 1 female, 25; 1 male, 25; 1 female, 10; 1 male, 9; 1 male, 6; 1 male, 6; 1 male, 4; 1 female, 3; 1 female, 1; 1 female, 8/12. Total: 11.

1860 CENSUS, LOWNDES COUNTY, ALABAMA
Dacus, R. W., 42, male, farmer. Real estate value: $9,600.
Personal property value: $23,355. Born in South Carolina. Married within the year.
Dacus, S. E.[1] (Varner widow), female, 42 years old, born in Georgia.
Varner, William F., 14, male, born in AL. Attended school the past year.
Varner, Amaziah, 12, male, born in AL. Attended school the past year.
Varner, Elizabeth, 9, female, born in AL. Attended school the past year.
Varner, Martha M., 6, female, born in AL. Attended school the past year.
Varner, John F., 4, male, born in AL.
Varner, Marcela, 22, female, born in AL.
(Northern Division, Hayneville)

Varner, William F.[2], 37, male, farmer, born in AL.
Personal estate value: $5,775.
Varner, M. F., 35, female, born in AL.

---

[1]..S. E. Dacus was Susan Eliza Varner, daughter of John Varner of Coosa County, AL, and granddaughter of George Varner of Oglethorpe County, GA.

[2]..William F. Varner was a son of John Varner of Coosa County, AL, and grandson of George Varner of Oglethorpe County, GA.

Varner, William W., 8, male, born in AL.
Varner, B. J., 6, male, born in AL.
Varner, G. H., 4, male, born in AL.
All the children attended school within the past year.

Cook, I. C., 26, male, clerk. Real estate value $500, personal estate value $435. Born in AL.
  Cook, E. A., 20, female. Born in AL.
  Varner, S. C., 22, female. Born in AL.
  Varner, A.[1], 6, male. Born in AL.
(Northern Division, Hayneville)

Garrett, A. J., 32, male, farmer. Personal estate value $4,800. Born in AL.
  Garrett, Eliza, 25, female. Born in SC.
  Garrett, Lucinda, 1, female. Born in AL.
  Garrett, Alice, 2/12, female. Born in AL.
  Dawson, J. M., 18, male. Born in AL.
  Varner, James[2], 17, male. Born in AL.

1870 CENSUS, LOWNDES COUNTY

Rufus W. Dacus, 52, male, white, farmer. Value of real estate $5700. Value of personal estate $1,075. Born in SC.
  Susan E.[3], 52, female, white. Keeping house. Born in GA.
  Amaziah Varner, 21, male, white, farmer. Born in AL.
  Martha Varner, 15, female, white. Born in AL.
  John F. Varner, 13, male, white. Born in AL.
Beat # 1, page 201.

---

[1]..E. A. Cook, S. C. Varner, and A. Varner were Azariah Varner's orphans.

[2]..James Varner was an orphan of Azariah Varner. James was killed in battle in Virginia during the Civil War.

[3]..Susan E. Dacus was Susan Eliza Varner, daughter of John Varner of Coosa County, AL, and granddaughter of George Varner of Oglethorpe County, GA.

1900 CENSUS, LOWNDES COUNTY, ALABAMA

Varner, Amaziah, white, male, born Dec. 1848, 51, married 26 years. Born in AL. Parents born in GA. Owns farm.

Varner, Harriet W., wife, white, female, 45, born June 1854. Mother of 8 children, 5 living.

Varner, William A., son, white, male, 22, born May 1878, farmer.

Varner, Mary E., daughter, white, female, 19, born July 1880.

Varner, Robert L., son, white, male, 16, born Nov. 1883. Farm laborer.

Varner, Emma V.?, daughter, white, female, 13, born Oct. 1886.

All can read and write.

The Amaziah Varner family was in Hayneville Precinct 14, North Half. Amaziah Varner was enumerator for that district.

Vol. 37, ED 83, Sheet 1, Line 1.

Varner, John F., white, male, 44, born May 1856, widowed salesman. Born in AL. Father born in AL.

Dacus, Susan E.[1], mother (of John F. Varner), white, female, 82, born Jan. 1818. Widow. Born in GA. Parents born in GA. Both can read and write.

Evans, Lila, 70, black, cook.

O'Ree, Robert, 16, black, servant.

The John F. Varner family was residing in South half of Hayneville Precinct 14, E.D. #84, Sheet 10, Line 85. J. F. Varner was the enumerator for that district.

---

[1]..Susan E. Dacus was Susan Eliza Varner Dacus, daughter of John Varner of Lowndes and Coosa County, AL.

Supplement XV-B
Notes on Varners in Lowndes Co History

Lowndes Court House 1820-1900. A Chronicle of Hayneville, an Alabama Black Belt Village, by Mildred Brewer. 1951. The Paragon Press, Montgomery, Alabama.

Notes from that book about the Varners:

"During the incumbency of Peter Williamson as judge of the County Court, John Varner, an early settler of this section, and who died in Coosa County at an advanced age in 1869, was clerk of the court." Page 16.

The court first met Nov. 15, 1830. The first courthouse was built in 1832. Page 19.

Dr. George Esselman[1] was the first mayor of Hayneville. The city was incorporated in 1831. Page 21.

"On May 14, 1834, Rev. William Rice, James L. F. Cottrell, John Fisher, and John Varner were commissioned to build a Methodist-Protestant church. The lot, No. 18, according to the first plan of lots, and containing one-fourth acre, was purchased from George Givhan for $100. This church, Hayneville's first tabernacle in the wilderness, formerly stood on South Commerce Street, back of the residence of the late Dr. W. P. Russell." Page 22.

Rev. Peyton Smith Graves, a native of Oglethorpe County, Georgia, was the first minister of the Methodist Church. He came to Lowndes County in 1817. Page 23.

"These pupils went to school to me between the first of April 1848, and the first of October 1849. (Signed) J. J. Judge." Judge was principal of the Hayneville Female Academy during the late 1840's and early 1850's. The list

---

[1]..Esselman Varner, son of John Varner of Lowndes County, was probably named after George Esselman.

of pupils included: Martha Varner, Sarah Varner, Eliza Varner, and Harriet Varner. Pp. 28-29.

"In 1836, Hayneville was growing like a mushroom; everybody rich, or believed he might be by reaching forth his hand for it. A navigation company was organized, a charter obtained from the legislature, and work actually commenced on Big Swamp Creek for its navigation by keel boats, cutting logs, timber, etc., to be washed out by a rise of water. Much was said, and expectation ran high of the value of the lots at Varner's ford[1] on said creek, as a depot, or a warehouse for shipping, for Hayneville and the surrounding country. "Page 41.

"General orders, No. 1, Headquarters 58 Regiment, Hayneville, January 31, 1861: A Battalion parade, and drill of the First Battalion, 58th Regiment, A. M., is hereby ordered on the second day of March next, at Hayneville. Companies comprising said battalion are ordered to appear by 10 o'clock of said day, armed and equipped as the law directs. By order of H. M Larey, Commandant; A. Gilchrist, Adj't." Included in the list of privates was James Varner[2], who was killed fighting for the Confederacy. Pages 101-102.

Volunteers from Hayneville for the Spanish-American War included Lannie Varner. Page 142.

Author Mildred Brewer lists her schoolmates during the late 1880's. Names included Sam Varner, Maggie Varner, and Will Varner.

---

[1]..Big Swamp Creek is less than a mile from Hayneville where it crosses through what was then John Varner's plantation. Varner's ford that is mentioned here was probably about where AL Hwy 21 crosses Big Swamp Creek today.

[2]..James Varner was a son of Azariah Varner and grandson of John Varner of Coosa County.

"A partial list of the unmarried ladies and their escorts, attending the leap year ball of 1884, is copied from a newspaper of the time." Those listed included Miss Mary Folmar and Mr. Frank Varner.

Supplement XV-C
Varner Marriages in Lowndes County
LOWNDES COUNTY MARRIAGES
Varner, Eliza and Isaac C. Cook, Dec. 30, 1858.
  By Rev. William Rice.
Varner, Harriett and Rufus W. Dacus, May 14, 1857.
Varner, Elizabeth and Robert A. Blanks, March 29, 1833.
  G. W. Esselman, J.P.
Varner, Louisa and Leonard G. Waters, Dec. 7, 1849.
  By M. Hinkle.
Varner, Mary A. and James D. Hicks, May 30, 1856.
  By David Doneon.
Varner, M. E. and Jerry Light, Nov. 11, 1869.
  By John Enochs, J.P.
Varner, Susan E.[1] and William G. Varner[2], Dec. 21, 1837.
  By Rev. William Rice, MG.
Varner, A. and Miss H. V. Tucker, Oct. 29, 1873.
Varner, Charles A. and Miss A. J. Thomas, May 1, 1870.
Varner, Azariah and Maggie Folmar, Feb. 11, 1877.
Varner, Thomas J.[3] and Nancy S. Graves, July 24, 1832.
  By Rev. P. S. Graves, MG.

---

[1]..Susan E. Varner was a daughter of John Varner of Lowndes County, AL.

[2]..William G. Varner was a son of Frederick Varner of Lowndes County, AL.

[3]..Thomas J. Varner was a son of Frederick Varner of Lowndes County, AL.

Varner, Azariah[4] and Mary L. Pickering, Dec. 13, 1832. By G. W. Esselman, J.P.
Varner, Amaziah[2] and Martha Pickering, Feb. 7, 1833. G. W. Esselman, JP.
Varner, S. M. and E. B. Buchanan, Oct. 22, 1893.
Varner, Maggie and W. W. West, Nov. 8, 1896.
Varner, Mary and Charlie Norris, Dec. 16, 1900.
Varner, J. L. and Nina Powell Thomas, Dec. 15, 1903.
Varner, John F. and Miss Ella Thomas, April 3, 1885.
Varner, Charles A. and Daisy May Judge, July 14, 1905.

MONTGOMERY COUNTY MARRIAGES

Varner, Armenty[3] and Lewis Jackson, July 13, 1829.
Varner, William F.[4], and Margaret F. Bonham, 11/12/1845. G. W. Jeter, M.G.
Varner, Mrs. Susan Eliza[5] and Rufus W. Dacus, 2/21/1860. Luther L. Hill, M.G.
Varner, William and Georgia Thomas, 3/22/1916. Edward C. Moore, M. G.

---

[1]..Azariah Varner was a son of John Varner of Lowndes County, AL.

[2]..Amaziah Varner was a son of John Varner of Lowndes County, AL.

[3]..Amerenty Varner was a daughter of Frederick Varner of Lowndes County, AL.

[4]..William F. Varner was a son of John Varner of Lowndes County, AL.

[5]..Mrs. Susan Eliza Varner was a daughter of John Varner of Lowndes County, AL, and the widow of William G. Varner.

Supplement XV-D
Division of Land by William G. Varner's Heirs
WILLIAM G. VARNER HEIRS DIVIDE LAND
The State of Alabama, Lowndes County

Know all men by these presents that whereas we Amaziah Varner, Jennie Varner, Mattie Varner, John Varner, Jerre Light, and Mary E. Light, wife of the said Jerry Light, heirs and devisees of W. G. Varner, deceased, and Susan E. Dacus the widow of said deceased for the purpose of having a just and equitable division and partition of the lands of the Estate of W. G. Varner deceased and in consideration of the premises and in further consideration of the costs and expenses of a suit at law for the purpose of making a partition of said lands have entered into the following agreement hereby binding ourselves and each of us, our heirs and assigns to forever observe the terms, stipulations, and conditions of the same forever.

First, the above named children of said W. G. Varner deceased in consideration of the premises and of the sum of one dollar to them in hand paid by the said Susan E. Dacus the following described lands belonging to the Estate of their said father, viz, Fifty-one acres in the North End of the W 1/2 of NE 1/4 of S 22 and the SW 1/4 of the SE 1/4 of S 15 of T 14 R 15 lying in said county and containing ninety-one acres more or less to have and to hold to her the said Susan E. Dacus in fee forever. And the said Susan E. Dacus accepts the said land as her share of the said estate and in consideration of the premises hereby releases and forever quit claims to the above named children of said W. G. Varner deceased all the balance of the lands of said estate hereinafter particularly described.

And the above named children of W. G. Varner deceased agree and hereby appoint G. W. McQueen and W. D. Wiggins with power in case of disagreement between them to call in a third person to be selected by them whose acts shall have the same force and validity as if selected by the said children to partition and divide the remainder of the lands of said Estate, to wit: the NE 1/4 of SE 1/4 the NW 1/4 of SE 1/4 the E 1/2 of SW 1/4 and 30 acres off East side of West half of SW 1/4 & W 1/2 of NE 1/4 and E 1/2 of NW 1/4 of S 15 and 20 acres of the South End of W 1/2 of SE 1/4 of SE 1/4 Section ten all in T 14 R 15 into fair shares of equal value, to wit: one share for Amaziah Varner, one for Mary E. Light, one for Mattie Varner, and one for John Varner. Said persons shall divide said lands having regard to the quantity and quality of the land as well as of the improvements thereon so as to make the shares as nearly as equal of value for farms and shall assign to each share when it is practicable some of the wooded land on such tract.

After the land has been thus divided into four equal tracts such persons or commissioners shall determine by lot to whom the several lots shall belong and for that purpose shall give notice of the time set apart for drawing the lots to each of said children and said drawing shall be made at the residence of Mrs. Susan E. Dacus. When the drawing is completed the said commissioners shall make a report in writing of the action setting forth a description of each lot and to whom it belongs...

In witness whereof we have hereto set our hands and seals on this the 16th day of August 1877.

(Signed) M. E. Light, J. M. Light, John F. Varner, Amaziah Varner, H. V. Varner, Mattie Varner, Susan E. Dacus.

The commissioners divided the 370 acres into four parcels. The heirs drew lots from a hat at the Susan E. Dacus residence on August 23, 1877. J. F. Varner drew lot # 1; L. W. Varner drew lot # 2; Mattie Varner drew lot # 3; and J. F. Light drew lot # 4.

Recorded in Lowndes County Deed Book L, page 358.

Chapter XVI
Varner Records in Coosa County, AL

As noted earlier, John Varner, son of George Varner of Oglethorpe County, GA, and several of his children moved from Lowndes County, AL, to Coosa County, AL, during the 1840's. John established his fourth plantation near Providence Church in the Southwest quarter of Coosa County. His earlier plantations were in Oglethorpe County, GA (1810-1819), on the Alabama River in what was then part of Montgomery County, AL (1820-1830), and on Big Swamp Creek near Hayneville in Lowndes County, AL (1831-abt 1843). With the help of his sons, John Varner operated this plantation until his death in the waning hours of 1869.

This chapter includes documents that help tell the story of John Varner's life as a resident of Coosa County. These records cover the period from the time John Varner moved to Coosa County, AL, during the 1840's up until about 1900.

Supplement XVI-A
Coosa County, AL, Census Records, 1850-1900
1850 CENSUS, COOSA COUNTY, ALABAMA
Varner, John, 65, male, farmer, born in GA. Personal estate worth: $2000.
    Varner, Amanda, 40, female, born in GA.
    Varner, Amazia[1], 38, male, farmer, born in GA.
    Varner, Esselman[2], 15, male, farmer, born in AL.
    Varner, Lucy[3], 9, female, born in AL. Attended school the past year.

---

[1]..This was Amaziah Varner, one of John Varner's oldest sons, and a grandson of George Varner of Oglethorpe Co, GA.

[2]..Esselman was John Varner's youngest son.

[3]..Lucy was John Varner's youngest daughter.

VARNER RECORDS IN COOSA COUNTY, AL

Varner, Mary[4], 7, female, born in AL.
John Varner family enumerated in the Hatchet Creek District, Census enumerator's visit # 402. Enumerated 11/23/1850.

Varner, Edward[2], 28, male, farmer, born in AL. Value of real estate owned: $500.
Varner, Jane, 16, female, born in AL.
Varner, John?, 1, male, born in AL.
Edward Varner family enumerated in the Hatchet Creek District.

1850 SLAVE SCHEDULE, COOSA COUNTY, ALABAMA
Slaves belonging to **Varner, John**. Hatchett Creek District.
Listed in the order that they appear on the census tally sheet.
1 male, age 80; 1 male, 40; 1 female, 40; 1 female, 25; 1 female, 20; 1 male, 30; 1 male, 32; 1 male, 25; 1 female, 25; 1 male, 30; 1 male, 32; 1 male, 25; 1 female, 25; 1 female, 10; 1 male, 18; 1 female, 55; 1 female, 15; 1 female, 17; 1 female, 22; 1 male, 4; 1 male, 17; 1 male, 26; 1 male, 52; 1 female, 35; 1 female, 13; 1 female, 6; 1 male, 7; 1 female, 4; 1 female, 7; 1 male, 25; 1 female, 25; 1 female, 17. Total: 28.

Slaves belonging to **Varner, Edward**. Hatchett Creek District.
1 male, 8; 1 male, 14; 1 male, 21; 1 female, 17; 1 female, 25. Total: 5.

----

[1]..Mary Varner was a daughter of Amaziah Varner and granddaughter of John Varner.

[2]..Edward Varner was a son of John Varner and grandson of George Varner of Oglethorpe Co, GA.

VARNER FAMILIES OF THE SOUTH--XVI

1860 CENSUS, COOSA COUNTY, ALABAMA

Varner, J.,[1] 30, male, white, farmer, born in AL.
  Real estate value: $1600, personal property value: $7000.
  Varner, E., 26, female, white, housewife, born in AL.
  Varner, C., 7, male, white, born in AL.
  Varner, Sallie, 5, female, white, born in AL.
  Varner, L. A., 2, female, white, born in AL.
One member of the family attended school the past year. (Southern Division, Rockford Post Office, Coosa County, Census Family # 243.)

Varner, E. P.,[2] 37, male, white, planter, born in AL. Real estate value: $1200, personal property value: $15,000.
  Varner, Senora, 20, female, white, housewife, born in SC.
  Varner, Eulia, 11, female, white, born in AL.
  Varner, E. B., 7, male, white, born in AL.
  Varner, Ella, 5, female, white, born in AL.
  Garnett, James, 2, male, white, born in AL.
Two members of the family attended school the past year. (Southern Division, Rockford Post Office, Coosa County, Census Family # 261.)

Varner, J.,[3] 77, male, white, planter, born in NC. BLIND.
  Real estate value: $3,500; personal property value: $46,000.
  Varner, A., 54, female, white, housewife, born in GA.

---

[1]..This was John W. Varner, son of John Varner and grandson of George Varner of Oglethorpe County, GA.

[2]..This was Edward P. Varner, son of John Varner and grandson of George Varner of Oglethorpe County, GA.

[3]..This was John Varner, son of George Varner of Oglethorpe County, GA.

Varner, E.,[4] 26, male, white, farmer, born in AL. Real estate value: $700; personal property value: $350.
    Varner, L. A[2]., 18, female, white, housekeeper, born in AL.
    Varner, J.,[3] 10, male, white, born in AL.
One member of the family attended school the past year. (Southern Division, Coosa County, Census Family # 276.)

1860 SLAVE SCHEDULE, COOSA COUNTY, ALABAMA
Varner, John--33 slaves--8 slave houses.
    Ages of male slaves: 55, 51, 35, 34, 35, 26, 14, 10, 8, 3, 3, 5.
    Ages of female slaves: 68, 47, 47, 25, 38, 27, 26, 23, 13, 12, 12, 12, 10, 9, 5, 2, 5, 1, 23.

Varner, E. P[4].--10 slaves--3 slave houses.
    Ages of male slaves: 35, 33, 21, 3.
    Ages of female slaves: 24 (mulatto), 28, 15, 10, 5, 1.

Varner, John[5]--7 slaves--2 slave houses.
    Ages of male slaves: 60, 4, 3.
    Ages of female slaves: 26, 17, 6, 3/12.

----

[1]..This was Esselman Varner, son of John Varner and grandson of George Varner of Oglethorpe County, GA.

[2]..L.A. Varner was Lucy Varner, John Varner's youngest daughter.

[3]..This was John Varner, orphan son of Azariah Varner of Lowndes County, AL, and great grandson of George Varner of Oglethorpe County, GA.

[4]..This was Edward P. Varner, son of John Varner.

[5]..This was John W. Varner, son of John Varner.

1860 AGRICULTURAL CENSUS, COOSA COUNTY, AL
John Varner
400 acres improved land, 240 acres unimproved land. Value of farm land: $4,000.
Value of farm equipment and tools: $375.
Livestock owned at time of census: 3 horses, 4 mules and asses, 15 milch cows, 2 working oxen, 12 other cattle, 5 sheep, 30 swine.
Value of livestock: $1550.
Crop production during past twelve months: 800 bushels Indian corn, 10 bushels of oats, 20 bales of ginned cotton, 10 pounds of wool, 70 bushels of peas and beans, 2 bushels of Irish potatoes, 20 pounds of butter.
Value of manufactured goods made in the home: $20.
Value of livestock slaughtered: $50.

John Varner, Jr.
50 acres improved land, 70 acres unimproved land. Cash value of farm: $1500.
Value of farm equipment and tools: $100.
Livestock owned at time of census: 1 horse, 1 mule or ass, 2 milch cows, 2 working oxen, 2 other cattle, 25 swine. Value of livestock owned: $550.
Crop production past twelve months: 10 bushels of wheat, 150 bushels of Indian corn, 9 bales of ginned cotton, 5 bushels of peas and beans, 5 bushels of Irish potatoes. Value of manufactured goods made in the home: $5.

E. P. Varner
120 acres improved land, 120 acres unimproved land. Cash value of farm: $1500.
Value of farm equipment and tools: $75.
Livestock owned at time of census: 7 horses, 8 milch cows, 4 working oxen, 16 other cattle, 16 swine.
Value of livestock owned: $1500.
Crop production during past twelve months: 700 bushels of Indian corn, 30 bushels of oats, 5 bushels of peas and beans, 14 bales of ginned cotton, 10 bushels of Irish potatoes, 100 bushels of sweet potatoes, 10 pounds of beeswax, 200 pounds of honey.

Value of manufactured goods made in the home: $50.
Value of livestock slaughtered: $125.

1870 CENSUS, COOSA COUNTY, ALABAMA

Varner, Elizabeth[1], 35, female, white, keeping house, born in AL. Value of personal property: $395.

Varner, Cicero, 16, male, white, working farm, born in AL. Can read but cannot write.

Varner, Sally, 15, female, white, born in AL. Attended school the past year.

Varner, Lucy, 12, female, white, born in AL. Attended school.

Varner, William, 9, male, white, born in AL.

Varner, Alva, 1, female, white, born in AL.

(Elizabeth Varner family enumerated with Flint Hill Beat. Family # 114 on census enumerator's record.)

Varner, E.,[2] 36, male, white, farmer, born in AL. Value of real estate: $1200. Value of personal property: $1200.

Varner, Sarah, 29, female, white.

Varner, W. A., 9, male, white.

Varner, M. E., 3, male, white.

Varner, Nancy, 1, female, white.

(E. Varner family enumerated with Traveler's Rest Beat, family # 33 on census enumerator's record. Enumerated Aug. 24, 1870.)

----

[1]..Elizabeth Varner was the widow of John W. Varner, son of John Varner and grandson of George Varner of Oglethorpe County, GA.

[2]..This was Esselman Varner, son of John Varner and grandson of George Varner of Oglethorpe County, GA.

Varner, H.,[3] 40, male, white, farmer, born in GA. Real estate value: $1000. Value of personal property: $600.
    Varner, Amanda,[2] 63, female, white, keeping house. Born in GA.
        Varner, Agnez, 45, female, mulatto. Cannot read or write. Born in AL.
        Varner, Joseph, 7, male, mulatto. Born in AL.
Enumerated with Traveler's Rest Beat, family # 57.)

Varner, E. P.,[3] 46, male, white, foreman, born in AL.
    Varner, Senora, 28, female, white, keeping house, born in SC.
        Varner, Emmet, 19, male, white, working farm. Born in AL.
        Varner, Rachael, 16, female, white. Born in AL.
        Varner, Sina, 10, female, white. Born in AL.
        Varner, Annie, 9, female, white. Born in AL.
        Varner, Bell, 7, female, white. Born in AL.
        Varner, Lucy, 4, female, white. Born in AL.
        Varner, Sis, 1, female, white. Born in Al.
        Varner, Edmon, 30, male, white. Working farm.
(E. P. Varner family enumerated with Traveler's Rest Beat, family # 75.))

----

[1]..This was Hardaway Varner, son of John Varner and grandson of George Varner of Oglethorpe County, GA.

[2]..Amanda Varner was the second wife and the widow of John Varner.

[3]..This was Edward P. Varner, son of John Varner and grandson of George Varner of Oglethorpe County, GA.

Varner Records in Coosa County, AL

Varner, John,[4] 21, male, white, farmer. Real estate value: $100. Personal property value: $200. Born in AL.
    Varner, Matilda, 18, female, white, keeping house. Born in GA.
    Varner, Charley, 1, male, white. Born in AL.
(John Varner family enumerated with Traveler's Rest Beat, family # 82.)

1880 CENSUS, COOSA COUNTY, ALABAMA

Varner, Esselman, 46, white, farmer, born in AL, parents born GA.
    Varner, Susan E., wife, 40, born in AL.
    Varner, William A., son, 17, laborer. Born in AL.
    Varner, Manton E., son, 13. Born in AL.
    Varner, Nancy A., daughter, 11. Born in AL.
    Varner, James H., son, 9. Born in AL.
    Varner, John A., son, 7. Born in AL.
    Varner, Mary A., daughter, 5. Born in AL.
    Varner, George H., son, 3. Born in AL.
Vol. 7, ED 52, Sheet 21, Line 36. Beat # 15, Traveller's Rest, family # 182.

Varner, Edward P., 59, white, male, farmer, born in AL, father born in GA, mother born in VA.
    Varner, Senora, 40, born in SC. Parents born in SC.
    Varner, Bell, daughter, 16. Born in AL.
    Varner, Lucy, daughter, 14. Born in AL.
    Varner, Hattie, daughter, 11. Born in AL.
    Varner, Jeff D., son, 7. Born in AL.
    Varner, Alice, daughter, 5. Born in AL.
    Varner, Minnie, daughter, 3. Born in AL.
    Burk, Sidney. 23, male, black, servant.
    Manyfield, Harris, 19, male, black, servant.
Vol. 7, ED 52, Sheet 15, Line 1. Traveller's Rest Beat, family # 125. This is first entry in Traveller's Rest Beat.

---

[1]..This John Varner was a son of Azariah Varner of Lowndes County, AL, and great grandson of George Varner of Oglethorpe County, GA.

Varner, Hardaway, 50, single, white, farmer, born in AL, father born in GA, mother born in AL.
Dayton, Hard, 9, male, white.
Vol. 7, ED 52, Sheet 24, Line 42. Beat 15, Traveller's Rest, family # 218.

Varner, Matilda,[1] 30, female, white, widowed, farmer, born in GA, parents born in GA.
Varner, Charles T., son, 11, father born in AL. Laborer.
Varner, Amanda, daughter, 9, father born in AL.
Varner, Mary J., daughter, 7, father born in AL.
Varner, John A., son, 5, father born in AL.
Varner, Emma, daughter, 3, father born in AL.
Vol. 7, ED 52, Sheet 15, Line 46. Beat # 15, Traveller's Rest, family # 132.

1900 CENSUS, COOSA COUNTY, ALABAMA

Varner, Edward P., 80, white, born Oct. 1819 in AL. Both parents born in VA. Land lord, owns farm free. Can read and write.
Varner, Senora, 60, born May 1840. Born in SC. Parents born in SC. Mother of 11 children, 6 living.
Traveler's Rest, precinct # 15. Vol. 15, ED 28, Sheet 2, Line 87.

Varner, Esselman, 66, white, born Aug. 1833. Born in AL. Both parents born in GA. Land lord. Married 20 years.
Varner, Elizabeth, wife, 62, born Sept. 1837 in AL. No children.
Vol. 15, ED 28, Sheet 14, Line 61. Coosa Traveller's Rest, Precinct 15.

---

[1]..Matilda Varner was the widow of John Varner, who was a son of Azariah Varner of Lowndes Co, AL.

Varner, Hardaway, 71, white, born Jan. 1829 in AL. Farmer, owns land free. Can read and write. Married 11 years.
    Varner, Caroline, 50, born May 1850 in AL. Can read and write. No children.
Vol. 15, ED 28, Sheet 7, Line 5. Traveller's Rest Precinct 15.

Varner, William A., 37, white, farmer. Born in AL. Parents born in AL. Owns farm, not mortgaged.
    Varner, Amanda C., wife, 33. Born in AL. Parents born in GA.
    Varner, Dora L., daughter, 13, attended school 1 1/2 months.
    Varner, Birdie A., daughter, 12, attended school 1 1/2 months.
    Varner, Bell I., daughter, 10, attended school 1 1/2 months.
    Varner, Beattrice, daughter, 8, attended school 1 1/2 months.
    Varner, Lewis E., son, 6.
    Varner, Minnie I., daughter, 3.
    Varner, Maggie M., daughter, 1.
    Varner, George, brother, 22, farm laborer.
Vol. 15, ED 26, Sheet 4, Line 17. Coosa County, Weogufka Precinct 11.

Varner, John W., 38, white, farmer, owns land free. Born May 1862 in AL. Parents born in AL.
    Varner, Debby L., wife, 23.
    Varner, John A., son, 2.
    Varner, Rushie, 1, daughter.
Vol. 15, ED 26, Sheet 5, Line 14. Coosa County, Precinct 11, Weogufka.

Varner, Lucien A., 41, white, born June 1858, farmer, owns land free. Born in AL. Parents born in AL. Can read but not write.
    Varner, Katie E., wife, 33, born June 1866 in AL. Parents born in AL. Can read and write.

Varner, William A., son, 16, born Dec. 1883. Can read but not write. Attended school 1 1/2 months past year.
Varner, Mary E., daughter, 13, born Sept. 1886. Attended school 2 months past year.
Varner, Annie O., daughter, 12, born Oct. 1888. Attended school 2 months past year.
Varner, Laura L., daughter, 7, born Mar. 1893.
Varner, Alvie L., son, 5, born May 1895.

Vol. 15, ED 26, Sheet 4, Line 51. Coosa, Precinct 11, Weogufka.

Varner, Manton E., 32, white, farmer, owns farm. Married 10 years. Born July 1862.
Varner, Sarah E., 29, wife. Born Dec. 1870. Mother of 8 children, 6 living.
Varner, Adolphus W., son, 8.
Varner, Roxie M., daughter, 6.
Varner, Jones A., son, 5.
Varner, Nathan, son, 2.
Varner, George R., son, 1.
Varner, William A., son, 1/12.

Vol. 15, ED 28, Sheet 6, Line 94. Coosa Traveller's Rest Precinct 15.

Varner, Emmett B., 48, white, born Jan. 1852 in AL. Married 9 years.
Varner, Faithie B., wife, 42, born Aug. 1857 in AL. Mother of 1 child, none living.

Vol. 15, ED 28, Sheet 2, Line 89. Coosa, Traveller's Rest Precinct 15.

Varner, James, 28, white, farm mortgaged, born Aug. 1872 in AL. Married 5 years.
Varner, Nancy G., wife, 25, born July 1875 in AL. Mother of 2 children, none living.

Vol. 15, ED 27, Sheet 4, Line 93. Coosa, Lewis Precinct 14.

VARNER RECORDS IN COOSA COUNTY, AL

Varner, John A., 27, white, farmer, owns land free, can read and write. Born May 1873.
 Varner, Emma G., wife, 21. Born April 1879. Can read and write.
 Varner, Olga, daughter, 7/12.
Vol. 15, ED 28, Sheet 7, Line 2. Traveller's Rest Precinct 15.

Varner, Dolphus L., white, 3. Enumerated with William M. Meharg, grandfather.
 Vol. 15, ED 26, Sheet 10, Line 20. Precinct 11, Weogufka.

Varner, Cicero, 46, white, born Sept. 1853 in AL, Parents born in AL. Farmer. Owns land free. Married 19 years. Can read and write.
 Varner, Nancy E., wife, 38, born May 1862 in AL, parents born in AL. Can read and write. Mother of 9 children, all living.
 Varner, Alice E., daughter, 18, can read and write.
 Varner, Lanetta, daughter, 16, can read and write.
 Varner, Daisy A., daughter, 14, can read.
 Varner, Martha, daughter, 12, can read.
 Varner, Ella, daughter, 11.
 Varner, Susan F., daughter, 8.
 Varner, Martina, daughter, 5.
 Varner, Sally A., daughter, 2.
 Varner, Viola E., daughter, 2/12.
Vol. 15, ED 26, Sheet 5, Line 3. ED 26 is precinct 11, Weogufka.

Supplement XVI-B
Cemetery Records[1], Coosa County, Alabama

PROVIDENCE CEMETERY. Located near Kelly's Crossroads, west of Rockford.
    John Varner, 10 SEP 1783-31 DEC 1869.
    Hardaway Varner, 1 JAN 1829-22 APR 1903.
    Senora Varner, wife of E. P., 19 MAY 1840-22 APR 1913.
    E(dward) P. Varner, 20 OCT 1820-4 FEB 1906.
    J. D. Varner, son of E. P. & S., 30 APR 1872-28 JAN 1893.
    Lenora Varner, 20 AUG 1882-20 JUL 1883.
    Rosa Lee Varner, 29 OCT 1886-4 NOV 1886.
    Varner, Infant of E. P. and L. (no dates)
    Sallie R. Varner, 2 DEC 1870-4 APR 1905.
    Edmond R. Varner, 7 NOV 1892-3 NOV 1893.
    May E. Varner, 23 MAR 1896-6 MAY 1899.
    Varner, infant of Mr. & Mrs. Manton E., b. & d. 1921.
    Ida M. Varner, 14 FEB 1892-3 JUN 1926.
    Manton E. Varner, 5 JUN 1867-8 MAY 1955.
    R. Ella Varner, wife of J. M. Wyatt, 24 AUG 1854-26 MAY 1927.
    Lucy D. (Varner) Hughen, wife of George Hughen, daughter of E. P. & L. Varner, 24 SEP 1866-6 JUN 1886.
    Wife of E. Varner (SMV), 15 DEC 1839-10 JUN 1878.
    E(sselman) Varner, 30 AUG 1833-14 MAY 1907.
    Adolphus B. Varner, infant of E. & S. M. Varner, Oct. 1, 1861 - Jan. 1, 1862, aged 3 months.

MT. MORIAH BAPTIST CEMETERY. Located near Hillwood, AL, and Weogufka, AL.
    Willis H. Varner, 19 MAR 1903-4 MAY 1936.
    Daisy Varner, 15 MAR 1886-21 JUL 1911.

---

[1]..Most of this information was taken from <u>Coosa County Records CEMETERIES</u>, published by the Coosa County, AL, Historical Society in 1980. Additions/corrections were made after inspection of grave markers in the cemeteries.

C(icero) Varner, 8 SEP 1853-17 FEB 1933.
Nancy Varner, 3 MAY 1861-12 MAY 1928.
Elwyn Varner, dau. of Mr. & Mrs. F. L., 8 APR 1929-26 APR 1929.
Minnie C. Varner, wife of W. A., 9 JUN 1886-3 DEC 1906.
Birdie A. Varner, dau. of W. A. Varner, wife of G. W. Blankenship, 9 OCT 1887-2 DEC 1910.
Arval Ready Varner, 28 JUN 1910-2 SEP 1910.
I. D. Varner, wife of G. H., 16 JUN 1883-31 MAR 1935.
George H. Varner, 9 JUN 1877-9 SEP 1960.
Mae Varner, 13 AUG 1902-31 JUL 1961.
Floyd Jackson Varner (Son), 31 MAY 1902-12 JUL 1921.
William Varner (Father), 12 MAY 1861-3 MAR 1903.
Gene C. Varner, 20 FEB 1933-31 JAN 1951. AL PVT. 7 CAV (Inf). 1 CAV DIV (INF) Korea.
Cora B. Varner 13 MAY 1898-12 JUL 1976.
John E. Varner, 23 JUN 1897-9 AUG 1978.
John Mosley Varner, 4 AUG 1904-10 FEB 1974.
Reba (Harmon) Varner, 8 FEB 1908-22 Jan 1981.
Howard H. Varner, 20 AUG 1924-26 APR 1977. U.S. Marines WWII.
Alma C. Varner, 15 OCT 1926-_____.
Orris L. Varner, 2 MAR 1920-_____.
Lois M. Varner, 2 MAR 1924-14 MAY 1982.

OLD HATCHET CREEK CEMETERY. Located near Marble Valley. Also known as Dollar Cemetery.
J. P. Varner, b. 2 NOV 1914, d. 25 AUG 1918.
Infants of J. H. and N. G. Varner: 1903, 1897, 1899, 1905. (Four markers.)

STEWARTVILLE CHURCH OF GOD CEMETERY. Located about 1/2 mile off Hwy. 231.
William M. Varner, 1883-1957.
Rosie A. Varner, 1888-1976.

Supplement XVI-C
Varner Marriages, Coosa County, Alabama
COOSA COUNTY MARRIAGES--1834-1865
David Varner[1] and Mary Ann Ray, 9 FEB 1848.
Edward P. Varner, 28, and Jane Knight, 16, 14 DEC 1847.
Edward P. Varner and Senora Bonnet, 8 DEC 1859.
Esselman Varner and Sarah M. Wilson, Dec. 20, 1860.
Ceremony performed Dec. 20, 1860, in Weogufka, AL.
John W. Varner and Elizabeth Wilson, 23 SEP 1852.
 Ceremony performed by Elias Kelly, JP, Sept. 23, 1852.
Margaret Varner and George Finelly, 27 NOV 1855.
 (This record taken from a reference at Stamford Univ. It is not listed on the Coosa County marriage records.)
Mary S. Varner and William F. Garnett, Sept. 18, 1856.
Lucy A. Varner and John A. Wilson, 3 FEB 1861.
 (Written consent of parent of female, who was not of legal age.)
John Varner and Matilda W. Wyatt, 30 AUG 1868.
Allia Varner and Jacob A. Flourney, 18 OCT 1866.
R. Ellen Varner and John M. Wyatt, 24 DEC 1871.
Sallie L. Varner and Alfred J. Mooney, 22 DEC 1872.
Ellen Varner and Thomas Caffee, 1 JAN 1878.
Catharine Varner and Allison Janny, 20 DEC 1877.
 MARRIAGE BOOK D, VOL. 2
Esselman Varner and S. E. Glenn, 30 JAN 1879.
C(icero) Varner and Nancy Cranford, 14 JAN 1881.
Lucian A. Varner and Cassandra Meharg, 26 JAN 1883.
M. B. Varner and J. W. Hull, 23 DEC 1882.
William A. Varner and Amanda Hughen, 31 DEC 1884.
Miss Lucy Varner and G. W. Hughen, Dec. 30, 1884.
 Ceremony performed by Elder A. G. Raines. Note from E. P. Varner stated that he had no objection to his daughter Lucy marrying Mr. G. Hughen.
 COOSA COUNTY MARRIAGES 1884-1892
Hettie J. Varner and M. N. Ward, 15 NOV 1886.
Hardaway Varner and Miss Carolyn Glenn, 5 DEC 1888.

---

[1]..The identity of this David Varner is unknown.

M. E. Varner and Miss S. E. Raines, 2 DEC 1889.
Manton Esselman Varner and Sarah E. Raines, 8 DEC 1889.

COOSA MARRIAGES 1882-1885

Miss Rilla Varner and W. D. Vance, 3 FEB 1894.

COOSA MARRIAGES 1895-1900

J. W. Varner and Miss Debbie Phillips, 16 OCT 1895.
L. A. Varner and Miss Katie Morris, 12 MAY 1897.
John A. Varner (25 yrs.) and Alice Emma Gilmer Raines (over 18), 24 DEC 1898.

COOSA MARRIAGES 1900-1909

W. A. Varner, 20, and Miss Rosa Honeycutt, 8 NOV 1908.
G. H. Varner, 24, and Miss I. Della Jacks, 31 DEC 1900.
Miss Elta Varner, 19, and J. S. Bates, 19, 28 APR 1903.
Miss Mattie Varner and W. B. Fowler, 31 DEC 1903.
Annie O. Varner, 17, and David Deason, 19, 9 OCT 1904.
Ella Varner, 22, and J. E. Crumbley, 23, 19 Feb. 1908.

COOSA MARRIAGES--1909-1920

W. A. Varner, 40, and Liza Thornell, 28, 31 DEC 1911.
J. A. Varner, 19, and Miss Lilla Logan, 18, 15 NOV 1915.
John E. Varner, 18, and Miss Cora M. Burks, 19, 26 DEC 1917.
Nathan Varner, 21, and Ella Varner, 19, 2 FEB 1919.
Lizie Dora Varner and G. C. Jones, 22, 2 OCT 1910.
Roxie Varner, 16, and G. H. Glenn, 20, 25 NOV 1910.
Alvie Varner, 18, and W. L. Fowler, 23, 6 OCT 1912.
Olfie Varner, 17, and Clayton Barrett, 20, 26 DEC 1916.
Rushie Varner, 17, and Homer Ezekiel, 18, 31 JAN 1918.

COOSA MARRIAGES--WHITE--1925-1936

Fonzen L. Varner and Gracie Hughes, 2 JUN 1928.
Odie O. Varner and Olga Robinson, 30 JUN 1932.
Flossie Varner and Julius Palmer, 31 OCT 1926.
Mozell Varner (Vernon?) and Milton L. Tate, 2 APR 1927.
Vida Varner and J. L. Brown, 28 OCT 1928.

Supplement XVI-D
Land Purchases and Sales by Varners
Land purchases and Sales by John Varner:
    Oct. 9, 1848, John Varner bought 320 acres in Coosa County, AL (East 1/2 of S 30, T 22, R 17) from Joseph and Adaline Bradford for $800. John Varner was a resident of the county at the time. E. P. Varner was one of the witnesses. Book I Old Series, page 337.

    Feb. 25, 1856, John and Amanda Varner sold 320 acres in Coosa County, AL (East 1/2 of S 30, T 22, R 17) to William A. Wilson for $1500. Book N Old Series, page 186.

Edward P. Varner Land Purchases and Sales
    Jan. 19, 1855, Edward P. Varner acquired 40 acres of government land in Coosa County (NW 1/4 of NE 1/4 of S 27, T 21, R 17). Public Lands, Coosa County, page 49, entry 168.

    Dec. 10, 1868, E. P. Varner bought land in Coosa County (W 1/2 of SW 1/4 of S 16 and SE 1/4 of S 17 all in T 21, R 17) from J. W. E. Gulledge and his wife for $150. Book N?, Page ?

    Dec. 4, 1874, Ed Varner sold land in Coosa County (E 1/2 of NW 1/4 and NW 1/4 of NW 1/4 and NE 1/4 of SW 1/4 all in S 24, T 21, R 18) to J. G. Stephen for $600. Book T, page 188.

    July 19, 1900, E. P. Varner and his wife Senora Varner sold 120 acres in Coosa County (S 1/2 of SW 1/4 plus part of N 1/2 of SW 1/4 of S 21, T 21, R 17) to J. B. Bonnett. E. B. Varner was one of the witnesses. Book R, page 455.

Esselman Varner Land Purchases and Sales
    Dec. 30, 1869, E. Varner bought land in Coosa County (E 1/2 of S 1/2 of S 33, T 23, R 16) from W. A. Wilson for $500. Book N, page 231.

July 15, 1879, E. Varner sold land in Coosa County (SW 1/4 [except SE 1/4 of SW 1/4] and 20 acres in SE corner of NW 1/4 & 1/2 acre off of S 6, T 21, R 18) to A. H. Henderson for $1024. Book A, page 62.

Dec. 25, 1895, E. Varner sold land in Coosa County (W 1/2 of SW 1/4 [less 3 3/4 acres] of S 7, T 21, R 18) to A. J. Rich for $232.

Hardaway Varner Land Purchases and Sales

Jan. 7, 1860, Hardaway Varner of Louisiana sold 5 acres of land in Coosa County ((5 acres off of East side of NW 1/2 of S 6, T 21, R 18) to E. Logan for $29. Book K, page 132.

Jan. 10, 1873, H. Varner sold land in Coosa County (W 1/2 of S 15, 40 acres off being the NE 1/4 of the West half of S 15 and E half of NE 1/4 also west 1/2 of NE 1/4 and east 1/2 of SE 1/4 of S 16, all in T 21, R 17E) to Rutland and others for 8 bales of cotton. Book 28, page 295.

Sept. 2, 1876, H. Varner sold land in Coosa County (NE 1/4 of SW 1/4 of S 35, T 22, R 18) to H. Patton for $150. Book V, page 182.

Mar. 3, 1894, H. Varner sold land in Coosa County (1 acre deep on N side of SW 1/4 of NE 1/4 of S 10, T 21, R 17. Book D, page 504.

Mar. 3, 1894, H. Varner sold land in Coosa County (1 acre deep on N side of SE 1/4 of NE 1/4 of S 10, T 21, R 17) to W. A. Varner for $40. Book D, page 505.

Nov. 10, 1897, H. Varner and wife sold land in Coosa County (1 acre deep across N end of the NE 1/4 of the SE 1/4 of S 10, T 21, R 17) to W. A. Hilyer for $40. Book F, page 119.

Varner Families of the South--XVI

Other Varner Land Purchases and Sales

Oct. 3, 1859, David H. Varner acquired 80 acres of government land in Coosa County (NW 1/4 of NE 1/4 and SW 1/4 of NE 1/4 of S 20, T 21N, R 18E). Entries Public Lands, Coosa County, page 115, entry #'s 14643 and 14443.

Apr. 28, 1894, John Varner acquired 120 acres of government land in Coosa County (in S 12, T 21, R 16). Public Lands, Coosa County.

Dec. 30, 1869, Sarah M. Varner bought 160 acres in Coosa County (SE 1/4 & 1/2 of E 1/2 of S 30, T 22, R 17) from W. A. Wilson and wife Ann for $500. Book N, page 230.

INDEX

People whose names are mentioned in the text of this book are indexed. However, those whose names appear several times throughout the book and\or in multiple passages are not referenced for every occurrence of their names.

Counties and other localities where significant numbers of Varner families lived are also indexed. Places where only one or a few people were born, married, lived, and\or died are not indexed. As with the names of people, place names are not indexed for each and every time they are mentioned in the book.

Generally, women are indexed under their maiden names; some are also indexed under their married names. Place names are entered under state names. Names of slaves are indexed under the headings "Slave" and "Slaves." Federal census records are indexed under the heading "Census."

Generally, footnote references are not indexed. Thus most names of people, places, and events that appear in footnotes but not in the text are not indexed.

Abernathy
   Callie 223
   Jewel Pauline 223
Adams
   Cameron K. 273
   Gladys Winford 221
   J. B. 221
   John Quincy 221
   Keith 273
   R. B. 221
Adderton
   Lew 38
   Thomas 38
Alabama
   Alabama River 329
   Big Swamp Creek,
      Lowndes Co 120,
      342
   Birmingham 242

Alabama (continued)
   Birmingham Public
      Library 10
   Chambers Co 7
   Coosa Co 1, 7, 93, 122,
      127, 158, 170, 178,
      212, 217, 232, 234,
      254, 281, 284, 342
   Coosa County
      Courthouse 9
   Cypress Creek, Lowndes
      Co 120
   Dept of Archives and
      History 9
   Hayneville Cem,
      Lowndes Co 193
   Hayneville Female
      Academy 166, 336
   Hayneville, Lowndes Co
      111, 212, 337

Alabama (continued)
   Lowndes Co 2, 7, 93,
     108, 118, 119, 122,
     126, 144, 153, 157,
     164, 170, 186, 188,
     212, 232, 254, 288,
     292, 298, 329, 342
   Lowndes County Court
     120
   Lowndes County
     Courthouse 9
   Macon Co 7
   Marengo Co 7
   Mobile 231
   Montgomery 245, 329
   Montgomery Co 93, 108,
     118, 119, 288, 329
   Montgomery Public
     Library 10
   Mt. Moriah Church Cem
     354
   Perry County 170
   Providence Baptist
     Church 128, 148,
     160
   Providence Church Cem
     354
   Rockford, Coosa Co 145
   Shelby Co 244
   Sylacauga, Talledega Co
     237
   Talladega Co 1, 281
   Univ of AL Library 10
   Weogufka, Coosa Co 237
Allen
   Debra Renee 280
   Jordan 319
   Mike 280
   R. J. 140
Arkansas
   Cleburne Co 1
   Lincoln Co 7, 87
Arnold
   John 79, 80

Atchison
   McDaniel 206, 295
Atkinson
   Donna 243
Author
   a message from 1
Babb
   Robert M. 304
Bagley
   Everett 271
   Melissa Jo 271
Baker Williams & Co 183
Ballard
   Catherine 265
   Raymond 231
   RoDene 231
Balzorah
   Faithie 149
Banks
   John 327
Barganier
   Fin 199
Barnett
   Francis M. 74
   J. B. 162
   Joseph B. 162
Barrett
   Clayton 264, 357
   J. D. 148
Bartlett
   C. 317
   Cloey 317
   H. 317
   Helen 317
Barton
   Margaret Varner 3, 212,
     220, 229, 231
   Warren D. 231
Bates
   Irene Jones 238
   J. S. 238, 357
Beal
   E. 77
Bean
   Billie Eugene 229

INDEX

Beard
    Annie 220
Beasley
    Henry 55
Beeson
    Ashley Nicole 281
    Britanny Ryan 280
    Kelley Elizabeth 280
    Kristin Nicole 280
    Michael Ray 280
    Pamela Denece 281
    Patricia Lynn 280
    Richard 280
    Richard Keith 280
    Steven Wayne 281
Beheler
    Joseph Morris 228
    Velma Pearl 228
Bell
    Bro. Ellis 78
    Samuel 55
Bentley
    Erin F. 269
    Ted 269
Berry
    Brawley 90
Bilbrey
    Ben Kendall 230
    Bryce Kendall 231
    Carl Haskell 229
    Christopher Michael 230
    Elizabeth Kathleen 231
    Kari Diana 230
    Karl Dwayne 229, 230
    Keith Wayne 230
    Keith Wayne, Jr. 230
    Kelley D. 230
    Margaret Doris Varner 231
    Mary Kathleen 229
    Morgan Taylor 230
    Taylre Alexis 230
    Todd Dwayne 230
Birchfield
    Linda 226

Blackwell
    I. W. 301
    Major 73
Blankenship
    Abigail 249, 250
    Evelyn Ezekiel 249
    G. W. 259, 355
    Gregory Todd 249
    Grover Lloyd 249
    Ida Adams 249
    James Paul Edward 237
    Jim Wes 237
    John Grover 249
    Johnnie Grover 249
    Karen Lynn 249
    Pam 249
    Patricia Ann 249
Blanks
    Amarintha L. 293
    Elizabeth 303
    Frederick A. 293
    Harriet E. 293
    John W. 293
    Josephine 293
    Robert 142
    Robert A. 293, 338
Bledsoe
    Jesse 321, 322
Blocker
    A. B. 139
Bonham
    B. J. 163, 181
    Margaret F. 152, 155, 339
Bonner
    Robb 277
    Scott 277
    Todd 277
Bonnet
    Senora 151, 356
Bonnett
    Autumn Rebekah 243
    Benjamin Dwight 243
    Byron Joseph 242
    Carol Ann 243

Bonnett (continued)
   Conrad Austin 242
   Donald Aubrey 243
   Edna Varner 242, 245
   Erskine J. 242
   Gary Austin 243
   George Henry 263
   Janice Gail 243
   Jeffery Dwight 242
   Joseph Austin 243
   Ora Lee 263
Booth
   William 271
Bowdoin
   Audrey 277
   Mike 277
   Tina 277
Bradford
   Joseph and Adaline 358
   Mary A. 323
Bradley
   Berry 89
Brand
   Carolyn Ann 237
   Dale Huston 237
   Robert Otis 237
Braun
   Donald L. 225
Bray
   Pam 249
Brewer
   Mildred 193, 336, 337
Brown
   A. R. 116
   Angela 283
   David 268
   Governor 318
   J. L. 264, 357
   Ronald 283
   Sarah Zutella 195
   Valentine 58, 80, 325, 326
Bruce
   Billy Joe 231

Bruce (continued)
   Margaret Doris Varner 231
Bryant
   Barry D. 272
   Jeffrey Harold 250
   Michael Kenyoa 250
   Noah Taylor 272
Buchanan
   E. B. 339
Buchannan
   Christin Nicole 279
   Ryan Matthew 279
   Tim 279
Burk
   Sidney 349
Burks
   Cora Matilda 241
   Miss Cora M. 357
Burton
   Joy 250
Busch
   Alice Dorothy 224
Byrd
   Corey 247
   Dorothy 282
   Sutton 217
   Teddy 247
Caffee
   Thomas 356
Callahan
   John 327
Callaway
   Isaac 325
   Jo 275
   Lucy 324
   Martha 101
Calloway
   George M. 257
   J. 139
   Linda 276
Camp
   Frances Marie 229
   Kimberly 251

INDEX

Campbell
  Andrew 89, 90
  Franklin C. 90
  Mary 87, 323
Carns
  Charles Davis, Jr., 283
  Charlie 283
  Cody Dallas 283
Carr
  Madelyn 243
Castleberry
  Sonja 282
Caswell
  Richard 40
Cdmong
  Anthony 78
Cease
  Edward 327
Cemetery Records
  Coosa Co, AL 354
Census, 1800 Federal
  Oglethorpe Co, GA 308
Census, 1820 Federal
  Oglethorpe Co, GA 309
  Putnam Co, GA 310
Census, 1830 Federal
  Coweta Co, GA 312
  Henry Co, GA 312
  Jasper Co, GA 312
  Lowndes Co, AL 329
  Meriwether Co, GA 313
  Oglethorpe Co, GA 311
  Putnam Co, GA 313
Census, 1840 Federal
  Fayette Co, GA 314
  Henry Co, GA 314
  Lowndes Co, AL 330
  Oglethorpe Co, GA 315
Census, 1850 Federal
  Coosa Co, AL 342
  Fayette Co, GA 316
  Henry Co, GA 316
  Jasper Co, GA 316
  Lowndes Co, AL 332
  Pike Co, GA 317

Census, 1860 Federal
  Coosa Co, AL 343
  Lowndes Co, AL 333
Census, 1870 Federal
  Coosa Co, AL 347
  Lowndes Co, AL 334
Census, 1880 Federal
  Coosa Co, AL 349
Census, 1900 Federal
  Coosa Co, AL 350
  Lowndes Co, AL 335
Chambliss & Mundy 183
Cherry
  Lisa 280
Christopher
  Elizabeth 88
  John 86, 323
Ciardi
  Edward F. 230
  Maureen Ann 230
Civil Rights
  Movement 5
Civil War 5, 147, 175, 176,
  179, 219, 234, 255,
  292
Cobb
  Ann 280
  Thomas R. R. 89
  Thomas W. 325
Cole
  John M. 158, 188, 203,
    207, 295
  Josiah 52
Coleman
  Linda 275
Collier
  Charles B. 75
  Charles V. 58
Cook
  E. A. 334
  Edward H. 305
  Eliza 170
  Eliza Varner 175, 180
  George 223
  I. C. 334

Cook (continued)
   Isaac C. 170, 174, 175, 180, 338
   Nathan 299
   R. H. 163
Cooper
   Amber 247
   Benjamin 38
   Kent 247
   Rebecca 36
Corneil
   Aaron Crockett 278
   Andrew 278
   Regan Wyona 278
Cottrell
   James L. F. 336
Court Testimony
   by Allen Davis 205
   by John Varner 207
   by McDaniel Atchison 206
   by William A. Rice 206
Cox
   Geo. S. 181
   William 38
Crabb
   James B. 114
Cranford
   Nancy 356
   Nancy E. 235
Crawford
   J. A. 162, 286
Crockett
   Christopher Thomas 278
   Clyde D. 278
   Dawn Elaine 278
   Donna Lynn 278
   Gwendolyn Darcelle 279
   Patrick Bryan 279
   Tanya Jolan 279
Crookshanks
   George Campbell 101
Cross
   Christopher Brian 279
   Michael Keith 279

Cross (continued)
   Rusty 279
Crossley
   Carl 199
   Edward R. 199
   Karlyeen Varner 199
Crumbley
   Charlie 276
   Eddie 277
   Hillary P. 277
   J. E. 357
   Lottie 277
   Sarah E. 277
Culver
   Gail 248
   Nancy B. 244
   Sabrina 269
Curlee
   W. H. 138
Curry
   Barbara Jean 263
   William Alfred 263
Dacus
   R. W. 333
   Rufus W. 168, 170, 174, 334, 338, 339
   Rufus Wiley 175, 200
   S. E. 140, 333
   Susan E. 200, 334, 335, 340, 341
Daniel
   Henley 101
   James C. 101
   Robert Henley, Jr. 101
Daugherty
   Lamar 273
Davenport
   J. M. 327
Davis
   Allen 158, 189, 295
   Christy 280
   Edna 281
   Jean 277
   Norman E. 224
   Rebecca 18, 27

INDEX

Davis (continued)
    Thomas 38, 61, 80, 325
Dawson
    J. M. 334
Dayton
    Hard 158, 350
De Launey
    Louis 226
Dean
    B. F. 163
    Margaret 223
    Sarah Janette 223
Deason
    David 241, 357
Deaver
    Melody Deland 231
Decker
    Sharon 223
Deed Records
    Varner, George and Betsy 53
    Varner, George 39, 52
    Varner, John 131, 132
Dennis
    Arthur 253
Dent
    Emma 328
Dillow
    Mighi 32
Disney
    Alison Virginia 197
    Ronald Walter 197
Dobbs
    Carol Elizabeth 275
    Dewey Raymond "Butch" 275
    Kadie Michelle 275
Doneon
    David 338
Douglass
    A. 305
Doye
    Fred Theodore 227
    Frederick William 227
    Larry William 227

Dozier
    Thomas 264
Duffey
    Sonja 247
Duke
    Eleanor 87
Dunn
    Barnaba 42
Dupree
    Lewis L. 326
Echolls
    John 326
Eddy
    Tiffany 281
Edison
    James 79
Edmondson
    Michael Waid, Jr. 243
Edmondson
    Michael Waid, Sr. 243
Edward
    Sutherlin 73
Ellis
    James 86, 88, 324
    John 89, 324
    Radford 54
    Susan Varner 89
    William 54, 90
Elrod
    Biney 52
    Haner 52
    James 52
Englander and Brothers 203
Enochs
    John 338
Esselman
    George 336
    G. W. 338, 339
Estate Records
    Varner, Frederick of Oglethorpe Co, GA 69
    Varner, George of Oglethorpe Co, GA 325

Estate Records (continued)
  Varner, John F. of
    Henry Co, GA 102,
    115
  Varner, Thomas J. of
    Lowndes Co, AL
    304, 305
  Varner, William G. of
    Lowndes Co, AL 339
Estate Sales
  Varner, George of
    Oglethorpe Co, GA
    45, 50, 58
  Varner, John of
    Davidson Co, NC 37
  Varner, John of Coosa
    Co, AL 138
  Varner, William F., of
    Lowndes Co, AL 163
Estes
  E. E. 139
Etress
  Michael Chase 246
Eubanks
  Brian Jay 225
  Gary Stevens 225
  Jim 225
  Kimberly Machael 225
Evans
  Lila 335
Everett
  Bro. Francis 78
Ezekiel
  A. V. 246, 253
  Alan Wade 250
  Billy Floyd 246
  Bobby A. 247
  Bobby Adair 246
  Brandon Wade 250
  Carolyn 246, 251, 267
  Christopher 247
  Codey 247
  Curtis 246, 253
  Darrell Scot 251
  Donna M. 246, 248

Ezekiel (continued)
  Dwayne Earnest 251
  Earnest 246, 250
  Earnest and Bennie 250
  Evelyn 246, 249
  Homer 246, 357
  Judy L. 246, 248
  Kevin A. 247
  Kimberly L. 248
  Lester 246, 253
  Lodis V. 246
  Matthew W. 249
  Melissa Ruth 251
  Melodie Sue 251
  Myra Leigh 251
  Rhonda L. 247
  Robert 246, 253
  Samantha Lynn 251
  Timothy W. 247, 248
  Trent Dwayne 251
  Wanda J. 247
  Wayne S. 247
Family History Library
  Salt Lake City 9
Fargason
  Thomas H. 138
Faulkner
  Arthur and Naomi 245
  Clifford E. 245
  David E. 246
  Ellen Ruth Varner 245
  Laurie J. 246
  Lisa G. 246
Finelly
  George 356
Fisher
  John 336
  Michael 26
  Wm. P. 305
Florney
  Jacob A. 149
Flourney
  Eulia 161
  Jacob A. 356

INDEX

Folmar
  Maggie 338
  Margaret 180
  Mary 200, 338
Foshee
  Noah 140
Fowler
  Annie Belle 237
  Ava Dean 238
  Charlotte Renea 238
  Cora Lee 237
  Daisy Ressie 237
  Hershell Wade 238
  Hiram Keener 238
  Joseph Willis 238
  Larry Willis 238
  Lillie Marie 237
  Linda Jo 238
  Nancy Lucille 238
  Richard Lane 238
  Sherry 238, 274
  Victor Dawson 237
  Walter B., Jr. 238
  Walter B., Sr. 236
  W. B. 357
  W. L. 241, 357
  Wendell Kenneth 238
Freeman
  David 269
  George C. 181
French and Indian War 12, 14
Gaither
  Brandi 267
  Crystal 267
  Juanita 266
  Kenneth Richard 267
  Mary Ann 267
  Matthew Richard 267
  Robbie Jean 266
  Roy 266, 267
  Wanda 267
Galloway
  Kimberley 230

Gardiner
  Mary Pet 195
Gardner
  Betty Lois 237
  James Edward 237
  Judy Wynell 237
  Robert Lee 237
  Roland Victor 237
  Samuel 299, 301
Garnett
  Iwanna 136
  James 344
  John W. 145
  Mary I. 170
  Mary Iwanna 145
  Mary S. Varner 174
  Nelson 145
  William F. 145, 170, 174, 356
Garrett
  A. J. 334
  Alice 334
  Caswell 181
  Eliza 334
  Lucinda 334
Garron
  Catherine 35
  Catherine Varner 23
Gartsell
  Col. 319
Gazaway
  Lara 283
Georgia
  Athens 48
  Augusta 48
  Baldwin Co 7
  Cherokee Indians 98, 106
  County Line Baptist Church 43, 50, 65, 68, 76, 77, 84, 118
  Crop Production 44
  Decatur Co 7
  Dept of Archives and History 9

Georgia (continued)
  Eatonton, Putnam Co 66, 104
  Falling Creek, Oglethorpe Co 44, 83
  Franklin Co 1
  Henry Co 7, 100
  Henry County Public Library 10
  House of Representatives 97, 106
  Houston Co 99, 133
  Legislature 95
  Lexington, Oglethorpe Co 47
  Little River, Oglethorpe Co 118
  Long Branch 42
  Long Creek, Oglethorpe Co 117
  McDonough, Henry Co 101, 104, 122, 133
  Oglethorpe Co 3, 7, 30, 33, 41, 43, 45, 48, 63, 65, 66, 82, 84, 92, 93, 108, 117, 118, 212, 288, 308, 323, 329
  Oglethorpe County Courthouse 9
  Pike Co 100
  Pulaski Co 7
  Putnam Co 7, 48, 66, 94, 96, 99, 103, 109, 110, 319, 321
  Putnam County Courthouse 10
  Savannah River 13
  State Senate 106
  Univ of GA Library 9
  Wilkes Co 30, 41, 45, 63, 82, 83, 117, 288, 308

Georgia (continued)
  Wilkes County Courthouse 10
  Wilkes County Public Library 10
Gibbs
  Fay 196
Gibson
  Renee 227
Giddine
  Alan 272
Gilchrist
  A. 337
Gill
  Joseph 55
Givhan
  George 336
Glasgow
  J. 40
Glass
  Joshua 54
Glenn
  Caroline 157
  Ed 139
  G. H. 261, 357
  M. C. 287
  Miss Carolyn 356
  S. E. 356
  Susan Elizabeth "Betty" 283
Glover & Fairchild 183
Goodman
  Monica 269
Goodson
  Jerrell 268
  Mark 268
Goodwin
  Bessie E. 226
Goswick
  Amanda Jolan 282
  Andrew Gilbert 282
  Linda Varner 9, 265, 270, 273, 276, 277
  Ralph E. 282
  Shirley 269

INDEX

Gowens
    Melinda 252, 267
Graham
    Bro. 77
Graves
    Nancy "Ann" L. 290
    Nancy S. 338
    Peyton Smith 336
    Rev. P. S. 338
    Sally 186, 323, 329
    Sarah "Sally" 108, 288
    William 54, 290
    Young W. 306
Green
    Bradford 79
    Sula 277
Gregg
    Amelia 216
Greggs
    Amelia 213, 217
    Mary Ann 217
Gresham
    John 58
    John H. 58, 61, 325
Griffin
    Judge 55
Gross
    Wanda Joy 229
    William J. 229
Gulledge
    F. A. 137
    J. W. E. 358
    Joel 209
    R. H. 285
    W. A. J. 140
    W. A. 139
Gunn
    Radford 80
Guy
    James 139
Gwinnel
    John 55
Haden
    Mary Louise 221

Haigler
    Luther 194
Haile
    Margaret Wallis 70
Haisten
    Dora 275
Haley
    Mareta 227
    Marilyn Lockridge 225
Hancock
    Mary 316
Hardeman
    Isaac 61
Harder
    D. E. 139, 140
Hargraves
    Richard 55
Harmon
    Melinda 276
    Reba 270
    Tom 274
Harper
    John 35
Harrall
    Adam 209
Harrell
    Nellie 221
Harris
    Dora 250
    Henley Kay 271
    J. V. 162
    Jacob Drew 271
    Lendsey Necole 271
    Mary Emma 242
    Mordicai D. 306
    Thomas Jacob 270
    W. C. 162, 286
    Wendy Leigh 271
Harrison
    A. 111, 184
    James 306
Hartwell
    Thomas C. 306
Hawkins
    Benjamin 35

Hawkins (continued)
  Elizabeth 323
  Elizabeth Varner 24
Head
  Jesse H. 326
Heath
  Velda W. 227
Heddleston
  James William 227
Helm
  Billie V. 248
  Haley M. 248
  Jane 247
  Johnny R. 248
  Tiffany M. 248
  Toni M. 248
  Tony R. 248
Hemmet
  James 80
Henley
  Benjamin 223
  Betsy 109, 117
  Darby 32
  Elizabeth 43
  John 43
  John, Sr. 41
  Susannah 32, 43, 81, 82
Henry
  Bonnie Jean 272
  Iain D. 272
  John Richard 272
  Judy Kaye 271
  Marvin 271
  Mary Jo 271
  Ryan William 272
  Tammy A. 272
Henson
  Gregory David 223
  Jeffery David 223
  Marion Jack III, 222
  Marion Jack, Jr. 222
  Marion Jack, Sr. 222
Hepburn
  Anthony Wayne 283
  Carol Ann 283

Hepburn (continued)
  Donald 283
  Emily Ann 283
  Harold 282
  Harold Wayne 283
Hewitt
  Ann Grimes 247
  Charles 247
Hicks
  James D. 292, 338
Higgins
  B. F. 138-140
  W. D. 163
Hillyer
  Dryer 75
Hilyer
  Ann E. 161
  James 138
  Wash 151
Hinkle
  M. 338
  M. B. 207
  Morgan B. 211
  Morgan J. 202
Hogue
  Cara Leigh 252, 268
  Wade 252, 268
Holden
  Deborah 244
Holladay
  Charles Dickerson 195
  Mary Charles 196
  Robert Laslie 196
  Steve 195
Holland
  Floyd Franklin 228
  Myrna Jo 228
Holman
  Sara J. 266
Holmes
  Benjamin 79
Honeycutt
  Miss Rosa 357
  Rosa "Rosie" A. 240

INDEX

Hoover
    Jacob 28, 38, 39
    Joseph 35
    Philip 28, 39
Horn
    Edward Lee 229
    Henry Herman 229
Hottesfield
    Daniel 55
Howard
    Fay 228
    Joseph H. 306
Huddleston
    George 80
Hudson
    Martha 323
Huffman
    Katherine 39
Hughen
    Amanda 356
    Amanda C. 259
    G. W. 151, 356
    George 354
    Lucy D. (Varner) 354
    W. J. 259
Hughes
    Gracie 239, 357
    Mabel Inez 227
    Rev. J. D. 148, 160
Hull
    J. W. 151, 161, 356
    James 138
    Mary B. 161
    T. J. 140
    Thomas 138
Humble
    Jacob 304
Humphrey
    Shirley 269
Iler
    Melissa 220
    Melissa Melvina 219
Ingram
    John 140

Isbelle
    Annie Lori 238
Ivey
    Sherry 269
Jacks
    Annie 277
    I. Della 265
    Lisa 247
    Miss I. Della 357
Jackson
    Amarantha L. 303
    Amarintha 293
    Bro. E. 79
    Bro. Ephriam 79
    Daniel 53, 80, 103
    Elizabeth 292
    Emma 293
    Frederick 293
    Fredonia 292
    James L. 293
    L. B. 80
    Lewis 292, 304, 339
    Littleberry 48
    Martha 293
    Owen 79
    Patience 103, 323
    Saphronia 292
    Sarah 292
    Virginia 292
Janny
    Allison 356
Jennings
    Allen 73, 324
Jeter
    G. W. 339
Jirtle
    Bruce 271
    Jayne Lynn 271
    Nicole Ruth 271
Johnson
    Bartley 79
    Big John 55
    Nancy A. 262, 286
    William R. 87
    Wm. R. 324

Johnston
  Angela 272
  Fletcher 287
  John 29
Jones
  G. C. 357
  Robert 75
  T. 138, 139
Jones & Smith & Co 183
Jordan
  Fleming, Esquire 55
Jowers
  William C. 180
Judge
  Daisy May 178, 339
  J. J. 184, 336
  Jonathon 184
  Jonathon P. 166, 173
Kalisky
  Ashley Dawn 228
  Kristy K. 228
  Wayne D. 228
Kawaski
  Sammy 281
Kelley
  Charles R. 244
  Dickson 301
  Eugenia Lorraine 244
  Floyd M. 244
  Lindsey Blane 244
  Myrtice A. 244
  Phil Randal 244
  Robert Randal 244
  Ronald Steven 244
  Travis Carlton 244
Kelly
  Challice Ann 270
  E. 138, 139
  Elias 138, 356
  Hannah Margaret 270
  Janice Marie 238
  John 140
  Marilyn Fay 238
  Wilbur 238

Kennedy
  Kathy Lynn 229
Kinnebrew
  Littleberry 131, 132
  Mary L. 94
Kirby
  Normand Gilchrist 251
Kittlitz
  Emma Mader 227
Knight
  J. R. 139
  Jane 146, 149, 356
Knott
  David 114
Knox
  Dewey 266
Lacy
  Lester 77
Lambert
  William 32
Land Deed Records
  Coosa Co, AL 358
  George Varner Estate 325
Landrum
  John 326
Langston
  Virgil Erastos 227
Lanier
  J. B. 139
  J. T. 140
LaPrade
  Patrick 225
Larey
  H. M. 337
Larsen
  J. B. 139
Larson
  Dorothy 244
Latner
  Virginia 292
Lawson
  John H. 321

INDEX

LDS
  Genealogy Research
    Library 10
Ledford
  William 292
Lee
  Aida 221
Lester
  Bennie Sue 250
  Furman Farris 250
Letter
  Henley Varner to John
    Varner 133
Lewis
  John 140
  John H. 138
  John S. 325
Libby
  Brooke 198
Light
  Elizabeth 199
  J. F. 341
  Jerre 199, 340
  Jerry 338
  Jim 199
  Lillie 199
  Lyzinkie 199
  Mary E. 340
  Mytel Mason 199
  Tom 199
  Virginia 199
Littleton
  Helen Inez 237
  Lillie Marie 236, 237
  Melvin Maynard 237
  Melvin Philmore 237
Litton
  Marilyn 226
Liveoak
  Benjamin Kyle 271
  Thomas Blake 271
Logan
  E. 359
  Lilla 261
  Miss Lilla 357

Loudermilk
  Adam Grant 251
  Bobby Ray 251
  Rebecca Ann 251
Louisiana
  Caldwell Par 7, 108,
    122, 217, 288, 301
  Caldwell Parish
    Courthouse 10
  Columbia, Caldwell Par
    289
  Franklin Par 219
  Quachita River 108, 288
  Richland Par 219, 220
Lowery
  Minnie 246
  Simmie 246
Lowndes Courthouse Notes
  336
Luckie
  Alexander M. 183
Lumpkin
  J. W. 58
  John 53, 61
  Sarah 324
  Sarah Georgia 87
  Wilson 76, 77
  Wilson, Jr. 78
Luther
  Cassandra Varner 89
  Edmond 89
Lyons
  Helen C. 230
Macey
  John 32
Manghan
  Bryant 111
Manyfield
  Harris 349
Marchbanks
  Mary Susan 228
Marriage Records
  Coosa Co, AL 356
  Lowndes Co, AL 338
  Oglethorpe Co, GA 323

Marshall
  Jacob 203
Martin
  Cameron 248
  Colbey 248
  Colton 248
  Donnie 248
Maryland
  Baltimore 18, 81
Mascarella
  Jan 227
Masery
  Michelle 247
Mason
  Virginia 242
Mathews
  Andrew Jackson 223
Maxey
  Booze 324
May
  Polly 77
  Sister 69
  Talbot 58
McCade
  G. A. 221
McColluch
  Clough C. 292
  William C. 292
McComb
  M. D. 318
McDaniel
  Atchison 189
  L. 37
  Shirley 274
McGarry
  Francis Patrick 251
  Francis Patrick III 251
  Shane Michael 251
  Timothy James 251
McGuire
  Mattie May 263
McHoover
  James 78
McIlroy
  Andrew 55

McIlroy (continued)
  William 77
McKinney
  Henry Carl 226
  Henry Wayne 226
  James Glenn 226
  Jeff Garrett 226
  Steven Charles 226
  Terry Paul 226
  Timothy Carl 226
McLain
  J. C. 275
  Jimbo 275
  Lois 238
McLellan
  Susan 244
McQueen
  G. W. 340
Meharg
  Cassandra 240, 356
Mexican War 144, 147, 219, 302
Mickleborough
  Bro. James 78
Miller
  Rebecca 230
  Steven 38
  T. 139
Millikan
  William 15
Mississippi
  Franklin Co 123, 212, 213, 216, 219
Mitchell
  David B. 112
Moates
  Glen 281
  Jami Ruth 281
  Julie Samantha 281
Mooney
  Alfred J. 239, 356
  Christy 274
  Connie 273
  James Cecil 274
  James R. 275

INDEX

Mooney (continued)
  Janet 274
  Jerry Lee 273
  Judy Diane "Carolyn" 275
  Paul 274
  Paula Jean 274
  Roger D. 275
Moore
  Edward C. 339
  John 73, 323, 325
  Richard 55
Morgan
  Bro. Daniel 79
  Daniel 74, 79
  Danish 78
  Jeremiah 52
  Molly 52
  Sandra 197
Morris
  Donnie 275
  Katie E. 241
  Miss Katie 357
Mulkey
  Amanda 93
Murchison
  Joseph 238
  Leann Hewitt 247
Napier
  Martha Caroline 104
  Thomas 104
Neal
  Elizabeth 57
  Elizabeth (Varner) 92
  George V. 319
  James 56, 109, 323
  John 102, 134
  Martha A. 56, 109
  Susan V. 56, 109
  Susannah (Varner) 92, 105
  Thomas 57, 109, 323
NeSmith
  Saml. P. 203

Newbery
  Annie Josephine 221
  Annie Varner 221
  Benjamin Franklin 220
  Benjamin Ryan 221
  Clarence Franklin 221
  Daisy Lillian 220
  Frank 221
  Hiawatha 221
  Jane 221
  Jim 222
  Lucile Rebecca 222
  Mamie Elizabeth 221
  Mildred F. 222
  William 220
Nichols
  Grady H. II 196
  Grady Henry III 196
  Grady Henry IV 196
  Joshua Varner 196
  Wayne Varner 196
Norrell
  H. 138, 139
Norris
  Charlie 195, 339
  Erleen 195
Northcutt
  Linda E. 226
North Carolina
  Davidson Co 17, 26, 28, 34
  Davidson County Courthouse 10
  Randolph Co 14, 22, 29, 31, 41, 62
  Randolph County Courthouse 10
  Rowan Co 14, 18, 21, 28, 31, 33, 41, 62, 81, 92
  Rowan County Courthouse 10
  Rowan County Public Library 10
  NC State Archives 9

377

North Carolina (continued)
   Uwharrie River 14, 21, 22
   Yadkin River 16, 21, 26
O'Ree,
   Robert 335
Ogden
   Elijah 325
   Elisha 61
Overton
   Albert 140
Owen
   David 80
   Davis 79
   Glen 77
   Glenn 80
   Jacob 131, 132
   Robert 131, 132
   Thomas 323
Owens
   Glenn 52
P. B. Walton Co 184
Palmer
   Albert V. 275
   Albert, Jr. 275
   Arlie Alton 275
   Bertha O'Neal 273
   Betty Jean 275
   Janice 2
   Julius 273, 357
   Matthew 276
   Melvin 276
   Melvin Merrel, Jr. 276
   Michelle 276
   Mike 275
   Myles 276
   Sherry 275
   Terry 275
Paris
   William I. 90
Parker
   Jonathan 266
   Therald 266
Pence
   H. W. 138

Pennsylvania
   York Co 20
Perry
   Ethel 274
Phillips
   Debbie 241
   Miss Debbie 357
Pickering
   Alfred 170, 176
   Martha 142, 144, 145, 164, 339
   Mary L. 164, 173, 338
Pody
   Alma Clarice 270
   Bernice Louise 266
   Carolyn Ezekiel 252, 267
   Carlton Boyd 252, 268
   Cathy Denise 252, 268
   Clifford C. 269
   Donald E. 266
   Ester 252
   James Clinton 268
   James David 252, 265
   Jeff 268
   Jennifer Gale 265
   Kelly Challice 269
   Kenneth 270
   Kevin 269
   Lacey 269
   Larry Douglas 266
   Leigh Ann 269
   Lowell Edward 238
   Madonna Ann 268
   Michael Andrew 252, 268
   Michael Ashley 266
   Michael Ralph 252, 268
   Ralph E. 252, 267
   Regina Dawn 252, 268
   Sheila Diane 266
   Sherill 265
   Stuart 269
   Tara Jean 269
   Terri Lynn 268

INDEX

Pody (continued)
   Timothy Dupriest 269
   Wilma June 238
Porter
   Sister 79
Powell
   Drury 119
   Edward 117
   Edward W. 117
   Hudson 119
   John 117
   Lucy 117
   Nancy 92, 93, 117, 119, 126, 127, 142, 164, 186, 213, 232, 323, 329
   Polly 117
   Rebecca 117
   Seymour 119
   Seymour H. 306
   Thomas 117, 119
Preacher
   pioneer, notes from 160
Price
   Arpie 101
   Joseph 53
   Virginia Richardson 231
Pritchett
   J. T. 140
Proclamation Line of 1763 13
Prudence
   Jack L. 79
Pruitt
   J. A. 205-207
Pugh
   Mary Varner 24
Ragan
   Bro. John 78
   Jonathon 131, 132
   Jonathon, Jr. 131
   M. B. 79
Raines
   A. G. 356

Raines (continued)
   Alice Emma Gilmer 264, 357
   Augustus Goodwin 260
   S. E. 357
   Sarah E. 260, 357
Ramsey
   Randolph 326
Ray
   Jean 268
   Mary Ann 356
Reason
   William 55
Redwine
   John 37
Reed
   Edwin D. 228
   Edwin Kent 228
   Jerry Allen 229
   Jonja 273
   La Quita Dawn 228
   Maleia 272
   Melissa Deane 229
   William, Jr. 272
Reese
   Alfred B. 89
   Dr. Alfred D. 87
   Sarah Varner 89
Revolutionary War 12, 22, 24, 27-29, 31, 32, 62, 81
Rhoades
   Bro. Thomas 77, 78
   Thomas 77
   Bro. James 78
Rice
   W. A. 202
   William 336, 338
   William A. 189, 206, 208, 295
Richardson
   Annette 225
   Lt. 112
Riggins
   Martha 246

Roach
    Amy Suzanne 222
    Deena Ann 223
    Michelle 222
Robbin
    Pat 247
Robertson
    Present 75
Robinson
    Lucy 199
    Olga 240, 357
Rogers
    James Lafayette 226
    John R. 290, 305
    Mary A. (Graves) 290
    Myrtle 226
    Terry Smith 230
Rose
    Washington 319
Ross
    Margaret Jane 228
Rupert
    John 75
Ruppert
    John 325
Russell
    W. P. 336
Samples
    Hazel Velma 228
Samuels
    W. L. 304
Sanders
    Birdie Varner 70, 327
Sawyers
    Audrey 237
Schutz
    Caroline Magdalene 225
Self
    W. 39
Shuemate
    Mary Ellen 224
Siler
    Valerie 224
Simmons
    Randy 267

Slave
    Betsy 77
    Easter 77
    Glasco 102
    Hannah 77
    Harry 79
    London 215, 216
    Millie 119
    Milly 188, 203, 204, 295
    Peter 79
    Sidna 205, 206
    Sidney 207
Slave child
    Milly 187
Slave Milly
    returned to Susan
        Varner 204
    testimony concerning
        203
Slavery
    practice of 5
Slaves
    Aggy, Oney, Mose, and
        Joe 190, 210
    Alsey, Jerry, Billy,
        Georgia, and
        Margaret 115
    Andrew, Spencer,
        Hannah, Mariah and
        infant 305
    Bob, Milly, Bill, John,
        and Randal 303
    Butler, Sidna, and Milly
        187, 202, 203
    Caesar and Jane 26
    Cealy, Polly, Dianah,
        and Suzith 305
    Charles, Letty, and
        Linder 303
    Cheny, Caroline and
        Eaify 56
    Crawford, Robert, Jim,
        Henry, and Green
        88

INDEX

Slaves (continued)
  Daniel, Nehley, Edify,
    Reuben, and Burrel
    60
  Elder, Judge, Mary,
    Major, Nancy, and
    George 303
  Fillis, Elinder, Amy,
    Janett, Sarah, Avey,
    and Aram 60
  Flemming, Dinah,
    Andrew, Plenty, and
    Caty 305
  Forsyth, Harriet, Frank,
    Caty, and Plenty
    304
  Frank and Jerry 102
  Franklin and Poll 25
  Giles, Warren, Butler,
    Simon, Wat and
    Frank 60
  Handy, Charity, Ellen,
    and Cyrus 303
  Harry, Caroline,
    Adeline, Bob, and
    Jane 304
  Harry, Celia, Caroline,
    Bob, and Adaline
    305
  Identification of, 6
  Isaac, Jim, and Sophia
    77
  Jack and Juda 80
  Jacob, Tilly, Milly,
    Telvira, Tabby,
    Ciller, and Charity
    60
  Jane, Polly, Margaret,
    and one other child
    305
  Lindy, Priss, Edify,
    Jackson, Joe, and
    Charlotte 171

Slaves (continued)
  Margaret, Georgia,
    Alsey, Jerry, and
    Billy 102
  Mary, Sally, Cherry,
    Carolina, Dick,
    Adaline, and Charles
    60
  Millie and Haggar 77
  Newton, Major, Robin,
    Randol, Henry, and
    Nathan 60
  Priss, Lindy, Edefy, and
    Simon 165, 185
  Rob, Milly, Primos, Ben,
    Harry, Rhody 59
  Sall, Lucy, Caroline,
    Addeline, Burwell,
    Abram, and Clary 56
  Sam, Tilda, and Phillis
    303
  Sarah, Dick, Jim, John,
    Charles, and Harry
    59
  Sidney and Milly 208
  Suzette, Mariah,
    Harriett, Forsythe,
    Francis 305
  William, John, Abby,
    and Alabama 303
Slaves, Division of
  T. J. Varner's Estate
  305
Slaves
  gift of accepted
    by W. G. Varner 202
Slaves
  John Varner deeds to
    daughter 201
Slaves
  put in trust
    by John Varner 209
Slave Schedules, 1850
  Coosa Co, AL 343
  Lowndes Co, AL 333

381

Slave Schedules, 1860
    Coosa Co, AL 345
Sloan
    A. C. 116
Smith
    B. B. 203
    Ella 224
    Felix L. 287
    Florence 139
    Jeanette 267
    Joseph E. 90
    Keri Desnetta 230
    Lucy 36
    Peter 53
    Ted J. 250
    Vines 209
    William H. 327
Smythe
    James M. 318
Sonntag
    B. S. 222
    Bernice Winford 222
    Robert Banard 222
Sorrell
    Wiley 89
Sorrells
    Mahalia 88
    Mahalia Varner 89
    Wiley J. 86, 324
Sowders
    Debra 226
Spanish-American War 337
Stamps
    Brittain 74, 75
Stedman
    Jeanne 196
Stephen
    J. G. 358
Stewart
    Patricia 198
    Tara 282
Stocker
    Daniel 54
Stokes
    Young 77

Stone
    Harold 266
    Keith Allen 267
    Monty Bruce 266
    Thomas 55
Streety
    John P. 168
Suggs
    Addie Eudorah 226
Sutherlin
    Edward 323
Swafford
    Alexandra "Ally" 245
    Dirk L. 245
Swain
    George 54
Talin
    John 139
Tanner
    Susan 292
Tate
    Milton L. 357
Tavern keeping
    prices approved 324
Tax Records
    for Azariah Varner 182
    for William G. Varner 211
    Putnam Co, GA 319
Taylor
    Cindy 279
    James 53
    Orvella Kay 231
Tennessee
    Greene Co 29, 30
    Maury Co 30
    Rock Creek Baptist Church 30
    Sullivan Co 30
Texas
    McLennan Co 223
    Santa Anna 231
    Waco 225
    Waco, McLennan Co 228

INDEX

Thomas
    Amelia Jane 176
    David 266
    Elizabeth 102, 107
    Elizabeth Rust 107
    Ella 200
    Geo. 305
    Georgia 339
    Jeremy Wayne 266
    Miss A. J. 338
    Miss Ella 339
    Nancy 139
    Nina Powell 339
    Traci 267
Thomason
    A. J. 305
Thomasville
    Clyde 318
Thompson
    Jack 139
    W. R. 145
Thornberry
    Donnie Ebert 226
    Jennifer Lynn 226
    Kallie Doniel 226
    Kathy (Varner) 226
Thornell
    Liza 357
    Liza "Lizzie" J. 260
Thornhill
    Dale 280
Thornton
    J. J. 139, 140
    J. P. 138
    Maude Bee 263
Thrasher
    Joseph A. 107
Till
    Eloise 197
    John Henry 197
    Mary Louise Stabler 197
Timmons
    Brenda 196
Travis
    E. 317

Travis (continued)
    J. L. 317
    W. C. 317
Traywick
    Ashley Julian 279
    J. C. 138, 140
    Steve 279
Tripp
    Frank 222
    Nancy D. 222
Tucker
    Claranhappy 29
    Harriet Virginia 193
    Miss H. V. 338
Turgeon
    Robert 274
Turner
    John 267
    Lisa 267
    Michael 267
    Sharon Diane 267
    Tabitha 267
Turrell
    A. 138
Tye
    Lewis M. 114
Upmore
    Evelyn Margaret 225
    Thomas George 225
Urban
    Debbie 227
Vance
    Mary A. 287
    W. D. 287, 357
Vansandt
    Byron Glenn 250
    Cynthia Ann 250
    Mark Aaron 249
    Tommy 249
    Winston Craig 249
Varner
    (Unnamed infant) 261
    A. 334, 338
    A. C. 287
    Abbie M. 240

Varner (continued)
  Aby 324
  Adam 14, 15, 22, 23, 31, 34, 62
  Adelaide 261
  Adolphus B. 258, 354
  Adolphus W. 261, 352
  Agnez 158, 348
  Albert Ashby 224
  Alberta 241
  Alberta "Allie" 253
  Alexander, of Chambers Co, AL, 307
  Alexander Thomas 282
  Alfin G. 265
  Alice 349
  Alice B. 152, 161
  Alice D. 241
  Alice E. 236, 353
  Allia 356
  Alma 261
  Alma C. 355
  Alonzo 87
  Althia 264
  Alva 347
  Alvie 357
  Alvie L. 352
  Amanda 135, 138, 158, 164, 180, 254, 255, 342, 344, 348, 350
  Amanda C. 351
  Amarantha 289, 292
  Amarantha L. 108
  Amarentha L. 332
  Amaziah 124, 130, 136, 143-145, 147, 164, 193, 209, 254, 297, 299, 332, 333, 335, 339, 340, 342
  Amaziah, son of John Varner 142-146
  Amaziah, son of William G. and Susan E. Varner 193-199
  Ambrilla 280

Varner (continued)
  Amerentha L. 192, 297
  Andrew 23, 35
  Ann "Annie" E. 151
  Ann Eliza 328
  Annie 348
  Annie O. 241, 352, 357
  Armenty 339
  Arval Ready 276, 355
  Azariah 121, 122, 124, 125, 130, 136, 142, 144, 147, 154, 164-173, 179-182, 184, 232, 331-333, 338
  Azariah, law suits against 182
  Azariah, sale of land where he died 181
  Azariah, son of Azariah Varner 180
  Azariah, son of John Varner 164-185
  Azariah, trust to support his children 184
  B. J. 334
  Barbara 28, 39, 277
  Beattrice 260, 351
  Bell 348, 349
  Bell I. 260, 351
  Ben Henley 228
  Benjamin Henley 223
  Benjamin J. 156
  Benjamin Wayne 225
  Bernon Elmo 242, 243
  Bessie 272
  Bethel 157
  Betty 285, 287
  Billy Keith 280
  Birdie A. 259, 351, 355
  Blacks with Varner surname 6
  Bob 138
  Brandy Charmaine 225

INDEX

Varner (continued)
  Brian Gregory 225
  Bridget Margaret 225
  Bro. F. 76
  Bro. Frederick 79
  Bro. Mark 77
  Buelah Zutella 195
  Carol Ann 264
  Carol Howard 271
  Caroline 351
  Carrie 101
  Carry 113
  Casandra 323
  Cassandra 73
  Catharine 356
  Catherine 23
  Charity 28, 38, 39
  Charles 170, 175, 176, 179, 184, 332
  Charles A. 338, 339
  Charles Allen 176
  Charles Allen II 177
  Charles A., Jr. 178
  Charles T. 180, 350
  Charles Wayne 262, 263
  Charley 349
  Cicero 235, 344, 347, 353, 355, 356
  Cintha 324
  Clarence William 242
  Clarice Rebecca 270
  Clovis 23, 35
  Cooper 7
  Cora B. 355
  Cynthia 73
  Daisy 223, 354
  Daisy A. 236, 353
  Daniel Ray 264
  David 24, 25, 134, 356
  David H. 360
  David N. 100, 101, 113, 317
  Debby L. 351
  Deborah Lorraine 225
  Dolphus L. 353

Varner (continued)
  Dora E. 259
  Dora L. 351
  E. 138
  E. B. 161, 344
  E. P. 136, 138, 141, 159, 354, 356, 358
  E. R. 316
  Earl Emmett 224
  Earl Hardaway 263
  Early 316, 324, 328
  Ed 160, 358
  Edmon 348
  Edmond R. 354
  Edna Leona 242
  Edward 94-96, 105, 311, 312, 314, 316, 319, 320, 323, 328, 343
  Edward, son of Frederick Varner 65-67, 70-71, 94-96
  Edward Hugh 263
  Edward Lafayette 197
  Edward L., Jr. 198
  Edward P. 6, 130, 144, 146, 147, 149, 161, 233, 235, 344-346, 348-350, 356, 358
  Edward Scott 198
  Elender 316
  Eli 28, 36, 37
  Eliza 101, 166, 170, 174, 184, 332, 336, 338
  Eliza R. 113
  Elizabeth 24, 25, 51, 53, 86, 108, 109, 143, 194, 289, 293, 323, 324, 333, 338, 344, 347, 350
  Elizabeth "Betsy" Henley 92
  Elizabeth of Marengo Co, AL 7
  Ella 238, 261, 344, 353, 357

Varner (continued)
  Ellen 356
  Ellen Ruth 245
  Ellie Ruth 242
  Elmiry Sophrony 56
  Elwyn 355
  Emily Sophronia 51, 92,
    94, 112
  Emma 180, 316, 350
  Emma G. 353
  Emma V. 199, 335
  Emmet 348
  Emmett B. 148, 149,
    352
  Ernest Millar, Jr. 227
  Ernest Millar, Sr. 226
  Esselman 93, 130, 136,
    142, 235, 254-257,
    283-286, 342, 344,
    347, 349, 350, 354,
    356, 358, 359
  Esselman and Sarah 259
  Esther 261
  Eula 149
  Eulia 344
  Eunice Nell 263
  Evelyn 228, 261
  Evelyn Palmer 279
  Faithie B. 352
  Felix 87
  Flossie 273, 357
  Floyd A. 241
  Floyd Jackson 253, 355
  Fonza 239
  Fonzen L. 357
  Francis M. 108, 289,
    302, 303
  Frank 200, 338
  Frederick 16, 26, 30, 31,
    44, 46, 51, 57, 62,
    63, 66, 68-70, 73-77,
    80, 81, 83, 84, 92,
    96, 97, 108, 119,
    121-124, 129, 134,

Varner (continued)
  Frederick (continued)
    186, 217, 288, 289,
    293, 301-304, 308,
    309, 323, 326, 327,
    329, 330
  Frederick and Judah 51,
    70, 82
  Frederick Augustus 328
  Frederick, Jr. 108, 301,
    304, 323
  Frederick, of Oglehtorpe
    Co, GA 30, 62-80
  Frederick, son of George
    Varner 108, 123,
    217, 288-306, 329
  Freeman 8, 277
  G. H. 334, 357
  Gary Wayne 282
  Gene C. 355
  Gene Carlton 242, 245
  George 16, 26, 29-33, 39,
    41-43, 44, 46, 48, 49,
    53-55, 57, 61, 62, 64,
    65, 71, 72, 81, 83,
    84, 92, 94, 98, 103,
    108, 109, 117, 258,
    285, 288, 307-310,
    320-323, 327, 329,
    342, 351
  George and Betsy 50,
    53, 54, 82
  George and Della Jacks
    252
  George and Elizabeth 53
  George, jury service 54
  George H. 3, 122, 130,
    136, 142, 156, 158,
    212-214, 216, 217,
    219, 220, 231, 286,
    349, 355
  George H. and Amelia
    214
  George Henley 258, 264,
    277

INDEX

Varner (continued)
  George of Decatur Co, GA 7, 307
  George of SC 1, 307
  George, of Franklin Co, GA 1, 307
  George, Mr. 51
  George R. 261, 352
  George Roy 224
  George, Sr. 95, 325, 326
  George W. 108, 124, 298-301
  George W., Jr. 52
  George Washington 220, 223, 225
  George, Jr. 57, 92, 103, 105
  George, Jr., son of George Varner 102-103
  George, of Oglethorpe Co, GA 32, 33, 41-61
  George, Sr. 56, 58
  Giles 291, 302
  Giles T. 292
  Giles W. 305, 306
  Gregory Wayne 225
  Hardaway 93, 130, 136, 141, 157, 158, 205, 219, 255, 257, 285, 332, 347, 350, 351, 354, 356, 359
  Hardaway and Caroline 158
  Harriet 166, 168, 170, 174, 184, 332, 337
  Harriet Virginia 195
  Harriet W. 335
  Harriett 338
  Harvey Amaziah 195
  Hattie 152, 349
  Heather Ashley 281
  Henley 51, 92, 94, 100, 104-107, 108, 110, 113, 114, 116, 122,

Varner (continued)
  Henley (continued)
    133, 135, 156, 310, 312, 314, 317, 321
  Henley J. 101
  Henley, letter to brother John Varner 133
  Henley, son of George Varner 104-108, 133-135
  Henly 57
  Henry 16, 26, 28-30
  Herbert Kenneth 242, 243
  Hettie J. 356
  Hosiah "Hogy" 260
  Howard H. 355
  Howard Henley 270
  Huston 282
  I. D. 355
  Ida L. 261
  Ida M. 354
  Infant of E. P. and L. 354
  Infant of Mr. & Mrs. Manton E. 354
  Infants of J. H. and N. G. 355
  J. A. 286
  J. D. 161, 354
  J. F. 316
  J. L. 181, 339
  J. P. 264, 355
  J. W. 357
  J. A. 357
  Jacob 15, 16, 22-26, 28, 38, 39
  Jacob, Jr. 24
  Jacob, son of Adam Varner 23-25
  Jacob, son of John Varner 27, 28, 38
  James 170, 175, 184, 258, 332, 334, 337, 352

387

Varner (continued)
  James A. 261
  James Calvin 227
  James H. 262, 286, 349
  James Hardaway 259, 262
  James Madison 156
  Jane 343
  Janette 226
  Jason Morgan 197
  Jeff D. 152, 349
  Jefferson 302
  Jeffie 264
  Jennie 340
  John 14, 15, 16, 18, 19, 22, 26-28, 31, 34, 36, 37, 39, 43, 51, 57, 62, 81, 92, 93, 100, 108, 110, 117-119, 121, 122, 125, 126, 128-134, 136, 142, 143, 146, 154, 158, 164-166, 168-170, 172, 174, 178, 179, 184, 187-189, 201, 202, 207, 212, 217, 232, 235, 254, 257, 258, 284, 288, 294, 295, 323, 329, 331, 332, 336, 340, 342-346, 348, 354, 356, 358, 360
  John A. 180, 259, 264, 286, 349-352, 357
  John and Amanda 128, 144, 178, 181, 358
  John and Nancy 119, 186, 293
  John and Rebecca 27
  John E. 355, 357
  John Esmond 241
  John F. 100, 101, 108, 113, 115, 200, 297, 302, 303, 333, 335, 339, 341

Varner (continued)
  John Frank 200
  John Hardaway 220, 223
  John Henley 86
  John, Jr. 18, 19, 136, 174, 205, 332, 346
  John, Sr. 26, 35, 209
  John Moseley 270
  John Mosley 355
  John of Marengo Co, AL 7
  John R. 8
  John R. III 197
  John R., Jr. 197
  John Robert 196
  John Trice 231
  John W. 6, 130, 142, 158, 165, 232, 234, 345, 351, 356
  John William 241
  John, of Rowan Co, NC 16-20
  John, son of Adam Varner 22, 34, 35
  John, son of George Varner 6, 92, 117-141, 187, 190, 201, 217, 329, 342
  John, son of John Varner 26-28, 35-37
  Johnny Goldson 242, 244
  Jones A. 352
  Joseph 87, 158, 316, 348
  Joseph Eggleston 263
  Joseph Waller 197
  Josephine 271
  Josephine H. 220, 223
  Joyce May 242, 244
  Judah 68
  Judy 282, 312
  Kathryn 28
  Kathy Lee 279
  Kathy Lynn 225
  Katie E. 351

INDEX

Varner (continued)
  Kevin Paul 282
  L. A. 357
  L. W. 341
  Lana Jo 224
  Lanetta 236, 353
  Lannie 337
  Larry Wayne 281
  Laura L. 241, 352
  Lee 279
  Lenora 354
  LeRoy Monroe 107
  Lewis E. 260, 351
  Lillian 260
  Linda 281
  Linda Sue 225
  Lizie Dora 357
  Lois M. 355
  Lois Mae 227
  Lori Leighann 281
  Louisa 291, 292, 302, 338
  Lucian A. 356
  Lucien A. 239, 351
  Lucy 27, 316, 342, 347-349
  Lucy A. 130, 159, 344, 345, 356
  Lucy D. 151
  Lula F. 240
  M. A. 316
  M. B. 356
  M. C. 316
  M. E. 338, 347, 357
  M. F. 333
  Mae 355
  Maggie 193, 337, 339
  Maggie M. 260, 351
  Maggie P. 181
  Mahalia 86
  Manton E. 259, 286, 349, 352, 354
  Manton Esselman 260, 261, 357
  Marcela 333

Varner (continued)
  Marcus 94, 310, 313, 314, 320, 321, 323
  Marcus "Mark" 72
  Margaret 28, 39, 321, 356
  Margaret Doris 229
  Margaret F. 154, 163
  Maria 276
  Marilyn Diane 198
  Mark 77, 105, 316
  Mark Wilson 224
  Martha 166, 169, 170, 316, 332, 336, 353
  Martha A. 113, 114, 317
  Martha B. 260
  Martha C. 173, 184
  Martha Jeannine 197
  Martha M. 199, 333
  Martin E. 287
  Martina 239, 353
  Mary 24, 144, 168, 169, 302, 316, 339, 342
  Mary A. 259, 265, 286, 292, 305, 306, 338, 349
  Mary Ann 220
  Mary Bell 151
  Mary Belle 177
  Mary D. 356
  Mary E. 194, 240, 335, 352
  Mary Elizabeth 199
  Mary H. 260
  Mary J. 180, 350
  Mary L. 122, 332
  Mary M. 23
  Mary Magdeline 24
  Mary, Mrs. 170
  Mary S. 145, 356
  Mathew 38, 318, 323, 324
  Matilda 179, 349, 350
  Matthew 18, 19, 26, 27, 30-32, 34, 44, 46, 62,

Varner (continued)
  Matthew (continued)
    70, 81-86, 88, 308, 309, 311
  Matthew and George 70
  Matthew and Susannah 84
  Matthew Joseph 263
  Matthew, Jr., Esquire 90
  Matthew, Jr., son of Matthew Varner 85, 87-89, 315
  Matthew, son of John Varner 31, 32, 81-91, 315
  Mattie 340, 341
  Mattie Savina 236
  May E. 354
  Michael David 263
  Mickey Jeanette 224
  Millie 23
  Minnie 349
  Minnie C. 355
  Minnie I. 260, 351
  Minnie S. 152, 161
  Miss Elta 357
  Miss Lucy 356
  Miss Mattie 357
  Miss Rilla 357
  Mitchell Wayne 263
  Molly 23, 35
  Molly "Polly" 73
  Molvin F. 156
  Morgan Brittany 282
  Mozell 357
  Mulbrina Tatnell 156
  Myrtice Azarene 242, 243
  Nancy 24, 25, 27, 36, 118, 323, 347, 355
  Nancy A. 259, 261, 349
  Nancy E. 353
  Nancy G. 352
  Nancy L. Graves 290
  Nancy Lea 225

Varner (continued)
  Nancy Lee 264
  Nancy Powell 93, 123
  Nathan 261, 352, 357
  Nettie Pearl 224
  Nina 151
  Nora Virginia 198
  Norma Kathryn "Kay" Peterson 8
  Norma Lee 272
  Odie O. 240, 357
  Olfie 357
  Olga 353
  Olga (or Olfie) 264
  Olive 86, 324
  Onia "Onie" 73
  Orris L. 355
  Oscar Fletcher 8
  Patience 103
  Patty Ruth 281
  Polly 27, 28, 36, 39, 323
  Pormelia 155
  R. D. 357
  R. Ella 354
  R. Ellen 356
  Rachel 348
  Rachel Ella 149, 150
  Rachel Velma 227
  Ray 194
  Reba (Harmon) 355
  Rebecca 38, 224
  Rilla L. 240
  Robert 323
  Robert, U.S. District Judge 307
  Robert L. 335
  Robert Lafayette 195
  Rollie E. 261
  Ronnie Augusta 242, 245
  Rosa Lee 354
  Rose 227
  Rosie A. 355
  Roxie 357
  Roxie M. 261, 352

INDEX

Varner (continued)
 Rushie 351, 357
 Rushie L. 241, 246
 S. C. 334
 S. M. 339
 Sallie 344
 Sallie L. 239, 356
 Sallie R. 354
 Sally 324, 347
 Sally A. 239, 353
 Sam 337
 Sam Dent 317
 Sam M. 176
 Samuel Dent 328
 Sara Ester 265
 Sarah 51, 94, 99, 109, 121, 124, 136, 166, 170, 173, 179, 184, 289, 332, 336, 347
 Sarah E. 352
 Sarah Jumelle 198
 Sarah M. 360
 Sarah W. 86, 87, 324
 Senora 148, 161, 344, 349, 350, 354, 358
 Shelton 277
 Sherry Kim 279
 Sidney Oliver 1
 Sina 348
 Sis 348
 Steven Cody 282
 Sula 8
 Susan 100, 134, 188, 324, 349
 Susan E and Wm G 208
 Susan E. 191, 204, 205, 207, 297, 332, 338
 Susan Eliza 122, 124, 130, 136, 142, 157, 168, 175, 186-188, 190, 192, 200-202, 209, 216, 217, 293, 294
 Susan Eliza, Mrs. 339
 Susan F. 239, 353

Varner (continued)
 Susannah 23, 35, 51, 94, 105, 109, 323
 Susannah Henley 85
 Syntha 324
 Tabitha Ann 263
 Thomas 27, 36
 Thomas J. 291, 305, 338
 Thomas J. and Nancy L. 292
 Thomas Jefferson 108, 124, 289, 290
 Ula M. 261
 Unnamed infant 262, 264
 Unnamed son 156
 Valat "Vida" 264
 Vida 357
 Viola E. 239, 353
 Virginia Waller 8, 194, 196, 199
 W. A. 286, 347, 355, 357
 W. D. 316
 W. F. 181
 W. G. 330, 332, 333
 Wallis 157
 Wayne 281
 Widow 15
 Wife of E. 354
 Will 337
 William 23, 27, 30, 35-37, 51, 57, 73, 74, 86-88, 92, 94-99, 101, 105, 110, 112, 122, 133, 135, 136, 291, 292, 305, 306, 310, 313, 319-322, 325, 327, 339, 347, 355
 William "Ashby" 227
 William A. 194, 240, 259, 286, 335, 349, 351, 352, 356
 William Alfred 261
 William D. 102, 113

Varner (continued)
  William F. 122, 130, 152-155, 163, 164, 169, 172, 192, 333, 339
  William G. 123-125, 157, 187, 189, 191, 192, 202, 205, 207, 209, 211, 216, 217, 294-296, 298, 303, 338, 340
  William G. and Susan E. 206
  William Graves 108, 175, 186, 289, 293
  William, Jr. 302
  William L. 297, 332
  William M. 355
  William N. 260
  William W. 156, 334
  William, son of George Varner 94-100, 113, 310, 313, 319, 325
  Willis "Willie" H. 239
  Willis H. 354
  Winford Annie 220
  Wm G. 205
  Wm G. and Susan 206
  Wyona 278
Varner Collection of Family Papers 70
Varner Family Papers at GA Archives 327
Villareal
  Brenda Marie 281
  Joel 281
Virginia
  Appomattox Courthouse 179
Walker
  A. E. 318
  David 316
  Lincoln 77
  William 76, 77

Wallace
  Corey Ralph 252, 268
  Mark 272
  Paul 272
  Robyn 252, 268
  Sheila 272
Waller
  Ella 102
  John 102
  Lewis Edwin 196
  Martha 102
  Minerva J. 102
  Rosa Bell Gates 196
  Virginia 196
  William 102
Wallis
  Evelyn Mercede 224
  Lamar C. 224
Walton
  Drury D. 300
  Ruffin E. 300, 301
Walton Co
  P. B. 182
Ward
  Betsy 36
  Hattie 161
  George Wilburn III 198
  George W., Jr. 198
  Jonathon 38
  M. N. 152, 356
  Marilyn 198
  Michael Varner 198
Waters
  Lemuel G. 292, 305
  Leonard G. 338
  Louisa 305
Watson
  Ann Catherine 87
  W. T. 140
Webb
  Herbert E. 222
  Isaac 301
  Patricia Ann 222
Webster
  Jacob 326

INDEX

Werner
   Christopher 20
   Fronaney 20
   George 20
   Hans Adam 20
   Jacob 20
   John 20
   John Adam 20
   Katharina 20
West
   Agaster 194
   Herman 194
   James 80
   Margie 194
   Mary Lynn 194
   Maud 194
   Millie 35
   Millie Varner 23
   W. W. 193, 339
   William 194
White
   Dana 248
   J. B. 287
   J. R. 286
   Nancy G. 262
Whitfield
   George 57, 133, 324, 327
   George B. 99, 110, 111, 121, 124, 321, 327
   Sarah 57, 111, 133, 331
   Sarah (Varner) 92, 105, 109
   William 134
Whitman
   James K. 305
Whittaker
   Elvira 222
Wicks
   Gary 225
Wiggins
   W. D. 340
Williams
   F. M. 207
   Thomas M. 202, 208
   W. 40

Williamson
   Peter 336
Wills
   Varner, Edward P. of Coosa Co, AL 161
   Varner, Esselman of Coosa Co, AL 258, 285
   Varner, Frederick of Caldwell Par, LA 289, 302
   Varner, George of Oglethorpe Co, GA 49, 56
   Varner, Jacob of Rowan Co, NC 38
   Varner, John F. of Henry County, GA 113
   Varner, John of Coosa Co, AL 135
   Varner, John of Davidson Co, NC 35
   Varner, John of Randolph Co, NC 34
   Varner, Matthew of Oglethorpe Co, GA 85, 88
Wilson
   A. B. 139
   Amanda 136
   Angie 248
   Elizabeth 232, 356
   John A. 159, 356
   John Roy 224
   L. M. 239
   Mary Christine 224
   R. 138
   Sarah 256
   Sarah M. 254, 356
   W. A. 358, 360
   William A. 232, 358
Wood
   Lynn 272

Woodard
    Jennifer 248
    Jordin 248
    Norman R. 248
    Travis R. 248
Woods
    Carolyn T. 317
    James S. 316
    Mary L. 317
Wyatt
    J. M. 140, 354
    John 140
    John M. 150, 356
    Matilda 179
    Matilda W. 178, 356

Wyatt (continued)
    Rachael E. 161
Wyman
    Chadwick 53
Wynn
    Wilbur 194
Wynne
    John 326
Young
    Betsy 323
    George H. 326
Zak
    George 8, 245, 253
    Ronnie Varner 8, 245, 253

About the Author

Gerald Hubert "Jerry" Varner was born 8 Aug 1926 in Cleburne County, Arkansas. He is the second oldest of six children of Oscar Fletcher Varner and Olive Grace Allen Varner. He attended the rural 4-classroom Valley Special School in grades 1 through 9 and Heber Springs High School in grades ten through twelve. Both schools are in Cleburne Co, AR. He graduated in 1944.

Jerry then worked in a variety of odd jobs, mostly migrant farm work in the Midwest and on the West Coast, until he was called for military service in World War II.

After serving nineteen months in the army, with no overseas duty, Jerry returned to migrant farm work in Washington State, in Aug 1946. A few months later, after that season's crops were harvested, he enrolled in classes at Central Washington College (now Central Washington University), Ellensburg, WA, on the G.I. Bill of Rights. He graduated in 1950 and began his teaching career that fall.

In 1949, the author married one of his classmates, Norma Kathryn "Kay" Peterson, who also taught in the public schools for many years. Jerry and Kay have two children and two grandchildren.

Jerry taught high school classes in Vancouver, WA, for 14 years. He then moved with his family to the Beaverton, OR, School District, where he was a school administrator for 17 years and a high school teacher for 6 years. He taught U.S. history, journalism, and English. His administrative assignment was director of public information for the school district. He retired in 1987.

The author is working on Volume Two of <u>Varner Families of the South</u>. It will cover the Varner/Verner families of Pendleton District, SC, and their descendants. (Jerry is descended from this Varner line.) He plans to publish Volume Two in 1995 or as soon thereafter as he completes the manuscript for it.